READING
AND
WITHDRAWN LEARNING
IN
CONTENT AREAS

RANDALL J. RYDER

UNIVERSITY OF WISCONSIN, MILWAUKEE

MICHAEL F. GRAVES

UNIVERSITY OF MINNESOTA

Merrill, an imprint of Macmillan College Publishing Company
    New York
Maxwell Macmillan Canada
    Toronto
Maxwell Macmillan International
    New York • Oxford • Singapore • Sydney

Editor: Linda James Scharp
Production Supervisor: Custom Editorial Productions, Inc.
Production Manager: Francesca Drago
Text Designer: Proof Positive/Farrowlyne Associates
Cover Designer: Proof Positive/Farrowlyne Associates

This book was set in Palatino by Compset Inc. and
printed and bound by R.R. Donnelley & Sons Company.
The cover was printed by Phoenix Color Corp.

Macmillan College Publishing Company
866 Third Avenue, New York, New York 10022

Macmillan College Publishing Company is
part of the Maxwell Communication
Group of Companies.

Maxwell Macmillan Canada, Inc.
1200 Eglinton Avenue East
Suite 200
Don Mills, Ontario M3C 3N1

Library of Congress Cataloging-in-Publication Data

Ryder, Randall J.
    Reading and learning in content areas / Randall J. Ryder, Michael
F. Graves.
    p.   cm.
    Includes bibliographical references and index.
    ISBN 0-02-404945-X
    1. Content area reading—United States.   2. Communication in
education—United States.   3. Learning.   I. Graves, Michael F.
    II. Title.
    LB1050.455.R93   1994
    428.4'0712—dc20   93-38202
                                                                      CIP

Printing: 1 2 3 4 5 6 7   Year 4 5 6 7 8 9 0

In Memory of Our Parents:

Randall G. Ryder
Florence M. Ryder

Finley E. Graves
Pauline H. Graves

PREFACE

Reading and Learning in Content Areas presents ideas for assisting students in reading, thinking, learning, and communicating in all curricular areas. In a concise, practical style, this text suggests ways teachers can enhance students' ability to learn from reading, writing, discussion, classroom activities, and demonstrations. Several thematic and organizational features will assist you to read, consider, and apply the ideas presented here.

THEMATIC EMPHASIS

Integrated throughout this text are two overriding themes that have directed our presentation of the topics. The first is that **instruction includes a variety of communication processes.** We view reading, writing, and other forms of learning as complementary and integrated processes. Learning subject matter content involves not only reading, but various forms of writing, viewing films and videotapes, observing or engaging in experiments and demonstrations, and discussions. A second theme is **the potential for dynamic learning in the classroom**—students and teacher actively communicating with one another as they engage in common learning experiences that extend the role of teacher beyond that of information provider. This sort of instruction acknowledges the wealth of information and experience students bring to class. We view students as active learners who (1) have considerable knowledge they can share with each other as well as the teacher, (2) possess linguistic and cultural diversity that can be shared in the classroom, and (3) are capable of engaging in a variety of learning tasks including those that require higher level thinking. We have integrated these themes throughout the book by noting them within the context of a given topic or activity, and we have addressed them directly by including individual chapters on critical thinking, cooperative learning, writing instruction, and cultural and linguistic diversity.

CHAPTER FORMAT

Each chapter begins with a graphic overview and written narrative previewing the chapter's content. Scattered throughout each chapter are practice exercises which allow you to apply and reflect on your understanding of various topics. Answers to these practice activities are located at the end of the book. Although we have limited instructional activities to those that have been shown by research or practice to be effective, even the best activities have certain limitations. Accordingly, following descriptions of these activities, we provide commentaries focusing on their strengths and limitations. Finally, each chapter concludes with a summary and a "reflections" section designed to extend your understanding of the chapter's content and how that content may be tailored to the needs of your classroom.

APPLYING THE CONTENT OF THIS TEXT

Whether you are reading this text from the perspective of a teacher with classroom experience or as a student in a teacher preparation program, we hope you will carefully reflect on the content of this book to consider how it may be applied to your classroom. This will require you to adapt the instruction to your content, your students, your instructional objectives, and your teaching style. The instructional activities presented throughout this book offer diverse yet practical ways to facilitate students' understanding of the subject matter curriculum. Some of the ideas and techniques presented may be new to you. Your first efforts at involving students in cooperative groups or engaging them in critical thinking may be a challenge. Yet we are certain that with persistence and thoughtful evaluation you will recognize the merits of these efforts. We encourage you to reflect upon these efforts, to share them with your colleagues, and to discuss their effectiveness with your students.

ACKNOWLEDGMENTS

We would like to express our appreciation to four groups of people who have aided us in writing this text. First, we would like to extend our appreciation to the many classroom teachers and school administrators who, during the past twenty years, have shared with us their visions of teaching and their evaluations of many of the activities discussed in this text. These colleagues have challenged our thinking, suggested many creative ideas to improve students' learning, and provided us encouragement to pursue this text. Second, we would like to acknowledge the many scholars whose research over the past twenty-five years has made rich contributions to the knowledge base that has informed this text. Through their efforts to examine how students learn in the classroom, the teaching profession has acquired a much better understanding of instruction and learning. Third, we would like to extend our appreciation to the many talented individuals at Macmillan Publishing for their vision, their belief in the underlying constructs of this text, and their dedication to their craft. In particular, we like to acknowledge the efforts of Linda Scharp, Jeff Johnston, Sharon Rudd, and Laura Daly. Additionally, we would like to thank the following reviewers for their insightful suggestions, their timely feedback, and their words of encouragement: Patricia L. Anders, University of Arizona;

Ulrich H. Hardt, Portland State University; James E. McGlinn, University of North Carolina–Asheville; Michael McKenna, Georgia Southern University; Harry B. Miller, Northeast Louisiana University; Katherine E. Misulis, East Carolina University; Sue R. Mohrmann, Texas A & I University; Cathleen D. Rafferty, Indiana State University; Albert J. Shannon, St. Joseph's College; Lana Smith, Memphis State University; Judith Thelen, Frostburg State; Diane Truscott, Eastern Montana College; and Liane H. Willey, Central Missouri State University.

Finally, we would like to thank our wives, Pamela and Bonnie, and our children, Randall Patrick, Julie, and Erin, for their patience with our long nights at the computer, their humor when we were in need of it, and their gentle prodding when we got bogged down.

R. J. R.
M. F. G.

CONTENTS

CHAPTER ONE

. . . .

Introduction

CHAPTER OVERVIEW

This chapter is divided into four sections. In the first section, we provide a brief historical overview of content area reading instruction. In the second, we present guiding principles of content area reading instruction that serve as the underlying conceptual foundation for the topics presented throughout this book. In the third, we discuss the concept of functional literacy and the incidence of illiteracy from a historical perspective. Also in this section, we present a discussion of how well students are learning in school, noting in particular detail historical data on academic achievement. In the final section of this chapter, we provide a general model of the reading process.

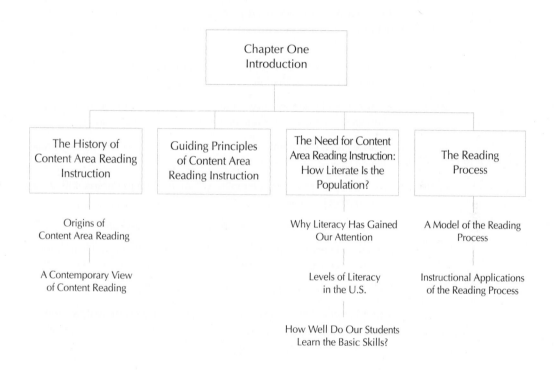

Chapter One
Introduction

The History of
Content Area Reading
Instruction

Guiding Principles
of Content Area
Reading Instruction

The Need for Content
Area Reading Instruction:
How Literate Is the
Population?

The Reading
Process

Origins of
Content Area Reading

Why Literacy Has Gained
Our Attention

A Model of the Reading
Process

A Contemporary View
of Content Reading

Levels of Literacy
in the U.S.

Instructional Applications
of the Reading Process

How Well Do Our Students
Learn the Basic Skills?

THE HISTORY OF CONTENT AREA READING INSTRUCTION

This section contains a brief history of content area reading instruction as well as a discussion of the contemporary view of the role of content area reading instruction in the subject matter classroom. It concludes with a set of guiding principles for content area reading instruction.

This book addresses techniques and issues directed at improving students' learning of subject matter curriculum. In reading it, you are likely to gain additional insight into how you personally acquire knowledge from text, and you may acquire strategies that assist your understanding as you read independently.

As you begin this chapter, consider the study strategies you will apply consciously. Then examine the following reader behaviors and check all those you believe most closely describe your own reading habits.

1. _____ Before I read I define a purpose or goal for reading, which allows me to generate questions that direct my reading.

2. _____ Before I read I skim or survey the material, then consciously activate knowledge I have that is related to the content of the reading.

3. _____ Before I read I set a limit to the amount of time I will devote to the reading.

4. _____ As I read I occasionally attempt to summarize the gist or main ideas that I encounter in the text.

5. _____ As I read I limit notes to details that I might be tested on.

6. _____ As I read I generate questions about information that is unclear or for which I need additional information.

7. _____ As I read I limit note taking to the use of a highlighter.

8. _____ After I read I attempt to summarize important points by writing brief summaries, generating an outline, or constructing a graphic representation to organize important ideas.

While this is a partial list of study behaviors, it may be surprising to learn that not all of them are particularly effective in improving students' understanding of text. Specifically, behaviors 3, 5, and 7 generally are not effective study strategies, especially when they are the sole strategy applied to a reading selection. The remaining behaviors are strategies commonly used by proficient readers. Unfortunately, study strategies like those identified are often absent from the school curriculum even though their use can enhance learning the text presented in various subject matter courses. Although the issues and activities addressed throughout this book are directed at teachers, recognize that it is the students who eventually will derive the benefits of what has been labeled content area reading instruction.

Origins of Content Area Reading

The origins of content area reading instruction can be traced back to the 1920s, when the U.S. Bureau of Education acknowledged that each subject matter area contributes directly to the development of reading competency (Gray, 1925). Accordingly, educators popularized the slogan "Every teacher should be, to a certain extent, a teacher of reading" (Whipple, 1925, p. 6). Although reading educators recognized the importance of providing instruction that would aid students' understanding of subject matter textbooks, an examination of classroom practice between the 1930s and 1960s failed to provide evidence that this sort of instruction was widespread (Austin & Morrison, 1963). The limited use of reading strategies in the subject matter classroom appears to be a result of the lack of teacher training in reading methods (Early, 1957), as well as teachers' perception that modification of their instruction was not necessary (Olson & Rosen, 1967).

The Past 20 Years.   During the past 20 years content area reading instruction has evolved in its instructional practice and its importance in teacher training. The first book dedicated exclusively to content reading, *Teaching Reading in the Content Areas* (Herber, 1970), helped to distinguish instruction to aid students in the reading of subject matter text from the instruction of reading within the confines of the basal reader program (the self-contained reading instruction from kindergarten through eighth grade consisting of graded student books and teacher instructional manuals). At the same time that the importance of content area reading instruction was being recognized by educators, attention was being drawn to the observation that test results on advanced skills of reading were showing small, yet consistent declines (Eckland, 1982; Harnischfeger & Wiley, 1975). No doubt, the increased awareness of students' reading performance had some influence on efforts to improve teacher preparation in reading. In 1973 eight states required coursework in content area reading instruction for secondary teacher certification (Estes & Piercey, 1973). Approximately a decade later, 31 states required coursework in content area reading instruction for all secondary teacher certification programs, and an additional 5 states required content reading coursework solely for English and language arts teachers (Farrell & Cirrincione, 1984). These preservice teacher training efforts directed at content area reading strategies have produced some measurable effects on teachers' perceptions of their own teaching. Teachers who integrated these strategies report greater confidence in their teaching (Pearce & Bader, 1986) and a sense that their lessons are more organized (Conley, 1986). There is also some evidence that certain strategies have a positive effect on students' achievement (Alvermann & Swafford, 1989; Bean, Singer, & Frazee, 1986), as well as their attitude toward the subject matter (Bean, 1981).

While the effect of content area reading strategies on students' learning is encouraging, obstacles remain. Students enrolled in secondary teacher cer-

tification programs display resistance to content reading coursework requirements (Memory, 1983; O'Brien, 1988), and inservice programs directed at improving teachers' knowledge of content reading strategies have a limited effect
on classroom instruction (Smith & Feathers, 1983).

A Contemporary View of Content Reading

For many years, reading instruction was based on the assumption that readers
were passive. As a more thorough understanding of the reading process developed from research conducted during the 1970s and 1980s, reading was no
longer viewed as a passive activity in which the reader memorizes information
from the text. Instead, reading was seen as a process in which the reader independently draws on strategies to construct meaning. The distinction between a
passive and constructivist reading activity is determined by the degree to
which a reader can retrieve and utilize prior knowledge. Passive reading requires the reader to commit text information to memory and to prepare for recall of that information in its original form. Constructivist reading, on the other
hand, requires the reader to have a purpose for reading, to activate available
knowledge that is related to that purpose, to read for additional information,
and finally to restructure knowledge on the basis of the new information. An
example of a study strategy using this approach, the What-I-Know (Heller,
1986) procedure, has students divide a sheet of paper into three columns. In
the first column, before reading, the students list the general concepts they
know that might be related to the reading. Then a purpose for reading is established and noted on the bottom of the paper. As the selection is read, information pertaining to the purpose of the reading is noted, and concepts not clearly
understood are listed in the third column. Once the reading is completed,
students may examine additional sources of information to clarify concepts
that were poorly presented or not understood. Finally, students may write
responses to the purpose-setting question or may work with several classmates to write a summary that reflects their combined understanding of the
selection.

Constructing Knowledge in Our Everyday Lives.   As adults, many of
our everyday problem-solving tasks require the construction of knowledge.
For example, consider the decisions required to buy a new car. The criteria applied to the purchase are often based on cost, fuel efficiency, riding comfort,
physical appearance, and legroom. It is unlikely that any single source will
provide enough information to guide the purchase of the car. An individual
may read reviews of particular models in trade magazines or consumer publications. Or the individual can take test drives to collect information to form an
opinion. Ultimately, however, a decision will be reached from information collected from a variety of sources. That decision is constructed from the collection of data, from the evaluation of that data according to defined criteria, and
from the comparison of data to prior knowledge.

Recognizing the importance of students' ability to consciously apply strategies to construct meaning from the subject matter curriculum, a set of guiding principles of content area reading instruction follows. These principles serve as an instructional and conceptual foundation for the topics and instructional activities addressed throughout this book.

GUIDING PRINCIPLES OF CONTENT AREA READING INSTRUCTION

The guiding principles presented in this section stress the importance of allowing the teacher to assist students in constructing knowledge, and the importance in recognizing the diverse intellectual, social, and cultural contributions that students bring to class. These principles reflect a view that content reading is functional and that it should recognize the various constraints that exist in the classroom.

Since the 1970s, considerable effort has been directed at obtaining a better understanding of the cognitive processes involved in reading and of reading instruction itself. Through the efforts of educators, psychologists, and linguists, a much clearer understanding of reading as a cognitive act has emerged. Coincidentally, efforts at examining the success of American schooling, the effectiveness of various forms of instruction, the factors within a classroom that affect learning, and the managerial structure of the school have provided a better understanding of factors external to the learner that influence the students' ability to acquire knowledge. Applying this knowledge to instruction in the subject matter classroom, we propose the following set of guiding principles:

1. **Content area reading instruction is based on the assumption that students acquire meaning through the application of strategies, skills, and prior knowledge to text material.** Content reading, therefore, is functional and driven by the learners' needs to acquire knowledge. The goal of the teacher is to create and direct an instructional sequence using activities and strategies that will enhance students' acquisition of knowledge. To the students, content reading is a strategic process to acquire meaning, not a set of skills or exercises taught in isolation of content. To the teacher, content reading instruction involves employing teaching strategies and instructional designs that direct students through the curriculum to accomplish the teacher's instructional objectives.

2. **The classroom is a dynamic social, cultural, and intellectual environment where students acquire information and construct knowledge.** Content area reading instruction draws on the teacher's ability to evaluate the diverse social elements involved in classroom learning, as well as the sources of information that contribute to that intellectual environment. Instruction within this environment draws on students' knowledge collectively and individually. Instruction should present learning activities similar to those encountered in everyday problem-solving tasks that demand social interactions among individuals of various educational and social backgrounds. The complex and di-

verse nature of the social environments in school is characterized by Greene (1989):

> Teachers must somehow conceptualize the scale and anonymity of society today, the pulsations of city streets, the protected enclaves of the suburbs, the persisting homogeneities in certain villages and towns. They must be aware of the privileged young's claims of entitlement, the complaint postures of those seeking upward mobility, the apathy and wariness of the disinterested. (p. 144)

Although the diverse needs and social backgrounds of students can pose a considerable challenge to teachers, unchallenged beliefs and stereotypes can interfere with learning (Oakes, 1986). The way students learn and the social patterns they follow in the classroom may reflect their cultural background (Barnes, 1989). We believe teachers should acknowledge the cultural and social diversity of the classroom on an ongoing basis. Furthermore, we advance instructional methods that incorporate the social, cultural, and cognitive diversity of the classroom in the confines of subject matter instruction.

3. Content area reading instruction allows students to learn from numerous sources of information. Although the primary source of classroom information is a single textbook, students are more likely to become actively involved in learning when they make use of multiple text sources, as well as such media as videotapes, films, slides, transparencies, audiotapes, and compact diskettes. We believe that learning from sources of information made available through computer technology (such as the videodisc and CD-ROM) will be increasingly evident in classroom instruction. Content area reading instruction should draw on new instructional technology and existing text-based sources of information to promote learning.

4. Content area reading instruction aims to facilitate active learning. Instruction in the subject matter areas traditionally has proceeded along the assumption that curriculum is shaped by the objectives and content identified in curriculum guides and textbooks and in guidelines established by state and local educational agencies. As a result, many teachers attend primarily to the content to be delivered rather than to the process of delivering that content. A likely outcome of this emphasis is that beginning teachers view the function of teaching as telling students what they need to know (Vosniadou & Brewer, 1987). Seasoned teachers, pressured by measures of accountability, focus their efforts at communicating the constructs of their subject matter area rather than the process that allows learners to use the constructs to acquire knowledge. As a result, the needs of the learners may not be addressed until the teachers have dealt with problems of management and their own evaluation of their teaching competencies (Fuller, 1969).

Active processing of information requires much more than committing information to memory because individuals differ in the way they organize and interpret information. Acknowledging students' diverse interpretations of information, the content area teacher can draw on students' ability to describe their strategies for constructing meaning, as well as model strategies that allow students to monitor their own processing of information. These strategies are functional. Over time, the teacher gradually reduces the amount of direct instruction to promote students' ability to independently monitor and direct their learning.

5. Instructional strategies and activities in the content areas are adaptable to the constraints of the classroom. Teachers experience considerable demands on their time. Faced with frequent additions to the curriculum, the pressure of accountability, the frustrations of balancing students' needs with the curriculum mandated by the district, and the increasing responsibility of the school to address innumerable societal ills, teachers are severely restricted in the amount of time they can devote to learning or applying new instructional strategies. Content area reading instruction acknowledges these constraints by advancing instructional strategies and activities that can be presented spontaneously or with a minimal amount of preparation.

To summarize, the purpose of content area reading instruction is to improve students' learning through the integration of instructional strategies in the subject matter curriculum, rather than to present strategies in isolation. It is functional, directed by the students' academic needs as well as their cultural and social background. Content reading is a process to facilitate learning. The locus of control is the teacher, who serves to provide information, to present strategies that facilitate learning, and to direct students' ability to become independent learners. To accomplish these goals, the teacher assumes much more than the role of information provider. In reality, the teacher now assumes the role of coach, maestro, and navigator. As a coach, the teacher models learning strategies in an effort to provide students insight into their own cognitive processes. In addition, the teacher must recognize the individual and aggregate characteristics of the learners, providing feedback and direction to both individuals and the group. As a maestro, the teacher must assess students' knowledge of the content and assist them as they engage in activities centered on classroom instruction. And as a navigator, the teacher facilitates discussions, questioning activities, demonstrations, and hands-on projects designed for the whole class, cooperative groups, or independent learning.

Content Area Reading Applications to Non-Text-Based Instruction. While the term *content reading* would seem to be limited to instruction centered on text, most of the topics and activities discussed throughout this book apply equally as well to subject matter areas where texts are used infrequently or are absent altogether. Teachers of mathematics, art, industrial or physical education, foreign languages, and English as a second language can improve non-text-based instruction by applying content area reading strategies. For example, applying strategies presented in Chapter Four, "Preparing Students to Learn," a physical education teacher could begin a unit on basketball by first presenting students with a graphic display of the various positions and their functions, then asking students to observe a film or videotape of professional basketball players. Similarly, an art teacher may consider having students engage in a cooperative learning activity (Chapter Eight) in which they generate written summaries (Chapter Seven) of the process for firing ceramics in a kiln. This activity would allow students to reflect on their learning, share their insights with their peers, and provide closure on the process and technique of firing clay. Activities such as these provide students with the background information necessary for learning, increase the likelihood that students will connect the lesson content to their everyday lives (either watching or playing sports or more closely examining a ceramic cup or mug), and provide the teacher with a means to assess students' understanding of a lesson's objectives prior to the instruction of that content.

PRACTICE ACTIVITY 1.1

Imagine that you are about to present a 40-minute lesson in your subject matter area. List types of activities you would use to help students understand this content. This lesson does not have to be based on a text selection.

THE NEED FOR CONTENT AREA READING INSTRUCTION: HOW LITERATE IS THE POPULATION?

This section contains a brief overview of the concept of literacy, a discussion of historical trends in the levels of literacy in the United States, and a description of recent assessment data on students' ability to read and write. Before continuing, carefully respond to the following statements. Answers to these statements can be found at the end of this section.

	Agree	Disagree
Levels of literacy have been relatively static over the past 100 years.	_____	_____
Standards applied to literacy are motivated primarily by social and economic considerations.	_____	_____
During the past 15 years the school-age population has significantly improved its ability to perform higher level reading tasks.	_____	_____
With technological advances, literacy demands will actually decrease by the year 2000.	_____	_____

Why Literacy Has Gained Our Attention

During the past decade Americans increasingly have become aware of the importance of literacy. This heightened awareness has been fueled by economic, educational, and social factors. Economically, business has shifted from the production of capital goods to the delivery of services, which in turn has required a higher level of reading and writing skills. The Department of Labor's *Workforce 2000* study (Johnston & Packer, 1987) calls attention to the growing literacy demands of the workplace. According to the report, in the year 2000 below-average skills will be good enough for only 27% of the jobs created between 1985 and 2000; this compares with 40% of the jobs in the mid-1980s. Although these projections have been questioned (Flynn, 1988; Rumberger & Levin, 1989), it is apparent that there is a steady increase in the number of occupations requiring individuals with higher levels of education (Bailey, 1991). The absence of comprehensive assessments of the nature and development of thinking skills necessary in the workplace make it difficult to assess changes in the total distribution of jobs. Certain segments of the work force, however, do serve as examples of these changes. In the textile industry, for example, generations of low-skilled workers who previously worked on mechanical looms are now required to handle sophisticated machinery run by computers. Operators of this new equipment are required to read and comprehend complex manuals and apply higher level thinking skills to conceptualize the equipment's operation. Similar examples can be found in other industries. The disparity between levels of literacy skills required in the workplace and the level of literacy skills available to the worker has raised serious concerns from the private sector. This sentiment is evident in the following statement appearing on the cover of a special supplement to the *Wall Street Journal* (1990):

Smarter Jobs, Dumber Workers: Is That America's Future?

Jobs are becoming more demanding, more complex. But our schools don't seem up to the task. They are producing students who lack the skills that business so desperately needs to compete in today's global economy. And in doing so, they are condemning students to a life devoid of meaningful employment.

Literacy and Economic Costs.   There is little doubt that literacy is important in the workplace, and that the level of proficiency in reading, writing, and mathematics has increased as part of an attempt to maintain our competitiveness in a global economy. Although many secondary students maintain that a high school diploma is not necessary and believe they can obtain a job as a means to escape academic tasks presented in school, most jobs require numerous literacy skills. In an examination of reading in the workplace, Mikulecky (1982) found that all categories of workers, except those in blue-collar jobs, read more than high school juniors. According to Mikulecky, workers read an average of 2 to 3 hours a day, whereas high school students read an average of 98 minutes each day. Moreover, the level of difficulty of the material read by workers was generally as high as the materials commonly read in high school. The level of literacy one attains has long-term economic consequences. Students who attain high levels of literacy will earn more income (Schwartz, 1988) and will achieve a higher level of job performance (Mikulecky & Ehlinger, 1986).

Social Consequences of Literacy.   As important as the economic consequences of literacy may be, the social consequences are equally significant. The ability to acquire and interpret text information and the ability to communicate one's thoughts in print are basic human rights (Freire, 1985; Kazemek, 1988). Tragically, these rights have been denied to certain groups during our history in order to limit social and political access. Prior to the Civil War, all but two states had laws prohibiting the instruction of reading or writing to slaves. During that same time, few women attended school; as a consequence, only a very small percentage of women could read or write. Today, all students are provided access to schooling to enhance literacy skills. Efforts directed at educational reform and instruction directed at literacy skills seem to have narrowed the gap between the reading achievement of minorities and white populations (Mullis, Owen, & Phillips, 1991). Shown in Figure 1.1, for example, are values representing the differences between the scores obtained by white and black 13-year-olds, and those of white and Hispanic 13-year-olds from 1971 to 1988 on the National Assessment of Educational Progress (NAEP). While the gains of minority students are encouraging, the difference in scores between minority and nonminority populations remains sizable. The average proficiency in reading for 13-year-olds in 1988, for example (based on scores that range from 0 to 500 with an overall mean of 250), was 261.3 for whites, 242.9 for blacks, and 240.1 for Hispanics. Efforts to reduce these differences must continue in order to ensure advanced educational opportunities and meaningful and sustained employment.

Levels of Literacy in the United States

The criteria for "being literate" depend on the type of reading and writing tasks required in society at any given point in time. While an individual was considered literate in 1979 if he or she had completed six years of education (Irwin, 1987), a 12th-grade standard has been suggested as more appropriate for the tasks required in today's society (Aaron et al., 1990). With 20% to 30% of the population having difficulty with common reading materials (Stedman & Kaestle, 1987), our awareness of the incidence of illiteracy is heightened and educational institutions are called upon to narrow the gap between the literacy tasks required in everyday life and the level of reading performance acquired in school.

FIGURE 1.1   READING DIFFERENCES IN AVERAGE PROFICIENCY SCORES ON THE NAEP FOR BLACK AND HISPANIC 13-YEAR-OLDS

	1971	1975	1980	1984	1988
Difference between white and black scores	39	36	32	27	18
Difference between white and Hispanic scores	—	30	28	23	21

Functional Literacy.   Functional literacy is the ability to engage in reading tasks encountered in the workplace, as part of our civic responsibility, or during leisure activities. Generally, it has been equated with school attainment levels: Students with more education are assumed to be better readers. The level of school attainment required to be functionally literate has risen rather dramatically over the past 60 years. In 1930 an individual was functionally literate if he or she had completed 3 or more years of schooling. In 1950 the criterion was 5 or more years; in 1960, 8 or more years. In 1980 the criterion was graduation from high school (Stedman & Kaestle, 1987).

There is, of course, some question as to the usefulness of school attainment as a measure of literacy. Years of school may not be a good measure of an individual's ability to engage in and succeed with essential reading material. Functional literacy is not an "all or nothing" condition. If, for example, the criterion for functional literacy is the completion of 12 years of education, it would be unreasonable to assume that an individual with 11 years of schooling would be unable to read such things as newspapers, common periodicals, and job-related materials. Furthermore, individuals in the workplace may receive considerable assistance with literacy tasks from peers or co-workers that could enhance their functional literacy skills over time. Functional literacy (level of school attainment necessary to perform essential reading tasks), therefore, cannot necessarily be equated with how well one actually engages in tasks requiring reading competency.

Many of the materials commonly encountered in our daily lives require a high level of understanding. Figure 1.2 presents a portion of the Internal Revenue Service's directions for completing the miscellaneous deductions portion of itemized deductions on Schedule A.

Understanding written instructions to federal tax returns can be a difficult task. Certainly, the information describing the conditions allowing uniforms or special clothing to be deducted as a miscellaneous expense is open to interpretation. In fact, our conversations with two CPAs and two representatives of the Internal Revenue Service produced a variety of responses to our original question. Clearly, not all functional reading tasks demand the degree of understanding required for IRS publications. Yet many common tasks can present problems for an individual who has inadequate reading skills, or who lacks background knowledge of the topic being read.

Criteria of functional literacy have increased steadily over the past century, with some of the largest increases occurring during the past 20 to 30 years. A century ago individuals were determined to be functionally literate if they could write their names. Current standards of functional literacy require individuals to read text containing unfamiliar information, and to acquire both the stated and the inferred information available from the text. The standards have reached levels that not long ago were achieved only by an elite, highly educated segment of society (Resnick & Resnick, 1977). Certainly technological advances will demand wider dissemination of information and the need to apply that information to advance societal goals. The findings of international comparisons of student achievement test scores indicate that students in several countries perform better than their American counterparts (Kutscher,

1989). Accordingly, government agencies and the private sector are likely to continue their interest in reforming the school curriculum in an attempt to better meet the literacy skills required in the workplace. As a result, the level of school attainment and the level of competency with reading and writing tasks will no doubt increase.

How Well Do Our Students Learn the Basic Skills?

This section presents a brief overview of how students' level of achievement has changed over the past 25 years. It begins with a presentation of the concerns that have gained widespread recognition in the media, then examines the results of two major sources of achievement test data that have been gathered over the past quarter century.

Since the mid-1960s a number of publications have addressed a purported crisis of learning in the schools. The study *Equality of Educational Opportunity* (Coleman et al., 1966), sponsored by the U.S. Office of Education, was one of the first to direct public attention to the state of the American educational sys-

---

FIGURE 1.2   EXAMPLE OF A READING TASK FROM THE INTERNAL REVENUE SERVICE

Question: *Could a member of a professional rock band who wears a neon blue leather jacket and green leather pants emblazoned with silver-spiked grommets deduct the cost of this clothing under miscellaneous deductions?*

Work Clothes and Uniforms

You can deduct the cost of upkeep and work clothes only if they are required as a condition of your employment and are not suitable for everyday wear. To qualify for the deduction, both conditions must be met. It is not enough that you wear distinctive clothing; it must be specifically required by your employer. Nor is it enough that you do not in fact wear your work clothes away from work; the clothing must not be suitable for taking the place of your regular clothing.

Examples of occupations in which you may be required to wear uniforms which qualify are: delivery workers, firefighters, health care workers, law enforcement officers, letter carriers, professional athletes, and transportation workers (air, rail, bus, etc.).

Musicians and entertainers can deduct the cost of theatrical clothing and accessories if they are not suitable for ordinary use.

However, work clothing consisting of white cap, white shirt or white jacket, white bib overalls, and standard work shoes, which a painter is required by his union to wear on the job, is not distinctive in character or in the nature of the uniform. Similarly, the cost and maintenance of blue work clothes worn by a welder at the request of a foreman are not deductible.

(Department of the Treasury, Internal Revenue Service, Catalog Number 10560, Publication 529, Miscellaneous Deductions)

tem. Claiming that differences in school quality were not closely related to differences in students' level of achievement, the report concluded:

> [O]ne implication stands out above all: That schools bring little influence to bear on a child's achievement that is independent of his background and social context; and that this lack of an independent effect means that inequalities imposed on children by their home, neighborhood, and peer environment are carried along to become the inequalities with which they confront adult life at the end of school. (p. 325)

On the basis of this report, Jencks and colleagues (1972) concluded that school reform would do little to affect the inequality in students' academic achievement and that teachers or schools had little influence on students' learning.

In the years following the Coleman report, a rather widespread decline in junior and senior high school students' standardized achievement test results became evident. Scores of 10th and 12th graders on the Iowa Test of Educational Development in 1978, for example, fell below those obtained in 1962 (Science Research Associates, 1978). At the same time, results of the Comprehensive Test of Basic Skills reading test showed declines from one third to one year depending on the grade level examined (CTB/McGraw-Hill, 1982). Similar declines were evident among students completing college entrance exams. Scores on the Scholastic Aptitude Test, for example, declined from an average of 466 verbal and 492 quantitative in the school year 1966–1967 to 434 and 472, respectively, in the year 1974–1975. With the publication of the *Nation at Risk* report (National Commission on Excellence in Education, 1983), politicians and the public were led to believe that the decline in test scores was of such significance that it threatened the economic security of the nation. This and other reports critical of the status quo brought sustained attention to the condition of education. Critics of the educational system attributed the cause of the decline in test scores to poor instruction (Cooperman, 1979; Ravitch, 1985), and many states enacted legislation for greater accountability through teacher competency testing and greater assessment of students' academic progress.

Was all this attention on students' academic progress justified? What evidence is there to substantiate the widespread belief that students' academic abilities were declining? In answering these questions, we draw on two sources of test results of students' academic achievement over the past 25 years. What follows is a description of the test results of the National Assessment of Educational Progress (NAEP) and the Scholastic Aptitude Test (SAT).

National Assessment of Educational Progress.   The NAEP is a congressionally mandated program that began in 1969 for the purpose of assessing students' performance in reading, writing, mathematics, history/geography, and other academic disciplines. It is the only ongoing national assessment of the academic performance of 4th, 8th, and 12th graders attending both public and private schools. A recent review of achievement trends over the past 20 years (Mullis et al., 1991) concludes that students' academic performance has been rather stable. Reading achievement in 1988 was as good as, if not slightly better, than that of 4th, 8th, and 12th graders assessed nearly two decades earlier. Fourth and 12th graders in the 1988 assessment were reading better than students in 1971, and 8th graders showed little change in their reading proficiency. Similar trends were seen in writing and mathematics tests. Not all results, however, showed improvement over time. In science, the performance of 7th graders was slightly below that of 1970, and 12th graders' performance in 1986 was well below that attained in 1969. In summary, the NAEP results suggest that students' academic achievement has been relatively stable over the past 20 years. These results fail to substantiate claims of a significant and persistent drop in academic achievement in our nation's schools; to the contrary, they provide evidence of stable academic progress.

Scholastic Aptitude Test.   A second source of achievement tests data collected over the past 25 years is the Scholastic Aptitude Test, which is administered primarily to college-bound students. Some individuals have interpreted the SAT scores, therefore, as a measure of our best and brightest students. The drop of scores from 1966–1967 to 1974–1975 raised speculation that academic achievement was falling. However, this decline in scores was more likely a result of changes in the composition of individuals who took the test and the age at which students were tested. The College Entrance Examination Board (1977) estimated that changes in the population of students taking the exam contributed to 20% to 30% of the decline in scores. Stedman and Kaestle (1987) attribute the effects to a drop in the age at which students completed the exam, accounting for 24% to 40% of the decline. More recent test results of college-bound students fail to support the perception of eroding college entrance examination scores. Scores on the College Board's achievement tests, completed by the same students who took the SAT, indicate an improvement in the 1970s in English, science, and foreign languages. And scores on the SAT (College Entrance Examination Board, 1983) and the ACT (American College Test, 1985) have either held steady or increased since 1978.

Examination of academic achievement scores over the past 25 years provides some solace in the finding that the school-age population's academic performance has been rather steady. Similarly, measures obtained on the academic achievement of students planning to enter institutions of higher education indicate a slight improvement in scores from those obtained a decade earlier. Comparisons of academic performance are useful in providing a global measure of trends in how well our students are learning basic concepts taught in the school curriculum. Somewhat disturbing, however, is students' performance on higher level thinking tasks. Results obtained from the 1988 NAEP reading assessment (Mullis et al., 1991; see Figure 1.3) indicate that the majority of students nationwide are capable of performing simple, discrete reading tasks. As we examine more complex levels of reading proficiency, however, a rather dramatic decline in performance is noted. The finding that only 4.8% of 12th graders can synthesize and learn from specialized reading

FIGURE 1.3   PERCENTAGE OF STUDENTS PERFORMING AT OR ABOVE CERTAIN READING
PROFICIENCY LEVELS ON THE 1988 NATIONAL ASSESSMENT OF
EDUCATIONAL PROGRESS READING ASSESSMENT

Task	Percent of Students at Level		
	Age 9	Age 13	Age 17
Can synthesize and learn from specialized reading materials	0	0.2	4.8
Can find, understand, summarize, and explain relatively complicated information	1.2	10.6	41.8
Can search for specific information, interrelate ideas, and make generalizations	17.9	58.0	86.2
Can comprehend specific or sequentially related information	62.5	95.1	98.9
Can carry out simple, discrete reading tasks	93	99	100

materials could portend profound economic and political consequences. American business groups have expressed the need for workers who possess reasoning and problem-solving skills (National Center on Education and the Economy, 1990), the need for at-risk populations to possess skills needed in the workplace (National Business Alliance, 1987), and the need for employees to have much higher math, language, and reasoning skills (Rumberger & Levin, 1989). If our students will be required to apply higher level thinking and reasoning skills in tomorrow's workplace, then our efforts should be directed at the necessary instructional and curricular modifications to aid them.

At the beginning of this section you were presented with four statements addressing literacy. These statements and their answers are as follows:

Levels of literacy have been relatively static over the past 100 years.
  Disagree (Literacy is a fluid term; it changes to meet the needs of society at a given time.)

Standards applied to literacy are motivated primarily by social and economic considerations.
  Agree

During the past 15 years the school-age population has significantly improved its ability to perform higher level reading tasks.
  Disagree (The level of performance on higher level reading tasks has remained relatively static.)

With technological advances, the need to be literate will actually decrease by the year 2000.

> *Disagree* (If present trends continue, technological advances will require workers and citizens with a higher level of literacy.)

THE READING PROCESS

For over 20 years cognitive psychology has attempted to describe the reading and writing process. The body of research that has accrued allows a more descriptive understanding of how an individual constructs meaning from print, and how meaning is communicated in print. The following section provides a description of the reading process. It begins with a presentation of a general model of reading, then proceeds to a discussion of the importance of the model on instructional practice. Finally, instructional applications leading from our understanding of the reading process are given.

A Model of the Reading Process

Reading can be described as an interactive process that allows the reader to construct meaning by using information obtained from various knowledge structures. These knowledge structures include knowledge of letters, knowledge of letter-sound relationships, knowledge of words, knowledge of syntax (grammar), and schematic knowledge (mental representations that organize knowledge in related parts). The interactive process allows the reader to move in two directions. Comprehension can be accomplished through an interaction between information provided from the reader's prior knowledge and information gleaned from the text (Rumelhart, 1977). Efficient readers learn to direct their attention to both text information and their prior knowledge as they read to adjust for the role that prior knowledge and text information may have in a given context or under certain learning situations. The interaction between text information and prior knowledge can be demonstrated by reading the following.

> The man wearing the mask was at home waiting for the other man to arrive.
> The other man was afraid of the man with the mask.

Interpretation of these sentences draws primarily on your ability to activate prior knowledge as the context of the situation is somewhat ill-defined. Most likely, you constructed an image of a robber in someone's home, or of a physician or dentist waiting for a patient at a home office. Yet if you are now instructed to read this passage with the understanding that you are observing the behavior of these two men in your box seat behind home plate at a ballgame, the context is more clearly defined, and your comprehension of the passage now shifts to the relationship between a catcher and a base runner.

Constructing meaning from text requires the reader to draw on prior knowledge, to monitor strategies directed toward gaining meaning, and to process information in an efficient manner. Lacking proficiency in these three elements of the reading process, the reader often fails to comprehend the text, or processes the information at a level that is limited to gaining facts or other surface information. What follows are a more thorough description of these three elements and a discussion of their importance in learning from text in the subject matter classroom.

Schemata.   One of the most important constructs influencing our understanding of reading has been schemata. As described by Rumelhart (1980), schemata are chunks of knowledge that exist in our head. All of our knowledge is packed into these units, and the units are activated in our attempts to make sense of the world. We use them to interpret information gained from sensory input, to construct actions we may take, to determine goals, and in general to direct the flow of information to the mind. Schematic units contain our knowledge of objects, situations, events, actions, and sequences of actions. At another level, schemata contain procedures for processing and organizing information (West, 1981). One useful analogy to explain a schema would be a soap opera. In the same way that a soap opera has a cast of characters that can be played by different individuals in different ways without changing the essential nature of the soap opera, so a schema has a set of variables that can be given different values in an individual's interpretation of it without changing its essential nature. Consider the following schema for the concept of greed.

> The Husband had been a failure in his attempt to capture large profits in the commodities futures market. Exploiting his Wife's trust, he secretly obtained and sold all her precious gems and furs. These assets were then applied toward the purchase of additional futures contracts. Within weeks he had recouped his initial loses into huge profits. No longer interested in his direct involvement in the gold market, he turned his account over to the Commodities Broker so he could spend more time with his Tennis Instructor. Within weeks the Tennis Instructor and the Unscrupulous Broker had seized his assets and set sail for Fiji.

There are a number of interpretations of this greed schema, that is, a number of ways in which the characters can vary. The Husband can be young, intelligent, or overbearing. The Wife can be attractive, resourceful, compassionate, or reflective. The Commodities Broker can be well schooled or slovenly. And the Tennis Instructor can be male or female. But regardless of how these variables are interpreted, they have to be realized if the schema is to be interpreted. But if one of the variables is not present, then the greed schema will not be fully realized. If the Commodities Broker and Tennis Instructor are missing, then we have no realization of how their greed influenced the husband.

Schemata are not just concerned with people or events, as illustrated in the preceding example. You have a schema for the color blue, the concept of a practical joke, and the ideas of peace, beauty, and respect. Schemata are also active processes. They are more than something that is there, readily available for use. They are recognition devices that actively work to evaluate the fit between the information perceived and themselves. In other words, schemata are actively involved in the process of determining whether or not the information perceived can be interpreted in terms of a particular schema. Schemata direct the process by which the mind takes a particular piece of information presented to our senses, calls up a particular schema in terms of which the information can potentially be interpreted, checks for congruence between the incoming information and the variables of the schema, and either determines that the information can be interpreted in terms of the schema or calls up another schema to be tested. Comprehending the following paragraph is relatively easy due to the congruence between the information and your available schema.

> It is truly amazing that our attention is drawn to those tabloids as we wait in the checkout line at the grocery store. How can we be so gullible as to believe headlines like MAN FINDS ALIEN SPACECRAFT UNDER TOENAIL, or MASSIVE NASA COVERUP: MOON ACTUALLY FOUND TO BE MADE OF GREEN CHEESE.

The information presented is congruent with our available schema of grocery stores and checkout lines. Interpretation of the variables in the passage comes readily and without a great deal of study. As the variables become less distinct, however, we experience increased dissonance between the schema we activate and our interpretation of the information presented. Take, for example, the following paragraph.

> The joint had been presenting problems for a number of years. He discussed the problem with his neighbor. He glanced out the window. How could one corner be so pristine and the other so dilapidated? Certainly its appearance could be enhanced by nailing the culprit. Or he could gradually chisel away at the problem to remove the decay.

The congruence between information in this paragraph and our schemata is not as cleanly defined as the first example. The words *joint, corner, chisel*, and *decay* could invoke different interpretations depending upon the particular schema activated. Drawing on our schemata of urban blight and neighborhood problems, we can construct a scenario of a dilapidated structure that presents problems to the quality of a neighborhood. On the other hand, if we were familiar with woodworking, we would likely generate a scenario of a wood joint in need of repair. In either case, our available schema directed our interpretation of the text information. Schemata do change. As the learner acquires more information, schemata are refined, reshaped, corrected, and restructured. A child's schema for beach is not the same as an adult's; a teenager's schema for telephone is not the same as a second grader's. It is important to note that a reader can find an interpretation of the text that allows him or her to make sense out of the passage, yet it may not be the interpretation intended by the author. But what happens when schemata cannot be activated? The following excerpt from *Scientific American* provides a vivid example of the importance of available schemata.

> The superconducting accelerator magnets posed major technical challenges. The magnets must confine particles within a one-centimeter region in the center of the vacuum tube as they steer the particles around a 6.3 kilometer orbit, 50,000 times a

second. The accelerator magnets generate a field as electric currents flow through superconducting wires. The quality of the field depends on the precision with which the superconducting wires are placed around the vacuum tube. (Lederman, 1991, p. 51)

Unless we are familiar with the Tevatron and the process by which it first produces antiprotons, then smashes them against protons through the use of superconductivity, our schemata do not direct our interpretation of the information.

Acceptance of the notion of schemata and of the importance of schemata in the process of comprehending what one reads leads to a myriad of instructional applications. How can we draw on our knowledge of schemata to improve students' ability to comprehend text? It is apparent that readers who have knowledge of different types of texts are more likely to comprehend material contained in those texts (Meyer & Rice, 1984; Stein & Trabasso, 1982). If children, for example, have little experience listening to or reading stories, their lack of knowledge of story structures (story schemata) will lessen comprehension. Similarly, in math, children lacking well-defined schemata for math problems will experience difficulty determining what factors or variables are relevant to problem solving (Kintsch & Greeno, 1985). In science it has been noted that the limited schemata for scientific concepts acquired from everyday experiences hinders students' understanding of scientific concepts (Anderson & Smith, 1987). In the classroom, teachers can find ways to build readers' schemata or background knowledge in order to help them interpret specific texts. Activities that provide information prior to reading—such as presenting films, videotapes, demonstrations, and experiments, reading sections of a text aloud to students, previewing important concepts or vocabulary, and presenting students with specific objectives as they read—will either activate available schemata or contribute additional data to those schemata. A thorough discussion and samples of activities to increase students' prior knowledge are discussed in Chapter Four.

Our knowledge of the importance of schemata in the reading process has made a significant contribution to our understanding of the reading process. More than any other factor, the reader's ability to draw on prior knowledge will determine whether a text is understood and how efficiently it is comprehended. Poor readers often are unable to draw on schemata when they read, or when they do draw on schemata, they are poorly organized. Schemata are mental representations of information. The reader must direct his or her attention to that information and to the information in the text to construct meaning. This awareness and regulation during reading is the second element in the reading process.

Metacognition.   The term *metacognition* refers to the reader's awareness of comprehension of a text, as well as the reader's regulation of the processes that lead to comprehension. Metacognitive awareness occurs when learners think about their own thinking. Recent interest in metacognition is founded in the view that active awareness of one's comprehension while reading, and the ability to use effective fix-up strategies when comprehension breaks down, are absolutely essential to learning effectively from reading. It is also argued that good readers exhibit metacognitive behavior, while poor readers do not (Paris, Lipson, & Wixson, 1983), and that good readers are better able to detect ambiguous, inconsistent text or material that is otherwise ill-structured (Garner & Kraus, 1982). The characteristics of a good reader involved in thinking about his thinking as he reads is described by Whimbey (1975):

> A good reader proceeds smoothly and quickly as long as his understanding of the material is complete. But as soon as he senses that he has missed an idea, that the track has been lost, he brings smooth progress to a grinding halt. Advancing more slowly, he seeks clarification in the subsequent material, examining it for the light it can throw on the earlier trouble spot. If still dissatisfied with his grasp, he returns to the point where the difficulty began and rereads the section more carefully. He probes and analyzes phrases and sentences for their exact meaning; he tries to visualize abstruse descriptions; and through a series of approximations, deductions, and corrections he translates scientific and technical terms into concrete examples. (p. 91)

Metacognitive strategies involve more than applying what readers know to the reading in a conscious manner. Readers must recognize not only how they learn, but also how certain factors are related to their knowledge of the content being studied, which procedures or strategies should be applied in that instance, and why a particular strategy is suited to one instance rather than another. It has been suggested that learners must activate an executive control center, a conscious cognitive effort directed at planning strategies in accordance with perceived goals and regulating progress toward the goals, as they are engaged in reading (Paris et al., 1983). Metacognition involves knowledge, control of the cognitive process, and self-control (Paris & Winograd, 1989). Self-control involves readers' ability to commit to the task, to acknowledge their attitude toward the task itself, and to direct attention to the task. It is important to note that although readers may possess adequate knowledge and skillful application of cognitive strategies, if they lack self-control, metacognition will not be realized. Teachers themselves, therefore, need to become aware of the importance of metacognitive behavior as a monitoring device as students assess their comprehension and to apply fix-up strategies when comprehension fails. Furthermore, students should be told the importance of metacognitive behavior and taught metacognitive strategies.

PRACTICE ACTIVITY 1.2

To better understand the metacognitive process, imagine the following instructional scenario. Assume that your goal in reading the following information is to define the advantages of metal gutters over those made of wood. As you read for that goal, note what information you attend to and how you fill in gaps in the text with prior knowledge; also note any rereading that you may find necessary.

Gutters and Downspouts

Several types of gutters are available to guide the rainwater to the downspouts and away from the foundation. Some houses have built-in gutters in the cornice. These are lined with sheet metal and connected to the downspouts. On flat roofs, water is often drained from one or more locations and carried through an inside wall to an underground drain. All downspouts connected to an underground drain should contain basement strainers at the junction of the gutter.

Perhaps the most commonly used gutter is the type hung from the edge of the roof or fastened to the edge of the cornice facia. Metal gutters may be the half-round (fig. 160,A) or the formed type (fig. 160,B) and may be galvanized metal, copper, or aluminum. Some have a factory-applied enamel finish.

Downspouts are round or rectangular (fig. 160,C and D), the round type being used for the half-round gutters. They are usually corrugated to provide extra stiffness and strength. Corrugated patterns are less likely to burst when plugged with ice.

Wood gutters have a pleasing appearance and are fastened to the facia board rather than carried by hangers as are most metal gutters. The wood should be clear and free of knots and preferably treated, unless made of heartwood from such species as redwood, western red cedar, and cypress. Continuous sections should be used whenever possible. When splices are necessary, they should be square-cut butt joints fastened with dowels or spline. Joints should be set in white lead or similar material. When untreated wood gutters are used, it is good practice to brush several generous coats of water-repellent preservative on the interior.

From L. O. Anderson, *Wood-Frame House Construction.* Washington, DC: U.S. Government Printing Office, Forest Products Laboratory, Forest Service, U.S. Department of Agriculture, 1970.

Automaticity.   An automatic activity is one that can be performed instantaneously and without conscious attention. At least some of the subprocesses that are part of the overall process of reading must be automatic if the reader is to construct meaning from text. There are several processes that occur. The reader must simultaneously process information at the letter, word, phrase, and sentence level. This, however, creates a potential problem. The mind's capacity to process information is limited; the reader simply cannot attend to too many things at once. In fact, he or she can really attend to only one thing at a time. Getting meaning out of sentences and longer units of discourse requires attention. If the reader must attend to other processes while reading, understanding will be restricted.

Two closely related subprocesses must be automatic; one of these is recognizing words (Laberge & Samuels, 1974; Perfetti, 1977). Readers must automatically recognize the vast majority of words they encounter. They cannot afford any sort of mental processes such as, "Oh, let's see. Yes, this word is *consterna-*

tion." The other process that must be automatic is that of assigning meaning to words. Readers must develop rapid access to word meanings. This means that in addition to recognizing words automatically, they must automatically—instantly and without conscious attention—assign meanings to words. Many words encountered by students are at a near-automatic level; a moment of reflection is required to recall the word's meaning. *Ubiquitous* might be such a word for many seventh graders. Some seventh graders could probably recognize the word in print, might even recognize it automatically, but then would need to go through a mental process such as, "Let's see. *Ubiquitous?* Oh, yes. That means something is everywhere." Readers cannot afford to go through such a process with very many words they encounter. If they do, text is processed slowly and comprehension is fragmented.

There are a number of instructional implications stemming from the notion of automaticity. First, students need to have ready access to word meanings. It is reasonable to assume that students should be encouraged to read widely, and teachers should be encouraged to teach word meanings directly and to instruct students in strategies for learning word meanings independently (Graves, 1987). Readers must recognize and readily access the meanings of the vast majority of words they encounter in an automatic manner. Lacking that automaticity, cognitive effort is devoted to the recognition of words, reducing the likelihood that readers will have complete comprehension.

PRACTICE ACTIVITY 1.3

The importance of automaticity in the reading process can be seen in the following example. Read the directions carefully to complete the exercise.

Directions: *Read the following inverted print three times aloud. Use a tape recorder to record each reading. When you have completed the third reading, listen to the tape. Record the time in seconds and the number of errors for each reading. Do not turn the page to view the print as "normal."*

Vitamin C

Forms and Sources. Ascorbic acid, the chemical name of vitamin C, is a shortened form of antiscorbutic (scurvy-preventing) factor. A relatively simple organic acid, vitamin C, having six carbon atoms in each molecule, is structurally similar to the single, six-carbon sugars such as glucose. It is the least stable of all vitamins, being easily oxidized to dehydroascorbic acid. (*Dehydro* means minus hydrogen;) in oxidation, the ascorbic acid loses two hydrogen atoms per molecule.) Both ascorbic acid and dehydroascorbic acid are found in foods.

Wenck, D. A., Maren, M., & Dewan, S. A. (1980). *Nutrition.* Reston, VA: Reston.

Instructional Applications of the Reading Process

In summary, reading can be viewed as an interactive process whereby information is obtained simultaneously from knowledge sources. These sources include letter-level knowledge, word-level knowledge, syntactic knowledge, and knowledge of the meaning of sentences and larger units. This interactive view of reading is also a compensatory model whereby inefficiencies at one level in processing text can be compensated for by using greater amounts of information from other levels (Stanovich, West, & Freeman, 1981). Thus, a reader who has difficulty decoding a text can, to some extent, use background knowledge to make the content more meaningful despite having difficulty with the pronunciation of certain words. Similarly, if a reader lacks specific background knowledge, metacognitive strategies may allow for the establishment of specific goals and constant monitoring to apply fix-up strategies that will enhance the accomplishment of those reading goals. The subject matter teacher must recognize that reading ability is not static. Comprehension and thinking strategies can be improved by presenting difficult vocabulary, establishing reading goals, and creating background knowledge.

CONCLUDING REMARKS

In this chapter we have addressed a number of topics that cover the need, the intent, and the focus of content area reading instruction. The goal of content area reading instruction today has changed little since the early 1900s: to facilitate students' ability to learn from subject matter text and nonprint sources of information. However, today's students and teachers are faced with challenges that are unprecedented in American education. The level of reading and writing ability required to be functionally literate has increased dramatically over the past 20 years, yet achievement tests over the past 25 years indicate that the level of performance on many basic skills has remained relatively stable. In the workplace, employees are expected to be able to express their thoughts in print, obtain information and construct knowledge from text, solve everyday work-related problems that require critical thinking, and work cooperatively with their peers. Today's high school graduates, therefore, must attain a high level of literacy, must be capable of making decisions that require higher level thinking skills, and must be able to work and communicate effectively.

With these increased literacy and academic skills have come numerous calls for educational reform. At the same time, subject matter teachers are confronted with the demands of students with increasingly divergent social, economic, and intellectual backgrounds. They are expected to cover more content than in the past and to integrate that content with other subject matter areas. They are also being held accountable for students' understanding of that content. To say that education is in a state of flux would clearly be an understatement.

This book offers practical activities to help students better comprehend subject matter content in print or through such nonprint media as demonstrations, discussions, hands-on activities, and visual presentations. It also offers activities that promote cooperative learning and that assist students in becoming more independent in their acquisition of information and their ability to construct knowledge.

REFLECTIONS

This section of the chapter offers some activities for considering the major topics presented in the chapter, how these topics apply to literacy tasks, as well as how those tasks occur in the classroom.

1. Interview a subject matter teacher to determine what steps are taken to meet the demands of (a) students who read at various levels of ability; (b) a multicultural classroom; (c) a constructivist form of instruction whereby students are actively involved in the learning environment; (d) an integrated curriculum involving interdisciplinary instruction, multiple sources of information, or cooperative learning environments.
2. Select a text you would read for an academic course. From this source select 5 to 10 pages of text to read. Before reading the selection, examine the title and headings to determine the gist of the content. In an attempt to become aware of your prior knowledge, write down facts, concepts, or generalizations that come to mind. Next, read the selection with the intent of becoming more aware of your own study strategies. Attend to and write down the various strategies that you use as you engage in reading, such as summarizing, questioning, reviewing, and note taking.
3. Monitor for a 24-hour period the types of literacy tasks you engage in outside those involved with your schooling. Note these tasks, then rate each on a scale of 1 to 10 to identify the level of difficulty of the task (10 being the most difficult). Discuss your findings with your colleagues, then hypothesize how well the population at large may engage in these various types of functional literacy tasks.
4. Examine a curriculum guide, textbook, or other form of instructional material that could be used in a subject matter classroom. Survey this material and complete the following questions:
   a. To what extent does this material draw on the reader's background knowledge? Is the student allowed to form conclusions or generalizations by using prior knowledge?
   b. To what extent does the material seem to focus on the needs of the learner? Does the instructional material consider the individual needs, interests, and background of the student?
   c. Does the material allow the student to apply the content to daily life and work experiences?

REFERENCES

Aaron, I. E., Chall, J. S., Durkin, D., Goodman, K., & Strickland, D. S. (1990). The past, present, and future of literacy education: Comments from a panel of distinguished educators. *The Reading Teacher, 43*(4), 302–311.

Alvermann, D. E., & Swafford, J. (1989). Do content area strategies have a research base? *Journal of Reading, 32*, 388–394.

American College Test. (1985). Table: ACT score means and SDs for successive years of ACT-tested college-bound students. Iowa City: Author.

Anderson, C. W., & Smith, E. L. (1987). Teaching science. In V. Richardson-Koehler (Ed.), *Educators handbook: A research perspective.* New York: Longman.

Austin, M., & Morrison, C. (1963). *The first R: The Harvard report on reading in elementary schools.* New York: Macmillan.

Bailey, T. (1991). Jobs of the future and the education they will require: Evidence from occupational forecasts. *Educational Researcher, 20*(2), 11–20.

Barnes, H. (1989). Structuring knowledge for beginning teachers. In M. C. Reynolds (Ed.), *Knowledge base for the beginning teacher.* Oxford, U.K.: Pergamon.

Bean, T. W. (1981). *Improving teaching and learning from texts in history and philosophy* (Final report). Fullerton: California State University Chancellor's Office for Educational Development and Innovation. (ERIC Document Reproduction Service No. ED 205 925)

Bean, T. W., Singer, H., and Frazee, C. (1986). The effect of metacognitive instruction in outlining and graphic organizer construction on students' comprehension in a tenth-grade world history class. *Journal of Reading Behavior, 18*, 153–169.

Coleman, J. S., et al. (1966). *Equality of educational opportunity.* Washington, DC: U.S. Government Printing Office.

College Entrance Examination Board, Admissions Testing Program. (1983). *National report on college-bound seniors, 1983.* New York: Author.

College Entrance Examination Board, Advisory Panel on the Scholastic Aptitude Test

Score Decline. (1977). *On further examination.* New York: Author.

Conley, M. W. (1986). Teacher's conceptions, decisions, and changes during initial classroom lessons containing content area reading strategies. In J. A. Niles & R. V. Lalik (Eds.), *Solving problems in literacy: Learners, teachers, and searchers.* Rochester, NY: National Reading Conference.

Cooperman, P. (1979). The achievement decline of the 1970's. *Phi Delta Kappan, 60*, 736–739.

CTB/McGraw-Hill. (1982). *Comprehensive tests of basic skills: Preliminary technical report, Forms U and V.* Monterey, CA: Author.

Early, M. J. (1957). What does research reveal about successful reading programs? In M. A. Gunn et al. (Eds.), *What we know about high school reading.* Champaign, IL: National Council of Teachers of English.

Eckland, B. K. (1982). College entrance examination trends. In G. R. Austin & H. Garber (Eds.), *The rise and fall of national test scores.* New York: Academic Press.

Estes, T. H., & Piercey, D. (1973). Secondary reading requirements: Report on the States. *Journal of Reading, 17*, 20–24.

Farrell, R. T., & Cirrincione, J. M. (1984). State certification requirements in reading for content area teachers. *Journal of Reading, 28*, 152–158.

Flynn, P. M. (1988). *Facilitating technological change: The human resource challenge.* Cambridge, MA: Ballinger.

Freire, P. (1985). *The politics of education: Culture, power, and liberation.* South Hadley, MA: Bergin & Garvey.

Fuller, F. F. (1969). Concerns for teachers: A developmental characterization. *American Educational Research Journal, 6*, 207–226.

Garner, R., & Kraus, C. (1982). Good and poor comprehender differences in knowing and regulating reading behaviors. *Educational Research Quarterly, 6*, 5–12.

Graves, M. F. (1987). The roles of instruction in fostering vocabulary development. In M. G. McKeown & M. E. Curtis (Eds.), *The nature of vocabulary instruction*. Hillsdale, NJ: Erlbaum.

Gray, W. S. (1925). *Summary of investigations relating to reading* (Supplementary Educational Monograph No. 28). Chicago: University of Chicago Press.

Greene, M. (1989). Social and political contexts. In M. C. Reynolds (Ed.), *Knowledge base for the beginning teacher*. New York: Pergamon.

Harnischfeger, A., & Wiley, D. E. (1975). *Achievement test scores decline: Do we need to worry?* Chicago: CEMEREL.

Heller, M. (1986). How do you know what you know? Metacognitive modeling in the content areas. *Journal of Reading, 29*, 415–422.

Herber, H. L. (1970). *Teaching reading in content areas*. Englewood Cliffs, NJ: Prentice-Hall.

Irwin, P. M. (1987). *Adult literacy issues, programs, and options*. Washington, DC: Education and Public Welfare Division, Congressional Search Service.

Jencks, C., Smith, M., Ackland, H., Bane, M. J., Cohen, D., Gintis, H., Hegnes, B., & Michelson, S. (1972). *Inequality: A reassessment of the effect of family and schooling in America*. New York: Basic Books.

Johnston, W. B., & Packer, A. H. (1987). *Workforce 2000: Work and workers for the 21st century*. Indianapolis, IN: Hudson Institute.

Kazemek, F. E. (1988). The self as social process: The work of George Herbert Mead and its implications for adult literacy education. *Adult Literacy and Basic Education, 12*(1), 1–13.

The knowledge gap. (1990, February 9). *The Wall Street Journal*, p. R1.

Kutscher, R. E. (1989). Projections, summary and emerging issues. *Monthly Labor Review, 112*, 66–74.

LaBerge, D., & Samuels, S. J. (1974). Toward a theory of automatic information processing in reading. *Cognitive Psychology, 6*, 293–323.

Lederman, L. M. (1991). The Tevatron. *Scientific American, 264*(3), 48–55.

Mehan, H. (1979). *Learning lessons*. Cambridge, MA: Harvard University Press.

Memory, D. M. (1983). Implementing a practicum in a required content area reading course. *Reading World, 23*, 116–123.

Meyer, B., & Rice, E. (1984). The structure of text. In P. D. Pearson (Ed.), *Handbook of reading research*. New York: Longman.

Mikulecky, L. (1982). Job literacy: The relationship between school preparation and workplace actuality. *Reading Research Quarterly, 17*, 400–419.

Mikulecky, L., & Ehlinger, J. (1986). The influence of metacognitive aspects of literacy on job performance of electronic technicians. *Journal of Reading Behavior, 18*(1), 41–62.

Mullis, V. S., Owen, E. H., & Phillips, G. W. (1991). *Accelerating academic achievement: A summary of findings from 20 years of NAEP*. Princeton, NJ: National Assessment of Educational Progress, Educational Testing Service.

National Alliance of Business. (1987). *The fourth R: Workforce readiness*. New York: Author.

National Center on Education and the Economy. (1990). *America's Choice: High Skills or Low Wages*. Rochester, NY: Author.

National Commission on Excellence in Education. (1983). *A nation at risk: The imperative for educational form*. Washington, DC: U.S. Government Printing Office.

Oakes, J. (1986). Keeping track: 1. The policy and practice of curriculum inequality. *Phi Delta Kappan, 68*(1), 12–17.

O'Brien, D. G. (1988). Secondary preservice teachers' resistance to content reading instruction: A proposal for a broader rationale. In J. Readence & R. S. Baldwin (Eds.), *Dialogues in literacy research: 37th yearbook of the National Reading Conference*. Chicago: National Reading Conference.

Olson, A. V., & Rosen, C. L. (1967). A study of teacher practices in reading. *Reading Improvement, 4*, 84–87.

Paris, S. G., Lipson, M. Y., & Wixson, K. K. (1983). Becoming a strategic reader. *Contemporary Educational Psychology, 8*, 293–316.

Paris, S. G., & Winograd, P. (1989). How metacognition can promote academic learning and instruction. In B. F. Jones & L. Idol (Eds.), *Dimensions of thinking and cognitive instruction* (Vol. 1). Hillsdale, NJ: Erlbaum.

Pearce, D. L., & Bader, L. A. (1986). The effect of unit construction upon teachers' use of content area reading and writing strategies. *Journal of Reading, 30,* 130–135.

Perfetti, C. A. (1977). Language comprehension and fast decoding: Some psycholinguistic prerequisites for skilled reading comprehension. In J. T. Guthrie (Ed.), *Cognition, curriculum, and comprehension.* Newark, DE: International Reading Association.

Ravitch, D. (1985). *The schools we deserve.* New York: Basic Books.

Resnick, D. P., & Resnick, L. B. (1977). The nature of literacy: An historical exploration. *Harvard Educational Review, 47,* 370–385.

Rumberger, R. W., & Levin, H. M. (1989). Schooling for the modern workplace. In *Investing in people: A strategy to address America's workforce crisis* (Vol. 1). Washington, DC: Commission on Workforce Quality and Labor Market Efficiency, U.S. Department of Labor.

Rumelhart, D. E. (1977). Toward an interactive model of reading. In S. Dornic (Ed.), *Attention and performance* (Vol. 6, pp. 573–603). Hillsdale, NJ: Erlbaum.

———. (1980). Schemata: The building blocks of cognition. In R. J. Spiro, B. C. Bruce, & W. F. Brewer (Eds.), *Theoretical issues in reading comprehension: Perspectives from cognitive psychology, linguistics, artificial intelligence, and education.* Hillsdale, NJ: Erlbaum.

Schwartz, J. (1988). Learning and earning. *American Demographics, 10*(1), 12.

Science Research Associates. (1978). *Iowa Tests of Educational Development* (Tech. Rep.).

Smith, F. R., & Feathers, K. M. (1983). Teacher and student perceptions of content area reading. *Journal of Reading, 1,* 354–384.

Stanovich, K. E., West, R. F., & Freeman, D. V. (1981). A longitudinal study of sentence context effects in second grade children: Test of an interactive-compensatory model. *Journal of Experimental Child Psychology, 32,* 185–199.

Stedman, L. C., & Kaestle, C. F. (1987). Literacy and reading in the United States, from 1880 to the present. *Reading Research Quarterly, 21,* 8–46.

Stein, N. L., & Trabasso, T. (1982). What's in a story: An approach to verbal comprehension and instruction. In R. Glaser (Ed.), *Advances in instructional psychology* (Vol. 2). Hillsdale, NJ: Erlbaum.

Vosniadou, S., & Brewer, W. (1987). Theories of knowledge structuring in development. *Review of Educational Search, 57*(1), 51–67.

West, C. K. (1981). *The social and psychological distortion of information.* Chicago: Nelson-Hall.

Whimbey, A. (1975). *Intelligence can be taught.* New York: Dutton.

Whipple, G. M. (ed.). (1925). Report on the national committee on reading: *24th yearbook of the National Society for the Study of Education.* Bloomington, IL: Public School Publishing.

CHAPTER TWO

Assessment

CHAPTER OVERVIEW

This chapter is divided into three sections. The first section presents a discussion of the need for classroom assessment and the characteristics of classroom assessment. The second section covers the use and interpretation of standardized, norm-referenced tests and defines both formal and informal tests. The third section discusses factors that affect text difficulty and concludes with strategies to assess textbooks and text readability.

...ts or criterion-referenced tests may be ad-
...on how well students have learned.

...pes of assessment: formal and informal. The dis-
...focuses on two measures: norm-referenced and
...is is followed by a supplementary section provid-
...teristics of formal tests. The second concludes with
...of informal tests in the subject matter classroom and
...s for administering two types of informal reading as-

...students' behavior using uniform or consistent proce-
...ing and scoring the tests (Mehrens & Lehmann, 1991) in an
...curate and reliable results. If the directions of a test, for ex-
...teacher to present a sample test item to students then con-
...sion of the process needed to solve the item, it would be rea-
...e that omission of the sample item could have an adverse
...ts' test performance. The administration of a timed test also
...performance. If a teacher allowed one group of students 15 min-
...te a set of problems and another group 35 minutes, it would be
...assume that the students given additional time would have
...ores. The clarity of directions also can affect student performance.
...r example, the following question:

...ons: *Circle the word that is not a noun.*
    a. flog
    b. medallion
    c. convalescence
    d. fragrance

...ost likely you had little difficulty recognizing that *flog* (to flail or beat) is
...and thus does not have the same grammatical function as the other three
...s. Now complete the following:

Directions: *Circle the best response from the following.*
    a. rendezvous
    b. summit
    c. parlance
    d. rebuttal

Ambiguous directions make this question more difficult. You may have assumed that the answer was derived from a comparison of the words' mean-

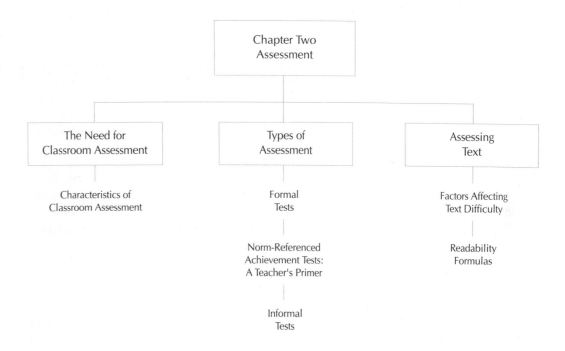

In the first section of the chapter we discuss the nature of assessment, addressing the need for and types of assessment, and conclude with a primer on testing in the schools.

THE NEED FOR CLASSROOM ASSESSMENT

Educational assessment is the process of gathering information about students, educational programs, or educational products. Mehrens and Lehmann (1991) assert that the term *assessment* "is used broadly, like evaluation; or it is often used to indicate the use of both formal and informal data gathering procedures and the combining of the data in a global fashion to reach an overall judgment" (p. 4). Although assessment is often associated with formal measures like norm-referenced tests, it also involves less formal measures, such as teacher observations, in-class questioning, student portfolios, and student self-reports. Formal assessment often is used as a measure of how well students in a school or district perform on certain academic tasks. These tests are often required by local or state agencies. Informal assessment is the day-to-day evaluation conducted by teachers to determine how well students perform on given objectives or to evaluate what students know about elements of the curriculum.

The process of gathering information about an individual or groups' performance or response to an activity is entrenched in our everyday lives. Whether it is our ability to drive a manual transmission automobile, to engage in a sporting activity, to prepare various types of foods, or to build or create an object, we all want some sort of feedback on our performance. For some, a personal evaluation will suffice; others seek the advice of peers or colleagues to define the level of performance or degree of satisfaction that was achieved. Most frequently we engage in assessment to provide ongoing feedback about our success in reaching an objective. Consider, for example, a home improvement activity. While painting the interior walls and trim of a room, we gather information about existing conditions as well as our performance in the task of painting. Initially we define our goal in terms of the color we want the walls and trim painted, and the finish we want the paint to display (flat, gloss, or semi-gloss). We examine the existing walls and trim to gather information that could affect the outcome of our efforts (whether the paint is blistered, scaled, or alligatored), then begin the process of preparing the surface and painting. As we continue painting, we continually monitor our work to determine if the new paint covers the existing paint, if there are visible brush marks, or if paint is splattering on adjacent surfaces. Based on feedback from this ongoing assessment, modifications may be necessary to accomplish our defined goal. An improperly sanded surface is resanded to allow the paint to adhere. Once the painting job is completed, we again assess the total impact of the effort and encourage others to provide verbal feedback on the finished product, trusting that they focus on our craft rather than on the blobs of paint on ourselves.

ings. If so, you would select the fourth response alternative, *rebuttal*, believing that the other terms dealt with people drawing together for the purpose of discussion, whereas *rebuttal* dealt with opposing views during debate. Your response would be incorrect, however, if the intent of the question was to select the term that is derived from a foreign word (*rendezvous*).

Formal tests can be either *norm referenced* or *criterion referenced*. Norm-referenced tests compare the performance of an individual with that of other individuals in what is termed the *norm group*. Generally, norm-referenced scores provide information on what percent of individuals performed above and below the level of the individual tested. Scores are often expressed in terms of percentiles (the percent of individuals who scored below a given point). A percentile score of 78 on the Iowa Test of Basic Skills (Hieronymus, Hoover, & Linquist, 1986) indicates that a student scored as well as or better than 78% of the individuals at that grade or age level.

Criterion-referenced tests do not compare students' scores; rather, they report a student's performance on a specified domain of educational or behavioral outcomes. For example, a criterion-referenced test may present a series of problems to determine if students have learned to add and subtract mixed fractions. These problems may present a wide range of difficulty to determine how well a student performs along the range of problems presented. Often called mastery tests, criterion-referenced tests provide information about a student's performance relative to the criterion of performance desired. Results of criterion-referenced tests, therefore, are reported on the basis of whether the student scored at the criterion level of performance. No comparisons are made between an individual's score and that of some norm group. Test results are examined instead on the basis of how well individual students or students as a whole perform on a test item. Consider, for example, a criterion-referenced test assessing students' ability to multiply mixed fractions. A teacher may receive results indicating that 89% of the students in a given class correctly multiply mixed fractions. No information is provided as to how well students in other schools performed, nor are scores reported as percentiles or grade equivalents.

Uses of Norm-Referenced and Criterion-Referenced Tests.   Student assessment is often conducted to compare an individual student's performance to others, or to compare the performance of a school district to other districts or the national average. Under these circumstances, a norm-referenced test may be the best choice. Norm-referenced tests are often used to predict students' potential to succeed and thus are frequently used as a criterion for admission to educational programs or institutions. They are also widely used by school districts to measure performance in comparison to national, regional, or local norms. These comparisons provide not only some measure of how well a school district stacks up against other districts, but also, over a period of time, some measure of students' level of achievement.

Criterion-referenced tests tend to measure more specific objectives; therefore, it may be possible to draw conclusions regarding an individual's performance on the objectives measured (Mehrens & Lehmann, 1991). In some subject matter areas students must master certain fundamental information before they can be presented with higher level concepts. In mathematics, for example, students need to master the concepts of circumference and radius before they can acquire concepts to determine the area of circles. Criterion-referenced tests are used to measure students' mastery of specific instructional objectives taught in the classroom, to assess those skills that are defined as minimal competencies for high school graduation, or to identify students who may require compensatory or accelerated instruction.

The decision of whether to use a norm-referenced or criterion-referenced test depends on the desired educational outcome. Criterion-referenced tests often assess a minimum level of performance. All practicing dentists, for example, must pass a criterion-referenced test to become licensed; yet among any group of dentists there are differences in how well they have mastered dentistry. Norm-referenced tests generally are more sensitive to individual differences and include items to indicate how well students learn defined skills.

Recognizing the importance that parents, administrators, school boards, and the public often place on formal, norm-referenced achievement tests, an overview of some of the important characteristics of these tests follows. This is not intended to be an exhaustive review of this topic, but a basic discussion to assist you in determining how you may use formal test results in your classroom.

Norm-Referenced Achievement Tests: A Teacher's Primer

Norm-referenced tests have been a fixture in our schools for over 100 years. During the past decade, the use of these tests increasingly has been questioned. In summarizing these concerns, Haney and Madaus (1989) note that formal, norm-referenced tests (1) provide false information on the status of learning in the schools (Gardner, 1985); (2) are biased against minority group students (Hoover, Politzer, & Taylor, 1987), those with limited English proficiency, and those students of low income (Taylor & Lee, 1987); (3) tend to reduce teaching to the preparation for test taking (Madaus, 1985, 1986); and (4) emphasize lower rather than higher order thinking skills. More recently, the validity of formal achievement tests has been questioned on several grounds. First, the most widely used achievement tests assume that learning can be examined by identifying isolated skills assessed outside the context of the classroom and the situations in which those skills are used (Paris, Lawton, Turner, & Roth, 1991). These tests do not consider the learner's motivation or the content or setting of the task; factors that have strong effects on learning. Second, achievement tests do not present tasks typically encountered in the classroom curriculum (Linn, 1987; Wiggins, 1989). Tasks that require students to read extended selections of text, to synthesize information drawn from various sources, or to solve problems through cooperative efforts with their peers are seldom evident in achievement tests.

Despite these criticisms, these tests are widely used as a measure of students' academic performance in an attempt to define individual's performance and to compare a school district's performance to the nation as a whole. While these tests assess aptitudes, interests, personalities, attitudes, and exceptionalities, the discussion of the characteristics and interpretation of scoring of these tests that follows will be limited to the most widely used type of formal, norm-referenced tests: those that assess achievement.

Interpreting Norm-Referenced Test Scores.   Scores on norm-referenced achievement tests are often reported as raw scores, percentiles and percentile ranks, stanines, and grade equivalents. Because each of these reported scores provides different information, it is important to understand what they represent and what their limitations are for purposes of reporting or interpreting test results.

Raw scores are the number of correct responses on a test. Raw scores alone provide little information on how well an individual or group performs relative to the school-age population; therefore, they are transformed to percentiles, percentile ranks, stanines, and grade equivalents.

Percentiles describe for a distribution of raw scores the percentage of the scores falling below a given point on that distribution of scores. For example, assume that Jennifer, an eighth grader, has obtained the following raw scores and percentile scores on a norm-referenced achievement test of reading consisting of 50 comprehension items and 71 vocabulary items.

Reading Comprehension

Raw Score	39
Percentile	87

Vocabulary Knowledge

Raw Score	51
Percentile	94

If the raw score of 39 on the comprehension test is transformed to a percentile of 87, then it can be stated that roughly 87% of the scores in the distribution of individuals in the normative group fell below the raw score of 39. Percentile scores provide information of a student's performance within a single age or grade level. Percentiles are useful in making comparisons between subtests. One limitation of percentile scores is presented in Figure 2.1. Note that the raw scores are equally distributed along the scale of scores from 0 to 50, whereas the percentiles bunch up toward the center of the curve. As a result, the interval between the 40th and 50th percentile corresponds to approximately one raw score point, whereas the interval between the 1st and 10th percentile corresponds to approximately 6 raw score points. A difference of 1 point in the raw score of an individual scoring anywhere between the 40th and 50th percentile will change the percentile rank approximately 7 points. A difference of 1 point at the upper or lower 10% of the distribution of the curve

FIGURE 2.1   PERCENTILES AND STANINES

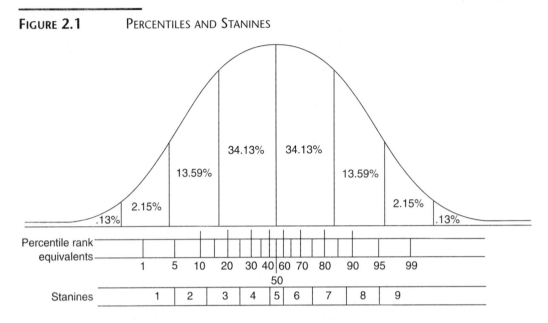

(90th to 99th percentile and below the 10th percentile) would change the percentile rank anywhere from 0.25 to 2.0 points. Caution must be exercised, therefore, when drawing conclusions from scores falling in the center portion of the distribution.

Stanine scores range from 1 to 9. Each score represents a range of the raw scores of a test. As seen in Figure 2.1, in a normal distribution, stanines 1 through 9 represent 4%, 7%, 12%, 17%, 20%, 17%, 12%, 7%, 4% of the scores, respectively. While stanines are more easily interpreted than percentiles, they tend to be gross measures of performance. Referring to Figure 2.1, note that students who score at the 61st or 76th percentile would be placed at the 6th stanine, although there is a range of 15 percentile points between the scores of the two individuals. On the other hand, students who score at the 76th percentile and those scoring at the 81st percentile are placed at the 6th and 7th stanines, respectively, although the range in their percentile ranks is 5 points. Because stanines are gross measures of student performance, their use should be limited to those instances in which a general estimate of achievement is desired.

The final type of norm-referenced achievement test score presented here is the *grade equivalent score.* Unlike raw scores, percentiles, and stanines, the grade equivalent score is not based on comparisons between students of the same grade level. Rather, grade equivalent scores are derived through a comparison of an individual's score to the average scores of students at various age or grade levels. A grade equivalent score, therefore, is a type of developmental level score because it can be used to compare a student's performance to a series of age or grade levels that will vary developmentally depending on the trait or characteristic being measured (Mehrens & Lehmann, 1991). A seventh grader obtaining a grade equivalent score of 7.8 would be performing at the level of the average student in the eighth month of the seventh grade. Grade equivalent scores frequently have been viewed as the standard of performance that should direct the school curriculum. It is not unusual, for example, to hear well-meaning educators, parents, administrators, or school board members state that they would like to "bring all students up to grade level." Recall that "at grade level" refers to the performance of the average student, or that raw score that falls at the 50th percentile. By definition the scores of a norm-referenced achievement test will be distributed so that half will fall below and half above the 50th percentile. The misuse of grade equivalent scores has resulted in a number of false assumptions regarding students' instructional placement. For example, the grade equivalent score should not be used as a guide to predict the grade level of the material a student can read—a student with a grade equivalent score of 7.0 may not necessarily be capable of reading seventh-grade material. Similarly, an eighth grader with a grade equivalent score of 10.0 may not necessarily read like an average tenth grader. As a result of the misuse of grade equivalent scores, the Delegates Assembly of the International Reading Association passed a resolution in 1981 advocating that publishers abandon the use of these scores.

Norm-referenced test scores are not precise measures. Each test has a *standard error of measurement*. This is the variation of test scores an individual would obtain if he or she took the test repeatedly. By adding and subtracting the standard error of measurement from an individual's obtained score, it is possible to determine the range of performance that the test measures. For example, if the standard error of measurement of a norm-referenced test is reported as a 0.75 grade-level equivalent, the actual performance of a student who scored at 7.0 is 6.25 to 7.75. This range was obtained by subtracting and adding the standard error of measure to the individual's score ($7.0 - 0.75 = 6.25; 7.0 + 0.75 = 7.75$). The standard error of measurement will vary between tests; thus, it is important to obtain this measurement from the test's technical manual. It is essential to obtain a test's standard error of measurement when assigning students to instructional groups or when using test results as measures of curricular accountability.

PRACTICE ACTIVITY 2.1

To make certain you understand the major points in this section on norm-referenced tests, respond to the following statements.

_____ Yes   _____ No   Percentile scores are sensitive to the performance of students at a specific grade level.

_____ Yes   _____ No   In a normal distribution of scores, the average raw score represents the 50th percentile.

_____ Yes   _____ No   Stanines range from 1 to 9 and represent an equal number of scores in each stanine.

_____ Yes   _____ No   If a test has a large standard error of measurement, care should be taken in using these scores for curricular or instructional decisions.

_____ Yes   _____ No   A formal, norm-referenced achievement test is a good measure of a student's mastery of the various skills or content taught in a subject matter area.

Informal Tests

This section presents a brief discussion of the use of informal tests in the subject matter classroom, followed by two forms of informal tests—the cloze test and the content area reading inventory. As you read this section, it may be useful to consider the advantages these two types of informal assessment have over standardized tests and the applications they may have in your classroom.

Informal testing has the advantage of being highly sensitive to student performance on the content addressed in a given classroom. The tasks students engage in, the material they use for the tasks, and the cognitive strategies these tasks may require are determined by the teacher. If, for example, a social studies teacher emphasizes students' ability to draw generalizations from multiple sources, a test can be constructed with perhaps five different reading selections to assess students' ability to construct generalizations. Informal tests can be administered at various times throughout the school year. At the beginning of the year an informal test may be used to assess students' knowledge of the content presented in a class. Results of this test can be used to identify each individual's ability, to form cooperative learning groups, to aid in the selection of supplemental reading material, and to determine the pace of instruction. Informal tests are also useful in gaining an understanding of a group's performance. By examining the average score of a class, the teacher can determine the level of students' background knowledge and their ability to engage in cognitive tasks required in the curriculum.

What follows is a description of two types of informal tests suitable for classroom use: the cloze assessment and the content area reading inventory.

Cloze Assessment.   The cloze assessment was first developed by Taylor (1953), who surmised that the concept of closure, a term referring to the tendency to make meaning of incomplete information, was a fundamental element in the reading process. To maintain coherence and understanding as we read, we tend to fill in those "vacuous slots" caused by words or concepts that may be unknown. In the following sentence, for example, it takes little effort to insert a word in the blank that is semantically and syntactically appropriate.

The horses entered the final turn on the dirt-covered _____ as they sped toward the finish line.

It is likely that you made closure by filling in the term *track* or *racetrack* with ease due to the familiarity of the content and the word itself. Sentences are not always this easy to understand. When the content of a passage or sentence is unfamiliar, the ability to supply the appropriate word can be difficult, as evident in the following sentence.

The body is capable of producing its own opiate-like compounds through a process in which neurotransmitters bind to opioid _____ , thus producing a sensation of pleasure similar to that obtained from opium.

Lacking a background in pharmacology or neurology, it may be difficult for you to reach closure with this sentence to produce the word *receptors*. Noting that the ability to attain meaningful closure was a function of the reader's background knowledge and skill at using cues in the text, Taylor proposed a form of reading assessment that draws on the reader's ability to interact with the text as it is being processed rather than testing the reader's understanding at the completion of the reading. The cloze procedure was later presented by Bormuth (1968, 1969) as a method to assess comprehension. Being an informal test, the cloze test is constructed, administered, scored, and interpreted by the teacher.

Constructing the Cloze.   Constructing a cloze test is easy. The first step is to select several passages from your classroom reading materials. Each passage should be approximately 200 to 300 words in length. The passages should be from the beginning of the text or a chapter to reduce the likelihood that students' understanding will be affected by concepts addressed in earlier portions of the text. Once you have selected a passage, you can construct the cloze test. Leave intact the first sentence or two of the selection. Next, delete every fifth word and replace each with a blank line. This line should be of an equal length for each of the deleted words to remove clues of any word's length. Delete a total of 50 words. Finally, leave the last sentence or two of the passage intact.

Administering the Cloze.   Many students are unfamiliar with the cloze procedure. It is advisable, therefore, that you model the process of selecting words to be placed in the blanks. Modeling can begin by presenting a simple example containing 5 to 10 deleted words. The content of this example should be familiar to students to ensure that their attention is directed to the process of completing the cloze rather than attempting to determine the meaning of the passage. Stress to students that in formulating their answers they should attempt to select the word used in the original text by considering the author's style and choice of words. Following the initial modeling, give students another passage that contains familiar content consisting of 10 or 15 deletions. This example should be completed by each student without time limits. Once completed, you can review the answers, provide a short discussion of the purpose of the cloze, then ask individual students for rationales for their responses. Both examples of the cloze should be administered without time limits. Once the sample cloze tests are completed, you can administer the cloze test. Administration of two or three cloze passages will increase test reliability and the accuracy of the procedure's results.

Scoring the Cloze.   As mentioned previously, correct responses are limited to the exact word appearing in the original passage. Spelling errors are acceptable. Synonyms or changes in the word's tense or inflection are not acceptable. While the acceptance of synonyms would increase students' scores, the relative difference between the scores would remain constant (Bormuth, 1968). Furthermore, scoring of synonyms has been shown to reduce test reliability (Henk & Selders, 1984), and exact replacement scoring has been shown to correlate significantly with informal reading inventories as well as standardized reading tests (Smith & Zinc, 1977). Therefore, it is recommended that to maintain the objectivity of scoring (McKenna, 1976) and to reduce the time necessary to determine if a synonym is acceptable, only the exact word be accepted. Once you have totaled the number of items scored correctly, multiply that sum by 2; this produces the percentage of items scored correctly.

Cloze scores are reported as one of three reading levels: independent, instructional, and frustration. These scores were derived by Bormuth (1968) in an analysis comparing the cloze scores with those of a standardized reading test and a multiple-choice comprehension test. According to Bormuth, a score of 57% on the cloze corresponded to a comprehension score of 90%, and a cloze score of 44% corresponded to a comprehension score of 75%. Bormuth suggested the following scoring criteria:

Reading Level	Cloze Test Scores
Independent	58%–100%
Instructional	44%–57%
Frustration	0%–43%

Students scoring at the *independent* level are assumed to be capable of comprehending the text and would not require instructional assistance from the teacher. Students scoring at the *instructional* level would require some assistance from the teacher. And students scoring at the *frustration* level would require either considerable assistance from the teacher or a less difficult text.

Commentary.   The cloze assesses students' ability to comprehend reading material used in the classroom. It is easy to construct, administer, and score. Results of the cloze have been shown to correlate highly with other measures of reading comprehension; thus, one can assume that it measures some of the same aspects of the reading process that are found in standardized reading tests. Because it measures students' ability to read classroom material, its results should be a good predictor of students' ability to learn from subject matter materials. Like any test, the cloze also has limitations, among these are the likelihood that it measures comprehension only at the sentence level (Shanahan, Kamil, & Tobin, 1982) and that it requires students to search for information to fill in the blanks rather than read for a more general understanding (Johnston, 1983). Finally, the cloze will not describe how well students apply higher level thinking strategies.

PRACTICE ACTIVITY 2.2

Now that you have read about the procedures to construct, administer, and score your own cloze test, complete the following sample assessment. Your objective is to write in each of the 50 spaces the exact word that you believe appeared in the text. Once you have completed the cloze sample, score your responses using the answers found at the end of the book.

Sample Cloze Assessment

Suntan: Your Skin's Natural Protection

Until relatively recent times, displaying one's suntan was not an attribute widely accepted by the population. In fact, for many years having a suntan denoted one as a laborer. Over time however, a _____ became fashionable as those _____ could afford to travel _____ maintain their tan by _____ in distant locations. More _____ , however, many individuals in _____ medical community have warned _____ excessive sun can cause _____ , premature aging of the _____ , and small wartlike growths. _____ individual's resistance to the _____ of sun is determined _____ the thickness of the _____ and the amount of _____ . Individuals who have thicker _____ are less likely to _____ . The extent of the _____ color is determined by _____ , a human skin pigment. _____ skin pigment is made _____ skin cells called melanocytes. _____ is these cells that _____ melanin, the pigment that _____ the skin from the _____ rays of the sun. _____ who have large concentrations _____ melanin are less likely _____ be affected by the _____ rays. Suntan as well _____ sunburn is caused by _____ invisible ultraviolet rays of _____ sun. These UV rays _____ the most intense between _____ A.M. and 2:00 P.M., _____ which time the sun's _____ are less likely to _____ deflected by the earth's _____ . The effects of the _____ are particularly strong the _____ time one is outdoors _____ a prolonged period of _____ indoors such as the _____ months. For those individuals _____ burn quickly, the first _____ to the sun should _____ limited to no more _____ 15 minutes a day. _____ subsequent exposures, the

duration _____ exposure can be increased _____ increments
of 15 minutes. _____ from the sun's UV rays can be obtained from sunscreens. These products contain chemicals to screen out portions of light in the UV
spectrum to prevent the skin from burning.

Content Area Reading Inventory.   The second informal reading assessment presented in this section is the content area reading inventory (CARI). It
can be used to (1) measure students' ability to use the learning aids in a textbook as well as more general reference aids, (2) assess students' vocabulary
knowledge as well as their ability to acquire word meanings from context, and
(3) determine students' understanding of literal and inferential comprehension
of text materials and their ability to understand the organizational structure of
text. Listed here are the skills and content assessed by the CARI. While this is a
rather comprehensive list, it is not necessary that the CARI contain all of the
following components. Because it is an informal test, you can construct the
CARI to assess learning behaviors you believe will be valuable to you and your
students. As stated at the beginning of this chapter, assessment should be flexible to meet the needs of your particular classroom.

Part 1: Components of a Textbook

1. Table of Contents
2. Index
3. Glossary
4. Chapter/Section Previews
5. Preview/Review Questions
6. Graphs and Statistical Charts
7. Pictures

Part 2: Reference Skills

1. Locating information from library sources
2. Locating information from classroom references

Part 3: Vocabulary Knowledge and Strategies

1. Recall of word meanings
2. Determining word meanings from context
3. Determining word meanings from morphological analysis
4. Obtaining word meanings from dictionary

Part 4: Comprehension

1. Locating and recalling literal information
2. Constructing inferences from text information
3. Constructing knowledge from multiple text sources

The CARI is constructed from the types of materials students generally
read and the tasks that they engage in while reading subject matter material.

Like the cloze test, the CARI is designed to be constructed and administered by the teacher, and many of its results are intended to reflect student performance on tasks unique to a specific area of study. Use of classroom reading material and the presentation of questions typical of classroom instruction contribute to the CARI's validity. Similarly, presentation of several questions for each of the four parts of the test contribute to its reliability; a greater number of text-reading tasks are measured. Construction, administration, scoring, and interpretation of the CARI are conducted as follows:

Construction

1. Select a text passage three to five pages in length. This passage should be obtained from materials typically read in the classroom and should not contain concepts presumed to have been covered in other portions of the text.

2. It is recommended that a total of 20 to 30 questions be constructed. Of these, 6 to 8 questions each should be constructed for Parts 1, 2, 3, and 4.

3. Questions should assess the same types of tasks required in the classroom, or those skills that you presume students possess. If, for example, most of the classroom activities focus on tasks that apply information from the text to everyday problems, questions assessing students' comprehension should reflect these sorts of cognitive skills. Examples of types of questions to ask are presented in Figure 2.2.

Administration

1. Administer the CARI to the entire class. It should be given over two sessions: Parts 1 and 2 are presented in the first section, Parts 3 and 4 in the second.

2. Give students directions, informing them of the purpose of the CARI and how the results of the assessment will be used.

3. As noted previously, the CARI should reflect the types of questions and materials generally presented in class. While it has been suggested that students be provided ample time to complete the test (Baumann, 1988), the time limits for Part 4 can reflect classroom practice. If, for example, students generally engage in comprehension activities outside class, then they should be allowed ample opportunity to complete this section of the inventory.

Scoring

Scoring the CARI should follow criteria that you consider acceptable performance. It is recommended that these criteria follow your practice in assessing student performance and what you consider to be acceptable performance on the types of tasks presented in the inventory designed for your students. It may be useful to examine individual items or groups of items that assess certain types of learning, then calculate a percentage of correct responses. For example, if you emphasize tasks that require students to construct inferences,

FIGURE 2.2   EXAMPLE OF CONTENT AREA READING INVENTORY

Part 1: Components of a Textbook

Directions: *Use the following table of contents to answer these questions.*

1. If you wanted to know more about fats and oils that you use in your kitchen, what page in the text would you turn to read about this topic?
2. Does the text provide a distinct chapter describing weight reduction methods for those people who are overweight?
3. If you were interested in including a lot of carbohydrates and fiber in your diet, with particular emphasis on breads and cereals, what page would you turn to to read about this topic?

CONTENTS

From D. A. Wenck, M. Baren, and S. P. Dewan, *Nutrition*. Reston, VA: Reston, 1980.

Part 2: Reference Skills

Directions: *List three standard reference sources you could use to learn more about nutrition.*

1. _____
2. _____
3. _____

FIGURE 2.2   CONTINUED

Part 3: Vocabulary Knowledge and Strategies

Directions: *Select the best definition for the following words.*

1. **heredity**
   a. one's relations
   b. one's genetic makeup
   c. one's physical appearance
   d. one's mental abilities

2. **malfunction**
   a. not working correctly
   b. not thinking appropriately
   c. not operating at best levels
   d. not producing enough

Read the following sentence, paying particular attention to the underlined word. After reading the sentence, select the best definition of the underlined word.

"To say that <u>obesity</u> is caused by overeating and inactivity is an oversimplification of a much more complex problem." (Wenck, Baren, & Dewan, 1980, p. 93)

obesity
a. being without exercise
b. being overweight
c. being malnourished
d. being underweight

Examine the following words. For each word, write the word's prefix and root and provide a meaning for each.

noncaloric
   prefix:
   root:

undernutrition
   prefix:
   root:

Read the underlined words in the sentences below, then examine the dictionary entries for those words. Write the dictionary definitions that apply to the context of the sentence.

The crisp, fibrous foods provide lots of chewing action for the dieter or nervous eater who needs constant mouth motion, but this may stimulate the <u>appetite</u> rather than satisfy hunger. Thus the <u>diet</u> that is based on large amounts of low-calorie, watery, fibrous foods may soon be discarded by the dieter.

appetite: 1. a desire for food or drink.   2. a desire to satisfy any bodily craving.   3. a desire for some taste.

diet: 1. food and drink considered in terms of nutritional qualities.   2. a particular selection of food, especially to improve one's looks or health.   3. the foods habitually eaten by a group of people or animals.   4. to feed.

FIGURE 2.2   CONTINUED

Part 4: Comprehension

Directions: *Read the following selection on diets. When you have finished, answer the questions at the end of the reading.*

WEIGHT LOSS DIETS

A person can lose weight on just about any diet if calories consumed are less than calories expended. But many fad-type diets are not nutritionally well balanced, may be unhealthful, and offer but a temporary solution to a permanent problem. An effective diet plan is one that will maintain a healthful level of nutrients and will teach new eating habits that can continue to be followed, with modification, after weight is lost.

A weight control diet that includes a wide variety of foods will not become monotonous and is more likely to be followed than one that severely restricts the kinds of foods that can be eaten. The diet needs to be low enough in calories so weight can be lost on it, but not so low that a person will be undernourished or hungry all the time.

An important criterion for choosing foods for a weight control diet is their caloric content. The energy values of foods depend on their composition, that is, the relative amount of fat, protein, and carbohydrate they have in proportion to the noncaloric components of water and fiber. Watery, fibrous foods such as vegetables and fruits have fewer calories per portion than such foods as fatty meats, whole milk, cheese, ice cream, and nuts, which have proportionately large amounts of fat, protein, sugar, and starch.

Another factor to consider in choosing foods for a diet, in addition to their energy value, is their satiety value—their ability to keep you feeling satisfied for a period of time. Fats and protein have the greatest satiety value.

From Wenck, Baren, & Dewar, 1990, p. 97.

1. What types of foods will satisfy your hunger for the longest period of time? (literal recall question)
2. Why do diets that contain a balance between carbohydrates, proteins, and fats seem to be the best for most people? (constructing inferences)
3. Refer to the reading on diets above and the following excerpt from Jane Brody's *Good Food Book* to answer this question: Once you have lost weight on a diet, why is it so difficult to keep that weight off? Can you maintain a lower body weight by diet alone?

According to one prevalent theory of weight control, your normal (that is, usual) body weight is like water—it constantly seeks its own level. The weight at which you stabilize when you make no special effort to gain or lose is called your body's *set point*. When your weight drops below that set point, chemical signals of starvation seem to trigger a corrective system into action to bring you back to "normal," even though normal by your definition means fat. This may be a major reason behind the failure of diets to produce long-lasting weight loss for most people.

From J. E. Brody, *Jane Brody's Good Food Book.* New York: Norton, 1985, p. 217.

yet results of the CARI indicate that only 30% of students demonstrate this ability, you can direct attention to this form of learning as you design your instruction. Similarly, examining individual student scores in these items will assist you in identifying students who may benefit from some additional assistance or who may benefit from group tasks that focus on cooperative efforts to discuss ways to draw inferences with the subject matter material presented in your class.

Interpretation.   Interpretation of student performance is determined from the scores obtained in each of the four parts of the test. Take, for example, the following class averages for two groups of students.

Class	Part 1	Part 2	Part 3	Part 4
Hour 5	23%	29%	67%	64%
Hour 7	21%	27%	87%	88%

Scores in Parts 1 and 2 draw attention to the difficulty both groups are experiencing with common reference materials and text structures. Scores on vocabulary and comprehension items indicate sizable differences between the two groups, thus suggesting different instructional approaches to each class. While the performance of the fifth-hour class would indicate that a less difficult text may be in order, the seventh-hour class may be better served with a text that is more difficult. If no alternate text materials were available, the fifth-hour class would require considerable assistance. You could present text in small chunks, design prereading activities that provide additional background information, and offer questions prior to reading small portions of the text to allow students to obtain a surface-level understanding of the material.

Before concluding the discussion of the CARI, it is important to call attention to its use in establishing cooperative learning groups. Because the CARI is constructed from text materials used in the classroom, the results provide a useful measure for creating cooperative learning groups. The type of grouping arrangement will depend on the nature of the learning task and the objectives of the teacher. For learning activities involving greater cooperative thinking and communication of explanations and for those requiring the reader to take a perspective obtained from the material, a heterogeneous grouping arrangement is advised (Johnson & Johnson, 1991). Homogeneous groups are recommended when students need to master specific skills or instructional objectives (Johnson & Johnson, 1991). Because the CARI offers one of the more accurate assessments of students' ability to learn from text materials, its results may be considered a useful measure for assigning students to cooperative learning groups.

Commentary.   The CARI offers a useful assessment of students' ability to use a textbook and reference materials, as well as their ability to learn vocabulary and to comprehend text information. Because the material presented in this informal assessment is the same as that read in class, and because the questions or tasks reflect those presented in class, the results of the CARI provide a good indication of students' ability to learn from the subject matter text. More-over, the CARI can highlight both the individual needs of students and the overall ability of a class or grade level. Results can be useful in planning in-structional activities that are best suited to the needs of the students, in estab-lishing cooperative learning groups (discussed in Chapter Eight), and in esti-mating the overall difficulty of text material. While the CARI can be a valid measure of those learning tasks presented in the classroom, its construction will require considerably more time than a cloze. Furthermore, care must be exercised in writing questions that reflect the various types of thinking re-quired in the classroom to ensure they are valid and reliable.

PRACTICE ACTIVITY 2.3

Take a few minutes to complete the CARI displayed in Figure 2.2. As you ex-amine this sample, note the variety of tasks presented and sources of informa-tion you are required to use in the various parts of the inventory.

ASSESSING TEXT

This section focuses on factors that influence students' understanding of text-books, with the goal of providing some reasonable criteria for assessing class-room reading material. The first part of the section presents a list of factors that affect text comprehension, followed by a checklist for adopting or selecting text for classroom use. The second part of the section discusses readability for-mulas with an emphasis on their use and limitations.

Factors Affecting Text Difficulty

The discussion of text difficulty that follows focuses on six factors that are largely inherent in the text itself. The factors considered here are vocabulary, sentence structure, length of text, elaboration, coherence and unity, and text structure. Two of these, vocabulary and sentence structure, are considered in readability formulas discussed later in this chapter. While these two factors are important, they cannot serve as the sole criteria for determining text difficulty. As has been pointed out by a number of authorities (Kintsch & Vipond, 1979; Ryder, Graves, & Graves, 1989; Zakaluk & Samuels, 1988), features of text other than vocabulary and sentence structure are certain to make a much greater difference than the combined effects of these two factors. The discus-sion of text difficulty begins, then, with a description of how vocabulary may affect text difficulty.

Vocabulary.   Vocabulary is one of the most easily identifiable characteristics of text difficulty. While there is sizable evidence to support the idea that texts containing many difficult vocabulary words are likely to present problems in comprehension (Anderson & Freebody, 1981), replacing difficult words with easier ones may not simplify a text; in fact, it may make a text even more difficult. If, for example, the term *herculean* is used, the simpler substitution "requiring a lot of strength" does not convey the same meaning. Replacing "The man lifted the car to free the woman. His *herculean* effort warranted a medal from the mayor" with "The effort that took a lot of strength warranted a medal from the mayor" leads to a sentence that conveys a much different meaning.

Encountering difficult vocabulary may impair understanding of small units of comprehension, such as details appearing in individual sentences, but it is not likely to interfere with understanding of the more central idea (Stahl, Jacobson, Davis, & Davis, 1989). Note, for example, the following:

> Luke had not won the admiration of the patrons. This *lout* from the outer reaches of the community had offended everyone with his behavior. Several individuals became particularly offended by his *prehension* of the refuse that had fallen to the floor. After a few minutes, many people began to leave.

Even if you don't know the meaning of *lout* (bumpkin) or *prehension* (act of grasping), you can readily understand the central idea that Luke was displaying behaviors that were offensive to a number of people.

Knowledge of vocabulary aids comprehension. But reading text that contains few new words does have its limitations. A reasonable number of words should be unfamiliar to students to provide the opportunity to learn new ones. Lacking those new words, students' ability to increase their vocabulary is reduced.

Sentence Structure.   The effect of sentence structure is relatively easy to assess. Very long, complex, or convoluted sentences make text more difficult to read. While it may seem reasonable to select a text based largely on short, simple sentences, sentences need to be complex enough to convey the meaning of the text clearly (Irwin & Pulver, 1984; Pearson, 1974–1975). If the intended meaning of a sentence is "Having lost his job, Ted had to return the new sports car to the dealer who would now lose his sales commission," then breaking the sentence into something like "Ted lost his job. He had to return his car to the car dealer. The car dealer would now lose his commission" is not going to result in more comprehensible text. Text that includes only short, simple sentences may lack logical connectives, thus placing the responsibility of inferring relationships on the reader. This added burden can cause problems for some students.

At the same time, even text that is written for beginning or less able readers often employs artificially short sentences, resulting in text that sounds stilted. These paragraphs are taken from *Run for Your Life and Other Stories,* a book in a high interest–easy reading series designed for less able adult readers.

> Henry Kissinger was born in Germany in 1923. He and his family had to leave in 1938. They were Jews. At that time the Nazis were running Germany. They were killing many Jews.

Henry and his family came to America. Life in the United States was different. Henry had to work hard to speak English well.

Henry liked school. He wanted to teach in school. And he did.

From J. Anderson, B. Longnion, and M. Gillis, *Run for Your Life and Other Stories.* New York: Cambridge Books, ND.

You may agree that the short, simple sentences produce text that is neither very interesting nor natural in its use of language. Many readers, even remedial ones, would benefit by more natural-sounding text. In fact, at least one study (Green & Olsen, 1988) has shown that less able readers comprehend original texts just as well as simplified ones. Moreover, the personal preference of these students is the original rather than the simplified version.

On the other hand, some long sentences are clearly difficult. Here is one from "Shooting an Elephant" by George Orwell.

Its mahout, the only person who could manage it when it was in that state, had set out in pursuit, but had taken the wrong direction and was now twelve hours' journey away, and in the morning the elephant had suddenly reappeared in the town.

Text containing a large percentage of complex sentences are likely to be difficult for less able readers.

Length of Text.   Often overlooked as a factor influencing the likelihood that a student will complete a selection with full understanding is the length of text. For students having problems reading, length alone can be a very formidable obstacle (Grobe, 1970). Although longer text can, at times, provide elaboration that may enhance understanding, longer text per se is not always better. In some cases, summaries or much reduced versions of complete text may produce better comprehension than longer ones (Carroll, Smith-Kerker, Ford, & Mazur-Rimetz, 1988; Reder & Anderson, 1982). Fortunately, the amount of material students are required to read is under the teacher's direct control. Sometimes short summaries may be more effective than longer selections. Similarly, the teacher may limit the amount of text read by directing students' attention only to key concepts.

However, shorter text, as noted below, is not always better. To cover new concepts adequately, illustrations and examples are often essential yet can increase text length.

Elaboration.   Elaboration is providing explanatory information beyond the basic facts presented. It extends thought, provides greater description, and qualifies statements. Because elaboration makes information more meaningful and understandable, it becomes more memorable. "Jason bought a new car" is certainly understandable, but it is not a very memorable sentence. Yet the elaborated sentence "Maria bought a new car that had a top speed of 140 miles per hour and was used in a James Bond movie" is more memorable.

While it has been shown that elaboration facilitates comprehension and recall (Bransford & Johnson, 1972), it has also been noted that shorter texts sometimes produce better comprehension and memory than longer ones. The matter of under which circumstances elaborated text hinders or aids the reader is not yet resolved. It appears, however, that shorter texts may be more effective if one needs to remember material, while elaborated text may be more effective if one needs to understand material thoroughly (Charney & Reder, 1988).

Coherence and Unity. Coherence refers to the clarity of each topic or subtopic and how well the various topics of a text relate to each other (Anderson & Armbruster, 1984; Beck & McKeown, 1988). For the young and inexperienced reader, text needs to be coherently written; each piece of information should fit together.

Unity is the text's focus on a single purpose. Well-written texts do not wander in their presentation of topics, nor do they contain chunks of irrelevant material. Text that abruptly shifts topics or themes or provides nonessential or unrelated illustrations or examples can be difficult to follow.

Text Structure. Text structure refers to the organization of the text. The majority of texts that students encounter in school can be categorized as belonging to one of two broad categories, narrative or exposition. These two types of text are organized quite differently (Drum, 1984). Narrative text (literature having characters, themes, plots, and events) is stressed throughout the primary grade years, and students do fairly well with this type of text structure. Exposition (text that informs the reader through explanation, compare/contrast, definition/examples, and problems/solutions) presents the reader with several problems. First, exposition does not provide the cues that narratives do. While narrative text generally has predictable sequences of problems-actions-resolutions, expository text generally lacks direct cues. A second problem with expository text is that very little children's literature is exposition; parents read primarily narrative text to their children, and basal readers usually contain narrative text selections. As a result, many students find expository text particularly difficult. Procedures for teaching students the various types of expository text structures are discussed in Chapter Five.

Text difficulty, as noted, can be affected by a number of factors within the text. Vocabulary, sentence structure, length, elaboration, coherence and unity, and text structure contribute to our understanding as we read. There are, however, factors outside the text—factors involving the reader—that also affect text difficulty. Briefly considered here are familiarity of content and background knowledge, and interestingness.

Familiarity of Content and Background Knowledge. Reading a selection on which we have little familiarity is a difficult task, and attempting to read a selection that is totally unfamiliar is impossible (Adams & Bruce, 1982). As was discussed in Chapter One, understanding text involves more than a degree of familiarity with the content; it requires whatever background knowledge is assumed by the author (Armbruster, 1986). Generally, we can approach most short stories and novels with the knowledge that we acquire from day-to-day experiences. However, many social studies, science, and mathematics texts require extensive background knowledge for comprehension. Lacking this information, reading becomes a laborious and frustrating task.

Although riding a bicycle is a familiar experience for most of us, reading about the function of the derailleurs can be difficult without considerable background knowledge, as described in this excerpt from *The All New Complete Book of Bicycling.*

> Some derailleurs, such as the SunTour, pivot freely on the mounting bolt that threads into the rear dropout or into the adapter bracket. This permits you to pull the derailleur back out of the way when removing the rear wheel. Without a spring in the mounting bolt, or rather attached to it, it's easier to pull the derailleur body back out of the way. Some rear derailleurs, such as the Champagnolo and some Shimano models, have the mounting bolt spring loaded, so this spring tension helps the main spring in the derailleur body maintain tension, which in turn helps keep the chain on the gear you have selected, and makes for somewhat snappier changes.
>
> From E. A. Sloane, *The All New Complete Book of Bicycling.* New York: Simon & Schuster, 1980, p. 546.

Unless you have experience with bicycle maintenance, lack of familiarity with the mounting bolt spring or the role the rear derailleur plays in maintaining chain tension makes this short passage difficult to understand. Texts that require a great deal of background knowledge, or those that presume the students have acquired prerequisite knowledge, are likely to be difficult to read and may discourage certain students from reading the text altogether. As was noted in the discussion of the reading process in Chapter One, if schemata are not available, students will experience difficulty comprehending material.

Interestingness.   This is a subjective factor referring to the degree of attention and intrinsic attractiveness of the reading. Although anecdotal information may sometimes lead attention away from important parts of text (Hidi & Baird, 1986), interestingness seems to have a significant effect on students' comprehension (Anderson, Shirley, Wilson, & Fielding, 1986; Graves et al., 1988). Here are samples of two texts. The first contains information that is familiar and centers on the discussion of commercials that have gained our attention over the years. While the content itself is not particularly useful, it is nonetheless interesting. The second sample contains content that is not particularly familiar to most of us and centers on the presentation of a topic that, while occasionally in the news, is not likely to have drawn our attention. Although the Federal Reserve System has a significant effect on our personal finances and the economy in general, for most of us the text is not interesting.

Image Can Be a Fickle Thing

One of the most image-dependent companies of the last generation has been American Express. In fact, its multi-year success has been due in no small part to sensational advertising. Recall Karl Malden (in his *Streets of San Francisco* cop alter ego), a perfect fit for the message at hand ("What will you do? What *will* you do?"). That was 1973. The company launched a classic the very next year with its "Do you know me?" campaign in which it achieved a rare reversal: The company was remembered long after the celebrities faces were forgotten. . . . The idea, of course, was to promote the American Express card as *the* prestige credit card, so that affluent consumers would pay more to own it and merchants worldwide would pay more to feature it. . . . In the '80's—the decade of prestige—American Express stock rose about 400%.

From Derrick Niederman, This is not your father's stockpicking method. *Investment Vision,* 1(5), 29.

The Most Watched Player: The Fed

The Federal Reserve System, the nation's central bank, was established by act of Congress in 1913. The Federal Reserve Act divided the country into 12 districts and provided for the creation within each of a *district Federal Reserve bank.* Responsibility for coordinating the activities of the district banks lies with the Federal Reserve's *Board of Governors* in Washington, D.C. The board has seven members appointed by the President and confirmed by the Senate. The main tools available to the Fed for implementing policy are open-market operations, reserve requirements, and the discount rate. On paper authority for policymaking at the Fed is widely diffused throughout the system. In practice, however, this authority has gradually been centered in the Federal Open Market Committee (FOMC), which was established to oversee the Fed's open-market operations.

From M. Stigum, *The Money Market.* Homewood, IL: Dow Jones Irwin, 1983, p. 227.

In general, it appears that texts that are intrinsically interesting are likely to facilitate comprehension; texts, however, in which the interesting material is an add-on or an aside are likely to impede comprehension.

Commentary.   The criteria for assessing text difficulty include six factors inherent in the text (vocabulary, sentence structure, length, elaboration, coherence and unity, and text structure) and two factors involving the reader and the text (familiarity of content and background knowledge, and interestingness). Note that this is not a checklist, in the sense that you quickly tally these factors and arrive at a score reflecting text difficulty. Instead, it represents a set of factors to consider carefully as you decide if a particular text is to be used for a given group of students. Moreover, a factor critical in one text situation may not be important in another. Sentence length, for example, may be important when the text is not interesting, when it requires considerable background

---

FIGURE 2.3   PROCEDURES FOR EXAMINING TEXT DIFFICULTY

Part 1: Factors Inherent in the Text

Directions: *Examine three or four parts of the text in answering each of the following questions. It is recommended that you first read each of these parts of the text, then respond to the questions.*

Vocabulary

	Yes	No
1. Does text allow students the opportunity to learn new words?	_____	_____
2. Can words be learned through context clues?	_____	_____
3. Does text provide definitions for new vocabulary in content or in glossary?	_____	_____
4. Does text contain a large number of new vocabulary in a given passage?	_____	_____

Sentence Length

1. Are sentences of a reasonable length?	_____	_____
2. Are meanings of sentences clearly conveyed?	_____	_____
3. Are there excessive numbers of short, fragmented sentences, or long, convoluted sentences?	_____	_____

Coherence and Unity

1. Do ideas presented in text fit together logically?	_____	_____
2. Does text contain irrelevant material?	_____	_____
3. Does text contain, where appropriate, summaries, and transitional or linking sentences?	_____	_____

Length

| 1. Are topics or sections of text of an appropriate length? | _____ | _____ |

---

knowledge, and when it is meant for students who are below average in reading ability. Conversely, sentence length would be unimportant in an interesting narrative selection that presents highly familiar themes and characters in a familiar style.

Matching students and texts requires careful attention to the factors outlined here, factors related to the students themselves, factors in the text, and the teacher's objectives in using a textbook. While assessing these factors through some sort of numerical scale is inappropriate, they play an important

------

FIGURE 2.3   CONTINUED

Part 2: Student Factors

Directions: *Provide students with passages or sections of the text examined in Part 1 and direct them to read the text. Then direct students to respond to each of the following questions.*

	Yes	No
1. Is the text interesting to read?	_____	_____
2. Does the text contain many concepts or ideas that are new to you?	_____	_____
3. Does the text provide enough detail or examples so that you can understand the information being presented?	_____	_____
4. Can you understand most of the individual sentences in the text?	_____	_____
5. Is this the sort of text that students in your grade could read and understand?	_____	_____

------

role in how well students learn from text selections. In an effort to address the points raised in this section, the following procedure should be helpful in assessing text difficulty in the subject matter classroom. This procedure is outlined in Figure 2.3. Note that factors of the text and of the students are addressed. While having students complete Part 2 of the text survey will require some additional effort, their evaluation can provide a valuable perspective in your efforts to assess a text's difficulty. Often text that may appear to the teacher to be interesting and of an appropriate level of difficulty is viewed in an entirely different manner by the students. Assessing potential problems in advance of students' reading will allow you to make modifications in the use of the text or obtain alternate selections that may be more appropriate for the students' ability, background knowledge, and interests. If the text contains numerous new words that cannot be defined from context, then it may be advisable to teach these words prior to reading. A variety of strategies for teaching words are presented in Chapter Three. Similarly, if portions of a text selection contain numerous new concepts, an absence of detail, or content that may seem uninteresting or irrelevant to students, then it may be advisable to engage students in activities that prepare them to learn the material. These types of activities are presented in Chapter Four. If sentences are excessively long to the point that they may interfere with learning, or if, on the other hand, they are excessively short, fragmented, or convoluted, then it may be advisable to use a different selection altogether.

Readability Formulas

The term *readability* has been used to describe texts' legibility, interestingness, and comprehensibility. However, readability is most often associated with formulas that provide grade-level estimates of text difficulty. These formulas were originally designed under the assumption that text difficulty can be predicted by limiting text analysis to measures of sentence length and word difficulty. Assessment of the reader's background knowledge and interestingness of the material were not considered. The following contains a short explanation of how these formulas were derived, examples of the use of two readability formulas, and a discussion of the limitations and use of the formulas.

Two of the original—and still widely used—readability formulas were derived by Dale and Chall (1948) and Flesch (1948). Both formulas were developed by analyzing how word difficulty and sentence length were related to text difficulty. It was assumed that as word difficulty and sentence length increase, text becomes proportionally more difficult. By examining the relationship between these two factors and material written at various grade levels, it would be possible to devise a formula to predict text difficulty. The source of graded text for this analysis was the *Standard Test Lessons* of McCall and Crabbs (1925). Each passage in these lessons was assigned a grade-level equivalent by its authors. By examining word difficulty with a count of the number of multisyllabic words or occurrence of words on a graded word list and by examining syntactic (grammatical) difficulty by tallying words per sentence, investigators were able to determine how these two factors varied over lessons assigned various grade levels. Thus, in a sample of a standard test lesson written for the fourth grade, one may find 14.5 sentences and 120 syllables for a 100-word sample. A passage from the seventh grade, on the other hand, may have 4.5 sentences and 165 syllables. As noted in the previous section on text difficulty, while vocabulary and sentence length can affect the understanding of text, these are only two of many factors affecting the ease or difficulty of text. To provide further understanding of the use of readability tests, here are two widely used formulas, the Fry graph (Fry, 1977) and FOG index (Gunning, 1979).

Fry Readability Graph.   This readability formula, shown in Figure 2.4, was designed to provide a grade-level estimate of text used in grades 1 through college. The grade-level estimate is based on two factors—word difficulty and sentence length. Calculation of readability begins with the sampling of three 100-word selections obtained from different parts of the text. For each 100-word sample, the total number of sentences and total number of syllables for all words, including proper nouns, are tallied. Initializations and numerals are counted as a syllable for each symbol. For example, *1993* would be counted as four syllables and *IBM* as three. The average number of sentences for the selection and the total number of syllables are then plotted on the graph. For example, a selection of 142 syllables and 6.3 sentences (indicated by the filled-in cir-

FIGURE 2.4   FRY READABILITY GRAPH

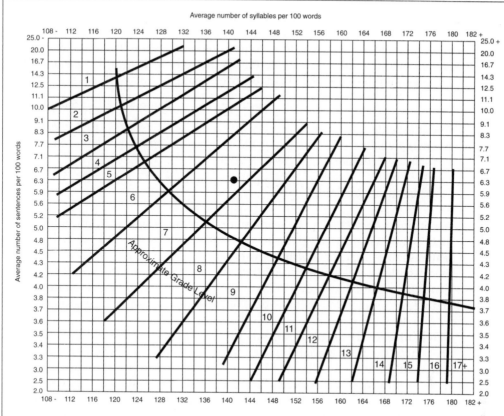

Average number of syllables per 100 words

1. Randomly select three (3) sample passages and count out exactly 100 words each, beginning with the beginning of a sentence. Do count proper nouns, initializations, and numerals.

2. Count the number of sentences in the hundred words, estimating the length of the fraction of the last sentence to the nearest one tenth.

3. Count the total number of syllables in the 100-word passage. If you don't have a hand counter available, an easy way is to simply to put a mark above every syllable over one in each word, then when you get to the end of the passage, count the number of marks and add 100. Small calculators can also be used as counters by pushing numeral 1 then push the + sign for each word or syllable.

4. Enter graph with *average* sentence length and *average* number of syllables; plot dot where the two lines intersect. Area where dot is plotted will give you the approximate grade level.

5. If a great deal of variability is found in syllable count or sentence count, putting more samples into the average is desirable.

6. A word is defined as a group of symbols with a space on either side; Thus, *1945* is one word.

7. A syllable is defined as a phonetic syllable. Generally, there are as many syllables as vowel sounds. For example, *stopped* is one syllable and *wanted* is two syllables. When counting syllables for numerals and initializations, count one syllable for each symbol. For example, *1945* is four syllables.

From Edward Fry, "Fry's readability graph: Clarifications, validity, and extension to level 17." *Journal of Reading,* *21* (1977): 242–252. Reproduction permitted—no copyright.

cle on the graph) would fall within the mid-range of seventh grade. Once the grade-level estimates are obtained for each of the three text samples, these values are averaged to provide a composite estimate of the text's readability. Shown below is the first sample that is plotted on the graph, two additional samples, and the composite readability estimate.

	Sample 1	Sample 2	Sample 3
Average Sentences	5.9	7.1	7.0
Average Syllables	142	136	144
Readability Estimate	7.75	7.0	7.5

$$\text{Composite Readability} = \frac{7.75 + 7.0 + 7.5}{3} = 7.4$$

According to Fry (1977), the readability graph is designed to provide an estimate of an instructional grade level. In other words, the Fry grade-level estimate assumes that the teacher assists students in reading. Fry also notes that the formula is accurate within 1.0 grade level of measuring text difficulty. If scores fall within the shaded areas of the graph, they are considered unreliable, and it is recommended that an additional 100-word sample be examined.

FOG Index.   The second formula presented here is the FOG index. Like the Fry graph, the FOG readability estimate is obtained by examining word difficulty and sentence length. Word difficulty is assessed by tabulating all words with three or more syllables. Sentence length is assessed by computing the average number of words per sentence for each text sample. To calculate the FOG, follow these steps:

1. Select a sample of text 100 words in length.

2. Determine the average number of words per sentence in the sample by dividing 100 by the number of sentences in the sample. If the 100-word sample includes a portion of a sentence, estimate the fraction of the sentence that is included in the sample.

3. Tally the number of verbs containing three or more syllables. Omit proper nouns, common compound words, or words whose third syllable would be an inflected form (provided, assuming).

4. Add the average sentence length to the total number of words containing three or more syllables.

5. Multiply the value obtained in Step 4 by 0.4. The result is the FOG readability estimate.

Computing readability estimates can be simplified through the use of various grammar checker software programs available for MS-DOS and Macintosh computers. Programs such as *RightWriter* (Que Software) and *Grammatik* (Reference Software) will provide readability estimates, using various formulas, on text created by most word-processing programs. These programs are widely available through local computer software dealers and mail-order firms. Here are some of the readability statistics provided by *Grammatik* on an analysis of the text paragraph below beginning "As noted...."

Readability Statistics	**Paragraph Statistics**	**Word Statistics**
Flesch reading ease: 44	Number of	Number of words: 262
Gunning FOG index: 17	paragraphs: 1	Average length:
Flesch-Kincaid grade	Average length:	4.8 letters
level: 17	11.0 sentences	Syllables per word:
		1.61

As noted, readability formulas are limited to the assessment of a few factors within the text. The level of a student's background knowledge, the interestingness and density of concepts of the material, the abstractness of the text, and the individual's motivation to engage in the reading are not considered. As a result, the estimates of text readability reported by these formulas may not accurately reflect the true difficulty of the material. As an example of the importance of various factors in the text and factors within background knowledge that affect the difficulty of text, consider the readability of the following excerpt from *The Republic* by Plato. Rather than analyze three samples of the text, as directed by the guidelines for the Fry graph and the FOG index, the calculations here will be limited to a single sample. To allow for a better appreciation of Plato's style of writing, the sample we have given exceeds 100 words. The 100-word sample is noted by the slash in the text. Limit your analysis to this sample. Spaces have been provided at the end of each line so you may note the number of syllables per line for the Fry graph, and the number of words having three or more syllables per line for the FOG. The line-by-line tally of syllables and words having three or more syllables and calculations of the readability estimates of these two formulas can be found at the end of the chapter. It is important that you complete this exercise before you continue reading the discussion of readability formulas.

Excerpt from *The Republic* by Plato

	Fry	*FOG*
And do you not suppose, Adeimantus, that a single boxer who was perfect in his	_____	_____
art would easily be a match for two stout and well-to-do gentlemen who were not	_____	_____
boxers? Hardly, if they came upon him at once. What, not, I said, if he were	_____	_____
able to run away and then turn and strike at the one who first came up? And	_____	_____
supposing he were to do this several times under the heat of a scorching sun,	_____	_____
might he not, being an expert, overturn more than one stout personage?	_____	_____
Certainly, he said, there would be nothing wonderful/ in that.	_____	_____

And yet rich men probably have a greater superiority in the science and practise

of boxing than they have in military qualities.

Likely enough.

Then we may assume that our athletes will be able to fight with two or three times

their own number?

I agree with you, for I think you right.

And suppose that, before engaging, our citizens send an embassy to one of the two

cities, telling them what is the truth: Silver and gold we neither have nor are

permitted to have, but you may; do you therefore come and help us in war, and take the spoils

of the other city: Who, on hearing these words would choose to fight against lean wiry

dogs, rather than, with the dogs on their side, against fat and tender sheep?

From The Works of Plato, trans. B. Jowett. New York: Tudor Publishing, 1937, pp. 135–136.

According to the Fry and FOG formulas, this excerpt from *The Republic* has a readability of 7.0 and 8.4 grade level, respectively. Recognize that these estimates were not an aberration; two additional samples taken from this work provided similar results. While the purpose of conducting a readability analysis on a piece of Plato's writing was intended to be illustrative of the process of using readability formulas, it may also have made you aware of some of the formulas' limitations. Undoubtedly, material written at the seventh- or eighth-grade level would be easier to understand than this selection of Plato's writing, even though the words are familiar and the sentences are not particularly long. What makes this a difficult piece of text to understand? It is Plato's style of writing. Phrases like "Before engaging, our citizens send an embassy" and the excessive use of colons and semicolons in the last sentence are uncommon stylistic features. You may also have noted that the thematic elements addressing states' rights, individual responsibilities, and the virtues and excesses of wealth are presented in a rather obscure manner.

In this excerpt, the readability formulas were unable to account for stylistic elements of text. Readability formulas are further limited in their inability to account for the reader's background knowledge, or the density of concepts presented in the text. Consider the following selection from an article on the Milwaukee Brewers appearing in the *Milwaukee Journal.* If you desire additional practice with these two formulas, the readability calculations for this article can be found at the end of the chapter.

It Just Goes On and On
By Bob Berghaus

Veteran Jim Gantner sounded like a frustrated fan after the Milwaukee Brewers' 14–5 loss to the Texas Rangers Saturday night at County Stadium.

"Trade the whole team and start over," Gantner said after his team was hammered for the second straight night by the Rangers.

It was another long, embarrassing night for the Brewers, who wound up using catcher Rich Dempsey as a ninth-inning pitcher for the second time this season. Dempsey and rookie Doug Henry tied for most effective Brewers pitchers of the evening; each allowed just a walk in one inning of work.

Other than that, the/ pitching was terrible and the defense lousy.

Milwaukee Journal, August 4, 1991

The readability of this article is 10.8 on the FOG index, and 10.0 on the Fry graph. Clearly, it is less difficult than the Plato excerpt. The style is informal, there are no difficult words, and the content is highly familiar. Again, attention is drawn to the importance of the author's style and the reader's background knowledge. Furthermore, this example demonstrates the importance of conceptual density. Most newspaper articles present relatively few concepts accompanied by a great deal of elaboration. Plato's writing, on the other hand, is ladened with many concepts presented in an uncommon style. While the readability estimates of the Fry and FOG formulas are quite similar, the application of different formulas on the same piece of text often produces sizable differences. As part of a study examining newspapers and books commonly read by adults from 1945 to 1980, Ryder and Smith (1981) found the following results of samples taken from the sports page of the *Milwaukee Journal* (see Figure 2.5). These figures present the mean readability of 15 samples taken from each of the years specified. Similar results were obtained from an analysis of periodicals as well as fiction and nonfiction on the *New York Times* best-sellers' list. The variations of grade-level estimates obtained from different formulas call attention to the fact that these truly are *estimates.* The utility of these estimates is best examined in the context of how well readability formulas directly assess those factors that affect text difficulty, a topic discussed in the next section.

FIGURE 2.5   READABILITY ESTIMATES OF SPORTS PAGE ARTICLES APPEARING IN THE MILWAUKEE JOURNAL, 1945–1980

	FRY	FOG
1945	11.0	12.8
1950	11.0	14.4
1955	10.0	14.3
1960	11.0	14.5
1965	7.0	9.4
1970	9.0	13.2
1975	7.0	10.5
1980	9.0	10.8

Commentary.   Readability formulas are only approximations of text difficulty. Because they assess a small number of the factors that affect text difficulty, no single formula will provide an accurate estimate. As noted by Bruce, Rubin, and Starr (1981), readability formulas do not address discourse cohesion, number of inferences, number of items to remember, complexity of ideas, rhetorical structure, dialect, and background knowledge required. Additional factors not directly assessed by readability formulas include density of concepts, style of the author, motivation of the learner, contribution of graphic aides to text understanding, and grammatical correctness of the text. Note, for example, that a readability formula would provide identical estimates for the following two sentences although the second sentence is incomprehensible.

Correct Text: As the young dog ran down the alley, she began to lose her stride, and soon the cat had escaped.

Incorrect Text: Soon the cat as the young dog ran down the alley had escaped she began to lose her stride.

As noted previously in this chapter, readability formulas have been used to write text that is presumed to be more easily understood. The outcome of writing to a readability formula is the production of material that is actually more difficult to understand (Pearson, 1974–1975; Davidson, 1984), as the writer attempts to omit logical connectives and construct short, simple sentences containing frequently appearing words. For this reason, writing text solely on the basis of factors assessed by a readability formula is discouraged (Giles, 1990; Klare, 1989; Marshall, 1970). When selecting text materials, attention should be directed to the sentence and word length. If you find sentences that are consistently short and unnatural, consider the following alternatives:

1. Complete the Procedures for Examining Text Difficulty in Figure 2.3.
2. Compare the text selection to other text presenting the same content. Note and compare the length of sentences, use of short words, and clarity of the writing.
3. Administer a cloze assessment on the selected text.
4. Collect four or five samples from a given textbook or reading selection and direct students to read and evaluate the relative ease of the text.

To summarize, readability formulas are general estimates of text difficulty, focusing on a few factors internal to the text while excluding the role of the learner in the process of comprehending text. These formulas are useful in screening text to determine its appropriateness for a particular group of students. Using the results of these formulas in conjunction with consideration of the level of objectives and study questions should provide a solid assessment of factors "outside the reader's head" (Zakaluk & Samuels, 1988). In a more direct method, Britton, Gulgoz, Van Dusen, Glynn, and Sharp (1991) recommend that learnability be gauged by students' judgments of text difficulty. On the basis of their research indicating that college students can usually select the most learnable texts, Britton and colleagues recommend that students judge text difficulty. This procedure begins by selecting excerpts from several texts addressing the same content. These excerpts are then presented to students with instructions to identify the selection that would best allow them to learn the specified content. The authors note that it is important to select multiple excerpts from different parts of a given text. This "learnability" procedure does not yield a score, but rather an indication from the students as to the suitability of the text material. This is a rather straightforward procedure and one that should yield results that are highly sensitive to the needs of the students. If results indicate that the students have mixed preferences for the reading material, these needs can be met by providing text they identify as most learnable. Both of these methods offer the advantage of assessing factors of the text and the learner. No doubt, as researchers continue to examine factors of the reader and the text that affect text difficulty, more precise readability measures will be devised.

CONCLUDING REMARKS

This chapter began with a discussion of standardized and informal assessments and the uses of these two types of assessments. We discussed two types of standardized tests: norm referenced and criterion referenced. We then considered the construction, administration, scoring, and interpretation of two types of informal reading assessments: cloze and the content area reading inventory (CARI). Next we discussed text difficulty by first pointing out those factors that make text difficult, then presenting procedures for assessing text difficulty.

In concluding this chapter we emphasize two points. First, assessment involves much more than creating tests; assessment can direct learning. The procedures we have outlined for reading assessment provide both teacher and student information to attend to certain behaviors. As you consider the techniques we have presented in this chapter, remember that assessment is an integral element of our ability to engage in those everyday learning tasks encountered outside the school. We believe that assessment should take on the same level of importance in your classroom.

Second, assessment should be ongoing and flexible. Assessing textbooks and students' reading are not one-shot matters. Classroom learning is often uneven. To monitor students' progress and to direct their attention to certain learning behaviors, you will need to draw on a variety of assessment tools during the course of the year. Initially, use of the cloze procedure or content area reading inventory will identify students' level of understanding of your content and knowledge of that content. Later on, as you begin to engage students in learning activities, you may need to monitor cooperative learning or have students engage in peer-mediated writing assessments, which are discussed in Chapters Seven and Eight. The form and frequency of assessments will vary according to the task at hand and the need to consider the social and intellectual factors in your classroom, as well as your instructional objectives. Implementing and maintaining effective assessment techniques may require substantial effort on your part. If you feel somewhat overwhelmed by the various assessment techniques we have presented, consider adopting one of the techniques each semester or one each year. Over time, the advantages of making these techniques part of your teaching will outweigh the initial effort.

REFLECTIONS

This section of the chapter offers some activities for considering the major topics presented in the chapter and how these topics apply to decisions you will make on the role of assessment in your class.

1. Interview a subject matter teacher to determine the various types of assessment used to measure students' ability to learn from reading material. Inquire about the use of formal and informal assessments, those assessments that are required by the school district or state government, and those designed or used by the teacher. Finally, inquire about the teacher's perception of how reading ability of students has changed during the course of the teacher's career.

2. Obtain the aggregate test score data on a norm-referenced achievement test from a school district. Examine and summarize the mean (average) reading performance at the various grade levels tested and report on how these results compare to national averages. If possible, break down the district test score data by schools and comment on factors that may account for any differences observed between schools.

3. Construct a CARI from reading materials in your subject matter area. Administer the device to several colleagues, then score and interpret the results. Summarize your colleagues' comments on the validity of the test and your own views on the strengths and limitations of this form of assessment.

4. Obtain several types of reading materials (textbooks, periodicals, newspapers) that you might read during the course of a year. Select two 100-word samples from each source, then, using your own judgment, estimate the grade level of each text sample. Next obtain a readability estimate of each text sample by applying a readability formula. Comment on any discrepancies between your estimate and that obtained from the formula.

5. Construct, administer, and score a cloze test using text selected from your subject matter area. Comment on what you perceive to be the strengths and limitations of this assessment device.

6. Obtain a copy of a formal, norm-referenced achievement test from a library or testing center, or from your instructor. Complete the test as if you were the test taker. Write a summary of the validity of this form of assessment, paying particular attention to the following questions:
   a. Does the test present the type of questions one typically encounters in school?
   b. Is the reading material itself similar in style to that encountered in the material written for your subject matter area?
   c. Does this test seem to measure tasks similar to those commonly presented in your subject matter area?
   d. Are passages long enough to obtain an accurate assessment of one's ability to learn from text?
7. Working with a group of your peers, apply the Procedures for Examining Text Difficulty (Figure 2.3) to a sample of text used in your subject matter area. Summarize your views on the qualitative aspects of the text's vocabulary, sentence length, and coherence and unity. Next present the text selection to another group of your peers and ask them to complete Part 2 of the text difficulty assessment (Figure 2.3). Compare your groups' views of the text with those of the group completing Part 2.

REFERENCES

Adams, M. L., & Bruce, B. (1982). Background knowledge and reading comprehension. In J. A. Langer & T. M. Smith Burke (Eds.), *Reader meets author: Bridging the gap.* Newark, DE: International Reading Association.

Anderson, R. C. & Freebody, P. (1981). Vocabulary knowledge. In J. Guthrie (Ed.), *Reading comprehension and education.* Newark, DE: International Reading Association.

Anderson, R. C., Shirley, L. L., Wilson, P. T., & Fielding, L. G. (1986). Interestingness of children's reading material. In R. Snow & M. Farr (Eds.), *Aptitude, learning and instruction: Cognitive and affective process analyses.* Hillsdale, NJ: Erlbaum.

Anderson, T. H., & Armbruster, B. B. (1984). Content area textbooks. In R. Anderson, J. Osborn, & R. Tierney (Eds.), *Learning to read in American schools: Basal readers and content texts.* Hillsdale, NJ: Erlbaum.

Archibald, D. A., & Newman, F. M. (1988). *Beyond standardized testing: Assessing authentic academic achievement in secondary schools.* Washington, DC: National Association of Secondary School Principals.

Armbruster, B. B. (1986). Schema theory and the design of content-area textbooks. *Educational Psychologist, 21,* 253–267.

Baumann, J. F. (1988). *Reading assessment.* New York: Merrill/Macmillan.

Beck, I. L., & McKeown, M. G. (1988). Toward meaningful accounts in history texts for young learners. *American Educational Research Journal, 25,* 31–39.

Bormuth, J. R. (1968). Cloze test readability criterion reference scores. *Journal of Educational Measurement, 5,* 189–196.

_____. (1969). Empirical determination of the instructional reading level. In J. Figurel (Ed.), *Reading and realism.* Newark, DE: International Reading Association.

Bransford, J. D., & Johnson, M. K. (1972). Contextual prerequisites for understanding: Some investigations for comprehension and recall. *Journal of Verbal Learning and Verbal Behavior, 11,* 717–726.

Britton, B. K., Gulgoz, S., Van Dusen, L., Glynn, S. M., & Sharp, L. (1991). Accuracy of learnability judgments for instructional texts. *Journal of Educational Psychology, 83,* 43–47.

Bruce, B., Rubin, A., & Starr, K. (1981). Why readability formulas fail. *IEEE Transactions of Professional Communications, 24,* 50–52.

Calfee, R. C. (1987). The school as a context for assessment of literacy. *The Reading Teacher, 40,* 357–375.

Carroll, J. M., Smith-Kerker, P. L., Ford, J., & Mazur-Rimetz, S. A. (1988). The minimal manual. In S. Doheny-Farina (Ed.), *Effective documentation: What we have learned from research.* Cambridge, MA: MIT Press.

Charney, D. H., & Reder, L. L. (1988). Studies in elaboration of instructional texts. In S. Doheny-Farina (Ed.), *Effective documentation: What we have learned from research.* Cambridge, MA: MIT Press.

Dale, E., & Chall, J. S. (1948). A formula for predicting readability: Instructions. *Educational Research Bulletin, 27,* 37–54.

Davidson, A. (1984). Readability formulas and comprehension. In G. G. Duffy, L. R. Roehler, & J. Mason (Eds.), *Comprehension instruction: Perspectives and suggestions.* New York: Longman.

Drum, P. (1984). Children's understanding of passages. In J. Flood (Ed.), *Promoting reading comprehension* (pp. 61–78). Newark, DE: International Reading Association.

Flesch, R. F. (1948). A new readability yardstick. *Journal of Applied Psychology, 32,* 221–233.

Flood, J., & Lapp, D. (1989). Reporting reading progress: A comparison portfolio for parents. *The Reading Teacher, 42,* 508–514.

Fry, E. (1977). Fry's readability graph: Clarifications, validity and extensions to level 17. *Journal of Reading, 21,* 242–252.

Gardner, H. (1985). *Frames of mind: The theory of multiple intelligences.* New York: Basic Books.

Giles, T. D. (1990). The readability controversy: A technical writing review. *Journal of Technical Writing and Communication, 20,* 131–138.

Graves, M. F., Slater, W. H., Roen, D., Redd-Boyd, T., Duin, A. H., Furniss, D. W., & Hazeltine, P. (1988). Some characteristics of memorable writing: Effects of revisions by writers with different backgrounds. *Research in the Teaching of English, 22,* 242–265.

Green, G. M., & Olsen, M. D. (1988). Preferences and comprehension of original and readability adapted materials. In A. Davidson & G. M. Green (Eds.), *Linguistic complexity and text comprehension.* Hillsdale, NJ: Erlbaum.

Grobe, J. A. (1970). Reading rate and study time demands on secondary students. *Journal of Reading, 13,* 286–288.

Gunning, R. (1979). FOG index of a passage. *Academic Therapy, 14,* 489–491.

Haney, W., & Madaus, G. (1989). Searching for alternatives to standardized tests: Whys, whats, and whithers. *Phi Delta Kappan, 71,* 683–687.

Henk, W. A., & Selders, M. L. (1984). A test of synonymic scoring of cloze passages. *The Reading Teacher, 38,* 282–287.

Hieronymus, A. N., Hoover, H. D., & Linquist, E. F. (1986). *Iowa test of basic skills.* Chicago: Riverside.

Hoover, M. R., Politzer, R. L., & Taylor, O. (1987). Bias in reading tests for black language speakers: A sociolinguistic perspective. *Negro Educational Review, 66,* 81–98.

Irwin, J. W., & Pulver, C. J. (1984). Effects of explicitness, cause and order and reversibility on children's comprehension of causal relationships. *Journal of Educational Psychology, 76,* 399–407.

Johnson, D. W., & Johnson, R. T. (1991). *Learning together and alone: Cooperative, competitive, and individualistic learning.* Englewood Cliffs, NJ: Prentice Hall.

Johnston, P. H. (1983). *Reading comprehension assessment: A cognitive basis.* Newark, DE: International Reading Association.

Kintsch, W., & Vipond, D. (1979). Reading comprehension and readability in educational practice and psychological theory. In L. Nilsson (Ed.), *Proceedings of the conference on memory.* Hillsdale, NJ: Erlbaum.

Klare, G. R. (1989). Understanding the readability of content area texts. In D. Lapp, J. Flood, & N. Farnam (Eds.), *Content Area Reading and Learning.* Englewood Cliffs, NJ: Prentice Hall.

Linn, R. L. (1987). Accountability: The comparison of educational systems and the quality of test results. *Educational Policy, 1,* 181–198.

Madaus, G. F. (1985). Testing scores as administrative mechanisms in educational policy. *Phi Delta Kappan, 66,* 616.

_____. (1986). *Testing and the curriculum: From complaint servant to dictatorial master.* Chestnut Hill, MA: Center for the Study of Testing, Evaluation, and Educational Policy.

Marshall, N. (1970). Readability and comprehensibility. *Journal of Reading, 22,* 542–544.

McCall, W. A., & Crabbs, L. M. (1925). *Standard test lessons in reading: Teacher's manual for all books.* New York: Bureau of Publications, Teachers College, Columbia University.

McKenna, M. C. (1976). Synonymic versus verbatim scoring of the cloze procedure. *Journal of Reading, 20,* 141–143.

Mehrens, W. A., & Lehmann, I. J. (1991). *Measurement and evaluation in education and psychology.* Fort Worth, TX: Holt, Rinehart and Winston.

Paris, S. G., Lawton, T. A., Turner, J. C., & Roth, J. L. (1991). A developmental perspective on standardized achievement testing. *Educational Researcher, 20,* 12–20.

Pearson, P. D. (1974–1975). The effects of grammatical complexity on children's comprehension, recall, and conception of certain semantic relations. *Reading Research Quarterly, 10,* 155–192.

Reder, L. M., & Anderson, J. R. (1982). Effects of spacing and embellishment on memory for the main points of a text. *Memory and Cognition, 10,* 97–102.

Ryder, R. J., Graves, B. B., & Graves, M. F. (1989). *Easy reading: Book series and periodicals for less able readers* (2nd ed.). Newark, DE: International Reading Association.

Ryder, R. J., & Smith, C. F. (1981, May). *An examination of the readability of materials commonly read by adults.* Paper presented at the Twenty-Sixth Annual Convention of the International Reading Association, New Orleans, Louisiana.

Shanahan, T., Kamil, M. L., & Tobin, A. W. (1982). Cloze as a measurement of intersentential comprehension. *Reading Research Quarterly, 17,* 229–255.

Smith, N., & Zinc, A. (1977). A cloze-based investigation of reading comprehension as a composite of subskills. *Journal of Reading Behavior, 9,* 395–398.

Stahl, S. A., Jacobson, M. G., Davis, C. E., & Davis, R. L. (1989). Prior knowledge and difficult vocabulary in the comprehension of unfamiliar text. *Reading Research Quarterly, 24,* 27–43.

Taylor, O. L., & Lee, D. L. (1987). Standardized tests and African-American children: Communication and language issues. *Negro Educational Review, 66,* 67–80.

Taylor, W. L. (1953). Cloze procedure: A new tool for measuring readability. *Journalism Quarterly, 30,* 415–433.

Tierney, R. J., Carter, M. A., & Desai, L. E. (1991). *Portfolio assessment in the reading and writing classroom.* Norwood, MA: Christopher Gordon.

Valencia, S. W. (1990). A portfolio approach to classroom reading assessment: The whys, whats, and hows. *The Reading Teacher, 43,* 338–340.

Wiggins, G. (1989). A true test: Toward more authentic and equitable assessment. *Phi Delta Kappan, 70,* 703–713.

Wolf, D. P. (1989). Portfolio assessment: Sampling student work. *Educational Leadership, 46,* 35–39.

Zakaluk, B. L., & Samuels, S. J. (1988). Toward a new approach to predicting text comprehensibility. In B. L. Zakaluk & S. J. Samuels (Eds.), *Readability: Its past, present, and future.* Newark, DE: International Reading Association.

ANSWERS TO FRY AND FOG READABILITY CALCULATIONS

Excerpt from *The Republic* by Plato

	Fry	FOG
And do you not suppose, Adeimantus, that a single boxer who was perfect in his	22	0
art would easily be a match for two stout and well-to-do gentlemen who were not	21	0
boxers? Hardly, if they came upon him at once. What, not, I said, if he were	19	0
able to run away and then turn and strike at the one who first came up? And	19	0
supposing he were to do this several times under the heat of a scorching sun,	20	1
might he not, being an expert, overturn more than one stout personage?	18	1
Certainly, he said, there would be nothing wonderful/ in that.	13	0

FOG

1. Number of verbs with 3
   or more syllables   2
2. Average sentence length   20
   $20 \times 0.4 = 8.8$ grade level

Fry

1. Total number of syllables   132
2. Number of sentences   4.9
From graph = 7.0th grade level

Excerpt from "It Just Goes On and On" by Bob Berghaus

	Fry	FOG
Veteran Jim Gantner sounded like a frustrated fan after the Milwaukee Brewers'	22	0
14–5 loss to the Texas Rangers Saturday night at County Stadium.	19	0
"Trade the whole team and start over," Gantner said after his team was hammered	18	0
for the second straight night by the Rangers.	10	0
It was another long, embarrassing night for the Brewers, who wound up using catcher	22	0
Rich Dempsey as a ninth-inning pitcher for the second time this season. Dempsey	20	0
and rookie Doug Henry tied for most effective Brewers pitchers of the evening;	20	0
each allowed just a walk in one inning of work.	12	0
Other than that, the/ pitching was terrible and the defense lousy.	5	0

FOG

1. Number of verbs with 3
   or more syllables   0
2. Average sentence length   <u>27</u>
                              $27 \times 0.4 = 10.8$ grade level

Fry

1. Total number of syllables   148
2. Total number of sentences   4.3
From graph = 10th grade level

• •

CHAPTER THREE

Vocabulary

CHAPTER OVERVIEW

In this chapter we describe ways of directly teaching vocabulary and ways of teaching students strategies they can use in improving their own vocabularies. We begin by briefly noting the importance of vocabulary and considering the huge store of words that students need to learn. Next come the two major sections of the chapter, "Teaching Specific Words" and "Preparing Students to Independently Learn Words." In the first section, we discuss various word-learning tasks that students face, consider different levels of word knowledge students can achieve, suggest ways to select appropriate vocabulary, and describe a variety of methods of teaching specific words. In the second, we discuss teaching students to use context and word parts to unlock the meanings of new words, using the dictionary and thesaurus, developing an approach to dealing with unknown words students meet while reading, and adopting a personal approach to building vocabulary.

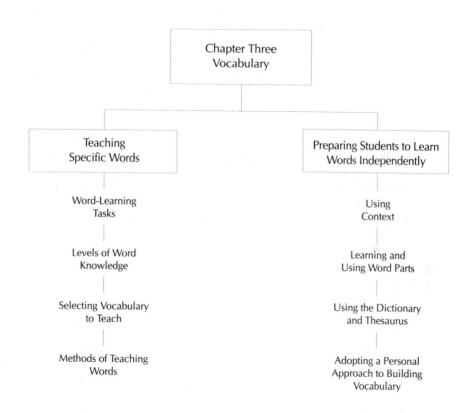

Students' vocabularies—the words they speak and write and those they understand when they read or hear them—are tremendously important to their success in school and in the larger world outside school (Graves, in press). Measurement experts have noted that vocabulary knowledge is one of the best predictors of verbal ability and that a vocabulary test might well be substituted for an intelligence test (Anderson & Freebody, 1981). Readability researchers have contended that vocabulary strongly influences the difficulty of texts (Klare, 1984), and even those who argue that readability formulas provide inadequate assessments of the difficulty of texts recognize that vocabulary is one important factor to take into account when considering whether or not a particular test is appropriate for a particular group of students (Ryder, Graves, & Graves, 1989).

Educators have shown that teaching vocabulary can improve students' comprehension and memory of selections containing the vocabulary taught (Beck, Perfetti, & McKeown, 1982). Educators have also shown that teaching vocabulary can improve students' writing on topics related to the words taught (Duin & Graves, 1986, 1988). Speech and writing researchers have shown that the vocabulary a person uses influences others' perceptions of his or her speech and writing as well as their judgments about the person (Bradac, Bowers, & Courtright, 1982; Neilsen & Piché, 1981). In fact, one noted author has claimed that if someone were to learn a word a day for a year—that is, learn about 350 words—then use those words in his or her speech and writing, he or she would be perceived as better educated, more intelligent, and more successful (Malloy, 1981).

Not only are students' vocabularies very important, they are also very large. The average first grader enters school with a listening vocabulary of something like 5,000 words (Graves, 1986) and by the end of the first grade can read approximately 4,000 words (White, Graves, & Slater, 1990). By the time students reach junior high school, many of them can read 20,000 to 40,000 words; by the time they complete high school, many can read 40,000 to 80,000 words, making the annual rate of growth 3,000 to 4,000 words (Miller & Gildea, 1987). At the same time, estimates indicate that the texts and other materials used by secondary school students contain over 100,000 different words (Nagy & Anderson, 1984) and that students might encounter 15 to 55 unknown words in a typical 1,000-word text (Nagy, Herman, & Anderson, 1985).

Clearly, there are a lot of words to be learned. Of course, teachers do not need to teach all the new words students encounter because students can usually understand selections even though they contain some unknown words (Freebody & Anderson, 1983) and can learn many words on their own. However, some of the words students need to learn should be taught directly. In addition, teachers need to help students develop more powerful strategies for learning words independently. In this chapter we consider these two major goals of vocabulary instruction—teaching specific words and preparing students to become independent word learners—and describe specific procedures for accomplishing each of these goals. Although these are ambitious goals, recent reviews of research (Baumann & Kameenui, 1991; Beck & McKeown, 1991) have suggested powerful approaches to accomplishing both of them.

TEACHING SPECIFIC WORDS

Teaching specific words is the goal that currently receives the most attention in schools. Yet instruction in specific words is often not as effective as it might be because vocabulary learning is frequently thought of as a single task for which there is a single instructional method. In reality, the task of learning words is a series of tasks that vary markedly depending on the word being taught, the learner's knowledge of the word and the concept it represents, and the depth and precision of meaning the student needs to acquire. The sort of instruction appropriate for accomplishing one of these tasks is often inappropriate for accomplishing others; teaching methods need to be matched with the learning tasks and with the students who are doing the learning. Ensuring this match is particularly important in multicultural classrooms, where students from different backgrounds may have different vocabularies.

All of this makes choosing vocabulary instruction appropriate for a particular situation a bit complex. In this section we minimize that complexity by taking matters step by step. We begin by describing six word-learning tasks. Next, we briefly discuss levels of word knowledge. Following that, we make some suggestions for choosing words to teach. Finally, we describe teaching procedures appropriate for each of the six different word-learning tasks. Together, these discussions will better prepare you to make informed decisions about which words to teach and how to teach them. The better the principles behind vocabulary instruction are understood, the more efficient and effective instruction will be.

Word-Learning Tasks

This section presents the following word-learning tasks:

1. Learning to read words in students' oral vocabularies.
2. Learning new labels for known concepts.
3. Learning words representing new and difficult concepts.
4. Clarifying and enriching the meanings of known words.
5. Learning to actively use words in speaking and writing.
6. Learning new meanings for already known words.

These tasks vary a great deal depending on students' prior knowledge of the target word and depth of word knowledge desired. More specifically, the nature of these tasks will be influenced by such factors as whether the words to be learned are already in students' oral vocabularies, whether students have prior knowledge of the concepts represented by the words, how well students will know the words, and whether it is desirable for students to actually use the words in their speech and writing.

Learning to Read Words in Students' Oral Vocabularies. For students just beginning to read, the primary task is learning to recognize in print words they already know when they hear them. Words like *picnic, circle,* and *laughter* are ones that students might learn to read during their first three years of school. By about the time they reach fourth grade, good readers can read nearly all the words in their oral vocabularies (Graves, in press). However, learning to read words in their oral vocabularies remains a task that poor readers may face even in the secondary grades. They know the words when they hear them, but they don't recognize them in print. For example, poor readers might not recognize such words as *ache* and *wrench* because of their unusual spelling.

It is worth noting that this first word-learning task is much different from the other tasks considered here because students need only recognize the printed form of a word they already know. With the others, they must deal with learning or refining word meanings.

Learning New Labels for Known Concepts.   Learning new labels for concepts they already know is a word-learning task all students face. For example, the word *patina* would be unknown to most junior and senior high students, but these same students would have internalized the concept of "film or covering appearing on some surface" or of "ornamental metal turning green." This task often requires students to do some fine-tuning of known concepts to the label being learned. Thus, for the word *patina*, students would need to learn that a distinguishing characteristic of the term is that the film or covering appears gradually as a result of age or long use.

Learning Words Representing New and Difficult Concepts.   Learning to read words that are in neither their oral nor their reading vocabularies and for which they do not have available concepts is one of the most challenging word-learning tasks students face. Learning the full meanings of such words as *fusion, anarchism,* and *proteins* is likely to require the development of new concepts for even senior high students. In fact, in many ways learning words representing new and challenging concepts is more demanding than and quite different from any of the other word-learning tasks considered here. The learner's task is to master a new idea, not just a new label for a familiar idea. Learning a new concept is likely to involve a host of subtasks—defining the new concept, recognizing instances of the new concept, distinguishing between the new concept and other similar concepts, and dealing with a great deal of information about the contexts in which the new concept is embedded. As later sections in the chapter will illustrate, it takes very robust instruction to fully teach new and challenging concepts.

Clarifying and Enriching the Meanings of Known Words.   Another word-learning task is refining the meanings of already known words. The meanings students originally give to words are often vague and imprecise. Initially, for example, students might not recognize any difference between *sad* and *morose,* or be able to distinguish a *trumpet* from a *cornet,* or understand that the term *watershed* is usually applied to a critical point that serves as a dividing line in some historic event. As students repeatedly encounter words they know in a variety of contexts, they will gradually expand and enrich their knowledge of them. However, more direct approaches can help guarantee that students add to the depth of their word knowledge.

Learning to Actively Use Words in Speaking and Writing.   The task here is to learn words well enough to actually use them, moving words from students' listening and reading vocabularies to their speaking and writing vocabularies. Twelfth graders, for example, might have a fairly thorough understanding of the word *omnipotent* when they hear it or read it, yet never use the word themselves. Certain methods of vocabulary instruction can stimulate students to actively use the words they do know.

Learning New Meanings for Already Known Words.   The last task considered here is learning new meanings for words that students already know. The target words are ones students can pronounce and know one meaning for but for which they need to learn an additional meaning. The multiple-meaning words that need to be dealt with in content classes are those with both common meanings and specialized meanings in particular content areas. The words *mean* in mathematics, *charter* in history, *sash* in carpentry, and *resistance* in physics are examples.

PRACTICE ACTIVITY 3.1

Listed here are two sets of words that present students with various word-learning tasks. Assume that you are considering teaching the first set to a class of average eighth-grade students and the second set to a class of average eleventh-grade students. Consider each word, then identify the word-learning task that it probably represents. We say probably because the learning task represented by a particular word may not be the same for all students even in a fairly homogeneous class. Moreover, identifying the word-learning task particular words represent requires a judgment, a hypothesis. Because doing this exercise requires you to hypothesize, it's a good one to do with a colleague so that you can talk over your decisions. Our judgments about the word-learning task each word represents are listed in the answers to practice activities section.

Words for 8th Graders

fling (a wild time)   _____ a new concept

    _____ a new meaning for a known word

rational number   _____ a word in students' oral vocabularies

    _____ a new word for a known concept

pneumonia   _____ a word in students' oral vocabularies

    _____ a new concept

finite   _____ a new concept

    _____ a new word for a known concept

Words for 11th Graders

fluke   _____ a new concept

                         _____ a new word for a known concept

languish   _____ a word in students' oral vocabularies

                         _____ a new word for a known concept

fugue   _____ a word in students' oral vocabularies

                         _____ a new concept

taxonomy   _____ a new concept

                         _____ a new word for a known concept

Levels of Word Knowledge

Not only are there different word-learning tasks, but there are also different degrees to which students can know words. Beck, McCaslin, and McKeown (1980) identify three levels of word knowledge: unknown, acquainted, and established. An unknown word is obviously just that. The word *levorotatory* (an adjective pertaining to a chemical solution that rotates the plane of polarized light counterclockwise), for example, is almost certainly unknown to both junior and senior high students. A word at the acquainted level is one that students need to deliberately think about to recall its meaning. The word *fiesta* is probably at the acquainted level for many junior high students, the word *raucous* at the acquainted level for many senior high students. Finally, a word at the established level is one students recognize and give a meaning to easily, rapidly, and perhaps automatically. The word *library* is at the established level for nearly all secondary students.

Students also need to learn many words at an in-depth level, a level at which they are thoroughly understood. When a word is thoroughly understood, students are able to associate it with a range of experiences, articulate their understanding of it, use it flexibly, and recognize synonyms, metaphors, and analogies that employ the word (Calfee & Drum, 1986). The word *prom* would be at the in-depth level for many senior high students, the word *school* at that level for both junior and senior high students. A significant goal of content classes is to move students' knowledge of such words as *tariff, tangent, mass,* and *sonnet* to the in-depth level.

Any vocabulary instruction is likely to move students' knowledge of a word beyond the unknown level. But to learn a word thoroughly requires students to be exposed to that word in a variety of contexts (Beck & McKeown, 1983). Of course, one instructional encounter with a word will often not leave students with a rich or deep meaning of that word. However, one encounter with a word should not be viewed as the only exposure students will have to it.

Vocabulary learning should be viewed instead as a series of encounters that will eventually lead students to mastery of words. Sometimes instruction will be relatively brief, serving primarily as an introduction, preventing students from stumbling over unknown words when reading. But this is just the first step on the long road to full mastery of words. There will be many more opportunities for students to deepen their knowledge of words, both through repeated exposure in their reading and listening and through further instruction.

PRACTICE ACTIVITY 3.2

Listed here are four words for junior high students and four words for senior high students. Classify each as likely to be at the unknown, acquainted, established, or in-depth level. Our classification is shown in the answers section.

Words for Junior High Students	Words for Senior High Students
harmony	examinations
languid	pi
fast food	erstwhile
triangle	aerobic

Selecting Vocabulary to Teach

As you become familiar with the various word-learning tasks students face and the knowledge they are expected to gain, you should direct your attention to selecting specific words to teach. Two steps are helpful here: Find out just which words students are likely to know, then set up criteria for selecting words to teach.

The best source of information about the words students know is the students themselves. One way to get this information is to select some of the words in upcoming selections that will be difficult and create matching tests to check your perceptions. Such tests will be most effective and efficient if you follow certain guidelines in developing them. First, the words tested and the alternatives should be the same part of speech. Second, the alternatives should be simpler than the word being tested. Third, there should be one and only one clear match for each word being tested. Grouping the words to be tested in four word sets with five alternatives provides a convenient format for students to respond to. Here is a sample matching item for some words from a high school American history text.

_____ atrocity	a. something huge
_____ colossus	b. the right to vote
_____ plight	c. something horrible
_____ suffrage	d. a group of companies
	e. a difficult situation

Of course, constructing tests requires a good deal of time and cannot be done for every selection, nor should it be. The experience of identifying potentially troublesome words and then checking students' performance against your perceptions, however, will give you a better understanding of which words might cause difficulty.

Besides constructing tests to identify difficult vocabulary, you can query students on which words they know. Recent work (White, Slater, & Graves, 1989) has suggested that students can be quite accurate in checking words on a list to indicate those that they do and do not know. Giving students a list of words and having them indicate whether or not they know each word is certainly less time consuming than preparing and administering a test.

Another option is to have groups of students skim through upcoming selections and pick out words they think will be important in the selection and difficult for their classmates. This is an excellent opportunity for cooperative work, and heterogeneous groups of four work well for this task. Divide students into groups and then explain that each group's task is to skim through a part of the upcoming selection, looking for difficult words that seem important to understanding the selection. When they find such words, they are to define them and be prepared to give the sentences in which the words occurred and their definitions to the class. Assign each group member a definite role. One student can skim the passage for difficult words. Another can write down the words selected. A third can look up the words in the dictionary and write down an appropriate definition, and the fourth can check to see that the definitions given are appropriate for the way the words are used in the passage. Each group is assigned a particular part of the selection and teaches the words they have highlighted to the class.

The suggestions thus far in this section have been aimed at helping you to identify potentially difficult vocabulary. Many times your job in selecting vocabulary does not end here because there may be more words than you will have time to teach. Thus, once potentially difficult vocabulary is identified, criteria for identifying the most important words to teach need to be established. The following guidelines are useful in determining these critical words.

1. Understanding the word is important to understanding the selection in which it appears.
2. If students can use their context or structural analysis skills to glean a meaning for the word, they ought to be allowed to do so. Having students use their word-learning skills whenever possible will both help them solidify these skills and reduce the number of words taught.
3. If the word is likely to be useful outside the selection currently being taught, that is, if students are likely to come across it in other reading, it is important to teach it. The word *incumbent*, for example, is one that is fairly often unknown but is likely to be encountered again. On the other hand, such words as *ganister* and *laches* are infrequently used.

Still another matter to consider in choosing words to teach is that of how many can reasonably be taught for a single selection. For a chapter, article, or short story of 10 to 20 pages, 10 words is about as many as should be taught. This does not mean that you need always teach this number of words for a selection. Sometimes you will teach none, sometimes only a single word representing a difficult new concept. Of course, for longer selections, such as books, it may be necessary to teach more than 10 words; but if many more than 10 words are taught, they should be taught in several sessions.

PRACTICE ACTIVITY 3.3

Compose a matching test for the words *sensationalist, surreal, inflated,* and *neutral.* As before, check your items against our sample in the answers section. Share your test with a colleague and ask him or her to critique it.

Methods of Teaching Words

This section describes teaching procedures that can be used for each of the word-learning tasks we have described.

Learning to Read Known Words.   In order to learn to read words that are in their oral vocabularies, students need to associate what is unknown, the written word, with what is already known, the spoken word. To make this happen, they need to see the word at the same time they hear it; once the association is established, they need to rehearse it until the association becomes automatic:

1. Students see the word.
2. Students hear the word pronounced.
3. Students rehearse that association.

There are many ways to accomplish each of these steps. Students can initially see the word in the context of their reading material, on a handout, on the board, on a screen, or on a computer. They can hear the word when you say it, another student says it, or a computer speech synthesizer says it. Students can rehearse the association by seeing and pronouncing the word in a variety of contexts, by using it in their writing, or by playing games that require them to recognize printed versions of it.

The best form of rehearsal, and an essential part of students' mastering words, is using reading materials that contain numerous repetitions of the words. In fact, wide reading is almost certainly the most powerful force in developing vocabularies, and it would be difficult to overestimate the value of getting students to do as much reading as possible. Remember that, when teaching students to read words that are in their speaking and listening vocabularies, there is no need to teach meanings. By definition, these are words students already know; they simply cannot read them.

Learning New Labels for Known Concepts.   Two quite different sorts of instruction are discussed here. First, several types of introductory instruction are described—relatively brief instruction that teaches the basic meanings of words. Then, several types of intensive instruction are described—relatively lengthy instruction that teaches deep and full word meanings and often stresses the interrelationships among sets of words and concepts.

Introductory Instruction.   Described here are three approaches to teaching new words representing known concepts. These require different amounts of teacher preparation time, different amounts of class time, and different amounts of student time and effort; they are likely to yield different results. All, however, include more than one step and involve some sort of interaction and feedback from you as the teacher. Recent research suggests that giving students only a definition of a word, giving them only the word in a brief context, or simply telling them to look up the word in the dictionary is ineffective (Herman & Dole, 1988; Stahl & Fairbanks, 1986). Consequently, each of these procedures includes a definition and the presentation of the word in context.

1. Giving students the word in context, asking them to look it up in the dictionary, then discussing the definitions they come up with

   subscript

   Nicole, a student in Ms. Greene's third-hour mathematics class, had used the term x to refer to three different quantities; thus, she used *subscripts* to distinguish the three terms.

2. Giving a synonym or definition of the word, presenting a rich context, and discussing the word's meaning

   detriment (DET re ment)—damage, harm, or loss

   Smoking, not eating properly, and not getting enough sleep has been a real *detriment* to Alex's football-playing ability. The coach has been very concerned about Alex's unhealthy lifestyle, and the fans have been disappointed in his performance this season.

3. Using the context/relationship procedure (see Aulls & Graves, 1985) This procedure presents the target word three or four times in a brief paragraph, which is followed by a multiple-choice item designed to check students' understanding of the word.

   rationale

   The *rationale* for exposing students to a variety of words and their meanings is to help them become better thinkers who are able to express their ideas more clearly. Part of that *rationale* includes my belief that words themselves are fascinating objects of study. My *rationale* for doing something means my fundamental reasons for doing it.

   Rationale means

   _____ a. a deliberate error.
   _____ b. the basis for doing something.
   _____ c. a main idea for an essay.

In presenting each word, explain the procedure's purpose, pronounce the target word, read the paragraph containing the word, read the multiple-choice items, then ask students to select the best definition by putting a check next to their choice. Finally, give students the correct answer and respond to any questions they have.

Note that these approaches do not involve merely handing students a worksheet and asking them to complete it independently. Instead, each approach involves some interaction between the teacher and students, a discussion that gives students the opportunity to express what they know about a word's meaning and offers the teacher an opportunity to probe students' understandings of the word being taught and clear up any misconceptions that may exist.

Intensive Instruction.   Three forms of intensive instruction are presented here—rich and thorough instruction that provides rich and thorough understanding of the words taught.

The first form of intensive instruction considered is called *semantic mapping* (Heimlich & Pittelman, 1986). Using this method, the teacher puts a word representing a central concept on the board; asks students to volunteer words related to the central concept; writes these on the board and groups them in broad categories; has students name the categories; and concludes by discussing the central concept, the related words, the categories, and the relationships among these elements. Semantic mapping is particularly appropriate for selections that have a single central concept and when students have fairly substantial prior knowledge relevant to the central concept. Figure 3.1 shows a semantic map for the word *telecommunications*.

The second method of intensive instruction is called *possible sentences* (Moore & Moore, 1990). Possible sentences is intended primarily for informational texts rather than for narratives. It is a particularly useful approach because, in addition to teaching vocabulary, it provides for very active student involvement, creates interest and curiosity in the upcoming selection, and gives students some information about the upcoming selection. The following is an outline of the procedure.

1. **Select six to eight words that are central to the selection and that students may not know, as well as four to six words that are familiar to students.** Words from a geography chapter dealing with the environment might include *pollution, pesticides, atmosphere, particulates, hazard, recycling, organic, ozone, carbon dioxide, fertilizer,* and *feasible*.

2. **Write the words on the board, have volunteers define those they know, then define any that they do not.**

3. **Ask students to create sentences that include at least two of the words and that might appear in the upcoming selection.** These sentences should be written on the board, with the words from the list underlined. The process should continue until all of the potentially difficult words have been used in sentences. Some of the possible sentences that might be generated for the

---

FIGURE 3.1   SEMANTIC MAP FOR THE WORD *TELECOMMUNICATIONS*

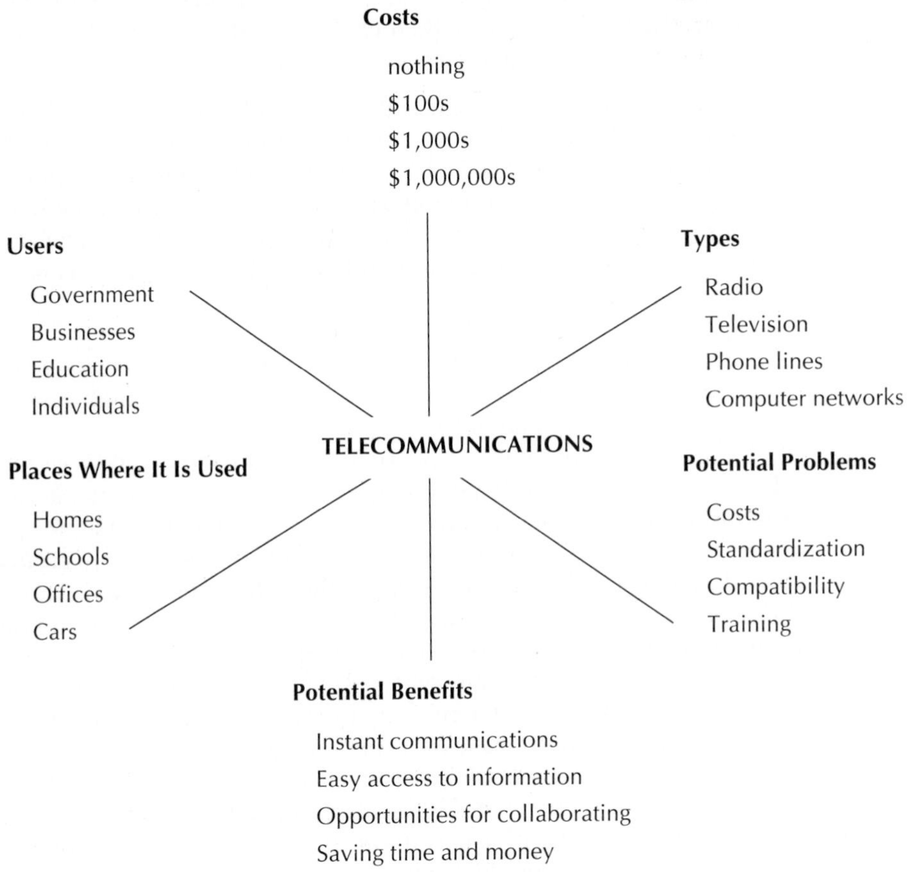

Costs

nothing
$100s
$1,000s
$1,000,000s

Users

Government
Businesses
Education
Individuals

Types

Radio
Television
Phone lines
Computer networks

TELECOMMUNICATIONS

Places Where It Is Used

Homes
Schools
Offices
Cars

Potential Problems

Costs
Standardization
Compatibility
Training

Potential Benefits

Instant communications
Easy access to information
Opportunities for collaborating
Saving time and money

---

above words are *"Pesticides* are a serious *hazard* to people" and "The *ozone* layer in the *atmosphere* is rapidly being depleted."

4. **Have students read the selection for general understanding and to evaluate the accuracy of the sentences.**

5. **Return to the sentences on the board and discuss with the class whether or not each of them could or could not be true based on the selection.** This, of course, is a crucial phase and an excellent opportunity for students to read closely and critically and articulate their points of view.

6. **Delete or modify sentences that are inaccurate, and have students volunteer additional sentences if they are needed to deal with the central concepts of the selection.** If, for example, the sentence *"Recycling* will never be

economically *feasible* on a large scale" was inconsistent with the information presented in the chapter, it would be rewritten.

While the possible sentences approach is certain to stimulate students' active involvement and curiosity, care must be taken to ensure that students generate appropriate meanings and relationships *before* they have read a selection. Otherwise, students may attach an incorrect label to a word as they are reading, making comprehension more difficult and possibly frustrating them.

The third type of intensive instruction suggested here was developed by Ryder (1985) and is referred to as *student-activated vocabulary instruction.* As described here, the procedure has two phases, *conceptual assimilation* and *lexical refinement,* each of which includes several steps. Together, these two phases require a substantial amount of teaching time. In cases where time is limited, the conceptual assimilation phase can be used by itself. Both phases are described here.

Conceptual Assimilation

1. Select 5 to 10 important words (in the upcoming selection) that are probably unknown to students. Words from a multicultural lesson in art and social studies dealing with the Dias de los Muertos (Day of the Dead) in Hispanic cultures might include *conquistadors, secularized, evangelizing, colonialism, mosaics, serapes, altar,* and *jadeite.*

2. Construct four word cards for each word. On the first card, write the word phonetically. On the second, write the word and its definition. On the third, give a sentence that presents the word in a rich context. On the fourth, write the word itself. For example, for the word *secularized* you would do the following:
- Card 1: sek´ yə lə rīzd
- Card 2: secularized = to have separated from religious connections or influences, to have made worldly
- Card 3: Urban Hispanics today tend to be somewhat secularized. They have removed themselves from many of the traditional religious observances of the Day of the Dead.
- Card 4: secularized

3. **Have students create lists of words related to each of the words to be learned.** Give each student one of the cards from Step 2. Have students compare cards and form groups made up of the four students whose cards form a set. Then have each group create a list of words related to the word being studied. If the word is an adjective or noun, they should list attributes and nonattributes. If the word is a verb, they should list synonyms and antonyms. At first, you probably will want to model these sets of related words. Once a group has completed their list, they should put the new word, its definition, and the related words on the board or an overhead. An example of such a list for the word *secularized* is shown here.

• secularized = to be separated from religious influence

spiritual	nonreligious
priest	supreme court judge
government	churches
parishoners	worship

4. **Have one member of each group teach the group's word to the class.** The student should present the word, its definition, and the list of related words on the board or overhead. After reading the word and its definition, he or she should then call on class members to indicate whether each related word is either an attribute or synonym, on the one hand, or a nonattribute or antonym, on the other.

Lexical Refinement

1. **Refine students' knowledge of the new word by using it to describe something they are familiar with.** Put a new word and its definition on the board or overhead, then ask several yes/no questions about whether or not the word applies in a situation students are familiar with. For example, with the word *serape,* you might ask, "Would you be likely to wear a serape in the summer?" or "Would a serape be more likely to be made of wool or nylon?"

2. **Conduct a sentence-combining lesson in which students first list attributes or nonattributes of the new word in kernel sentences, then combine these sentences to form more complex ones.** For example, you might present the prompt "The altar is central to observing the Day of the Dead. The altar is maintained to ensure good relations between the family on earth and the family in the afterworld" and get such kernel sentences as "The entire family gets involved in the construction of the altar," "Foods, ornaments, and objects that the deceased enjoyed are placed on the altar," and "Religious images are placed on the altar in the hope that the souls of the departed will travel safely on the journey to the afterworld." Students would then combine these sentences to yield something like "The altar, constructed by the family, is central to celebrating the Day of the Dead as foods, ornaments, and objects the deceased enjoyed are placed on the altar."

Student-activated vocabulary instruction requires a great deal of student involvement. By drawing on the concepts and background knowledge they associate with the words presented, students of all abilities and backgrounds will benefit from this form of instruction. Furthermore, the presentation of words through various learning modalities increases the likelihood that all students will acquire some knowledge of the words presented. This activity is likely to arouse students' curiosity, maintain participation, and present words in contexts that are meaningful and relevant to the students.

When considering using any form of intensive instruction, it is important to realize that it takes a good deal of preparation and class time and is not something that can or should be used continually. However, it is certainly worth the effort on some occasions. Results of several studies (Beck & McKeown, 1983; Johnson, Pittelman, Toms-Bronowski, & Levin, 1984; Stahl & Kapinus, 1991) have indicated that intensive instruction helps students gain deep understanding and mastery of the words taught and that this in-depth knowledge enables them to better comprehend materials containing the words.

Learning New Words Representing New Concepts.   As noted earlier, learning new words representing new concepts is a very demanding task. Just how demanding the task is will depend on the difficulty of the new concept and on how unfamiliar students are with that concept and others related to it. For example, in the area of literary analysis, the concept of *plot* will be understood by most upper-elementary students and the concept of *characterization* by most secondary students, while the concept of *theme* will continue to prove difficult for many college students. Similarly, in the area of physics, the concept of *weight* will be available to many elementary students and the concept of *volume* to many secondary students, while the concept of *mass* will continue to puzzle many college students.

Semantic mapping, one of the intensive instruction methods just described, can also be used to teach new concepts, particularly if students have some knowledge related to those concepts. One procedure particularly appropriate for very challenging concept learning was developed by Frayer and colleagues (see Frayer, Frederick, & Klausmeier, 1969) and is sometimes referred to as the *Frayer method*. The major steps of the method as it might be used to teach the concept of *perseverance* are shown here.

1. **Define the concept, giving its attributes.**
Perseverance is a trait that a person might possess. A person demonstrates *perseverance* when he or she remains constant, despite obstacles, to some purpose or task over an extended period.

2. **Distinguish between the concept and similar concepts with which it might be confused. When doing this, you may need to point out some of the nonessential features of the new concept that might falsely be considered necessary features.**
Perseverance differs from *stubbornness* in that *perseverance* is typically seen as a positive quality, and the goal toward which one perseveres is typically a worthwhile one. Conversely, *stubbornness* is usually seen as a negative quality, and the goal pursued by a person who is being stubborn is often not worthwhile.

3. **Provide examples of the concept and reasons explaining why they are examples.**
A person who graduates from college despite financial responsibilities that require him or her to work full time would be demonstrating *perseverance* because the goal is worthwhile and takes a long and steady effort to achieve.
A person who learns to ski after losing a leg in an accident is demonstrating *perseverance* for similar reasons.

4. **Provide nonexamples of the concept and reasons explaining why they are nonexamples.**
Someone who goes fishing a lot just because he or she enjoys it is not demonstrating *perseverance* because there is no particular purpose here and no obstacles.

Someone who waters his or her lawn once a week is not demonstrating *perseverance* because there is no particular challenge in doing so.

5. Present examples and nonexamples to students. Ask them to identify which are and are not instances of the concept and to explain why. Give feedback on their responses.
- Reading an interesting book that you thoroughly enjoy (nonexample)
- Completing a canoe trip from the headwaters of the Mississippi to New Orleans (example)
- Eating a dozen donuts because you are really hungry (nonexample)
- Completing a 3-mile cross-country race even though you were out of breath and were dead tired after less than a mile (example)

6. Ask students to generate their own examples and nonexamples, let them talk about why they are examples and nonexamples, and give feedback.

Using the Frayer method obviously takes a substantial amount of effort and time on both the instructor's and learners' part. In fact, while some concepts could be taught in part of a class period, really difficult concepts may require several days of instruction. However, the effort and time expended yield rich rewards. This method provides students with full, precise understandings of important concepts.

Clarifying and Enriching the Meanings of Known Words.   Two of the procedures already described—semantic mapping and the Frayer method—are appropriate for clarifying and extending word meanings. The procedure described here, *semantic feature analysis* (see Pittelman, Heimlich, Berglund, & French, 1991), can be used to teach in-depth meanings and new concepts. However, it is especially appropriate for refining word meanings.

Semantic feature analysis involves presenting students with a grid that includes a set of related words on one axis, and a set of attributes that each of the words may or may not have on the other axis. Figure 3.2 illustrates the method using words describing roads and walkways. The plus signs indicate the presence of a characteristic and the minuses its absence.

In their first work with such a grid, students are shown a completed example, such as this one. Next, they are shown grids with the terms and attributes filled in, but without the pluses and minuses, and are asked to insert them. Later, they are given grids with some terms and attributes and asked to add to both the list of related words and the list of attributes, then fill in the pluses and minuses. Finally, after becoming proficient in working with partially completed grids you supply, students can create grids for sets of related words they suggest. In all cases, there should be a good deal of discussion, for the essence of semantic feature analysis lies in the discussion. With the above grid, for example, discussion of the fact that *boulevards, freeways,* and *turnpikes* share the same features should lead to a discussion of whether additional attributes should be added in order to distinguish among these or whether the three terms are synonymous.

FIGURE 3.2   SEMANTIC FEATURE ANALYSIS FOR ROADS AND WALKWAYS

Roads and Walkways	Typical Characteristics					
	Narrow	**Wide**	**Paved**	**Unpaved**	**For Walking**	**For Driving**
path	+	−	−	+	+	−
trail	+	−	−	+	+	−
road	+	+	+	+	−	+
lane	+	−	+	+	+	+
boulevard	−	+	+	−	−	+
freeway	−	+	+	−	−	+
turnpike	−	+	+	−	−	+

Moving Words Into Students' Expressive Vocabularies.   Any sort of intensive vocabulary instruction is likely to move some words into students' expressive vocabularies. Additionally, students can be encouraged to add words to their expressive vocabularies by providing them a model of precise word use. Students can also be encouraged by recognizing and rewarding precise and mature word usage in their speech and writing through praise and other kinds of positive feedback. Also, providing time and encouragement for various sorts of word play that prompt students to work with words they might otherwise not say or write can have positive results in terms of students' actually incorporating these new words.

Another approach to promoting expressive vocabulary has been developed by Duin (see Duin & Graves, 1986, 1988). The major features of this instruction are described here.

1. Words are taught in a set of 10 to 15 related words presented over a week or so. The words need to be carefully selected so that they lend themselves to writing on a particular topic. A set of words Duin used with an essay about space exploration included *accommodate, advocate, capability, configuration, criteria, disarray, envision, feasible, habitable, module, quest, retrieve,* and *tether.*

2. Students work extensively with the set of words. About half an hour a day is spent with the 10 to 15 words taught during the week, and students are actively engaged in a dozen or so activities with each word.

3. Instruction is purposely varied, and the activities are designed to accomplish a variety of goals. Students give definitions for words orally and in writing, create sentences containing the words, do timed trials with them, make affective responses to them, make comparisons of target words and similar concepts, keep a journal of their work with them, are encouraged to use them outside class, and do several short writing assignments with them. Instruction for each word centers on the concept it represents, its relationship with other words, and the possibilities for its use when writing on a particular subject.

In Duin's lesson students discussed whether or not a particular *quest* would be *feasible.* They were asked what sort of *criteria* they would use in choosing people to build a space station. They distinguished between new words such as *quest* and known words such as *dream* by choosing the more colorful word and explaining why it was so. And they worked in cooperative groups writing short essays on such topics as how to make a space station enticing to tourists, being sure to employ their new vocabulary.

Research has shown that students who received this instruction used a number of the taught words in their writing and that their writing was judged superior to that of students who did not receive the instruction. Research has also shown that students really enjoy working with words in these ways. It should be noted, however, that the students Duin worked with were seventh graders, and in general this approach is better suited to junior high than to senior high students. There is, though, one way in which the approach can be used with senior high students without fear of its seeming too juvenile, and that is to treat it as a game. That is, work with a set of words and ask students to see how many of the words they can use in a one-page paper. This sort of playing with words is likely to spark their interest and encourage more word play.

Learning New Meanings for Already Known Words.   Learning new meanings for known words may or may not require students to learn new concepts; thus, acquiring such words can represent different word-learning tasks. For example, all 7th graders will know that the word *pole* means a long piece of wood. However, many students still need to learn that *pole* also refers to the positive and negative ends of a magnet; teaching this meaning thoroughly may mean teaching what positive and negative poles are, which would be a new concept for most students. Or consider the word *police.* All 7th graders know that *police* are law officers; however, most 7th graders and many 12th graders will not know that *police* is also a verb meaning to clean up an area. In this case, the new meaning represents a readily known concept. Or consider the word *lot,* meaning a plot of land. This meaning is known by virtually all 7th and 12th graders. However, the word *lot,* meaning one's fate in life, is known by very few 7th graders and only some 12th graders. Again, this new meaning represents a readily known concept.

Because teaching new meanings for known words represents a variety of learning tasks, many of the techniques already described can be used. If the new meanings to be taught do not represent new and difficult concepts, the simple procedure described here is effective.

1. State the known meaning.
2. Present the new meaning.
3. Point out similarities and differences between the meanings.

For example, for the verb *reduce*, meaning to lose weight, present the new meaning "to change the form of a mathematical expression to something more easily understood." Point out that in both instances, something is lessened. In the first case, it is weight; in the second, it is the complexity of a mathematical term. This procedure has proven successful both in teaching new meanings and in reminding students that many words have multiple meanings.

Some Inappropriate Techniques for Teaching Vocabulary. We close this section by briefly discussing some techniques that, although commonly used, are generally ineffective.

The most frequently used inappropriate technique is that of giving students a list of words out of context and telling them to look up the meanings in the dictionary. Three facts argue against this. First, most words have several meanings and many shades of meaning. Taken out of context, there is no way for students to decide which dictionary definition is most nearly appropriate. Second, unless a learner has some knowledge of a word and its meaning already, dictionary definitions are often inadequate. In general, dictionaries are more useful for students to use in checking the meaning of a word they think they know than in determining the meaning of a totally unfamiliar word. Finally, asking students to do something does not constitute instruction; before students are asked to look up words in the dictionary, they need to be taught how to do so. Such instruction is described later in this chapter.

Another frequently suggested technique is giving students the words in context and asking them to figure out the meanings. This, like the previous technique, is a practice activity rather than an instructional activity; students are being asked to use context, not taught how to use it. Before asking students to use context to discern word meanings, be certain to teach them how to do so. (Teaching students to use context cues is discussed in the next section of this chapter.) Also, although context by itself reveals some meaning and is certainly something that students need to learn to use in unlocking word meanings, a single occurrence in context seldom reveals the whole of a word's meaning. Students will usually need rich context and a definition to master a word's full meaning.

Still another frequently suggested technique is doing speeded trials with flash cards or some device that rapidly displays a word. Students do need to learn to make rapid and automatic responses to words, but for the most part they learn to do this by repeatedly reading the words in the context of fairly easy and definitely enjoyable reading. Somewhat related to this technique is that of having students search letter mazes—rows and columns filled with letters—for words. This resembles no realistic reading task and is simply busy work.

Finally, there is the matter of teaching spelling. Learning to spell is something that students certainly need to do. However, teaching spelling and teaching vocabulary are two different tasks. In teaching vocabulary, the task is to teach students the meanings of words they don't know or (but not very frequently in secondary school) teach students to read words that are already in their oral vocabularies. In teaching spelling, the task is to teach students to spell words they can already read. Therefore, when vocabulary is taught, teach students words that are in one way or another unknown to them. When spelling is taught, students will be learning to spell words they already know; the words that students need to know how to spell are those words that they actively use in speech and writing. Of course, if the goal is to move words into students' writing vocabularies, it is important to ensure that students can spell the words.

PRACTICE ACTIVITY 3.4

1. Construct a semantic map for the word *fear* by filling in appropriate words under the given categories. Our response, which is based on a semantic map presented by Nagy (1988), is given in the answers section.
   - Reactions to fearful places
   - Antonyms for *fear*
   - Synonyms for *fear*

2. Create Frayer model material for teaching the concept of *textbook*. Our response is given in the answers section.

3. Shown here is a partial grid for planets in the earth's solar system. Note that the planets are listed alphabetically. Complete the grid by adding the missing planets and inserting pluses and minuses (or question marks if you're not sure of the answer). A completed grid is given in the answers section.

Characteristics

Planet	Closer to Sun Than Earth	Larger Than Earth	Has Moon(s)	Has Rings	Orbits the Sun	Inner planet
Earth						
Jupiter						
Mars						
Mercury						
Neptune						

4. Choose one of the classes you teach or plan to teach, select a phrase describing a cluster of words appropriate for using Duin's expressive vocabulary instruction with the class, and generate a set of 10 or so words forming the cluster. Then share your list with a colleague, and see which of you can use the most words in a short essay or narrative. We suggest that you do this in writing and keep it as part of your notes on this chapter. You may be able to use it in introducing work on building writing vocabulary to your students.

5. Listed here are some multiple-meaning words and a meaning for each. For each word and grade level given, indicate whether the meaning

probably represents an available concept or a new and most likely difficult one. Our response is given in the answers section.

12th grade	medium	sources of information such as print, television, and radio
7th grade	review	a critical report
7th grade	issue	children
12th grade	force	the capacity to do work or cause change
9th grade	scan	to mark poetic meter

PREPARING STUDENTS TO LEARN WORDS INDEPENDENTLY

As noted in the beginning of this chapter, students learn approximately 4,000 words each year, many more than could be taught directly. Thus, even if instruction in individual words were as widespread and rich as one could possibly make it, students still need to learn much of their vocabulary independently. In this section, we consider four skills that students need to become independent word learners: using context, learning and using word parts, using the dictionary and thesaurus, and developing a personal approach to learning words.

Using Context

Most words are learned from context; no other explanation can account for students' learning 3,000 to 4,000 words each school year (Sternberg, 1987). At the same time, wrestling a word's meaning from most contexts is often very challenging. Still, it has been estimated that average students acquire over 1,000 words—roughly one third of the words learned during the year—in the context of their normal reading (Nagy, Anderson, & Herman, 1987). If students can develop better than average skills in learning words from context, they can learn even more words from their reading.

Given the importance of using context, it is useful to help students learn to use context more effectively. The remainder of this section presents various ways in which context can reveal meaning and offers a plan for introducing the notion of context cues. We suggest that you periodically embed brief lessons on context cues when challenging words come up in subject matter lessons.

Ways in Which Context Can Reveal Meaning.   As Sternberg and Powell (1983) have pointed out, the text surrounding an unknown word can provide a variety of cues to that word's meaning. The following sentences illustrate many of the ways in which this is done.

Temporal Cues: The sentence "Whenever I see a movie set in the fifties, I'm swept by nostalgia for my high school years" indicates that I feel "nostalgic" when I "see a movie set in the fifties."

Location Cues: The sentence "She carried a small nosegay to the prom" indicates that a "nosegay" is something a girl might take "to the prom."

Value Cues: The sentence "Gathering the sustenance to keep their families alive is one of the top priorities of many parents in developing nations" indicates that "sustenance" is a "top priority of many parents."

Attribute Cues: The sentence "The equitable distribution of wealth is one prerequisite of a just society" explicitly states that "equitable distribution of wealth" is a feature of a "just society."

Functional Cues: The sentence "The defendant was exonerated by the judge because there was not enough evidence" indicates that "exonerating" defendants is one function of a "judge."

Causal Cues: The sentence "Three years of apprenticeship in a welding shop left Jackson with a lot of experience in welding" indicates that an "apprenticeship" provides a person with "a lot of experience."

Class Membership Cues: The sentence "The only sound in the empty house was a faint rasping that could occasionally be heard" indicates that "rasping" is a type of sound.

Definition or Synonym Cues: The sentence "The crew anchored the boat in a cove, a small bay on the uninhabited side of the island" defines a "cove" as "a small bay."

Contrast or Antonym Cues: The sentence "The war had been a harrowing experience for some men, but a few soldiers actually found the war exciting and exhilarating" contrasts the word *harrowing* with "exciting and exhilarating."

Note that the list of cues here is intended for the teacher rather than for students. With students, the cues should be introduced one at a time and rather informally; students should not be required to learn the list of cues. For example, if a selection contains a number of location cues, take the time to point out that sometimes other words in a sentence indicate something about the location of an unknown word and knowing the location associated with an unknown word can provide a cue to its meaning.

Presenting the Notion of Context Cues.   Almost all secondary students have had some instruction in using context cues, and so presenting the notion of context cues generally means reminding students of something they have already had some experience with. The following steps will be useful in promoting the use of context cues.

1. **Introduce the concept of context cues.** The introduction should be short and to the point. Tell students that they need to become adept in using context cues because most words are learned from context. Explain further that while most of the time context will not give them a precise definition of a word, it will often give them hints to its meaning. Also, tell them that context cues in-

clude the words, phrases, and sentences that surround an unknown word, and that context cues can come before or after an unknown word.

2. **Point out useful cues.** Next, suggest that when they are reading a passage and come to a word they do not immediately know, they should consider the words and phrases within the sentence that surrounds the word to deduce enough of the word's meaning to understand its use in the passage. Next, suggest that the students examine the sentences surrounding the sentence containing the new word. It is often useful to first define the new word, then ask students to find the cues in the sentence in which the word appears as well as in the surrounding sentences. By providing the definition, students' attention will be focused on semantic and syntactic cues rather than the word's meaning.

3. **Think aloud the process of using context cues.** After this introductory explanation, describe one or two of the types of cues context can provide. For example, consider cues to attributes of an unknown word or to its functions. Select a few sentences that include difficult words and some informative cues illustrating the cue types described, and explain how these cues help reveal the difficult words' meanings. For example, the sentence "The defendant was exonerated by the judge because there was not enough evidence" could be presented with the following think aloud:

> Let's see. Exonerated. It's something a judge does, and it's something that happens to a defendant. Maybe it means convicted. But no, that's not right because the defendant got exonerated because there wasn't enough evidence. I think exonerated means something like let off, because when there isn't enough evidence, a judge is likely to let the defendant off.

Following the presentation of a few examples, let students find a few of their own and explain how the context cues help reveal the meanings of difficult words. This brief session would constitute the introductory instruction.

4. **Allow for further work with context.** After this introductory lesson, provide further work with context when students need to figure out unknown words in their reading or when the material contains some revealing context cues. Here again, briefly describe a cue type, talk through the way context provided cues to one word's meaning, and let students talk through the way it provides cues to a few other words' meanings. Students should benefit from instruction designed to teach them to analyze cues within paragraphs through the following procedure outlined by Ryder (1986).

- Underline the key context cues in a paragraph. Students then define the vocabulary from the underlined cues.
- After a period of time, reverse the procedure. First, define the vocabulary term, then ask students to locate and identify cues within the paragraph that contribute to the defined word's meaning.
- If students have difficulty locating cues within the paragraph, it is often helpful to read each sentence to them, then ask if they can locate any cues in that sentence for the defined word.

These periodic mini lessons will keep students conscious of the value of context cues and gradually extend their ability to use context to uncover word meanings.

PRACTICE ACTIVITY 3.5

To gain some practice in identifying context cues, get together with a colleague, select a text representative of those you and your colleague use in your classes, then select a sentence illustrating each cue type. Again, it would be a good idea to write out these sentences and keep them as part of your notes for this chapter.

Learning and Using Word Parts

Using word parts—prefixes, suffixes, and roots—is another approach that can help students acquire the thousands of words they need to learn independently. In fact, evidence (White, Power, & White, 1989) suggests that by the time they enter junior high and are reading material that contains a large proportion of affixed words, students are likely to learn a very substantial number of words from structural analysis. In this section, we discuss selecting word parts to teach and procedures for teaching them.

Selecting Word Parts to Teach.   Until a few years ago, one of the most difficult aspects of teaching word parts was selecting those that are worth teaching. Fortunately, White, Sowell, and Yanagihara (1989) have recently identified the most common prefixes and suffixes. These are shown in Figure 3.3.

The first column contains the most frequently used prefixes and suffixes, the second column the next seven most common, and the third the next six most common. Thus, for example, un- is the most frequently used prefix, re- the next most frequently used, and over- the eighth most frequently used. Together, these 20 prefixes are used in nearly 3,000 words, the 20 suffixes in over 2,000 words. Less common prefixes and suffixes are very rare and we do not recommend teaching them. On the other hand, recognizing these 40 prefixes and suffixes is tremendously useful in building vocabulary.

Because these are very common prefixes and suffixes, secondary students already know many of them. Before presenting any instruction, therefore, find out what students already know. To get an idea of students' knowledge of prefixes, give some prefixed words, have students remove the prefixes, then have them define those prefixes. To get an idea of their knowledge of suffixes, give them some words with suffixes, have them remove the suffixes, then have them alter the spelling of the remaining root if necessary so that the spelling is correct. Because suffixes generally have grammatical meanings that are very difficult to define and because students typically have tacit knowledge of these

---

FIGURE 3.3   THE 20 MOST COMMON PREFIXES AND SUFFIXES

Prefixes

un-	over- (too much)	trans-
re-	mis-	super-
in-, im-, ir-, il- (not)	sub-	semi-
dis-	pre-	anti-
en-, em-	inter-	mid-
non-	fore-	under- (too little)
in-, im- (in or into)	de-	

Suffixes

-s, -es	-al, -ial	-en
-ed	-y	-er (comparative)
-ing	-ness	-ive, -ative, -itive
-ly	-ity, -ty	-ful
-er, -or (agentive)	-ment	-less
-ion, -tion, -ation, -ition	-ic	-est
-ible, -able	-ous, -eous, -ious	

---

grammatical meanings even before they enter school, it is both unnecessary and inappropriate to ask students to define suffixes.

Latin and Greek roots are other word parts you may consider teaching. These include such elements as *ject*, meaning to throw and used in such words as *inject* and *reject*, and *tele*, meaning far and used in such words as *telephone* and *telegraph*. Unfortunately, identifying Latin and Greek roots to teach is more difficult than identifying prefixes and suffixes because there is no short list of Latin and Greek roots that need to be learned. There are many more Latin and Greek roots than there are prefixes and suffixes, and many roots are seldom used or are used only in certain fields. Thus, choose Latin and Greek roots to teach from the materials students read in class. However, if you desire to have an idea of the roots that may come up in subject matter materials, Fry, Polk, and Fountoukidis (1993) have provided very useful lists of those that tend to be used in various content areas.

Teaching Word Parts.   In typical content classes, where there is a limited amount of time and a good deal of material to cover, the following procedure suggested by Moore, Moore, Cunningham, and Cunningham (1986) and by Irvin (1990) is quite appropriate. It requires relatively little time and uses words obtained from the subject matter content. The procedure has four steps.

1. **Write two familiar words containing the word part on the board or overhead, and have students define them.** Consider the word *subterranean* and emphasize the prefix *sub-*. Most students know what a submarine is and what subzero weather is, so these would be appropriate words to use here.

2. **Underline the word part and note its spelling. Then, if the word part is a prefix or a root, point out its meaning to students, or have them give its meaning.** *Sub-*, of course, means below.

3. **Write the word you want to teach in a sentence on the board or overhead.** With the word *subterranean*, you might use the sentence "Stories of subterranean creatures, monsters that come to the surface and terrorize entire cities, are fairly common in science fiction literature." Ask students to use their knowledge of *sub-*, the elements that remain when the prefix is removed (in this case, *terra*, a Latin root meaning earth, and *-ean*, a suffix), and the context of the sentence to arrive at a meaning of the word. *Subterranean* means beneath the earth's surface. At this point, it's a good idea to check the meaning in the dictionary and to caution students that although both word parts and context are useful in identifying word meanings, neither is completely reliable. Thus, if one wants to be absolutely certain of a word's meaning it is necessary to check the dictionary.

4. **Give an example of a word students know in which the letter group just taught does not represent the meaning taught; caution them that letter groups that look like prefixes, suffixes, or roots are sometimes just groups of letters.** The letter group *sub-* does not mean below in the word *substantial*.

PRACTICE ACTIVITY 3.6

This would also be a good point at which to stop and jot down some of the Latin and Greek roots that come up in your subject area. You will probably need to scan one of your textbooks to identify these. Also, you may want to look through a list of Latin and Greek roots such as that provided by Fry et al. (1993) to suggest some roots to look for. In any case, jot down those you identify and keep them with your notes on this chapter.

Using the Dictionary and Thesaurus

Elementary school students routinely learn some key points on using the dictionary. Instruction is usually given in alphabetizing, in using guide words, in using pronunciation keys, and, perhaps, in choosing meanings appropriate for the context of the word. However, such instruction does not adequately prepare students to effectively use the second most popular book in the English language.

Quite possibly the most important thing students need to learn is which dictionaries are appropriate for them. Students also need to know the characteristics and features of the particular dictionary they use: what the entries for individual words contain and how they are arranged, what aids to its use the dictionary provides, and what features beyond the basic word list the particular dictionary includes. Much of the important information appears in the front matter of the dictionaries themselves, but it is very seldom read, and simply asking students to read it is hardly sufficient instruction. Thus, direct instruction in how to use specific dictionaries is needed.

Students must also be instructed to scan all definitions for a given word. Too often they pick the first definition regardless of the context of the word. Since many words have more than one meaning, a definition appropriate for the context is needed. If, for example, the word *latitude* is encountered in the sentence "The judge agreed to give the prosecutor some *latitude* because the witness was being very uncooperative," then the appropriate dictionary definition is "freedom from limitations," not "position in relation to the equator." Although this appears obvious, it is something that many students seem not to realize, and taking the time to mentally model the process used in choosing a definition appropriate to the context is definitely worthwhile.

If available, students need to be made aware of computerized dictionaries, convinced of their power and ease of use, and taught how to use them. For example, the *American Heritage Electronic Dictionary* (Houghton Mifflin, 1990) contains the complete word set of a pocket dictionary and can be very easily accessed by students as they are writing on a word processor. It provides definitions, pronunciations, parts of speech, and spelling information—in seconds and without leaving the computer. Many students who would all too rarely go to a bookshelf and look up a word will routinely access a computerized dictionary.

Students also need instruction in using a thesaurus. Specific attention is worthwhile because a thesaurus is used for a somewhat different purpose than a dictionary. In general, a dictionary is useful when a word has already been identified. A thesaurus, on the other hand, is much more likely to be used when an alternate word is desired. It helps students find new ways of saying things. Getting students in the habit of using a thesaurus is a step toward helping them enlarge their active vocabularies, as well as becoming interested in words.

As with dictionaries, students need to be made aware of and taught how to use computerized thesauruses. The *American Heritage Electronic Dictionary*, for example, is also a thesaurus. Students can identify synonyms for words with a simple keystroke or click of a mouse. Most powerful word-processing programs also contain very useful thesauruses. *Microsoft Word* (Microsoft, 1991), for example, comes with an integrated thesaurus that will provide a list of synonyms and then let a student automatically replace a word in a text he or she is working on with a selected synonym. As with computerized dictionaries, students who would rarely take a thesaurus off the bookshelf will readily use a computerized thesaurus.

Adopting a Personal Approach to Building Vocabulary

As noted at the beginning of this section, regardless of how much instruction you provide, students will actually do most of their word learning independently. It therefore makes sense to encourage students to adopt personal plans to expand their vocabularies over time. Options include learning word parts, looking up novel words and keeping a file of them, making a commitment to learn a word a day and actually using those words, making a commitment to use the thesaurus when writing, using vocabulary-building books, doing crossword puzzles, and playing word games of various sorts.

Although one could certainly argue for some of these approaches being better than others, what probably matters most is that a student adopt some approach—some conscious and deliberate plan for improving his or her vocabulary.

Concluding Remarks

In all, we have listed ten areas in which you can assist students in gaining increasing control of English vocabulary—six sorts of tasks students face in learning specific words and four generative skills that students need if they are to become independent word learners. In concluding the chapter, we emphasize several points common to all of these tasks.

First, most instruction should involve active teaching that includes explicit teacher talk, modeling, giving students opportunities to actively manipulate the ideas and procedures introduced, listening to students' responses, and assisting students in reaching more accurate interpretations when their understanding seems to be wrong or slightly askew.

Second, effective vocabulary instruction requires teachers who themselves appreciate words and the English language more generally, who are knowledgeable about language, and who are precise in their diction and articulate in their speech and writing. Without such teachers, the plan outlined here would be of no value; with such teachers, students can master the English vocabulary and skillfully use their vocabulary knowledge in understanding what they read as well as in communicating in speech and writing.

Third, it needs to be recognized that instruction directed at any of the goals fosters achievement of the others as well. Thus, for example, instruction that teaches students individual words strengthens the likelihood that they will learn other words from context, and teaching students prefixes makes it easier for them to learn and remember individual words employing those prefixes.

Finally, the plan described is intended to be a long-term one implemented across a number of grade levels. The goals listed here cannot be accomplished by a single teacher or in a single year. Reaching these goals requires the efforts of teachers in various content areas and at various grade levels. However, you can contribute to your students' vocabulary growth and growth in literacy skills more generally by selecting some parts of the plan for emphasis in your classroom. In the "Reflections" section, we suggest an approach for deciding that emphasis.

REFLECTIONS

This section offers you an opportunity to review some of the major topics of the chapter, consider how they apply to your content area, and make some decisions about the vocabulary instruction you will include in your class.

1. A point made early in the chapter was that students need to learn to read a tremendous number of words. Select a chapter, article, or short story typical of the reading students do in your content area. Then go through it and pick out the words you suspect some of your students won't know.
2. Your search for challenging words is likely to have yielded more words than you have the time to teach or need to teach, that is, more than 10 or so words. If so, next apply the three criteria we have suggested for selecting words to teach and identify the most important ones.
3. Once you have selected the most important words to teach, identify the word-learning task that each word probably presents to your students.
4. Now that you have identified the most important words to teach and the word-learning task or tasks they represent, select a teaching method to use. Note that we say *method* rather than *methods*. Typically, you will probably use only one method in teaching the words for a particular selection. If the method is not appropriate for all of the words you selected to teach, you will need to decide whether to skip some of the words you originally selected, use the method with all of the words even though it is not a perfect match, or use more than one method—probably an infrequent choice.
5. Now that you have gone through the process of selecting words and a teaching method, consider again each of the methods described in the chapter and identify two or three that you are most likely to use repeatedly in your class.
6. Consider the four approaches to preparing students to learn words independently, then decide which best fit your content area, students, and teaching priorities; make a commitment to work with your students on those approaches.

REFERENCES

Anderson, R. C., & Freebody, P. (1981). Vocabulary knowledge. In J. Guthrie (Ed.), *Comprehension and teaching: Research reviews*. Newark, DE: International Reading Association.

Aulls, M. W., & Graves, M. F. (1985). *Quest: New roads to literacy*. New York: Scholastic.

Baumann, J. F., & Kameenui, E. J. (1991). Research on vocabulary instruction: Ode to Voltaire. In J. Flood, J. M. Jensen, D. Lapp, & J R. Squire (Eds.), *Handbook of research on teaching to English language arts*. New York: Macmillan.

Beck, I. L., McCaslin, E. S., & McKeown, M. G. (1980). *The rationale and design of a program to teach vocabulary to fourth-grade students* (LRDC Publication No. 1980-25). Pittsburgh: University of Pittsburgh, Learning Research and Development Center.

Beck, I. L., & McKeown, M. G. (1983). Learning words well: A program to enhance vocabulary and comprehension. *The Reading Teacher, 36,* 622–625.

_____. (1991). Conditions of vocabulary acquisition. In R. Barr, M. Kamil, P. Moselthal, & P. D. Pearson (Eds.), *Handbook of reading research* (Vol. 2). New York: Longman.

Beck, I. L., Perfetti, C. A., & McKeown, M. G. (1982). The effects of long-term vocabulary instruction on lexical access and reading comprehension. *Journal of Educational Psychology, 74,* 506–521.

Bradac, J. J., Bowers, J. W., & Courtright, J. A. (1982). Lexical variations in intensity, immediacy, and diversity: An axiomatic theory and causal model. In R. N. St. Clari & H. Giles (Eds.), *The social and psychological contexts of language.* Hillsdale, NJ: Erlbaum.

Calfee, R. C., & Drum, P. A. (1986). Research on teaching reading. In M. D. Wittrock (Ed.), *Handbook of research on teaching* (3rd ed.). New York: Macmillan.

Duin, A. H., & Graves, M. F. (1986). Effects of vocabulary instruction as a prewriting task. *Journal of Research and Development in Education, 26,* 7–13.

_____. (1988). Teaching vocabulary as a writing prompt. *Journal of Reading, 22,* 204–212.

Frayer, D. A., Frederick, W. D., & Klausmeier, H. J. (1969). *A schema for testing the level of concept mastery* (Working Paper No. 16). Madison: Wisconsin Research and Development Center for Cognitive Learning.

Freebody, P., & Anderson, R. C. (1983). Effects on text comprehension of differing proportions and locations of difficult vocabulary. *Journal of Reading Behavior, 15,* 19–40.

Fry, E. B., Polk, J. K., & Fountoukidis, D. (1993). *The reading teacher's book of words* (3rd ed.). Englewood Cliffs, NJ: Prentice-Hall.

Graves, M. F. (1986). Vocabulary learning and instruction. In E. Z. Rothkopf (Ed.), *Review of research in education* (Vol. 13). Washington, D.C.: American Educational Research Association.

_____. (in press). Vocabulary knowledge. In A. C. Purves (Ed.), *Encyclopedia of English studies and language arts.* New York: Scholastic.

Heimlich, J. E., & Pittelman, S. D. (1986). *Semantic mapping: Classroom applications.* Newark, DE: International Reading Association.

Herman, P. A., & Dole, J. (1988). Theory and practice in vocabulary learning and instruction. *The Elementary School Journal, 89,* 41–52.

Irvin, J. L. (1990). *Reading and the middle school student.* Boston: Allyn & Bacon.

Johnson, D. D., Pittelman, S. D., Toms-Bronowski, S., & Levin, K. M. (1984). An investigation of the effects of prior knowledge and vocabulary acquisition on passage comprehension (Program Report 84-5). Madison: Wisconsin Center for Educational Research, University of Wisconsin.

Klare, G. R. (1984). Readability. In P. D. Pearson (Ed.), *Handbook of reading research.* New York: Longman.

Malloy, J. (1981). These remarks were heard on a radio broadcast in the Los Angeles area January.

Miller, G. A., & Gildea, P. M. (1987). How children learn words. *Scientific American, 257* (3), 94–99.

Moore, S. A., & Moore, D. W. (1990). Possible sentences. In E. K. Dishner, T. W. Bean, & J. E. Readence (Eds.), *Reading in the contents areas: Improving classroom instruction* (3rd ed.). Dubuque, IA: Kendal Hunt.

Moore, D., Moore, S., Cunningham, P., & Cunningham, J. (1986). *Developing readers and writers in the content areas: K–12.* New York: Longman.

Nagy, W. E. (1988). *Teaching vocabulary to improve reading comprehension.* Urbana, IL: National Council of Teachers of English.

Nagy, W. E., & Anderson, R. C. (1984). How many words are there in printed school English? *Reading Research Quarterly, 19,* 304–330.

Nagy, W. E., Anderson, R. C., & Herman, P. A. (1987). Learning word meanings from context during normal reading. *American Educational Research Journal, 24,* 237–270.

Nagy, W. E., Herman, P. A., & Anderson, R. C. (1985). Learning words from context. *Reading Research Quarterly, 20,* 233–253.

Neilsen, L., & Piché, G. L. (1981). The influence of headed nominal complexity and lexical choice on teacher's evaluation of writing. *Research in the Teaching of English, 15,* 65–73.

Pittelman, S. D., Heimlich, J. E., Berglund, R. L., & French, M. P. (1991). *Semantic feature analysis: Classroom applications.* Newark, DE: International Reading Association.

Ryder, R. J. (1985). Student activated vocabulary instruction. *Journal of Reading, 29,* 254–259.

_____. (1986). Teaching vocabulary through external context clues. *Journal of Reading, 30,* 61–65.

Ryder, R. J., Graves, M. F., & Graves, B. B. (1989). *Easy reading: Book series and periodicals for less able readers.* Newark, DE: International Reading Association.

Stahl, S. A., & Fairbanks, M. M. (1986). The effects of vocabulary instruction: A model-based meta-analysis. *Review of Educational Research, 56,* 72–110.

Stahl, S. A., & Kapinus, B. (1991). Possible sentences: Predicting word meanings to teach content area vocabulary. *The Reading Teacher, 45,* 36–43.

Sternberg, R. J. (1987). Most vocabulary is learned from context. In M. G. McKeown & M. E. Curtis (Eds.), *The nature of vocabulary acquisition.* Hillsdale, NJ: Erlbaum.

Sternberg, R. J., & Powell, J. S. (1983). Comprehending verbal comprehension. *American Psychologist, 38,* 878–893.

White, T. G., Graves, M. F., & Slater, W. H. (1990). Development of recognition and reading vocabularies in diverse sociolinguistic and educational settings. *Journal of Educational Psychology, 82,* 281–290.

White, T. G., Power, M. A., & White, S. (1989). Morphological analysis: Implications for teaching and understanding vocabulary growth. *Reading Research Quarterly, 24,* 283–304.

White, T. G., Slater, W. H., & Graves, M. F. (1989). Yes/no method of vocabulary assessment: Valid for whom and useful for what. *Cognitive and social perspectives for literacy research and instruction.* Chicago: National Reading Conference.

White, T. G., Sowell, J., & Yanagihara, A. (1989). Teaching elementary students to use word-part clues. *The Reading Teacher, 42,* 302–308.

. . . .

CHAPTER FOUR

Preparing Students for Learning

CHAPTER OVERVIEW

In this chapter we present activities that prepare students for learning. The first section, "The Importance of Preparing Students to Learn," focuses on the role of background knowledge in the learning process and the goal of activities that prepare students to learn. The next section, "Planning Prereading Instruction," discusses the factors that need to be addressed as you engage in lesson planning. The third section, "Establishing a Purpose for Reading," discusses ways to have students generate objectives and the use of teacher- or student-generated summaries. In the final and major section of this chapter, "Activities to Enhance Background Knowledge," we present a number of instructional strategies that build students' background knowledge.

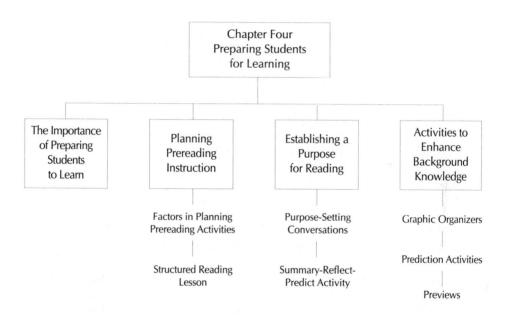

This chapter presents activities that prepare students to learn in the subject matter classroom. Consistent with the view of the reading process described in Chapter One, most of the activities stress the importance of allowing students to draw on their existing knowledge, to engage in activities that allow for co-operative learning and the construction of knowledge, and to instill an appreciation for knowledge beyond the memorization of facts. Because many of the activities presented here may be unfamiliar to you, it is important to carefully examine the examples and exercises provided throughout the chapter.

THE IMPORTANCE OF PREPARING STUDENTS TO LEARN

As noted in the beginning of this book, how much your students learn depends upon their schemata, or "packets or bundles in which the mind stores knowledge" (West, Farmer, & Wolff, 1991, p. 7). Schemata allow us to interpret new information, to construct actions or thoughts, to determine goals, and in general to direct the flow of information to the mind. Note, for example, how schemata affect your understanding of the following paragraph.

> John was on his way to school. He was terribly worried about the mathematics lesson. He thought he might not be able to control the class again today. He thought it was unfair of the instructor to make him supervise the class for a second time. After all, it was not a normal part of a janitor's duties.

> Adapted from Sanford & Garrod, 1981, p. 10.

The first two sentences in this example were easy to follow. Most of us have rather vivid associations of our schooling, so activating schemata is rather straightforward. Continuing with this paragraph, the phrase "to control the class" in the third sentence redirects attention from that of a student to a schema for teacher. Indeed, from the perspective of a teacher the first two sentences make sense. The fourth sentence, however, presents information that is incongruent with a teacher schema. As a result, a schema for janitor is activated as the final sentence is read. This example demonstrates how our attention is continually redirected by drawing on schematic information to reduce uncertainty and make text more meaningful. As you read the paragraph, available knowledge of teachers, testing, and janitors allowed you to "fix up" inconsistencies to construct an understanding of the paragraph.

Reading materials presented in the content area are easier for students to comprehend when they can draw on relevant prior knowledge. When schemata are readily available, the flow of information proceeds smoothly and students are able to comprehend the material. But what if schemata are not available for information encountered in text? How can we learn when we lack prior knowledge? Consider the following.

> The double haul can be done efficiently only with weight-forward or shooter-taper lines. Both of these lines utilize thirty feet of head or thicker line; the remainder of the line is thin-diameter running line. It's easy to see this junction in a shooting-

taper line, since the head and fly line are different types of materials, and sometimes different colors. With weight-forward lines this junction is not immediately apparent, because the head and running line are continuous, the demarcation being where the head tapers down quickly. . . . (Rosenbauer, 1984, p. 67)

Unless the techniques of fly-fishing are familiar—knowing the technique of casting and the properties of the line—this paragraph has little meaning. Encountering text containing new concepts can be a frustrating experience. Because it is hard to construct meaning from text of this sort, many students refrain from reading the material altogether, relying instead on information they obtain from class discussion or their peers.

Prereading activities are designed to enhance students' learning by drawing on students' existing knowledge and relating that knowledge to the lesson objectives, and by providing information that may be lacking in students' background knowledge. Text can become more meaningful when students are actively engaged in the gradual construction of meaning through numerous exposures to the content in a process in which known information is integrated with new information (Duffy & Roehler, 1989). As shown in Figure 4.1, prereading activities can be used to (1) facilitate learning, (2) activate and enrich prior knowledge, and (3) present lesson content. Goals and objectives are established through predicting, formulating questions, and defining overall learning goals. Numerous activities can be used to tap students' prior knowledge, relate that knowledge to new information, and establish goals to direct students' attention as they read. Gaps that exist in students' knowledge can be

---

FIGURE 4.1   GOALS OF PREREADING INSTRUCTION

Facilitating Learning

- Define goals and objectives
- Direct attention
- Arouse curiosity

Activating and Extending Prior Knowledge

- Draw on students' existing knowledge
- Fill in gaps in students' knowledge
- Clarify misconceptions

Presentation of Lesson Content

- Identify and present essential concepts and information
- Preview vocabulary
- Engage critical thinking

---

filled in with activities that present new information by relating it to their existing knowledge. Lesson content should become more meaningful when new concepts are discussed or demonstrated, important information is summarized, and hands-on activities are presented prior to reading, or when nonprint information such as videos, films, or computer software is used to build background knowledge. This departure from more traditional approaches to classroom instruction is predicated on the following observations:

1. **Learning may require sources of information other than textbooks.** Textbooks are the primary tool for classroom learning (Applebee, Langer, & Mullis, 1987; Smith & Feathers, 1983); they provide the content for 98% of classroom instruction (Jackson, 1981), and they determine how this content is taught (Elliott & Woodward, 1990). The efficiency of textbook learning is limited by textbooks themselves and by factors related to the learner's ability to construct meaning from these texts. Despite their widespread use, textbooks have been labeled as "narrow and limiting" (Applebee, 1984, p. 579) and "choppy, stilted, and monotonous" (Tyson-Bernstein, 1988, p. 9). Problems arise when texts present disorganized themes and poorly arranged headings, paragraphs, and sections. Even if a text is well written, students may falter due to a lack of knowledge of the text structure (Taylor & Samuels, 1983), or due to their inability to activate prior knowledge (Roller, 1990). Prereading activities can fill in gaps in students' prior knowledge, facilitate their understanding of text structure, and provide assistance in dealing with poorly organized texts.

2. **Students need to know what is important.**   Recognizing the importance of text requires readers to draw on what they know, their knowledge of author biases, intentions, and goals, and their knowledge of how information contained in the text is used to construct a meaningful message (Dole, Duffy, Roehler, & Pearson, 1991). When students fail to cue on signals provided by the text structure, key concepts are not recognized and prior knowledge is not activated. Prereading activities direct attention to important information, draw on and build students' prior knowledge, and define goals or objectives for reading. Through their use students gain a good idea of what is important before they read.

3. **Motivation and attention can be enhanced by prereading activities.** The amount of effort students direct to learning is, to some degree, determined by the level of interest in the task, available prior knowledge, and ability to learn. Prereading activities can motivate students by piquing their curiosity, reducing anxiety, and providing activities that allow them to engage actively in learning.

4. **Prereading activities can assist in establishing goals.**   Establishing goals can enhance the acquisition of skills, information, concepts, or strategies. Goals also increase motivation to learn, and when a goal is defined, students are more likely to believe they can accomplish the learning task (Bandura, 1982; Schunk, 1983). Student-defined goals increase students' resolve to learn, particularly when those goals are short-term and are perceived by students as

being attainable (Schunk, 1991). Prereading activities can help the teacher define goals to students; in addition, they can provide students the opportunity to generate their own goals.

5. **Prereading activities allow the teacher to tailor instruction to the needs of the students.**   Traditionally, students' knowledge is assessed immediately following the completion of a unit of study to determine the extent of their learning or mastery of instructional objectives. While this provides useful information on what students know, it is not always clear whether this reflects prior knowledge or what was learned from instruction. Becoming familiar with students' knowledge prior to reading can aid the teacher in constructing objectives tailored to students' background knowledge and in discarding or modifying objectives to be within their level of understanding.

By now it should be evident that prereading activities are an important part of instruction in the subject matter classroom. Both teacher and student can benefit from their use. Students gain knowledge, establish goals for learning, apply the appropriate prior knowledge to a unit of study, and learn activities that can be applied to independent reading. Teachers gain a better understanding of students' knowledge of the content and become more involved in facilitating students' learning. However, these benefits should not be viewed as an end in themselves. Subject matter lessons involve activities before, during, and after reading that are connected by common instructional goals. Activities, therefore, must address common goals throughout the various stages of instruction.

PLANNING PREREADING INSTRUCTION

Selection and application of prereading activities are an important part of instructional planning. Careful lesson planning will increase the likelihood that an activity is successful, that students have a positive learning experience, and that lesson objectives are accomplished. Attention should be directed to each of the following: (1) the nature of the content presented, (2) the students' prior knowledge, (3) the learning objectives, and (4) the available time and resources. Note from Figure 4.2 that these are not isolated factors. Attention to one factor will affect others. For example, the number of lesson objectives depends on the time available for instruction and the extent to which the structure of the text and students' prior knowledge facilitate those objectives. Following is a brief description of these factors and how they may be used in planning for prereading activities.

Factors in Planning Prereading Activities

Nature of Content Presented.   There are two considerations here; one deals with the structure and content of the text, the other with the match between the content of the text and your instructional goals. First, regarding text

FIGURE 4.2   PLANNING PREREADING ACTIVITIES

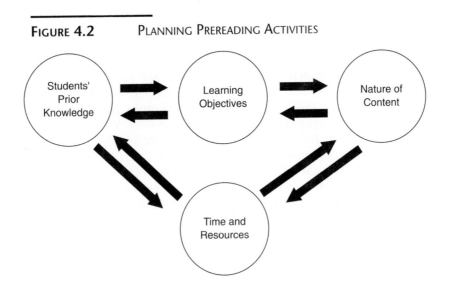

structure and content, refer to the procedures for examining text difficulty presented in Chapter Two. Consider the number of new words, the sentence length and structure, the coherence of information and concepts, and the length or depth of the presentation of information. Second, examine the content of the selection to determine if it will facilitate defined instructional goals. If, for example, an art teacher defines an instructional goal that includes teaching students' to understand and apply techniques for shaping a clay sculpture, but the selection examined primarily contains information on the properties of clay, then a mismatch exists between instructional goals and text content. When a mismatch exists, consider an alternate selection or directly teach the information absent from the selection.

Students' Prior Knowledge.   As noted throughout this book, students' prior knowledge plays an integral role in learning. There are times when students' lack of prior knowledge will interfere with their ability to understand a selection. In this case, you may want to select prereading activities that teach this requisite information. At other times, students may possess adequate prior knowledge, but it may be necessary to structure this knowledge to facilitate objectives requiring high-level cognitive skills. Knowing the nature of students' prior knowledge will help determine which prereading activities are most suitable for lesson objectives.

There are several practical techniques to assess students' background knowledge. One is to ask students if they know the concepts, facts, or vocabulary essential to understanding a given selection. Constructing this form of prior knowledge assessment is a straightforward task. First, list the concepts, facts, or vocabulary you believe students should know. Next, present this list to students with the directions to examine each item, then respond if they

FIGURE 4.3   EXAMPLE OF PRIOR KNOWLEDGE ASSESSMENT: SOCIAL STUDIES LESSON ON FORMS OF GOVERNMENT

Directions: *Examine each of the following items, then respond whether you know* or don't know *the meaning of that information.*

	Know	Don't Know
Presidential government	_____	_____
Party systems	_____	_____
Parliamentary government	_____	_____
Separation of powers	_____	_____
Plurality	_____	_____
Coalition	_____	_____

know or don't know its meaning. An example of this form of assessment is depicted in Figure 4.3.

A second technique is to conduct an informal assessment through classroom discussion. One such approach, the Prereading Plan (PreP; Langer, 1982), presents a procedure for assessing students' understanding of text concepts and steps to enhance prior knowledge. This approach begins with the teacher identifying three to five concepts in the text. Next, each concept is presented in the form of a word, phrase, or picture to determine students' initial association with the concept:

- **In English:** What do you think of when you see the word *conflict?*
- **In Physical Education:** What do you think of when you hear the word *hyperventilation?*
- **In Vocal Music:** What comes to mind when you think about harmony?

Following the association activity, the teacher asks students to reflect on their associations.

- **In English:** Why do you say that conflict is what happens when people get angry with one another, Marie?

  Marie: Well, it seems that you can tell if something was a conflict after it happens. Usually, if people are very angry, then it's a conflict.

- **In Vocal Music:** Toni and Tyronne, you indicated that harmony is when people sing in a way that is pleasant, is on key, is at the right pitch. Why is that important in vocal music? How do you feel when something is not in harmony?

  Toni: It isn't that easy to be in harmony. Sometimes you really have to listen to the other person and then change your pitch based on their voice. Practice is really important if you want to be in harmony.

Tyronne: Bad harmony is bad music. Not that many people sing in harmony anymore. I'm not sure why. If you don't sing in harmony, people won't care to listen to you.

In the final step of PreP, the teacher prepares students for the reading by
developing their background knowledge.

- **In Vocal Music:** Today we are going to learn about what is called functional harmony. In this type of harmony all chords are related to one of
  the three basic chords of a key. This type of harmony was abandoned by
  many composers in the early 1900s in favor of different forms of harmony that we will examine later on. Once I have provided you some examples of functional harmony, we will listen to some music written in
  the 1800s that makes use of functional harmony, then we will produce
  and sing our own lyrics that make use of functional harmony.

PreP can be a practical and efficient way to assess students' prior knowledge. Care must be exercised, however, in drawing generalizations solely from
classroom dialogue. Frequently, students have a grasp of concepts but experience difficulty expressing themselves in language that is readily understood
by adults. This potential problem can be addressed by probing students' understanding with questions requiring them to provide examples, or elaborate
and justify a response.

Learning Objectives.   Learning objectives define the outcomes or products of instruction. Constructing objectives is central to successful prereading
activities. Effective teachers have a firm grasp of what they want students to
learn and communicate these objectives to students before instruction is initiated (Rosenshine & Stevens, 1986). However, for many teachers, planning
tends to be limited to identifying activities that will be presented to students.
These teachers have failed to first define learning outcomes, then develop activities that will facilitate those outcomes (Clark & Yinger, 1980). Beginning
teachers are likely to remove themselves from planning altogether, relying instead on published curriculum materials as their planning guide (Clark & Peterson, 1986). Instructional planning should begin with a clear definition of
lesson objectives. Whether these objectives are selected from an external
source (e.g., a textbook or curriculum guide) or constructed by the teacher,
they should be tailored to meet the needs of students and be presented in a
form that is informative and purposeful.

One form of communicating objectives is the central question (Anderson
& Roth, 1989). Displayed in Figure 4.4 are examples of central questions
from a variety of subject matter areas. Objectives presented in the form of
central questions clearly communicate what students will learn, arouse
prior knowledge, and stimulate discussion. They also establish a purpose
for reading—directing students' attention to selected content as they read.
Regardless of the form used to describe lesson objectives, recognize that it
may be necessary to modify or abandon those objectives during the course

FIGURE 4.4   EXAMPLES OF CENTRAL QUESTION OBJECTIVES

High School Biology

How are the circulatory systems of species that have a rapid rate of movement (such as a jaguar or hummingbird) different from species that have a low rate of movement (such as an armadillo or opossum)?

Middle School Home Economics

What are the long-term health benefits of following a balanced diet?

High School English

Why do writers of fiction often reflect the political and social events of their time in their writing?

Middle School Art

Why is clay a good medium for learning how to sculpt?

High School Physical Education

Which sports are good for lifelong activities? What are the advantages of playing these sports?

---

of a lesson as students' progress is assessed and additional needs become apparent.

Available Time and Resources.   A common concern of teachers is the lack of instructional time to cover the prescribed content over the course of the year. There is little doubt that subject matter curricula have the tendency to expand over time; each year it seems there is more content to teach. Textbooks are more lengthy, and greater amounts of time are placed on curricular issues that are integrated within all subject matter areas. With less time available for instruction, some sort of priorities must be assigned to instructional objectives. There are numerous ways to reduce instructional time. An alternate source of information, including supplemental resources such as films, videotapes, trade books, periodicals, and demonstrations, may be used instead of a single textbook. In other instances the amount of reading students engage in can be reduced by directing them to read selectively. Or it may be advisable to assign specific topics to groups of students who then summarize and present their information to the entire class. Finally, as noted, generating lesson objectives tailored to students will reduce instructional time. Rather than reading an entire chapter, for example, students may read only those sections or pages related to your objectives.

Structured Reading Lesson

The structured reading lesson (SRL) is an organizational tool for planning instructional activities that occur (1) prior to reading, (2) during reading, and (3) after reading. While this chapter is limited to activities to prepare students to learn, it is important to note that instructional planning should consider all facets of a lesson. Activities that prepare students for learning should facilitate activities students engage in during and following a reading. For example, questions (whether directed by the teacher or generated by the student) addressed during recitations and discussions during and following a reading (see Chapter Five) become more relevant and purposeful when students engage in activities prior to reading that either build background knowledge or draw on and relate students' existing knowledge. The SRL provides a mechanism to plan the scope and sequence of instructional activities to accomplish the stated lesson objectives. The components of the SRL are the following:

Before Reading	During Reading	After Reading
Establish a purpose	Focus attention	Allow for reflection
Draw or build on students' knowledge	Stimulate discussion	Engage in higher levels of thinking
Present vocabulary	Relate prior knowledge to text information	Facilitate written and oral summaries
Build motivation		

Note that the before, during, and after reading stages of the SRL are mediated by the lesson objectives and by the ongoing assessment of students' learning. The lesson is structured to facilitate lesson objectives, then modified (when necessary) according to how well students perform during the three stages of instruction. This model acknowledges several of the guiding principles of content area reading addressed in Chapter One. First, the model recognizes that students acquire meaning through the application of strategies, skills, and prior knowledge to the text material. The SRL allows planning based on the students' need to acquire knowledge—instructional activities are tailored to meet the needs of the students, allowing them to interact with the content of the reading. Second, the SRL provides for the exchange and interpretation of information and knowledge between students who possess different intellectual and cultural backgrounds through active learning. The sharing of background knowledge and construction of objectives prior to reading and the active involvement in discussions during and after reading promote the exchange of ideas and recognition of the contributions of all students in the class. Third, the SRL allows the teacher to plan activities that are adaptable to the time constraints of the classroom. The prereading activities presented in this chapter, the comprehension activities during and after reading presented in Chapter Five, and the critical thinking activities to promote higher levels of understanding during and after reading presented in Chapter Six are viable instructional alternatives to directing the reading lesson. The nature of instruction during each of the three stages of the SRL include the following:

Before Reading

- Prior to reading activities are structured to establish a purpose for learning, to instill curiosity and motivation, to draw on or build background knowledge, and to present vocabulary that may be unfamiliar to students.
- A purpose for reading is established through a process shared by the teacher and students. Two of these types of activities—purpose-setting conversations and summary-reflect-predict activities—are presented in the next section in this chapter. Curiosity and motivation are essential elements in maintaining students' attention and maintaining a positive classroom environment. Students are more likely to become curious and motivated when they become active participants in the learning process, when they are provided reasonable purposes to learn, and when the instruction is seen as relevant. Most of the activities presented in this chapter can increase students' motivation and stimulate their curiosity.
- The success of these activities, however, is dependent upon the teacher's ability to be aware of the students' needs and interests and to display a sense of enthusiasm for the content and the shared learning process.
- Building and drawing on students' background is a primary goal of pre-reading instruction and its importance has been noted throughout this book. Many of the activities discussed throughout this chapter were designed for this purpose. In preparation of these activities, it is important to consider the concepts and ideas required to meet stated objectives, whether this information is adequately addressed in the reading, and then to consider ways to draw on students' background knowledge that may contribute to an understanding of this information.
- Finally, before reading activities can be designed to teach students vocabulary essential to acquiring an understanding of the reading selection. Procedures for selecting words to teach and strategies for vocabulary instruction are discussed in detail in Chapter Three.

During Reading

- During reading activities are structured to focus students' attention on lesson objectives, to stimulate discussion centered on lesson objectives, and to relate prior knowledge to information in the text. Typically, students' attention is directed to lesson objectives through questioning. This can take the form of questioning by the teacher to the students, questioning by the students to the teacher, or by students questioning themselves.
- Questions focus on information, point out relationships between this information, and draw on background knowledge and text information to engage students in critical thinking. Preparation for questioning activities requires an understanding of the goals and limitation of questions, and the types of questions that can be presented to students.
- Questions can also draw students' attention to various types of text structures as they read. A thorough discussion of ways to construct, present, and engage students in questioning activities is presented in Chapter Five.

After Reading

- After reading information and ideas obtained during reading are used to reflect upon the meaning of the text, to engage students in higher levels of thinking that go beyond surface-level information, and finally to facilitate written and oral summaries of what was learned.
- Many of these activities involve questioning through recitation and discussion. These questions often tend to cover more content than during reading questions, to require the learner to understand relationships between ideas, to apply text information to other contexts, or to engage students in critical thinking activities where they are allowed to construct their own meaning from a reading selection.
- After reading questions can be used to assess students' understanding. When gaps in students' understanding are apparent, it may be necessary to restructure questions to redirect students' attention to information that was not understood, or to provide students supplemental sources of information in the form of readings, visuals, demonstrations, or teacher-led discussions.
- Activities to extend understanding through teacher-directed questions or self-questioning are presented in Chapter Five. Guidelines and activities to engage students in critical thinking are presented in Chapter Six.

Here is an example of an SRL for a social studies unit dealing with minority groups.

Lesson Objectives

1. Students will understand the definitional characteristics of racial minorities.
2. Students will understand the definitional characteristics of ethnic minorities.
3. Students will understand how racial and ethnic minorities have difficulty assimilating into the dominant groups in a culture.

Before Reading Activities

1. The teacher determines that an anticipation guide (discussed in detail in this chapter) will serve to motivate students, draw on their background knowledge, and provide an informal assessment of students' knowledge of the lesson objectives. Students are asked to examine the following statements, then indicate whether they agree or disagree with each of them.

Anticipation Guide

Agree	*Disagree*	
_____	_____	All students in this class have the same body structure.
_____	_____	All students in this class speak only one language.

Agree   *Disagree*

———   ———   All students in this class belong to the same religion, and practice the same customs during holidays or other special occasions.

———   ———   It is not uncommon to refrain from social contact with people who have different customs.

———   ———   It is not uncommon for those in the majority to ostracize those who might hold views different from their own.

Once students have completed the anticipation guide, the teacher reads each statement, tallies students' responses, then enters into a discussion to have students justify their responses for each item.

2. The teacher now presents a concept map that previews the major concepts in the lesson. (See Figure 4.5 for an example.) As the concept map is presented, the teacher continually seeks to clarify information presented in the map and to add information to the map that is obtained from the students during the discussion.

During Reading Activities

Prequestions

1. The teacher asks students to read the text selection on ethnic and racial minorities in order to answer the following questions:

   • What are some of the characteristics of racial and ethnic minorities?
   • What are the differences between racial and ethnic minorities?

FIGURE 4.5   SAMPLE CONCEPT MAP

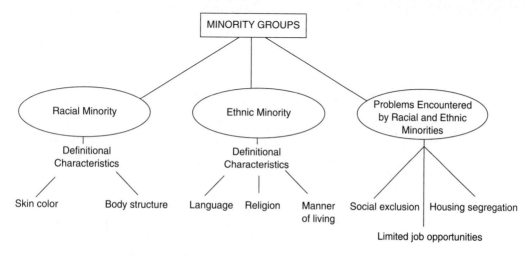

- What is the dominant group? How is the dominant group different from a minority group?

As students read the text selection, each of the above questions is answered. Once they have completed the reading, the whole class discusses each question.

Prior Knowledge

2. Students are asked to work in cooperative groups to answer the following questions:

- What are some of the racial and ethnic minorities in the area we live in?
- Examine some of the neighborhoods in the area we live in to determine where ethnic and racial minorities live or go to school. Have these groups been assimilated?
- Consider what you believe to be the dominant group in your community. Where do these people live? What types of jobs do they hold? With whom do they tend to socialize?

After Reading
Critical Thinking

1. Students are asked to use the information they acquired from the reading and class discussion to respond to the following assignment:

- Obtain articles on civil rights legislation during the past twenty years. Use this information to predict what sorts of legislation will be passed over the next five years that would lessen the economic and social consequences experienced by racial and ethnic minorities.

Reflective Writing

2. The teacher asks students to reflect upon the information they have learned about ethnic and racial minorities, then write a written summary of that information by addressing each of the following topics:

- What are the characteristics of racial and ethnic minorities?
- What are the effects of being a member of these minorities?
- What is the dominant group and how does this group influence the lives of those who belong to a racial or ethnic minority?

The SRL is a tool for planning experiences that prepare students for learning, engage them in the content of the lesson, and allow them to reflect upon or extend their understanding. By structuring each aspect of the lesson in a manner that integrates students' knowledge, information contained in the text, and the teacher's instruction, students should acquire a better understanding of the content and the process to learn new information and construct meaning.

This section has presented some of the factors involved in planning prereading instruction. No doubt, dealing with these factors presents a rather formidable challenge. For teachers who may be unfamiliar with the content of a particular class or grade level, the students' background knowledge, or expectations of what the students should learn, planning will require some additional effort. However, attention to these factors eventually should allow the teacher to become more familiar with instructional materials and students' readiness to learn.

ESTABLISHING A PURPOSE FOR READING

In our daily lives most of us routinely construct a purpose for the cognitive tasks we engage in. Knowing what we want to learn focuses attention on specific information we draw from prior knowledge, and it helps define the sorts of additional information we may need to complete our task. For students, learning is not always so purposeful. Many assume that all information in a textbook or reading selection is of equal importance and therefore attempt to commit everything to memory. Discussing with students *what* they will learn, and *why* they will learn it, will help them acquire an understanding that reading should be selective and purposeful. Defining objectives need not be directed exclusively by the teacher. Eventually, students can actively engage in activities that define a purpose for reading. This section contains two procedures for generating objectives in collaboration with your students. Both define objectives through some form of prereading activity that engages students in the lesson content.

Purpose-Setting Conversations

A purpose-setting conversation is designed to facilitate students' ability to generate purpose-setting questions from global objectives established by the teacher. This process consists of the following steps:

1. Present the central objective.
2. Skim material to answer the central objective.
3. Clarify the purpose through class conversation.
4. Generate purpose-setting questions or tasks.

Purpose-setting conversations begin with the teacher defining lesson objectives in the form of questions. In the next step, students are asked to skim the selection to generate responses to the questions. As part of an interdisciplinary lesson dealing with basic economic concepts, for example, the authors of this text observed a middle school mathematics teacher introduce the lesson with this central question objective: "How can statistical measures be used in running a retail business?" Working in cooperative groups, students then skimmed a chapter containing a description of the concepts of means and weighted averages, then generated a response to the central question. In the third step, the teacher engaged the class in a conversation to clarify and refine objectives:

Teacher: What are some of the ways that owners of retail stores would make use of statistics in their daily operations?

Julius: We thought that means could be used to figure out which days are busy or slow. That is, you can look at the mean daily sales over a month, then look at which days are above or below that mean.

Teacher: That's an interesting idea. That procedure certainly would be a good use of the mean and would help the owner identify high-volume days. What are some other ways we can use statistics?

Anita: We thought that weighted averages could be used to determine people's wages.

Teacher: Can you tell me how you would use weighted averages to determine wages?

Anita: Well, we thought that you could take the wages of people who worked, say, five years, four years, three years, two years, and one year to figure out how people who worked longer were making more money.

Teacher: That's an interesting approach. It does require the use of statistics in running a retail business. What did your group come up with, Kim?

Kim: We thought we could use the mean to find out how much money we made.

Teacher: How would you do that? Tell me how you could use the mean to calculate profits.

Kim: Well, we would add up all the money we took in, then subtract how much we paid for the products, and that would give us the profit.

Teacher: That would give you a rough idea of profits. Are there other things that you must consider when determining profits?

Kim: No, I don't think so.

Teacher: How did you use the mean to figure out the profit? Just to refresh your memory, the mean is a mathematical average. Why don't you and your group take a few moments to talk about how you might be able to use the mean in calculating profits.

Note that this step of purpose-setting conversations allows an informal assessment of students' understanding of text concepts and their background knowledge. Kim's group, for example, displayed an apparent lack of understanding of the concept of a mean (the group was not able to clarify its meaning after a second effort) and limited background knowledge of the various costs of operating a business. At this point, the teacher may clarify misconceptions, fill in gaps in students' background knowledge, or consider modifying the initial objectives in light of student feedback.

In the final step, the teacher and students engage in a dialogue to construct purposeful questions or activities that will direct their reading. These questions should acknowledge the stated central question objective, although they may not be limited to the information in the reading. For example, students may need to use supplemental readings or other resources of information to answer their questions. The product of this step for the mathematics class discussed above was an activity centered on the creation and maintenance of a popcorn stand designed to allow students to work directly with the various elements of running a retail business, then apply the concepts of means and weighted averages. As they engaged in this activity, students were asked to re-

---

FIGURE 4.6   EXAMPLE OF A PURPOSE-SETTING CONVERSATION

We are about to operate a popcorn stand after school for the following two weeks. Now that we have ordered all of our supplies and have advertised our business, we will need to collect information that will determine how efficiently we are running our business and whether we are making a profit. As we engage in the operation of the popcorn stand over the next two weeks, you will complete the following two activities that involve the use of the mean and weighted average.

Activity 1

Each day, determine the number of bags of popcorn that have been sold. From this data, determine the mean for the two Mondays, Tuesdays, Wednesdays, Thursdays, and Fridays. Make a graph to represent the mean number of bags of popcorn that are sold on these days.

Activity 2

Each day, record, then total the number of customers and the sales. At the end of two weeks, compute the weighted averages for number of customers and sales.

---

spond to the purpose-setting questions that were generated through the teacher-student dialogue. An example is given in Figure 4.6.

Purpose-setting conversations have the advantage of allowing students to understand the gist of the lesson content before reading by directing their attention to global objectives presented by the teacher. The teacher, therefore, maintains some control of the lesson content, but students tailor that content by shaping questions that reflect their interest and background knowledge. The conversational dialogue provides an informal assessment of students' background knowledge and their understanding of the text they examined. Information obtained from the conversational dialogue can then be used to structure additional prereading activities.

Summary-Reflect-Predict Activity

A second procedure to establish a purpose for learning is the summary-reflect-predict (SRP) activity. The first step of this three-stage process begins with the teacher presenting a brief summary of the reading assignment. This synopsis contains the main ideas or themes of the reading and, where possible, should attempt to relate that information to students' background knowledge.

In the second step students reflect on the summary, then respond to the following questions:

• What do I know about the concepts presented here?
• Why is this information important?

- What don't I understand?
- What more do I need to know?

Finally, students are asked to generate questions they believe could be answered from reading the material that has been summarized. The students and teacher then discuss these questions with the goal of selecting those that might best serve the interests and needs of the students. An example of an SRP activity on an English lesson introducing science fiction is presented in Figure 4.7.

As with the purpose-setting conversation, the SRP activity provides an informal assessment of students' background knowledge and allows for an interchange of ideas and hypotheses testing with the teacher. The structured questions set a purpose for reading and the summaries provide essential background information, a structure for examining the content as it relates to students' interests and experiences. One drawback of this activity is students' tendency to generate purpose-setting questions removed from defined lesson objectives. Students will generate numerous creative and thought-provoking questions. And while it is tempting to recognize their efforts, the lack of instructional time will not permit questions that direct students away from essential concepts.

The purpose-setting activities presented in this section recognize the importance of actively involving students in establishing learning objectives.

FIGURE 4.7   EXAMPLE OF AN **SRP** ACTIVITY

Step 1. The teacher presents the following summary.

Science fiction is a type of imaginative literature. Themes of this genre address topics such as space exploration, travel in the third dimension, and futuristic or amazing inventions. In science fiction, most themes are not fantasy. Generally, the themes can be supported from accepted theory or scientific practice. The beginnings of science fiction can be traced as far back as prehistoric myths, although modern science fiction began in the 1600s. Science fiction has been popularized in the last twenty years through such films as *Star Wars* and *E.T.* and through a wealth of paperbacks that fill the bookstores.

Step 2. Students are asked to answer the following questions.

1. What experience do you have reading or viewing science fiction?
2. Why do you think science fiction might be an important type of literature?
3. From what you know from the summary, what don't you understand about science fiction?
4. What additional things do you think it would be important to know about science fiction?

Step 3. Students are asked to respond to the following question.

From what we have learned about science fiction, what questions should we be able to answer when we finish reading this selection that addresses the nature and development of science fiction?

Stephen: I'd like to know why people write it or read it.
Janet: Perhaps we could find out why it is so bizarre.
Sara: I'm not certain that it is written as well as other types of literature. Are science-fiction writers as talented as those who write novels?

These activities provide an insight into students' understanding of the lesson content and their ability to formulate questions or activities that will direct their learning. Finally, the information students obtain from summaries, question generating, and conversations will enrich their background knowledge and increase their understanding of the lesson content.

ACTIVITIES TO ENHANCE BACKGROUND KNOWLEDGE

This section presents a variety of strategies designed to increase students' background knowledge. These activities have been divided into three groups: graphic organizers, prediction activities, and previews. All are forms of advance organizers, a general approach for the improvement of students' understanding of subject matter material. Advance organizers were originally conceived as a means to link new information to that already known by the learner by providing a basis on which more detailed information can be added (Ausubel, 1968). More recently, it has been suggested that advance organizers can be used to activate relevant schemata for the material to be learned, and modify schemata on the basis of the new information presented (Mayer, 1984). It should be emphasized that the advance organizers that follow are those that will teach students content and will likely be created by students as they engage in independent learning.

Graphic Organizers

Graphic organizers are pictorial representations of hierarchical relationships between facts and concepts (Barron, 1969). Generally, they are presented prior to exposure to new information. Three types of graphic organizers will be presented here: (1) frames, (2) concept maps, and (3) list, group, label.

Frames. A frame is a grid, matrix, or framework that represents knowledge (West et al., 1991). Its purpose is to display the organization of information in the form of a two-dimensional matrix where concepts are depicted in both rows and columns. An example of a two-dimensional frame is shown in Figure 4.8. Frames show relationships between concepts, identified in the columns and rows, and information, which is represented in the boxes or slots. In the

---

FIGURE 4.8   TWO-DIMENSIONAL FRAME FOR TREES

	Leaf Shape	Size	Growth Rate
Aspen			
Maple			

FIGURE 4.9   MATRIX FRAME OF THE CIRCULATORY SYSTEM

	Veins	Arteries	Capillaries
Function			
Location			
Size			

FIGURE 4.10   GOAL FRAME FOR DEVELOPMENT OF MICROCOMPUTER

	Goal	Plan	Result	Final Outcome
Apple Computer				
IBM				
Compaq				

FIGURE 4.11   PROBLEM-SOLUTION FRAME OF MILITARY CRISES

	Problem	Action	Results
Cuban Missile Crisis (1962)			
Iraqi Invasion of Kuwait (1990)			

frame for trees, for example, the columns list means of identification (leaf shape, size, and growth rate) and the rows list two types of trees (aspen and maple). In the column for size, one would insert "up to 90 feet" in the box for aspen and "15 to 20 feet" in the box for maple.

Frames can be constructed using the following steps adapted from West and colleagues (1991):

Step 1. Identify the major ideas, concepts and principles in the selection. Note and list topics, transition statements, introductions, and summaries.

Step 2. Once the text material has been identified, determine if it lends itself to the *matrix frame* (Figure 4.9), the *goal frame* (Figure 4.10), or the *problem-solution frame* (Figure 4.11). Matrix frames are particularly suited for information that displays comparisons/contrasts, simple cause-and-effect relationships, forms/functions, or advantages/disadvantages. Goal frames are useful for organizational structures of material that display linear relationships in the form of goal-plans-actions-outcomes (Armbruster & Anderson, 1984). These frames are useful for narrative and expository text that contain information presented in a temporal or sequential order. Finally, problem-solution frames are effective when a problem or issue is identified, action is taken to address that issue, and a resolution or consequence of that action is given.

Step 3. The final step is to draw the frame by creating and labeling the rows and columns. Most often characteristics or relationships are identified in the columns, and topics, major ideas, or concepts will be identified in the rows.

How the frame is used depends upon your purpose and the level of background knowledge of your students. Initially, the frame should contain labels for the columns and rows. Students actively involve themselves in examining and manipulating information to be placed in the boxes or slots. If students are not familiar with the concepts, information, or vocabulary that is placed in the slots, then you may consider providing a brief explanation of that information, listing items in random order, then asking students to place them in appropriate slots. An example of this application of the frame is provided in Figure 4.12.

FIGURE 4.12   EXAMPLE OF THE USE OF A FRAME FOR STUDENTS WITH LIMITED BACKGROUND KNOWLEDGE

Consider the information under each of the following categories. This information can be used to complete the frame dealing with types of storms. Note that the information appearing in these categories has been arranged in a random manner. Decide which information under the three categories (development, produces, season) would best describe the three types of storms, and write that information in the appropriate slot.

Development	Produces	Season
clash of two different air masses	high winds/blowing snow	summer/fall
rotation of air around a deep low pressure	high winds/some rain	winter
intense low pressure with overrunning cold air producing high winds and cold temperatures	high winds/heavy rain	summer

	Development	Produces	Season
Thunderstorms			
Blizzards			
Hurricanes			

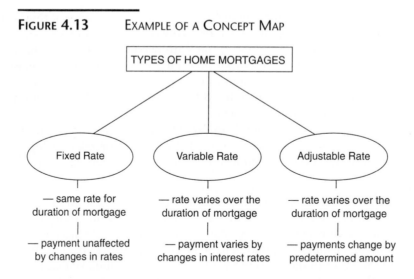

FIGURE 4.13   EXAMPLE OF A CONCEPT MAP

Another application of the frame is to structure information presented in previews or demonstrations. Here, students are provided an empty frame with labeled columns and rows. As information is presented in the form of an oral summary, demonstration, or discussion, students examine the labels, then note the information in the appropriate slot.

Finally, the frame is an effective means for improving students' writing (Armbruster, Anderson, & Ostertag, 1987). As a writing strategy, the frame provides an excellent tool to organize and structure information. Written summaries generated from the content of the frame allow students to reflect upon the content of the frame, to elaborate on its application, and to note relationships or draw distinctions between concepts and information. Here is a paragraph summary composed by a ninth grader using the frame presented in Figure 4.12.

> Thunderstorms, blizzards, and hurricanes are all forms of severe weather. Thunderstorms, which develop from the rapid development of clouds during the hot, humid weather of summer, produce high winds, widespread lightning, and heavy rain. Blizzards are winter storms that develop from large low-pressure systems and the clash between very cold air and air that carries moisture. Blizzards produce strong winds, cold temperatures, and snow. Hurricanes, in the U.S., are large storms that develop out of the equator during the fall. These storms produce high winds and waves, and heavy rain.

Concept Maps.   A concept map is a graphic display of concepts and the relationship or links between them (West et al., 1991). Generally, information presented in a concept map proceeds in a hierarchical manner from the more general (superordinate) to the more specific (subordinate). Common types of concept maps include the structured overview (Barron, 1969), semantic webs

(Heimlich & Pittelman, 1986), and information mapping (McAleese, 1986). An example of a concept map is given in Figure 4.13.

There are several notable features to the concept map presented in this example. First, conceptual linkages are clearly established through the use of lines. Second, a variety of graphic forms are used to set off information at coordinate, superordinate, or subordinate levels. Finally, the overall organization of the map reveals a structured (in this case, proceeding in a hierarchical manner) pictorial presentation that can be accommodated readily both visually and conceptually. Here are the steps in the construction and presentation of the concept map.

Step 1:

Identify the most important concepts in the material. Constructing a concept map begins with a thorough reading of the material to be presented to the students. As you read, note concepts (a class label for objects, events that share certain characteristics) and words or phrases that show information that can be linked to the selected concepts. A concept map is not an outline; *only concepts and information that are important to your lesson objectives should be noted.* Identifying concepts can be a difficult task when using poorly written text that embeds concepts and related information, and contains excessive amounts of irrelevant information. It may be useful, therefore, to draw on your own background knowledge to identify and include concepts that may not be clearly identified in the reading selection. If the content is not familiar, consider examining several selections that address the selected topic.

Step 2:

Organize concepts and identify linkages. Begin by creating a title that is descriptive of the map's content. A well-written title can stimulate curiosity, focus attention, and generate associations or predictions from prior knowledge. Presume you are sitting in an auditorium about to hear a presentation from an entomologist. Take a moment to reflect on the title "Insects." What do you associate with this term? Does the title pique your curiosity? Does it inform you of the content you might learn? Now consider the title "Insects That Are Dangerous to Your Health and How to Avoid Them." Most likely your associations are narrowed, your curiosity somewhat heightened; you now have a good sense of the content of the entomologist's presentation.

Once an appropriate title is constructed, the lesson's concepts can be organized according to whether they are superordinate, subordinate, or coordinate. Initially, write down each concept on a slip of paper, place the papers on a large flat surface, then, proceeding from the title, arrange them to display a hierarchical order. Finally, information that is linked to the concepts should be identified and placed under the conceptual label.

FIGURE 4.14 EXAMPLES OF ORGANIZATION OF CONCEPT MAPS

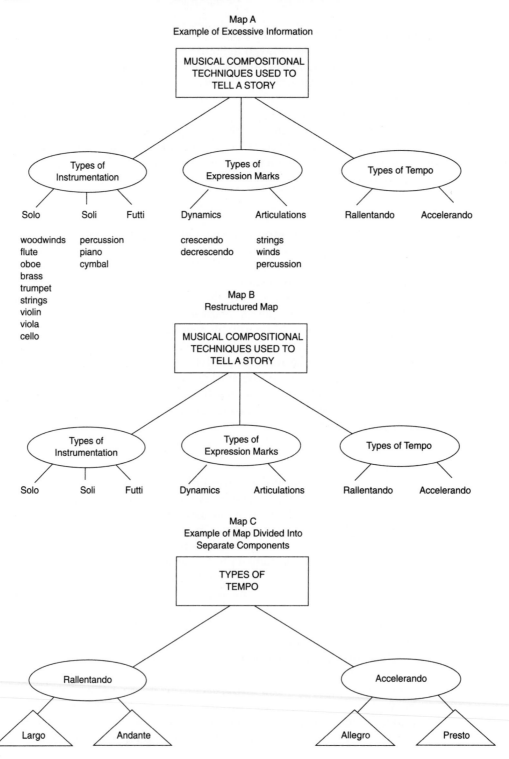

Map A
Example of Excessive Information

Map B
Restructured Map

Map C
Example of Map Divided Into
Separate Components

Step 3:

Refine and elaborate. The final step in constructing a concept map involves attention to factors that will refine and enhance its structure and appearance. First, keep the amount of information presented in the map to a minimum. The effect of a map containing excessive information is shown in Figure 4.14. By reducing the amount of information presented in Map A, Map B is more clearly organized and easier to understand. If the amount of information displayed in a map cannot be reduced, you may find it necessary to restructure concepts so they are displayed in separate maps, as shown in Map C. Second, where possible, assign distinct graphic symbols to the coordinate, superordinate, and subordinate information. Shapes or forms are more likely to draw students' attention to key conceptual categories and distinguish those categories from others representing different conceptual relationships. Finally, provide some additional space in your map to accommodate information presented by your students. Most teachers find that maps are most effective when both they and their students contribute to their construction.

At first, constructing a concept map can be relatively time consuming, and you may find that your final product requires some amount of modification as it is presented and discussed with your students. For those unacquainted with concept maps, the majority of preparation time is often directed at learning the material and identifying concepts related to lesson objectives. Over time, as you become more familiar with the reading selections and as lesson objectives become more refined, you will be able to construct maps spontaneously during classroom instruction.

To present a concept map, consider the following steps.

Step 1:

Introduce the map. Begin with a clear description of the title of the concept map, the purpose of the map, and a brief explanation of how the map can be used as a learning tool. Next, describe each concept and related information as the map is presented on an overhead or chalkboard. If the map is displayed on a transparency, consider displaying the concepts one at a time by covering the transparency with a sheet of paper that is gradually moved down as you discuss each concept. This technique reduces the amount of visual information and focuses attention on the concepts as they are presented.

Step 2:

Direct student elaboration. A concept map is more effective when students become actively involved in its construction. Sharing their knowledge adds to the relevance of the map and heightens their attention and motivation to learn. The product of students' efforts also provides insight into their understanding of the lesson's content and gives you an opportunity to clarify any misconceptions and to evaluate students' familiarity with the map's content. Once the entire map has been displayed and discussed, encourage students to examine each concept and identify information from their background knowledge that they could add to the conceptual linkages.

Step 3:

Follow up with application. The map can be used during reading as a study guide. As they encounter concepts in the text, students can refer to the completed map for clarification, or they may use the map as a note-taking device to highlight additional content or elaborate on concepts already presented.

A concept map can also be used to promote writing prior to reading. Here is a collaborative writing activity to preview lesson content and draw on students' background knowledge.

Step 1:

Present a skeletal concept map. Display a concept map containing a title and concept labels. Ask students to provide associations or information for each concept from their background knowledge. As information is presented by the students, add it to the map.

Step 2:

Elaborate on the concept map. Assign students to cooperative groups. Give each group a specific portion of a selection and ask them to find information that can be added to the map. At the conclusion of the lesson, have each group add their new information to the map.

Step 3:

Generate sentences. List conceptual headings from the map on an overhead or chalkboard. Beneath each heading, place a topic sentence that provides a main idea or generalization that is drawn from the information contained in the map. Have students then write sentences describing the attributes or relationships of the information contained under the conceptual headings. These sentences should be written on slips of paper that can be placed beneath the appropriate topic sentence.

Step 4:

Write paragraphs. Assign each group of students one of the conceptual headings. Then ask them to examine the sentences assembled under that heading and write a cohesive paragraph containing the information presented in the individual sentences. One member of the group should assume the role of transcribing the paragraph as the other group members review the headings and sentences generated in Step 3. Students can then present the paragraph orally to the class. An illustration of this activity is given in Figure 4.15 (pp. 130–131).

Concept maps are powerful tools that can help students locate, select, sequence, integrate, and restructure information (Jones, Palinscar, Ogle, &

Carr, 1987). Their uses prior to reading include establishing lesson objectives, drawing on students' prior knowledge, and acquainting students with essential concepts and information contained in the reading. Initially, concept maps may seem to be quite similar to traditional outlining. While both are structured representations of concepts that may be hierarchical and linear, there are important distinctions between the two. Maps allow for inclusion of information beyond that found in a reading because students and the teacher are encouraged to add information from their background knowledge. Furthermore, maps are more visual than traditional outlines. They display multiple and coordinating relationships, often through the use of graphic symbols.

Finally, the use of maps is not limited to prereading activities. Maps have also been found to be effective learning tools when constructed by students during or after the study of subject matter selections (Bean, Singer, Sorter, & Frazee, 1986; Boothby & Alvermann, 1984; Hawk, 1986; Holley & Dansereau, 1984). Following a reading, discussion, demonstration, or visual presentation, maps can be employed to organize and review important information.

PRACTICE ACTIVITY 4.1

Listed here are a number of concepts and pieces of information for a map entitled "The Effects of Oil Spills on Society." Take a moment to write them on slips of paper, then arrange the terms in a hierarchical manner. Compare your results with our version in the answers section.

economic costs	destruction of animals and	environmental costs
cleanup	plants	reduction in tourism
polluted water supply	health costs	

List, Group, Label.   The list, group, label (Taba, 1967) activity is a reflective learning activity in which students construct conceptual arrangements from their prior knowledge. The activity requires little teacher preparation, promotes cooperative learning, and is well suited for students with diverse needs and backgrounds. The list, group, label activity begins as the teacher presents a word or phrase that describes the topic or theme of a lesson, then asks students to suggest words they associate with the specified topic. These words are listed on an overhead or chalkboard. If students produce words seemingly unrelated to the topic, they are asked to provide a rationale for their response and, if necessary, are encouraged to provide an alternate response. If students have difficulty generating words, it may be necessary for

---

FIGURE 4.15   EXAMPLE OF CONCEPT MAP USED IN A WRITING ACTIVITY

Step 1: Skeletal Map

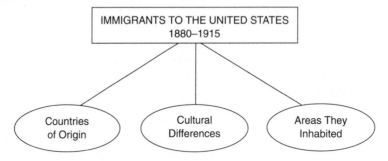

Step 2: Elaboration of Concept Map

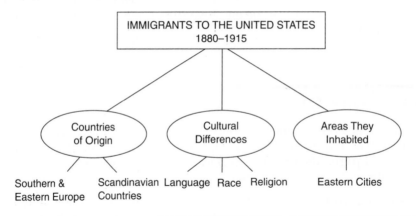

---

the teacher to provide additional clues or prompts. If these prompts fail to generate additional responses, the teacher may need to provide the relevant terms. Here are words dealing with a lesson on the Navajos. The list has been generated by students and supplemented with words provided by the teacher (marked with an asterisk).

The Navajos of the American Southwest

Arizona	sheep	farmers	craftwork
desert	blankets	sand painting*	Utah*
New Mexico*	tribal religion*	horses	pottery
hogans*	healing	medicine men	weaving
wool	hunting		

In the next step, students work in small groups to organize the terms into categories sharing common attributes or features. They then construct a label

---

FIGURE 4.15   CONTINUED

Step 3: Sentence Generation

Example of sentence generation from conceptual category "Cultural Differences"

- Before the 1880s most immigrants spoke English.
- Immigrants arriving between 1880 and 1915 spoke a variety of languages.
- Many of the new immigrants retained their native language.
- The new immigrants spoke their native languages in public.
- The new immigrants read newspapers in their native language.
- Many U.S. citizens who spoke English resented the new immigrants because they failed to speak English.
- Many of the new immigrants were Catholics who had migrated from Italy and what is now Poland.
- Jewish immigrants, who came from Russia, lived apart from the rest of the population.

Step 4: Paragraph Writing

The U.S. experienced a new wave of immigrants from 1880 to 1915. These immigrants, who came from the Scandinavian countries and southern and eastern Europe, did not become part of the "melting pot" as readily as earlier immigrants.

Topic Sentence: A number of cultural differences between the new immigrants and the rest of the population prevented them from being readily accepted in society.

   A. Language Barriers
   B. Religious Diversity
   C. Racial Diversity

---

for each category. Here is one example of the groups and labels for the words listed above.

Location	Spiritual Practices	Making a Living	
Arizona	medicine men	farmers	hunting
Utah	healing	craftwork	horses
New Mexico	sand painting	blankets	weaving
desert		wool	pottery

In the final step, each group presents a rationale for its categories. This is followed by a large group discussion focused on reaching group consensus on the categories and their respective words. During this final step it is likely that students will generate additional words for the various categories, or they may decide to restructure by deletion, consolidation, or division. The teacher should limit students' attention to words and concepts that facilitate lesson objectives. Inclusion of words or concepts not addressed in the lesson may establish learning expectations that cannot be met. Coaching students to provide a rationale for their groupings is another important function of the teacher. As students discuss their rationale for their groupings, additional associations are likely to be triggered, producing a spiraling effect. The more students describe and elaborate on their constructed topics, the more associations will be triggered by other students.

The list, group, label activity may also be used at the conclusion of a lesson to review and reinforce text concepts (Moore, Readence, & Rickelman, 1989). The procedure is the same as that outlined above, but the process now focuses on knowledge gained from the lesson in addition to the students' prior knowledge. This offers students an opportunity to reflect on the lesson content, to integrate information discussed prior to the lesson, and to deal with higher level relationships. As a postreading activity, the list, group, label also serves as an authentic form of classroom assessment. Students' description of the concepts they have learned and their ability to present a rationale for the relationships between these concepts provide the teacher with rich and meaningful insights into students' learning strategies and their knowledge of the lesson content.

Commentary: Graphic Organizers.   Graphic organizers provide a flexible strategy to promote learning. As a prereading tool, they can be used to acquaint readers with the information in text and provide clues about how that information is structured. They can direct the readers' attention as they are studying a text, and they can be used to review and extend their thinking at the conclusion of a reading, regardless of the age group or content area (West et al., 1991). As a prewriting tool, they can be used to help students organize information (Armbruster et al., 1987; Van Patten, Chao, & Reigeluth, 1986) and improve thinking, creativity, and decision making (West et al., 1991).

Although graphic organizers are effective instructional devices for the subject matter classroom, they do have certain shortcomings. First, benefits of their use may not be evident immediately. For example, Jones and colleagues (1987) report that some studies of graphic organizers showed effects only following weeks or months of sustained instruction. For that reason, you may consider initiating instruction with the most straightforward of the strategies outlined here—the list, group, label. It is easy to use, it is readily adaptable to most groups of students and subject matter areas, and results are attained quite readily. It also provides a good transitional step to the introduction and application of frames and concept maps.

The second shortcoming is that graphic organizers are sometimes difficult to apply to certain types of material or learning objectives. In circumstances in which students have little or no background knowledge, the use of frames and the list, group, label activity may produce frustration and confusion. Similarly, when learning objectives rely on knowledge acquired through direct experience (demonstrations, discussions, experiments, visuals, etc.) you may find that the effect of graphic organizers prior to these experiences is limited. In those circumstances, it may be necessary to first engage students in the activity, then use the graphic organizer as a form of review or reinforcement.

Finally, graphic organizers may produce disappointing results in those circumstances in which you fail to identify objectives or are not thoroughly familiar with the content of the reading selection. As noted earlier, graphic organizers are constructed to reflect teacher objectives and text information that will facilitate those objectives. If objectives are not defined, the use of graphic organizers usually leads to products that outline the entire content of a selection and that fail to engage students in learning activities beyond the memorization of surface-level information.

Prediction Activities

Prediction refers to the prior reduction of unlikely alternatives (Smith, 1978). In the subject matter classroom, prediction serves to aid comprehension by activating schema, thus making text more predictable and familiar. Its use, according to Anderson (1984), allows students to integrate what they know with what is presented in print. Prediction may also enhance students' critical thinking by drawing their attention to key concepts in order to hypothesize logical relationships (Nessel, 1988) and by drawing their attention to known concepts that may conflict with those presented in the text (Frager & Thompson, 1985). Instructionally, students can generate predictions prior to reading by drawing on their existing knowledge; when their background knowledge is limited, students may generate predictions from information they acquire from surveying titles, headings, subheadings, or short passages (Brozo & Simpson, 1991). Prediction can help students set a purpose for reading, increase their attention to text objectives, and increase their motivation to read (Nichols, 1983).

This section contains a discussion of two prediction activities: anticipation guides and the K-W-L (Ogle, 1989). The usefulness of prediction activities will be enhanced by making certain the material students read is meaningful and by encouraging students to draw on their prior knowledge as they generate predictions (Harris & Cooper, 1985).

Anticipation Guides.   Anticipation guides consist of a series of statements that cause readers to draw on their prior knowledge, then use that knowledge interactively with information in the reading. Prior to reading, students examine a series of statements, respond whether they agree or disagree with them, then discuss their responses to provide justification or add information. Following this discussion, students read the selection, then return to the statements to consider modifying their responses in light of the information pre-

---

FIGURE 4.16　ANTICIPATION GUIDE FOR "TRAPDOOR," A SHORT STORY
BY RAY BRADBURY

Directions: *Read and carefully consider the statements provided below. Determine whether you generally agree or disagree with each statement and mark the appropriate response. When you encounter a "Why?" in the item, please provide a brief explanation for your response.*

1. Strange noises are more frightening when one is alone.

_____ Agree　_____ Disagree　Why?

2. Generally, conditions of fear of the unknown are evident more often under conditions of darkness than light.

_____ Agree　_____ Disagree　Why?

3. Homes, at times, seem to take on human characteristics.

_____ Agree　_____ Disagree

4. Often when we are confronted with a circumstance that is strange, or different, we attempt to place the event in a context that is meaningful or familiar to us.

_____ Agree　_____ Disagree　Why?

5. Trapdoors are usually associated with illusions, magic, or evil events.

_____ Agree　_____ Disagree

6. Inanimate objects sometimes appear to have a soul.

_____ Agree　_____ Disagree

---

sented in the reading. Figure 4.16 is an example of an anticipation guide constructed for a high school English class.

Here are the steps for constructing an anticipation guide.

Step 1:

Identify major concepts. Examine the reading to identify the major concepts or information, then select those that are essential to your learning objectives. The following concepts were identified from an interdisciplinary lesson in science and social studies.

- Governmental funding of AIDS research has increased as a result of public and political pressure.
- Inclusion of AIDS preventive measures in the curriculum is often based on social norms of the community.
- As a wider segment of the population contracts AIDS, efforts to prevent its spread and find a cure have increased.

Step 2:

Translate lesson concepts into thought-provoking statements. Concepts now need to be translated into a form that is short, clear, and interesting and that reflects the everyday world of the students. Avoid narrow statements focusing on details or factual information. Statements should be general enough to elicit diverse points of view. Recognize that translating dry, abstract concepts into statements that attract students' attention and stimulate discussion can, at first, be difficult. The statement "Congress has the constitutional authority to impeach the President" is tedious, mechanical, and rather lifeless. Replacing it with "The people should always have the authority to remove people in positions of power and influence" would more likely gain attention and promote an interaction reflecting diverse opinions. Here are some statements generated from the concepts identified in Step 1.

People in government are more likely to act if a lot of people call out for action.
_____ Agree   _____ Disagree

It's not easy to support something that goes against your beliefs.
_____ Agree   _____ Disagree

A tragedy would have a lot more impact on me if it occurred to someone I know as opposed to someone I read about in the newspaper.
_____ Agree   _____ Disagree

Step 3:

Present and discuss statements. Direct students to examine each statement, consider that statement based on their experience and knowledge, then select an appropriate response that they may be asked to defend during class discussion that will follow. Statements may be listed on a chalkboard, displayed from a transparency, read aloud, or given on a handout. Response solicitation to statements may follow several methods. First, responses may be elicited prior to reading, as shown in the statements listed under Step 2. Instruct students to examine the statement, then respond on the basis of their background knowledge. Tally students' responses, then engage in a discussion focusing on the point of view and justification of their response. Have students read the selection, then reflect on that statement to determine if the text information would justify modification of their initial response. Using an earlier example:

A tragedy would have a lot more impact on me if it occurred to someone I knew as opposed to someone I read about in the newspaper.

        Before Reading   After Reading
_____ Agree   _____ Disagree   _____ Agree   _____ Disagree

An alternate method would be to have students answer the statement before reading based on their own judgment, answer the statement following reading based on the information provided by the author, then provide a writ-

---

FIGURE 4.17   EXAMPLE OF PROCEDURE FOR JUSTIFYING RESPONSE
TO ANTICIPATION GUIDE

Directions: *Based on what you know about the environmental movement, respond to the
following statement.*

Environmentalists' main goal is to gain political and economic power on a worldwide
basis.

Your Response   Author's Response

_____ Agree   _____ Disagree   _____ Agree   _____ Disagree

Next, read the following excerpt of an editorial appearing in the Wall Street Journal, *then
determine how the author of this article would respond to the statement above.*

> There have been Western elites in the past who believed that the hordes of hu-
> manity in developing countries should be beaten back and controlled. Following in
> their footsteps today are the environmental elites who want to prevent the Third
> World's economies from ever using the industrial techniques that will make them
> First World countries. They'll do this by imposing an international tax on carbon
> dioxide emissions and a freeze on human procreation. [*Source:* Editorial, *Wall Street
> Journal,* June 1, 1992].

*Consider the statement you responded to above. Now that you have read the selection,
provide a justification for what you believe is the* best *response to the statement.*
JUSTIFICATION: _____
_____

---

ten justification for what they consider to be the best response. This method
recognizes that there may be occasions when students construct a view that,
while logical and informed, may not agree with that presented in the text. Allowing students to justify their response should encourage class discussion,
stimulate critical thinking, and encourage students to regulate their own thinking. Figure 4.17 is an example of this method.

The anticipation guide is an effective tool for activating and relating
prior knowledge to themes or constructs presented in a reading, film,
videotape, filmstrip, or audio recording. Engaging in the statements is
likely to focus attention on important concepts, to arouse curiosity, and to
promote participation. And, as class discussion centers on individuals' ability to defend or explain their positions, you are afforded an opportunity to
engage in a meaningful and authentic form of assessing students' prior
knowledge. Results of this assessment can be used to identify students who
could profit from further enrichment activities or alternate readings (Moore
et al., 1989).

Since the anticipation guide relies on predictions constructed from prior
knowledge, statements based on material containing new and difficult concepts are likely to arouse little more than frustration as the students respond to

FIGURE 4.18   K-W-L STRATEGY WORKSHEET FOR EIGHTH-GRADE LESSON
ON CANCER

What We Think We Know	What We Would Like to Know	What We Learned and What We Still Need to Learn

Step 1-A

Cancer kills a lot of people each year	Is there more cancer in older people?	There are ways to reduce your risk for getting cancer
We don't have a cure for cancer	Do animals get cancer?	
	Why can't we find a cure?	There are many ways to treat cancer
People get cancer from smoking	How do I know if I have it?	There are many kinds of cancer
Throughout the world people get cancer	Are there different types of cancer?	People need to learn the warning signs of cancer
There seems to be more cancer now than in the past		Smoking and what you eat can influence cancer
There are some ways to help people that have cancer		Some kinds of cancer are inherited

Step 1-B

Categories We Think We Might Use

- a. Causes of cancer
- b. How many die from cancer
- c. Ways to treat cancer
- d. Who gets cancer

information that is seemingly dry and difficult. Similarly, material that is primarily factual or that contains information unlikely to stir emotion, raise debate, or be open to interpretation may not be suitable for this prereading strategy.

Know, Want to Know, Learn Strategy (K-W-L).   The K-W-L activity (Ogle, 1989) is a three-step procedure. It begins with a prereading activity for engaging students in retrieval of their prior knowledge, followed by a question-generating activity and an after-reading activity for reflecting and elaborating on what was learned. The procedure is guided by a worksheet composed of three columns reflecting the three steps of the activity (Figure 4.18).

The first column contains information students believe they know, the second what they want to learn, and the third what they have learned from the selection. The three steps proceed as follows.

Step 1:

What students know. The first step has three components: brainstorming, categorizing, and anticipating. The first two components, brainstorming and categorizing, are similar to the list, group, label procedure outlined earlier in this chapter. Brainstorming begins by eliciting students' associations with the topic of study. Topics should be specific and likely to draw on the appropriate prior knowledge. List responses on the board or overhead. Students, working individually, should be directed to indicate what they think they know under the first column of their guided worksheet (Step 1-A in Figure 4.18). Next, ask students to examine the information compiled during brainstorming in order to identify common attributes and characteristics. Categorical labels are then generated from the common attributes and displayed on the guided worksheet (Step 1-B in Figure 4.18). The purpose here is to have students predict and anticipate themes, main ideas, and general information contained in the reading. Because students may be unaccustomed to categorizing information, it will be useful to model a few familiar examples. Another approach involves group problem solving. Beginning with the procedure outlined above, have student groups brainstorm, then sort information listed in the first column of their guided worksheet. Direct them to write this information on small slips of a transparency. Then collect the slips and place them on an overhead; the class can sort, delete, and add information to derive categories. This process allows you and your students to model the thinking process for constructing categories.

Anticipating is the third and final component of Step 1. The purpose here is to show students how to anticipate categories that may be included by the authors of the selection to be read. Ogle (1989) recommends that the teacher generate questions that place students in the position of writing the selection. Thus, if students were about to read a selection on blues music, you may ask, "If we were going to write an article on the blues, what topics would you want to include? Why would you need to include these topics? What topics could be included but might not add a great deal to the article?" Anticipating topics should provide a structural framework to which information obtained during reading may be added. Ideas and information in the reading are more likely to be meaningful if students can relate them to preassigned themes or main ideas.

Step 2:

What students would like to know. Prior to reading, generate student-initiated questions. Questions are constructed from information addressed during the brainstorming, categorizing, and predicting components of Step 1. Your role here is to address areas of partial knowledge, resolve conflicting information or points of view, and direct students' attention to important information through the use of probing questions (Ogle, 1989). Instruct students to jot down questions in the second column of their worksheet. Students tend to ask factual, surface-level questions, like "In what year did they begin composing blues?" or "How many blues records have been produced in the past twenty years?" It may be necessary for you to discuss how to construct higher level questions by focusing on the central purpose ("Why did?"), causal relations ("How did . . . affect . . . ?"), or hypotheses ("What do you think will be the result of . . . ?" or "While not stated in the text, what evidence is there that . . . ?").

Step 3:

What we still need to know. During reading students perform two tasks. First, they attend to the questions listed in the second column of their worksheet. As they generate answers, they stop, reflect on what they have learned, write a response in the third column of their worksheet, then proceed to the next question. Second, students generate additional questions as they encounter new information or are unable to understand concepts or information presented in the text. For example, students may ask "What distinguished Billie Holiday as a great singer of the blues?" or "How is the blues different from some country western music?"

Following the reading, direct students to the first two columns of their worksheet to revise, delete, or modify any information as necessary. This encourages students to view learning as an ongoing process that undergoes revision. Encourage students to discuss any questions they were unable to answer from information in the selection and to summarize what was learned.

The K-W-L activity can improve the learning of classroom material (Dewitz & Carr, 1987; Ogle & Jennings, 1987) and material read independently (Carr & Ogle, 1986). One modification to this activity is to begin with a statement of learning objectives by discussing them with your students, then listing them on the K-W-L guided worksheet. These objectives should be expressed in general terms; otherwise students will tend to refrain from generating their own questions, relying instead on restructuring the objective into a question. In a world geography class, for example, general objectives for a lesson on Western European countries might include an understanding of how topographical features affect the economies of these countries and the influence that climatic conditions have on the production of foodstuffs. Objectives such as these tend to focus questions more directly on the concepts contained in the reading. Without these objectives, students' questions are likely to be so widely focused that there is little chance they will be addressed in the selection. Consider the questions that might be generated from the learning objectives in a lesson on Western Europe. For the first objective you might ask, "What are the various topographical features of Western Europe?" or "What countries are located in Western Europe?" or "What are the economies of Western Europe?" The inclusion of objectives facilitates each step of the K-W-L activity. Brainstorming and categorizing become more focused, and the questions generated are more likely to be addressed in the reading.

Commentary: Prediction Activities.   Generating predictions can instill curiosity (Shablak & Castallo, 1977) and heighten motivation (Lunstrum, 1981) as students draw on prior knowledge to anticipate outcomes. Predictions also establish objectives for reading and promote the active exchange of ideas and information between students. As a result, readers are encouraged to monitor and regulate their reading in an effort to make it purposeful and selective. Prediction may also enhance critical thinking. The presentation of objectives that address critical thinking problems on the K-W-L worksheet or anticipation guide encourage class discussion and debate on issues well beyond the literal level of understanding.

While prediction activities are a powerful instructional tool, their use is conditional. Material containing concepts and information far removed from students' background knowledge may not be well suited for prediction activities. Responding to statements or generating questions based on unfamiliar material can be a difficult and frustrating experience. Under these conditions, it may useful to first preview the material using prereading strategies that will provide students with some acquaintance with the material, then involve them with prediction activities. Recognize that certain types of material may not be suited for prediction activities. Highly scientific or factual selections as well as those containing information unlikely to stimulate discussion, debate, or interpretation may be inappropriate.

Previews

The final type of prereading activity presented in this chapter is the written preview. This is a script of moderate length that you read aloud before students engage in an expository or narrative selection. The preview is particularly useful for difficult material, or lengthy material containing a great deal of information. Once presented, students gain background knowledge, a purpose for reading, and the opportunity to discuss or question information prior to reading. Graves, Prenn, and Cooke (1985) recommend that the preview be constructed to reflect three components: discussion questions, the written summary, and purpose-setting questions. A preview written for Shirley Jackson's short story "Charles" is given in Figure 4.19.

Constructing a preview requires attention to the content of the selection, knowledge of the students' background, and clearly defined objectives. Consider these steps. First, become familiar with the selection by reading it several times. As you read, note important concepts, characters, events, and so on, then define what you consider to be the major themes or ideas. Next, consider how you can make this information relevant and practical to your students.

FIGURE 4.19   EXAMPLE OF PREVIEW FROM "CHARLES," BY SHIRLEY JACKSON

Try to remember your first day of kindergarten. How did you act and feel? Going to school for the first time is an important experience for most children. It's often the first time they are really away from their families and have a chance to develop their own personalities. It's also a chance to meet many new classmates. Some parents may worry about the kids their son or daughter associates with. Were there any troublemakers in your kindergarten class that might have had a bad influence on you?

In the story that you are about to read entitled "Charles," the main character is a boy named Laurie who is just starting kindergarten. He seems eager to go to school because he doesn't even stop to wave goodbye to his mother when he leaves on the first day.

After his first day of kindergarten, Laurie rushes home to report to his mother and father that a boy got spanked at school for being fresh and talking back to the teacher. When asked who the boy was, Laurie thinks for a while and then says, "It was Charles."

For the next two weeks, Laurie comes home everyday with news of Charles' new crimes and punishments. Charles was spanked for hitting the teacher; deprived of blackboard privileges because he threw chalk, kept after school for yelling, and kept out of gym class for kicking the gym teacher. Laurie's mother and father become so curious about Charles that they forget to ask Laurie what he does in school. Each day they can hardly wait to hear what Charles has done.

Laurie's parents also don't notice that Laurie's behavior at home is getting worse. They just ignore Laurie when he spills the baby's milk, talks back to his father, and pulls a wagon of mud into the kitchen. After all, he isn't as bad as Charles!

Read to see what happens when Laurie's parents find out more about Charles, and about Laurie.

The purpose here is to construct an introductory statement that can link information in the selection to the background and interest of your students. Questions may also be presented to draw on students' prior knowledge. The next section of the preview, the summary, should include the main ideas, supporting information, and other content relevant to your objectives. In the final section of the preview, provide purpose-setting questions and brief notes about the structure of the selection. For example, you may direct students to omit certain portions of the selection, or you may draw their attention to a particularly important section or to a poorly written passage.

Presentation of the preview, generally requiring 5 to 10 minutes, follows these steps as described by Graves and colleagues (1985):

Step 1:

Present an introduction. Inform students that you are about to provide an introduction to a reading selection. For example:

We are about to begin a unit on the study of water. Over the next two weeks, we have combined your science and geography class so we may learn about the distribution and use of water as well as some of its chemical properties. Today, we will learn about the need that living things have for water.

There is water in all living things. What percent of the following living things do you suppose is composed of water? (Offer the examples humans, corn, mice, and elephants.)

You may be surprised to learn that all of these living things are composed of 60% to 70% water. Why is such a large percentage of our body composed of water?

Step 2:

Preview important background information. Provide information that is unfamiliar to students. For example:

Your body is like a machine. You need fuel (food, air), you need something similar to oil to cleanse your body (blood), and you need an exhaust pipe to remove wastes (excretory system). Today we will concentrate on the importance of water in keeping your body functioning like a machine.

Step 3:

Read the preview. Read the remaining portion of the preview, then immediately direct students to read the selection.

All living things need water to stay alive. Surprisingly, living things are composed of a lot of water. Your body is about 65% water, about the same as a mouse, an ear of corn, or an elephant. Water is necessary to carry on the functions of taking in food, breaking down the food into its usable nutrients or food substances, then carrying away waste products. Solutions in your body that are composed of a great deal of water, like your blood, transport nutrients. Water also helps in the chemical reactions that break down food into materials you need to grow and repair body tissues. While you could survive about two months without food, you could live only about a week without water.

Step 4:

Provide purpose-setting questions and study aids. Provide students a purpose for reading and offer suggestions that may facilitate their understanding of the selection.

Now read the selection entitled "Body Functions: The Importance of Water." As you read, determine how water is used to break down food and remove wastes from your body. You may skip the second page of the reading because it addresses an issue we aren't concerned with. Also, before you begin reading, study the illustrations on pages 41 and 42. Looking at those illustrations will make the reading easier to understand.

Commentary: Previews.   The presentation of previews prior to reading has been shown to be an effective means for establishing an organizational framework to stimulate the appropriate background knowledge and to provide new information about the selection that will be read (Graves, Cooke, & LaBerge, 1983; Graves & Palmer, 1981; Graves & Prenn, 1984). Moreover, previews stimulate curiosity, enhance the motivation to read, and provide a means to link text material to background knowledge. Intuitively, while it would seem that previews would reduce interest in reading a selection, students appreciate receiving them. According to Graves and colleagues, students report that previews help them to read and understand the selections without ruining the story or selection. Note, however, because they are intended to provide background information, their use should be limited to material that is unfamiliar to students or that exhibits organizational schemes that may cause confusion.

CONCLUDING REMARKS

This chapter has addressed the importance of preparing students to learn by planning and implementing prereading activities, establishing a purpose for learning, and providing activities for enhancing background knowledge. In summarizing this chapter, three points should be emphasized.

First, prereading activities are essential to sound classroom practice. Many students experience uncertainty or frustration as they attempt to define a purpose for independent reading. By activating and building upon students' schema, reading becomes more purposeful and focused. And, as the teacher models the process of relating prior knowledge to new or difficult content, students begin to acquire a greater awareness of the process for generating questions, sharing information, and obtaining information from sources outside the textbook.

Second, students should increasingly assume responsibility for establishing objectives, relating background knowledge to these objectives, and enhancing background knowledge through cooperative efforts with their peers. The gradual release of instructional responsibility from the teacher to the student increases the likelihood that activities in this chapter can become part of the individual's repertoire of reading strategies. Some students will be able to apply these strategies on their own, while others will require the continued assistance of their peers. Yet all students will have a better understanding of the process of establishing goals and the importance of drawing on prior knowledge.

Finally, it should be noted that prereading activities are an important element in improving students' attitudes toward learning. Many of the activities presented in this chapter rely on group learning. This context fosters an appreciation of each student's contribution to the learning process and the diverse points of view evident in a classroom. Group activities also increase the likelihood that students will engage in risk taking and generate knowledge from information provided from the teacher, peers, and reading material.

REFLECTIONS

Now that you have become more familiar with ways to prepare students for reading text, complete the following questions as a review of some of the topics addressed throughout this chapter.

1. Construct a purpose-setting conversation activity for a lesson that could be presented to a class of students. Script each step of the procedure, then administer the lesson to a class in your subject matter area.

2. Select content appropriate for a unit of study in your subject matter area. Construct and list instructional objectives, then construct a series of concept maps that could be used to preview the lesson content to a group of students. Present these maps to a group of students or peers and solicit their feedback on the usefulness of the maps in building prior knowledge.

3. Obtain a reading approximately three to four pages in length. Construct a series of frames for the article, adhering to the guidelines discussed in this chapter. Present the frames to a group of your peers. Next, ask your peers to generate a written summary by referring to the frames you constructed. Finally, ask your peers to comment on the merit of using the frames for writing.

4. Construct an anticipation guide for a portion of a chapter in this text. Ask one of your peers to complete the anticipation guide prior to reading the chapter, then ask him or her to comment on the usefulness of this activity in establishing a purpose for reading.

5. Examine the teacher's edition of a subject matter textbook to determine the scope and nature of prereading activities recommended for instruction. Summarize these activities by noting (1) the types of activities suggested, (2) the frequency that the activities are presented, and (3) the degree that the activities allow students to become actively involved. Finally, note any suggestions you may have for improving or modifying these activities.

6. Use K-W-L as a study strategy. Apply its use to a selection of text, then write a summary noting its strengths, limitations, and any questions you may have regarding its use.

7. Construct a prereading lesson that would consume approximately 1 hour of class time. In constructing this written lesson, define your learning objectives and the rationale for selecting the prereading strategies used, and describe how you would present these strategies. If possible, administer this lesson to a group of students. Ask a peer or a teacher to evaluate the effectiveness of this lesson by (1) examining how well the activities addressed your stated objectives, (2) evaluating the extent that your activities allow for students' active participation, and (3) evaluating if the lesson followed the procedures for administrating the activities as discussed in the chapter.

REFERENCES

Anderson, C., & Roth, K. (1989). Teaching for meaningful and self-regulated learning in science. In J. Brophy (Ed.), *Advances in research on teaching,* Vol. 1. Greenwich, CT: JAI Press.

Anderson, R. C. (1984). Role of the reader's schema in comprehension, learning, and memory. In R. Anderson, J. Osborn, & R. Tierney (Eds.), *Learning to read in American schools: Basal readers and content texts.* Hillsdale, NJ: Erlbaum.

Applebee, A. N. (1984). Writing and reasoning. *Review of Educational Research, 54,* 577–596.

Applebee, A. N., Langer, J. A., & Mullis, I. V. S. (1987). *Literature and U.S. history: The instructional experience and factual knowledge of high school juniors.* Princeton, NJ: Educational Testing Service.

Armbruster, B. B., & Anderson, T. H. (1984). Mapping: Representing informative text diagrammatically. In C. D. Holley & D. F. Dansereau (Eds.), *Spatial learning strategies: Techniques, applications, and related issues.* New York: Academic Press.

Armbruster, B. B., Anderson, T. H., & Ostertag, J. (1987). Does text structure/summarization instruction facilitate learning from expository text? *Reading Research Quarterly, 22* 331–346.

Ausubel, D. P. (1968). *Educational psychology: A cognitive view.* New York: Holt, Rinehart & Winston.

Bandura, A. (1982). Self-efficacy mechanism in human agency. *American Psychologist, 37,* 122–147.

Barron, R. (1969). Research for the classroom teacher: Recent developments on the structured overview as an advance cognitive organizer. In H. Herber & J. Riley (Eds.), *Research in reading in the content areas: The fourth report.* Syracuse, NY: Syracuse University Reading and Language Arts Center.

Bean, T. W., Singer, H., Sorter, J., & Frazee, C. (1986). The effect of metacognitive instruction in outlining and graphic organizer instruction on students' comprehension in a tenth-grade world history class. *Journal of Reading Behavior, 18,* 153–169.

Boothby, P. R., & Alvermann, D. E. (1984). A classroom training study: The effects of graphic organizer instruction on fourth graders' comprehension. *Reading World, 26,* 325–339.

Brozo, W. G., & Simpson, M. L. (1991). *Readers, teachers, learners: Expanding literacy in secondary schools.* New York: Macmillan.

Carr, E., & Ogle, D. (1986, December). *Improving disabled readers' summarization skills.* Paper presented at the annual meeting of the National Reading Conference, Austin, TX.

Clark, C., & Yinger, R. (1980). *The hidden world of teaching: Implications of research on teacher planning* (Research Series No. 77). East Lansing, MI: Institute for Research on Teaching.

Clark, C. M., & Peterson, P. L. (1986). Teachers' thought processes. In M. C. Wittrock (Ed.), *Handbook of research on teaching* (3rd ed.). New York: Macmillan.

Dewitz, P., & Carr, E. M. (1987, December). *Teaching comprehension as a student-directed process.* Paper presented at the annual meeting of the National Reading Conference, St. Petersburg, FL.

Dole, J. A., Duffy, G. G., Roehler, L. R., & Pearson, P. D. (1991). Moving from the old to the new: Research on reading comprehension instruction. *Review of Educational Research, 61,* 239–264.

Duffy, G. G., & Roehler, L. R. (1989). Why strategy instruction is so difficult and what we need to do about it. In G. Miller, C. McCormick, & M. Pressley (Eds.), *Cognitive strategy research: From basic research to educational applications.* New York: Springer-Verlag.

Elliott, D. L., & Woodward, A. (Eds.). (1990). *Textbooks and schooling in the United States* (Part 1). Chicago: University of Chicago Press.

Frager, A. M., & Thompson, L. C. (1985). Conflict: The key to critical reading instruction. *Journal of Reading, 28,* 676–683.

Graves, M. F., Cooke, C. L., & LaBerge, M. J. (1983). Effects of previewing difficult short stories on low ability junior high school students' comprehension, recall and attitudes. *Reading Research Quarterly, 18,* 262–276.

Graves, M. F., & Palmer, R. J. (1981). Validating previewing as a method of improving fifth and sixth grade students' comprehension of short stories. *Michigan Reading Journal, 15,* 1–3.

Graves, M. F., & Prenn, M. C. (1984). Effects of previewing expository passages on junior high students' comprehension and attitude. In J. Niles & R. Lalik (Eds.), *Changing perspectives on research in reading/language processing and instruction.* Rochester, NY: National Reading Conference.

Graves, M. F., Prenn, M., & Cooke, C. (1985). The coming attraction: Previewing short stories. *Journal of Reading, 28,* 594–599.

Harris, T. L., & Cooper, E. J. (1985). *Reading, thinking and concept development: Strategies for the classroom.* New York: College Board Publications.

Hawk, P. P. (1986). Using graphic organizers to increase achievement in middle school life science. *Science Education, 70,* 81–87.

Heimlich, J. E., & Pittelman, S. D. (1986). *Semantic mapping: Classroom applications.* Newark, DE: International Reading Association.

Holley, C. D., & Dansereau, D. F. (1984). *Spatial learning strategies: Techniques, applications and issues.* Orlando, FL: Academic Press.

Jackson, S. A. (1981). About publishers, teachers, and reading achievement. In J. Y. Cole & T. Sticht, (Eds.), *The textbook in American society: A volume based on a conference at the Library of Congress on May 2–3, 1979.* Washington, DC: Library of Congress.

Jones, B. F., Palinscar, A. S., Ogle, D. S., & Carr, E. G. (Eds.). (1987). *Strategic teaching and learning: Cognitive instruction in the content areas.* Elmhurst, IL: North Central Regional Laboratory and the Association for Supervision and Curriculum Development.

Langer, J. (1982). Facilitating text processing: The elaboration of prior knowledge. In J. Langer & T. Smith-Burke (Eds.), *Reader meets author: Bridging the gap.* Newark, DE: International Reading Association.

Lunstrum, J. P. (1981). Building motivation through the use of controversy. *Journal of Reading, 24,* 687–691.

Mayer, R. E. (1984). Twenty-five years of research on advance organizers. *Instructional Science, 8,* 133–169.

McAleese, R. (1986). Computer-based authoring and intelligent interactive video. In C. W. Osborne & A. J. Trott (Eds.), *International yearbook of educational and instructional technology.* New York: Kogan Page.

Moore, D. W., Readence, J. E., & Rickelman, R. J. (1989). *Prereading activities for content area reading and learning.* Newark, DE: International Reading Association.

Nessel, D. (1988). Channeling knowledge for reading expository text. *Journal of Reading, 32,* 225–228.

Nichols, J. N. (1983). Using prediction to increase content area interest and understanding. *Journal of Reading, 27,* 225–228.

Ogle, D. (1989). The know, want to know, learn strategy. In K. Muth (Ed.), *Children's comprehension of text.* Newark, DE: International Reading Association.

Ogle, D., & Jennings, J. (1987, December). *Teaching comprehension as a teacher-directed process.* Paper presented at the annual meeting of the National Reading Conference, St. Petersburg, FL.

Roller, C. M. (1990). The interaction between knowledge and structure variables in the processing of expository prose. *Reading Research Quarterly, 25,* 79–89.

Rosenbauer, T. (1984). *The Orvis fly-fishing guide.* New York: Nick Lyons Books.

Rosenshine, B., & Stevens, R. (1986). Teaching functions. In M. C. Wittrock (Ed.), *Handbook of research on teaching* (3rd ed.). New York: Macmillan.

Sanford, A. J., & Garrod, S. C. (1981). *Understanding written language: Explorations in comprehension beyond the sentence.* New York: Wiley.

Schunk, D. H. (1983). Developing children's self-efficacy and skills: The roles of comparative information and goal setting. *Contemporary Educational Psychology, 8,* 76–86.

_____. (1991). *Learning theories: An educational perspective.* New York: Merrill/Macmillan.

Shablak, S., & Castallo, R. (1977). Curiosity arousal and motivation in the teaching/learning process. In H. L. Herber and R. T. Vacca (Eds.), *Research in reading in the content areas: The third report*. Syracuse, NY: Syracuse University Reading and Language Arts Center.

Smith, F. (1978). *Understanding reading* (2nd ed.). New York: Holt, Rinehart and Winston.

Smith, F. R., & Feathers, K. M. (1983). The role of reading in the content classroom: Assumptions vs. reality. *Journal of Reading, 27*, 262–267.

Taba, H. (1967). *Teacher's handbook for elementary social studies*. Reading, MA: Addison-Wesley.

Taylor, B. M., & Samuels, S. J. (1983). Children's use of text structure in the recall of expository material. *American Educational Research Journal, 20*, 517–528.

Tyson-Bernstein, H. (1988). *A conspiracy of good intentions: America's textbook fiasco*. Washington, DC: Council for Basic Education.

Van Patten, J. R., Chao, C. I., & Reigeluth, C. M. (1986). A review of strategies for sequencing and synthesizing information. *Review of Educational Research, 56*, 437–472.

West, C. K., Farmer, J. A., & Wolff, P. M. (1991). *Instructional design: Implications from cognitive science*. Englewood Cliffs, NJ: Prentice Hall.

CHAPTER FIVE

Comprehension

—By Judith Winn with Randall Ryder

CHAPTER OVERVIEW

This chapter presents activities that help students understand and learn from subject matter reading material. The first section, "Activities to Structure Subject Matter Content," begins with a discussion of questioning, then presents teaching activities that assist students' learning of particular content. The second, "How Proficient Readers Comprehend Text," describes the processes, or strategies, used by proficient readers to guide their own reading. The third, "Activities to Promote Independent Reading," discusses activities that help students learn from texts on their own through strategic reading and studying. The final section, "Planning Comprehension Activities," addresses planning considerations teachers make to help their students understand and learn from subject matter reading material. This chapter should be viewed as a continuation of the comprehension activities discussed in Chapter Four, "Preparing Students for Learning." Similarly, this chapter is closely connected with Chapter Six, "Critical Thinking," which addresses activities to enhance students' ability to engage in higher level thinking.

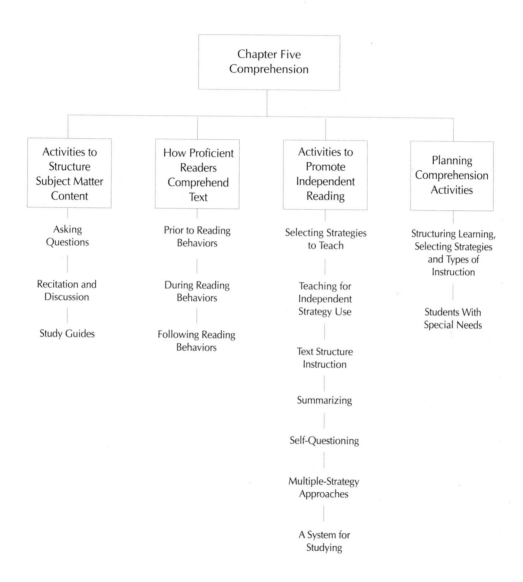

Many students find the reading material in their subject matter classes difficult to understand. As a result, it is not uncommon to find students who don't read the text, relying instead on the information they acquire from in-class lectures, discussions, or demonstrations, or who go through the motions of reading but are able to construct very little meaning. Comprehending text is difficult when students lack background knowledge of and interest in the material, when the texts are poorly written, or when the students do not have well-developed reading comprehension behaviors. Here are two examples of comprehension difficulties likely to be encountered in content area classes. Both are taken from a senior high school history class, in a school located in the mid-Atlantic states, that is about to begin reading about the Anastasi pueblo culture that resided in southwestern Colorado from A.D. 750 to 1300.

Kim

Kim has been assigned to a group of students who have been directed to engage in a problem-solving question. Their task is to read about the topographical and climatological characteristics of the region the Anastasi inhabited to determine how this culture survived for such a lengthy period. Kim has never traveled beyond the mid-Atlantic states. She has little understanding of the semiarid steppe climate of the Colorado plateau; the effect of the intense solar radiation at an altitude of 7,100 feet, where the Anastasi lived; or the relationships among altitude, climate, and vegetation. Lacking the background knowledge of these concepts, she experiences considerable difficulty reading about them.

Paulo

Paulo is a member of Kim's group. He lived most of his life in Cortez, Colorado, just a few miles from the present-day ruins of the Anastasi culture. He has visited these ruins on numerous occasions. Paulo locates six sources of information dealing with the climate and typography of southwestern Colorado. He reads these sources in the manner he is accustomed to—focusing on facts and figures that he then lists in his notes. Once these notes are completed, he turns them over to his group, assuming that they will somehow be able to apply the information to their problem-solving task.

Kim typifies a student who has difficulty comprehending text due to limited background knowledge. Lacking an understanding of concepts that many students of her age have acquired, reading for the purpose of gaining a higher level of understanding can be a frustrating experience. Paulo, on the other hand, has considerable prior knowledge of the concepts contained in the reading selections, yet he fails to adapt his note-taking strategy to meet the demands of the problem-solving task presented by the teacher. Neither of these students is likely to be able to successfully comprehend and learn from their content area reading material on his or her own, albeit for different reasons. Instruction that concentrates on building and activating background knowledge, as discussed in the preceding chapter, helps students construct meaning from the text by organizing and making sense of new information in terms of what they already know. Instruction can also help students develop control of their understanding and learning from reading in content area classes so that they can use the information in the reading material to meet the varied demands of their content classes.

Two types of instructional activities will be presented in this chapter. The first type comprises those that help structure the subject matter content of the text to enable students to meet the learning objectives. The second includes those that can be used to guide students toward becoming more proficient independent readers in subject matter areas. These activities address both the subject matter content and the processes of reading.

ACTIVITIES TO STRUCTURE SUBJECT MATTER CONTENT

This section begins with a discussion of the role and use of questioning. Following this are two comprehension activities: (1) recitation and discussion and (2) study guides.

Asking Questions

Questions have a variety of functions in the classroom. Used prior to reading, they can generate discussion that directs students to think about important concepts or values contained in reading selections. Both prior to and during reading, questions can help to establish a purpose for reading and to consolidate and extend the concepts or information presented. Following reading, questions presented in the text or by the teacher can assess each student's understanding as well as elicit discussion that involves drawing together or applying concepts presented in the reading.

While teachers initiate a lot of questions in the classroom, most of these tend to direct students' attention to factual-level information in the text (Bloome, 1987; Smith & Feathers, 1983; Wiley, 1977). A good set of questions can engage students in reasoning activities when they integrate that material with background knowledge to think about the text in novel ways. By sharing their approaches to these sorts of questions with the teacher and their peers, all students gain a better insight into the thinking process. Encouraging students to ask questions, whether it be an individual or cooperative effort, is likely to enhance their involvement in learning and increase the likelihood that they will gain a better understanding of the processes involved in constructing questions. This understanding can result in the students' independently generating their own questions to guide their reading.

Facilitating Learning/Thinking.   While questioning can serve a number of purposes (e.g., assessment and management), the one most relevant to this chapter is facilitating learning and thinking. The goals of these questions are to

1. **Highlight lesson content.** Questions can be used to direct students' attention to particular information in the text that is relevant to the learning objectives.

In Science: Describe the process of homeostasis.
In Physical Education: Describe three types of defense in basketball.

In Art: Describe the difference between color, hue and color saturation.
In English: From *Of Mice and Men*, describe Lennie's physical characteristics.

2. **Integrate lesson content with material learned previously.** Questions can assist students in applying previously learned material to the content of a particular reading.

> **In Science:** What effects does the aging process have on homeostasis?
> **In Physical Education:** What is the relationship between the weight, height, and speed of basketball team members and their ability to engage in a full-court press?
> **In Art:** Why do the various levels of saturation evoke different types of emotional reactions?
> **In English:** Compare and contrast the problems faced by the main characters in *Of Mice and Men* with the main characters in *The Grapes of Wrath*.

3. **Structure higher level understanding.** Questions can be sequenced in a manner that encourages students to apply that information to novel situations or contexts.

> **In Science:** How can our knowledge of homeostasis help us explain the functioning of the circulatory system?
> **In Physical Education:** How will the Milwaukee Bucks need to adjust their defense when they play the Los Angeles Lakers?
> **In Art:** What colors would you select for a police station waiting area?
> **In English:** Presume that you were to rewrite *Of Mice and Men* to take place in a contemporary urban setting. How would the characters and setting change?

4. **Promote the integration of students' knowledge, values, and cultural background with lesson objectives.** Learning can become more relevant and meaningful when students are encouraged to draw on their knowledge and background. Questions that encourage students to construct meaning using their values, their knowledge, and their own cultural perspective can provide a rich and stimulating environment for all students.

> **In Science:** What are some of the differences among groups of people living in different geographical regions in terms of how their bodies maintain homeostasis in light of their environments?
> **In Physical Education:** Think about your own neighborhood. How many kids play basketball and how often do they play?
> **In Art:** Certain cultures use different levels of color saturation in the clothes they wear. What are some of the traditional colors worn by your family or your ancestors?
> **In English:** If the character Lenny in *Of Mice and Men* were to move into your neighborhood, how would he be treated?

It is apparent from this list that questions can address much more than the mastery of specific factual content.

Developing questioning activities requires decisions about what types of questions to ask, when to ask them, and how to help students answer them. The following is a guide for question asking based on levels of thinking. In these next sections, question placement and ways of supporting students as they respond to questions will be addressed. Helping students generate their own questions will be covered in a later section, "Activities to Promote Independent Reading."

Cognitive Levels of Questions.   Costa's (1991) taxonomy of questions outlines a way of developing questions according to the type of thinking that is likely to be involved in answering them. The taxonomy is composed of three categories, or levels, of questions. Examples of questions in each of the categories are presented in Figure 5.1.

FIGURE 5.1   EXAMPLES OF COSTA'S QUESTIONING STRATEGY

Food irradiation is the process of bombarding food with gamma rays in order to kill insects, molds, and bacteria present in the food. While this process uses a form of radiation that in large quantities could be harmful, food irradiation does not make food radioactive. Proponents of irradiation note that it is an effective process in killing salmonella bacteria, which are responsible for millions of food poisoning cases each year in the United States. Opponents of irradiation note that it destroys nutrients and that the process exposes workers to excessive amounts of cobalt, which, over time, could lead to health problems. Eventually, acceptance of this process will be determined by the consumer, who will decide if the benefits of pest-free foods outweigh the potential risks.

Gathering and Recalling Information

- During the process of irradiation of food what do gamma rays kill?
- How many people in the United States develop food poisoning each year?

Making Sense of Gathered Information

- Why would workers at food irradiation facilities be exposed to larger amounts of cobalt than other workers?
- Why is it necessary to kill insects that may be present in food?

Applying and Evaluating Actions in Novel Situations

- How could food-producing procedures be changed so that irradiation would not be necessary?
- Why would food processors refrain from adding nutrients that may be lost in the irradiation process?

Questions in the first category involve the students in *gathering and recalling information*. In responding to these questions, they are required to name, define, observe, match, select, and describe important information. Answers to these questions can be taken directly from the reading material. The second category of questions, *making sense of gathered information*, contains questions that ask students to form relationships between concepts presented; this is done through summarizing, identifying cause and effect, classifying, organizing, and forming analogies. Questions in the third category, *applying and evaluating actions in novel situations*, ask students to use the information they have gathered to predict, plan, hypothesize, and evaluate new situations. Providing students the opportunity to engage in higher order thinking through responding to questions from Costa's Levels 2 and 3 fosters their ability to reason about what they read.

The majority of questions teachers ask involve gathering and recalling information. Gall (1970), for example, found that about 60% of questions teachers ask are fact questions, 20% are procedural questions (e.g., What page do we start on?), and only 20% are higher level thinking questions. Findings such as these may help explain why students experience difficulty engaging in higher level questions—limited practice or exposure to these types of questions certainly reduces students' ability to engage in higher level thinking. Recognize that factual questions, or those involving gathering information, should not be eliminated but should be used to ultimately support higher level thinking, and that questions from Levels 2 and 3 should be asked with greater frequency.

Sequencing Questions.   Well-designed questions fit together in a sequence. Most often, this sequence includes questions from all three levels. However, sometimes it may be best to concentrate only on questions at the higher levels. At other times, Level 1 questions may be emphasized, perhaps to establish a base from which to reason about the material. Even if only Level 1 questions are asked, it is important to sequence them carefully, according to the concepts on which students are to focus. A well-planned sequence of Level 1 questions can foster insight (Good & Brophy, 1987), as seen in the following example.

Unsequenced Questions

1. When did people in the United States begin moving out of large cities and into suburbs?
2. How do people move their households?
3. How many people living on farms during the 1950s left agriculture?
4. How many people lived in the central part of cities in 1950?
5. Where did the people who lived on farms move to?
6. List different types of farms.

Sequenced Questions

1. What was the rate of growth of population in the central cities and the suburbs from 1950 to 1960?
2. What factors drew people to the suburbs from the cities?
3. How was life in the suburbs different from that of cities?

4. With all the people moving to the suburbs, what types of problems soon emerged for the new suburbanites?

The unsequenced questions encourage random collection of facts about moving. They do not build on each other, nor do they lead to a key point. In comparison, the sequenced questions encourage the students to use the facts they collect to think about reasons for moving to the suburbs and the problems that occurred once the suburbs became more populated.

In sequencing questions asked on one or multiple levels, think about the following:

- *The need for students to see connections among questions.* Well-sequenced questions have a logical connection; each question builds toward a final conclusion.
- *The supporting information the students will need to answer each question and whether or not this information should be highlighted through other questions.* For example, if students will be asked to make judgments about the value of two different meals, it may be necessary to first ask them how to determine nutritional content of foods. Supporting information may come from the text or reference sheets, but it may also come from questions posed by the teacher.
- *The highest level thinking the students will use in answering the series of questions.* The main question requiring the highest level of thinking may be asked last or first. Generally, it is asked first if the teacher needs to highlight supporting information through questions.

Pivotal and Emerging Questions.   Sequences of questions cannot be completely planned in advance. Students' responses play a large role in determining question sequence. Sometimes more Level 1 questions need to be addressed than were originally planned. Similarly, sometimes Level 2 and 3 questions need to be clarified, based on students' responses. It has been suggested that teachers write four to five major, or pivotal, questions prior to lessons (Ornstein, 1988). These questions can help keep the lessons focused on the learning objectives. As the students respond, the teacher can formulate emerging questions, or questions that stem from the students' responses to the pivotal questions. Here is an example of a pivotal question and the questions that emerged in a physical education class examining the effects of aerobic exercise.

Teacher: Based on the readings on various types of exercise and the demonstrations we have conducted in class, why would cardiologists recommend that individuals who may be slightly overweight and have very low LDL cholesterol readings engage in some form of aerobic exercise? (Pivotal question)

Student A: As people get older, they need more exercise. Aerobic exercise is good for you.

Student B: Aerobic exercise conditions the body, and as the body is in better condition there is less chance that one will have heart problems associated with high cholesterol.

Teacher: So far you have mentioned that aerobic exercise seems to have some benefits to your body. That is useful information, and it certainly will help us as we try to solve the question I have raised. Let's think about some of the information we read about the relationship between LDL cholesterol levels and exercise. Now, here are two questions we need to think about. First, what is LDL cholesterol? Second, what effect does aerobic exercise have on the body's production of LDL? (Emerging questions)

In this example, the students' initial responses suggested that they were not attending sufficiently to the text information but were instead relying too heavily on their background knowledge. Thus, the teacher presented additional Level 1 questions to direct the students back to the text. Other factors besides lack of attention to the text could influence the choice of emerging questions. These include students' lack of understanding of the material or misinterpretation of it, as indicated in their responses, and students' identification of related topics or lines of reasoning that the teacher had not considered in designing the pivotal questions but that would enrich the lesson.

PRACTICE ACTIVITY 5.1

You are planning a lesson about China with this learning objective: *Students will identify ways in which China can improve its economy.* After students read the following paragraph, you decide to ask one pivotal question. From the list of questions below, select the one that is a pivotal question, given the learning objective. Compare your answer to ours in the answer section at the end of the book.

The growth of industry depends largely on minerals. China has much underground wealth. It ranks high among the countries of the world in coal, tin, and iron ore. However, many of China's mineral resources have not yet been developed. These resources include oil and natural gas.

Source: Theodore Kaltsounis, *The world and its people: States and regions.* Morristown, NJ: Silver Burdett, 1984, p. 183.

1. What is a mineral?
2. How can China become more industrialized?
3. Why do you suppose China has not developed many of its mineral resources?

Suggestions for Classroom Questioning.   There can be no hard-and-fast rules regarding questions to guide students' comprehension and learning; the students' own background knowledge and interest in the subject matter will vary, as will the learning objectives and the subject matter texts. However, there are some general guidelines for asking questions. The ones that follow have been adapted from Grossier (1964) and Wilen (1986).

1. **Ask questions that are clear and specific.** Much time is wasted when students try to respond to such vague questions as "What do you see here?" Although the students should not be directed to the answer by the question, they should receive some direction for their thinking.

"What is the situation here with Josie?" is an example of a rather vague question, as *situation* is a very broad term. A clearer way of phrasing this question would be "What problems is Josie having?" or "What seems to be the cause of Josie's anxiety?"

2. **Ask questions in natural language.** Avoid "textbook" language. Rather, use phrasing that would be common if the question were raised outside the reading assignment.

In asking students to justify their statements, a question like "How do you support your position?" may be too formal. "What evidence do you see for that?" or "Why do you think that is so?" is more natural and thus likely to lead to more natural dialogue.

3. **Engage all students in responding to questions.** Responding to questions engages the students with the material. Encourage all students, even the more reticent ones, to become involved in thinking about responses to questions.

Discussing responses in cooperative groups provides opportunities for more students to participate. Students can compose a group response and in the process ask each other to provide justifications for their contribution, relying on the text as well as their background knowledge. In providing the justifications, students are helped to "put together" more information than they may do when responding directly to a question. The group may consider several alternatives, again something less likely to occur if the students are responding on their own.

4. **Ask questions that encourage more than yes or no answers.** Yes/no questions encourage students to guess and promote impulsive thinking and "right answer" searching rather than conceptual thinking (Ornstein, 1988). They also provide little information to the teacher about mastery of information or understanding.

5. **Provide adequate time for students to respond to questions.** Rowe's (1986) research has pointed to dramatic effects of extending the amount of time that teachers wait at two points: (a) after they ask a question and (b) after students respond. Rowe reports that the typical "wait time" for students to respond to a question or to ask a subsequent question is 1 second. When wait time is extended to 3 seconds, the following changes have been found:

- Students' responses are longer (between 300% and 700%).
- Students are more likely to support inferences with evidence and logical argument.

- Students engage in more speculative thinking.
- Students ask more questions.
- Students talk more among themselves.
- Students' failure to respond decreases.
- Students are more attentive and cooperative.
- More students participate.
- Students appear more confident.
- Teachers ask fewer questions, but those they do ask are more likely to invite the students to provide clarifications or elaborations.

As is true for all suggestions in this section, the use of wait time is flexible. If the goal is drill and practice, a rather quick pace may be appropriate. However, if the goal is for students to reason about the material rather than simply recall it, longer wait times seem especially important (Good & Brophy, 1987).

Commentary: Questions.   Questions can be used to focus students' attention on critical information in the text and direct them to reason with this information and apply it to new situations. Frameworks such as those based on cognitive levels of thinking can help in designing questions that guide students to integrate their background knowledge with the text as they reason about the material.

There are two points to keep in mind when planning instructional questions. First, although questions can help students focus on relationships, the relationships they are likely to identify are those suggested by the questions rather than those they identify on their own. At times, therefore, the questions may constrain the ways in which the students reason about the text. For example, in reading a text that describes a computer program, students may focus only on its disadvantages if they are asked to list cautions about buying the program.

Later in the chapter, we offer alternatives to asking questions. These are not suggested as a way to totally eliminate questions, but as a means to encourage students to respond more fully to the text.

The second point concerns the overreliance on teacher-generated questions. Proficient readers generate their own questions to keep track of their comprehension. Besides answering questions, then, students need to learn to ask them, a difficult endeavor for many. Procedures for teaching question generation will be covered in the section "Activities to Promote Independent Reading." Before then, however, we will present teacher-directed activities that use questioning to help students understand and learn particular subject matter from reading material.

Recitation and Discussion

Recitation.   Recitation is a question-answer/teacher-student exchange. Each question has a predetermined correct answer. In a typical recitation, the teacher asks the questions, the students provide the answers, and the teacher evaluates the answers. As a result, the teacher talks approximately two thirds of the time (Dillon, 1988). Purposes of recitation, as outlined by Dillon (1988), are listed here. As can be seen, they mainly involve assessing students' grasp of information.

Increase participation   Drill and practice
Check homework   Quiz
Introduce new material   Lead up to a point
Probe   Challenge
Solidify knowledge

Student Involvement in Recitation.   Recitation is used quite often in classrooms. For example, Gage and Berliner (1984) note that one third of instructional time in math and social studies classes is devoted to recitation. Although recitations have several advantages, such as in assessing mastery of factual material, they can limit students' input. One way to increase students' engagement in recitations is to have students respond in cooperative groups. Another way is to have students generate questions that are then used along with those developed by the teacher. Dillon (1988) suggests the following instructional process:

1. **Preparation.** In the first stage, the students are instructed to write five questions that can be answered from information in the text. For at least four of the five questions, the students also write answers; they can write one question for which they truly do not know the answer. The teacher also writes recitation questions.

2. **Exchange.** At this point, a student asks one of his or her questions, selects another student to answer the question, then evaluates the answer. The student who answered the question asks his or her question, and the process continues. Other students may offer their answers or similar questions. A rigid sequence of ask, answer, evaluate does not need to be adhered to strictly. The teacher's main task is to listen for what the students understand about the text, as revealed in their questions and answers. However, the teacher can also make connections among questions, suggest different answers and evaluations, as well as different ways to pose the questions. Students, too, can make suggestions for ways of stating questions more clearly; this gives them valuable experience in thinking about the wording of questions.

3. **Quiz.** The teacher now asks questions, either orally or in writing. If the quiz is written, the teacher's first question becomes number six on the students' papers so that their own questions are part of the quiz. The teacher's questions can focus the students' attention on points that their questions omitted. The students can either answer the questions on the spot or at a later time.

4. **Evaluation.** Evaluation by the teacher most likely occurs throughout the question-asking and -answering process, especially during Phases 2 and 3, and also after the lesson. An important part of evaluation involves commenting on the questions that the students have asked. This should help them learn and

study on their own by asking questions. For example, the teacher can point out the value of asking questions about main ideas and comment on those questions that do so.

The student-generated questioning approach to recitation is highly recommended because it involves the students with the text in more depth than occurs in typical teacher-led recitations.

Recitations can well serve the purposes listed earlier. In addition, they can be a useful means for gaining students' attention and increased participation. This approach does have drawbacks, the main one being the emphasis on correct responses. For some questions, this is appropriate. If overused, however, the focus on correct answers can restrict students' creativity (Bellon, Bellon, & Blank, 1992), as well as their reasoning about the information and search for relationships.

While recitations commonly focus on factual-level questions (Costa's Level 1), discussions focus on higher level thinking (Costa's Levels 2 and 3) and encourage students to use their textbooks as more than fact sources. Recitation questions have predetermined correct answers; discussion questions generally do not. According to Dillon (1988),

> The source of the answer does not lie in the teacher, text, lesson, or assignment; the content of the answer is not predetermined, and its rightness is not foreordained. There may or may not exist a "right" answer; there is at least more than one answer that is right; the student is to get some right or useful answer (rather than the one right answer); and there may be different right answers for various students (rather than one and the same right answer for all students). (p. 126)

Through discussion, students become more responsible for understanding concepts (Alvermann, Dillon, & O'Brien, 1987). Guidelines for conducting discussions are presented in the next section.

Discussion.   Discussion has at least the following three criteria (Alvermann et al., 1987):

1. Discussants present multiple points of view and then must be ready to change their minds after hearing convincing counterarguments.
2. The students must interact with each other as well as with the teacher.
3. A majority of the verbal interactions, especially those resulting from questions that solicit student opinions, must be longer than the typical two to three word phrases found in recitation. (p. 3)

Use of Texts in Discussions.   Alvermann, Dillon, O'Brien, and Smith (1985) have identified different ways that teachers use textbooks in discussions, and the advantages and disadvantages of each. The first use is for *verification*. Students can be guided in the use of the text to check the accuracy of what they say or to back up their points. Verification can help students differentiate between directly stated and inferred information, thus helping them identify instances in which they may be overrelying on background knowledge.

If verification is overused, however, it can curtail students' independent thinking.

The second use is for *indirect reference,* or clues, which can help students compare and contrast present and past information. It is important to employ this if students can recall the correct information but are unsure of the material in the text.

Refocusing discussions, the third and most frequent use of the text, keeps the discussion centered on the learning objectives. Care must be taken, however, to emphasize students' ability to draw on their own knowledge and problem-solving abilities, rather than placing too much importance on the text.

The fourth use of the text is for *paraphrasing.* Paraphrasing, Alvermann and colleagues point out, can help students feel more confident about their responses and can aid their comprehension and recall of the material. Again, students should be encouraged to draw on their own knowledge.

Finally, teachers can have students keep their *books closed,* recalling text information rather than referring to it during discussion. Such *closed book* exercises can encourage reading in preparation for discussion as well as assessment. One problem with a closed book discussion, however, is that it may deter students from thinking critically about the material as they focus on remembering the information.

Although it may seem that the disadvantages cancel out the advantages of each use of the text, this does not have to be the case. Taking into consideration all of the uses presented, there are several general guidelines for deciding how to use the text. First, try to establish a balance between textbook information and students' own background knowledge. Second, encourage students to become more aware of different ways they can use the text in their contributions to discussions. They can be asked to identify the sources of their answers as well as whether using those sources is warranted, given the question asked.

Besides considering how to use the text for discussion, it is important to think about which sections of the text to use. Alvermann et al. (1987) make several suggestions for using the textbook to support the discussion's purpose. If the purpose of the discussion is to focus on ideas that are counterintuitive to what the students think, then it is important to use the portion of text containing these new ideas. For example, a text that explains the reason water droplets form on the outside of a glass containing a cool liquid most likely will challenge students' conceptions that somehow the moisture is coming from the liquid inside the glass, not from the humidity in the air. If the purpose is issue oriented, the portion of the text selected for the discussion should stimulate thinking about that issue. If the discussion will focus on a problem (initiated by the teacher or by students), the part of the text that links with the problem should be used.

Use of Text Structure in Recitation and Discussion.   The organization or structure of the text itself can be used to guide students' understanding of reading material. Teachers can use questions that correspond to structures to develop questions for the class (Anthony & Raphael, 1989). These questions can focus the students' search for answers to recitation questions and help them justify their responses to discussion questions. Students can also be taught patterns of questions that correspond to structures (e.g., Piccolo, 1987; Raphael, Kirschner, & Englert, 1986); they then can use these questions to guide their independent reading as well as their writing.

There are five common expository text structures. The first is *description*, or "a grouping of ideas by association" (Richgels, McGee, & Slaton, 1989, p. 168), as exemplified in this paragraph.

> In the near future buildings will be heated by energy produced within a structure, or "free heat." This is heat that is produced by people's bodies, the lights in the building, and the equipment that uses energy in the building, such as refrigeration, electrical appliances, and computers. While this source of heat isn't free—there is a cost involved in running the equipment generating the heat—it is existing heat that can be stored and used when heating equipment normally would be turned on to warm a building.

The second structure is *collection*; here, ideas are grouped by order.

> There are a number of ways to reduce energy used for illuminating buildings. First, sunlight can be employed as a source of illumination. Buildings in Japan now have fiber-optic cables that carry sunlight throughout the structures. Second, photosensitive sensors can be used to operate blinds, constantly adjusting them to maintain a certain level of light. Third, reflectors can be placed on windows to direct light to locations within a building.

Causation, the third structure, emphasizes causal connections between ideas.

> A rather cost-effective procedure for reducing the energy consumption of a building is to shade it with trees and shrubs and paint it a light color. At a temperature of 85 degrees Fahrenheit a light-colored building that is shaded by trees causes the reflection of the sun's rays to the point of reducing the energy needed for cooling by about 300%.

The fourth structure is *problem/solution*. The ideas expressed in the solution are a result of the problem.

> The biggest problem in reducing home energy consumption is increasing the energy efficiency of lighting and refrigeration. One low-cost solution is to replace incandescent lighting with fluorescent lighting, which consumes 75% to 85% less electricity than incandescent sources. Another solution is to purchase one of the new line of highly efficient refrigerators, which, on average, consume 80% to 90% less electricity than conventional models.

The fifth structure is *comparison/contrast*, in which similarities and differences between elements or ideas are noted.

> Energy conservation can be achieved through more prudent use and application of technology. While prudent use is an individual decision and may require changes

in one's lifestyle, the application of technology normally involves the outlay of capital to obtain immediate reduction in the consumption of energy. Long-term, radical reduction in energy consumption will require more widespread prudent use and application of technology.

Figure 5.2 presents questions based on the different text structures.

Text structures can be used to develop questions when the text is well structured or when it is more loosely organized. Many students, however, are unfamiliar with these structures. During class discussions and recitations, the teacher can generate questions that direct students to the text structures listed here and draw students' attention to clue words in the text that often signal the existence of structures embedded in the text.

Alternatives to Questions.   You do not have to be limited to asking questions in discussions. The following alternatives to teacher questions can be used to stimulate students' thinking, to foster discussion, and to model appropriate discussion behaviors (Dillon, 1988).

1. **Make statements.** There are several kinds of statements that can be made during discussion. The first is a *declarative statement;* rather than asking a

---

FIGURE 5.2   TEXT STRUCTURE QUESTIONS

Description

- What is being described?
- What did we learn about it?

Collection

- What happened first, second, last, etc.?

Causation

- What happened?
- What were the reasons for . . . ?
- What caused . . . ?

Problem/Solution

- Was there a problem? What was it?
- What was the solution to the problem?

Comparison/Contrast

- What was being compared?
- What are the similarities?
- What are the differences?

---

question after a student makes a contribution, state a "prequestion" thought, or a thought that would have stimulated your question. For example, rather than asking students if there is a difference between two candidates' positions on a certain issue, you can state that Candidate B claims that his position is the same as that of Candidate A. Declarative statements provide information to the students, ask them to think about the information in some way, and are open for them to respond to. The second kind is a *reflective restatement* in which you state, in one sentence, what you understand the speaker to have said ("So you are saying that Candidate A would be likely to veto a bill for stronger pollution control"). This typically encourages the student to elaborate on his or her original thought. A *statement of mind* is the third kind of discussion statement. This type includes statements about being confused, lost, distracted, or muddled. A statement of mind invites a student to clarify what he or she is saying; "I don't understand why the candidate's past voting record would predict such a veto" is an example. The fourth kind is a *statement of interest.* The interest may be in the student's reasoning, how he or she is defining something, or may call for examples ("Give us an example of what the candidate has said or done that makes her such a strong environmentalist"). *Student referral* involves making connections between what students are saying through such teacher comments as "John's point about her voting record provides evidence for Joanne's argument that the candidate does not vote along party lines." Finally, a *teacher rendition* statement involves sharing your own knowledge, experience, or feelings about the topic at hand. This in turn can stimulate the students to do the same. It is an excellent way of demonstrating or modeling thinking processes, as in the following: "One thing that always comes to my mind when I try to select a candidate is how her stand on education will affect the opportunities I can provide for the students in my classes."

2. **Encourage student questions.** Generally, students do not ask questions in classroom discussions. Encouraging them to do so can deepen their involvement with the material as well as with their classmates. Dillon (1988) points out that students' answers to questions asked by their classmates are longer and more complex than their answers to questions asked by the teacher. You can encourage *speaker's questions;* the student speaker who expressed confusion can be asked to pose a question. Besides providing classmates with a question to ponder, the student may begin to work through his or her confusion while formulating the question. You can then repeat the question and comment on it ("That question really gets at the main argument the author is making, which is difficult for me to understand"). You can also encourage *class questions* by asking if anyone in the class has been thinking about an issue raised by a fellow student and has a question about it. Finally, you can encourage *discussion questions.* With these, students are invited to suggest questions that should be pursued. For example, you can ask, "Given what we have discussed today about the advantages of no-fault insurance, what should we explore tomorrow? Why should we discuss that?"

3. **Use signals.** The function of signals is to encourage a student speaker to continue. One type are *phatics*, short phrases that convey feeling about the

topic or about what the student has said ("That's amazing, astonishing, surprising!"). The second are *fillers,* words or sounds that show the student you are interested ("I see," or "Hmm"). The third are *passes,* by which you indicate that it continues to be a particular student's turn to talk (through gestures or moving on to another student).

4. **Maintain silence.** As previously discussed, wait time can enrich students' contributions during discussions. Those few extra seconds of silence can encourage much more contribution from students.

Commentary: Recitation and Discussions.   While recitations can help students review and consolidate factual material, they can inhibit higher level thinking. Such thinking can be fostered, however, in well-run discussions. Initiating and maintaining discussions can be difficult. There is less teacher control, more ambiguity, and more on-the-spot decision making than in recitations. Since there usually are no "right" answers, it is sometimes quite challenging to weave students' interpretations and opinions together to keep the discussion flowing. An atmosphere of trust and encouragement of risk taking in the class is needed for discussion to be successful. If students understand that the goal of participation is not always to identify the correct answer but to share and justify their thoughts on a topic, and if they understand that their contributions are listened to and respected, they will be more likely to participate.

Recitation and discussion are methods to help students structure and organize textual information. The next instructional activity, the use of study guides, is another way in which you can help students reason.

PRACTICE ACTIVITY 5.2

The graphic organizer, found in Figure 5.3, is designed to highlight important points in the past sections on recitation and discussion. Complete the outline, adding to or modifying it so that it will be most helpful to you in reviewing and consolidating these sections. A completed organizer is found in the answers section.

Study Guides

Study guides are teacher-generated questions and activities that the students respond to during reading (Wood, Lapp, & Flood, 1992). Important concepts and information are highlighted as students read, rather than after they have finished. Research (Andre, 1987; Hamaker, 1986) has pointed to the positive effects of questions throughout the text on students' comprehension of the material. In addition to helping students comprehend the material, study guides can develop their metacognitive control of reading by signaling them to alter

FIGURE 5.3   RECITATION AND DISCUSSION

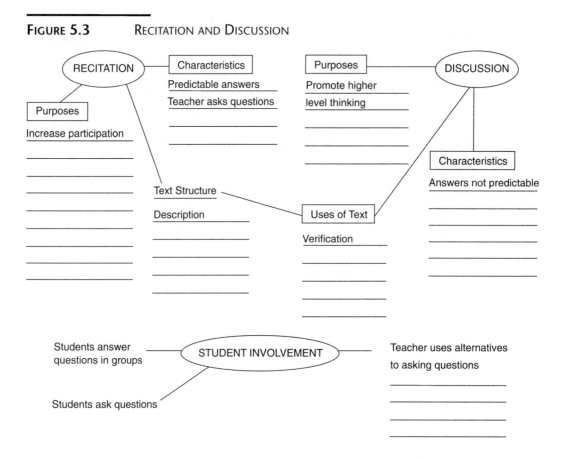

their reading rate, check for understanding, and think about what information is important (Wood, 1987).

Three conditions that make a study guide effective have been identified by Herber (in Wood et al., 1992):

1. The focus of a study guide is on the content of the material as well as on the processes of reading it. Thus, students learn the material and learn how to learn.
2. A guide supports students in their thinking about the material at more difficult levels than they could do on their own. If students can understand and apply the material on their own, a study guide is not needed.
3. A study guide can be used cooperatively by students. Although a guide can sometimes be valuable for independent work (preparing for class discussion, reviewing for a test), it is quite adaptable to group work. While completing a guide, students can support each other as they think about and apply the material in the text.

To make a study guide most beneficial, it is important to explain its purpose and demonstrate how it should be used (Wood, 1988).

There are many kinds of study guides. Determining which to use depends on the learning objectives, the nature of the text, and the students' preparedness to learn the material. The next section has descriptions of several different types of study guides. Following these are general considerations for developing guides appropriate for particular lessons.

Three-Level Study Guide. The three-level study guide (Herber, 1978) uses levels of comprehension seen in Costa's taxonomy: gathering and recalling information, making sense of gathered information, and applying and evaluating actions in novel situations. Each level has statements. To complete the guide, students identify which of the statements are supported in the reading material and discuss the evidence for their selections. An example of a three-level study guide is given in Figure 5.4.

To prepare the three-level guide, Herber recommends the following:

1. **Analyze content.** Read the material and determine the main ideas. Next, determine which information is critical for grasping these ideas. Then look for relationships among the information and between the material and students' background knowledge that will also aid in developing the principles. Finally, identify applications of the material.

2. **Use declarative statements.** Prepare the study guide, presenting statements students are to agree or disagree with. Level 1 statements can be supported by material found directly in the text. To support Level 2 statements, students need to put ideas together. To support Level 3 statements, students will need to rely heavily on their background knowledge in applying and extending the material in the text.

Textbook Activity Guide. A textbook activity guide (TAG, Davey, 1986) contains a variety of questions and activities about the subject matter, cues about the processes to use to respond to these, and a self-monitoring component. Students work in pairs using strategy and self-monitoring codes to complete the guide. Each question or activity directs the student to the relevant pages in the text. Davey (1986, pp. 490–491) suggests the following strategy and self-monitoring codes, although others can be substituted:

Strategy Codes

P = Discuss with your partner.
WR = Provide a written response on your own.
Skim = Read quickly for the purpose stated; discuss with your partner.
Map = Complete a semantic map of the information.
PP = Predict with your partner.

Self-Monitoring Codes

I understand this information.
I'm not sure if I understand.
I do not understand and I need to restudy.

FIGURE 5.4   THREE-LEVEL STUDY GUIDE FOR "A JONQUIL FOR MARY PENN"

Directions: *Check the sentence or sentences that best answer each question.*

Gathering and Recalling Information: What are some of the qualities or attributes of Elton Penn?

_____ 1. Elton raised horses.

_____ 2. Elton was a rather independent individual—he started his own farm at the age of fourteen.

_____ 3. Elton had a good sense of humor.

_____ 4. Elton was sensitive to the needs of his wife, Mary.

_____ 5. Elton worked hard and played hard—he lived life to its fullest.

Making Sense of Gathered Information: What did the author mean to say about life in the farmland of America during the Great Depression?

_____ 1. People were much more sensitive to the needs of their community and family.

_____ 2. Most farmers were well off and had considerable time for leisure activities.

_____ 3. The spirit of community and dedication to the land gave people assets other than money.

_____ 4. Some of Mary's strongest and most pleasant emotions came from the simple things in her life.

Applying and Evaluating Actions in Novel Situations: The theme of this story applied to our daily lives today would suggest that

_____ 1. People are often distracted from their true inner emotions by the demands of their daily lives.

_____ 2. You can't earn respect for yourself if you are unable to be compassionate and sensitive to those around you.

_____ 3. We really don't have a need for community in today's fast-paced world.

_____ 4. Some of our most pleasant experiences are gained from relatively simple pleasures.

Source: Berry, W. (1992). A jonquil for Mary Penn. *The Atlantic, 269*(2), 73–84.

Only parts of the text relevant to the learning objectives are focused on in the TAG, and only the strategy codes applicable to the tasks are suggested. An example of a TAG for a chapter on bluegrass music is given in Figure 5.5.

The following procedure is recommended for developing a TAG (Davey, 1986):

1. Identify the learning objectives.
2. Identify sections of the text, headings, diagrams, and so on, that are relevant to the learning objectives.
3. Select and sequence parts of the text that will be used in the TAG.
4. Select a study guide task that corresponds with each objective. Some objectives are best met by having the students discuss among themselves, others by drawing a diagram, still others by listing.

FIGURE 5.5 TEXTBOOK ACTIVITY GUIDE

Strategy Codes

P = Discuss with your partner.
WR = Provide a written response on your own.
Map = Complete a semantic map of the information.
PP = Predict with your partner.

Self-Monitoring Codes

√ I understand this information.
? I'm not sure if I understand.
X I do not understand and I need to restudy.

1. _____ PP Pages 332–340. Look over the headings, pictures, and charts. What do you think you will learn about in this chapter?

2. _____ P Pages 332–335. Read the first two sections and discuss the most important information in each.

3. _____ WR,P Pages 337–338. Read the third section and jot down the differences between bluegrass and country music.

4. _____ WR Pages 338–340. Read the fourth section and answer the question at the end. Be prepared to discuss your answer.

5. _____ Map With your partner, make an outline of the development of bluegrass music.

6. _____ P Page 340. With your partner, listen to the two songs on the tape. Which most clearly is an example of bluegrass music? What is your opinion of this song?

5. Identify a strategy code that signals how to respond to each question and activity. Sometimes more than one strategy code may be used for particular tasks. Write the tasks, strategy codes, and lines for the students to self-monitor on the guide.

Students complete the guide together, then check their work against an answer key. They can also discuss their responses with you, with other pairs of students, or with the whole class.

Collaborative Listening-Viewing Guide.   The collaborative listening-viewing guide (reviewed in Wood et al., 1992) is designed to help students take notes and reason about information they view or listen to, for example, a presentation or videotape. It is completed individually, in small groups, and as a class. There are five phases in completing the guide, as follows:

1. **Preview/Review.** In this phase, background knowledge is accessed or built. This can occur through brainstorming, teacher-directed vocabulary instruction, or any relevant prereading activities (adapted for listening or viewing). Students write the important previewed or reviewed information on their forms.
2. **Record.** As students watch or listen to the presentation, they individually write down brief notes about important ideas or events.
3. **Elaborate.** Students work in small groups to organize the notes they have taken and to add details to them.
4. **Synthesize.** As a whole class, students work together to identify and discuss the main concepts of the presentation. As in all phases, they record their conclusions on the form.
5. **Extend.** In pairs, students apply the information learned. This may be done in a variety of ways, including writing summary paragraphs, making semantic maps of the information, and identifying further research questions they would like to explore.

Graphic Organizers.   Recall that a graphic organizer (discussed in Chapter Four) is a pictorial representation of relationships. Used before reading, a graphic organizer can provide students with clues about how the material is structured; used during reading, it can serve as a study guide to focus the students' attention on important information and relationships. Students can complete and modify the graphic organizer as they read; in this way, the organizer can frame discussions about the text. The organizer can also be completed and modified in small groups in which students have to explain and justify the relationships they have identified. As with the other forms of study guides, students can complete the graphic organizer independently, in preparation for group discussion or review of the material they have read.

A graphic organizer can be combined with questions to focus attention on relationships. Before reading, students can be given a question that involves their reasoning about the material in the text. For example, they could be asked to think about the economic as well as the political factors that led to an increase in taxes. To assist them in addressing the question, they can then be given a graphic organizer, partially filled in. As a whole class or in small groups, they complete the organizer as they read.

Text structures can be portrayed in a graphic organizer. Figures 5.6 and 5.7 are sample organizers based on two text structures, problem/solution and description.

Refer to Chapter 4 for suggestions on developing a graphic organizer.

Figure 5.8 offers examples of two other forms for study guides, the questioning guide and the partially completed outline.

FIGURE 5.6   EXAMPLE OF USE OF A FRAME TO PRESENT PROBLEM/SOLUTION TEXT STRUCTURE

Endangered Species Birds' ingestion of DDT results in inability to produce shell for eggs	_____ _____ _____ _____ _____ _____
_____ _____ _____ _____ _____ _____	Provide wilderness habitat far removed from ranchers or farms

---

FIGURE 5.7   EXAMPLE OF DESCRIPTIVE TEXT STRUCTURE WITH CONCEPT MAP STUDY GUIDE

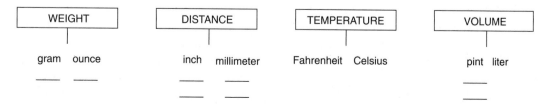

Types of Measurement

| WEIGHT | DISTANCE | TEMPERATURE | VOLUME |

gram   ounce   inch   millimeter   Fahrenheit   Celsius   pint   liter

---

FIGURE 5.8   EXAMPLES OF ALTERNATIVE FORMS OF STUDY GUIDES

Questioning Guide

Directions: *As you read the article on the schooling of black Americans, answer the following questions. Some of the questions ask you to form a response before you read a section of the article; other questions are designed to be answered during or after the reading.*

Before Reading

1. What are some of the obstacles you have encountered that you feel may have had an adverse effect on your education?
2. What role do your family and friends have in your desire to obtain an education? How has your parents' and relatives' level of education affected your desire to go to college or finish high school?

During Reading

1. Read the first two pages of the article. As you are reading, note the explanations provided by the author as to why blacks encounter so many obstacles in obtaining an education.
2. Read the final four pages of the article. Consider this question as you read, and write a response when you have finished the article: The author addresses the need to improve the self-esteem of black students in schools. Note the suggestions she provides, then write a summary of the actions you believe would be effective in improving self-esteem.

After Reading

Interview your school principal or a district administrator to determine what steps have been taken by the district during the past ten years to address some of the issues raised in this article. Based on the information you obtain, draft a plan of action you believe would address the problems raised in this article.

Partially Completed Outline

Directions: *As you read the information on nails and screws, fill in the information in the partially completed outline provided.*

I. Nails
   A. Sizes of Nails
      1. length designated in inches
      2. diameter designated _____
   B. Driving Nails
      1. length of nail should be three times thickness of wood
      2. nail should be driven through the _____ part of the wood
      3. factors that increase holding power of nail:
         a. _____
         b. _____
         c. _____
   C. Function of Nailheads
      1. spread load over surface
      2. _____
      3. _____

FIGURE 5.8   CONTINUED

II. Screws
    A. Sizes of Screws
        1. length designated by _____
        2. size designated by _____
    B. Types of Screws
        1. Dome head
            a. function = decorative screw
        2. _____ screw
            a. function = fasten end-to-end joints
        3. Hanger bolt
            a. function = _____
    C. When to Use Screws
        1. Need to increase fastening power
        2. When things need to be _____

Several factors can guide decisions on whether to employ a study guide and which format to use (Wood et al., 1992). These include

- the concepts, vocabulary, and information that are important to the lesson.
- the difficulty of the material, or portions of it.
- the skills and strategies students will need to understand and learn from the material.
- whether individual, small, or whole group activities are preferred.
- time constraints on both teacher preparation and instruction.

Commentary: Study Guides.   Study guides can focus students' attention on limited aspects of the content; this can be seen as both a positive and negative characteristic. The guides emphasize important ideas and concepts as identified by the teacher and help students organize their reading. Yet in so doing, the guides may inhibit students' own interpretation of the text and discourage them from generating their own questions about the material. Nevertheless, they serve as models for organizing information.

    Study guides can take considerable time and effort to prepare. An alternative to teacher-made study guides or graphic organizers are student-generated guides done in cooperative groups. Initially, the teacher shares his or her thinking in creating a guide, emphasizing the relationship of the text to the learning objective and the way in which he or she searches for important concepts in the text. Next, the teacher and students create a guide together; finally, the students, in groups, create guides for their peers. Each group can make a guide for a separate section of the text, or all groups can focus on the same section and compare the ways in which they reasoned about it. Besides reducing teacher preparation time, student-generated guides facilitate higher level thinking as the students look for important concepts and discuss these in their groups. A final benefit is the opportunity for assessment of the students' ability to identify the important points of the material. Recitation, discussion, and study guides have been presented as instructional activities to be used in guiding students to learn from and reason about subject matter content. Through the use of these activities, teachers can help students organize information. The activities also suggest ways in which students can reason about the material by examining relationships between text information and their prior knowledge.

The preceding sections have included suggestions for encouraging student responsibility for their learning. In the remainder of the chapter, the focus will be on instructional activities that prepare students to become independent learners who can reason about and learn from text in subject matter areas.

HOW PROFICIENT READERS COMPREHEND TEXT

Comprehension is a process in which readers attend to the information in the text and use this, together with their background knowledge, to construct meaning. Proficient readers know their purposes for reading, keep track of whether the purposes are being met, and take action if they are not. They accomplish this by using strategies, or plans of action, that they apply according to the demands of the reading tasks. Proficient readers know a number of strategies, know when and where to use those strategies, are motivated to use strategies, and have ample background knowledge to profit from strategy use (Pressley, Snyder, & Carigula-Bull, 1987). They continually modify the strategies they select and how they use them according to their personal characteristics as readers (background knowledge, interest, value they place on the reading task), the purpose for reading, and the text itself. Following is a more detailed description of strategy use by proficient readers before, during, and after reading, adapted from Jones, Palincsar, Ogle, and Carr (1987). Figure 5.9 offers a summary of the strategic behaviors discussed.

Prior to Reading Behaviors

Prior to reading, proficient readers actively set and/or think about their purposes for reading. Along with this, they activate relevant background knowledge. From their knowledge of the purpose for reading as well as their background knowledge, they develop expectations for what they will find out while reading. These expectations, modified as necessary during the reading process, serve as reading guides. To further guide their reading, proficient readers identify a probable text structure, using titles, headings, introductory paragraphs, and graphics. For example, in an article entitled "First Aid for Cuts and Sprains," the reader can expect a problem/solution text structure, in this case, with several problems and solutions included. Finally, based on knowledge obtained from all of the above sources, proficient readers select reading strategies.

Consider what you, as a proficient reader, do before reading a chapter on the school dropout rate to prepare for an upcoming class discussion. You may skim the chapter, predicting from the headings what the main points of the chapter are and making a mental note to watch for these. For example, you may decide from the headings that the chapter is going to focus on causes of the high dropout rate as well as attempts that have been made across the country to support students' staying in school. You prepare yourself to find out more about each of these topics. You remember a recent news item on the relation of the dropout rate to the overall economy and wonder if this chapter will cover that relationship. In thinking about how best to prepare for the upcoming discussion, you decide to first jot down notes on the main points of the chapter, then select controversial points that you will need to take a stand on in tomorrow's discussion.

During Reading Behaviors

While reading, proficient readers continually use strategies to guide and keep track of their reading (Jones et al., 1987). They check for sense making by using such strategies as asking themselves questions after reading sections of text. As confusing concepts or vocabulary are encountered, they seek clarifications by rereading and checking the context. They continue to use their knowledge of text structure to guide their reading, for example, by looking for an effect when they recognize a cause or looking for solutions when they recognize a problem. At various points, they summarize what they have read. They are continually checking and modifying their predictions as they read.

While you are reading the chapter for tomorrow's discussion, you jot down what you see as the important causes of the dropout rate as well as feasible ways of combating it. You wonder why the chapter does not cover the economy as a cause and look in the table of contents of the book, thinking the

---

FIGURE 5.9   STRATEGIES OF PROFICIENT READERS

Before Reading

Set purposes for reading

Activate relevant background knowledge

Identify probable text structure

Select strategies to use while reading

During Reading

Ask questions

Reread

Check context

Summarize

Check and modify predictions

Following Reading

Confirm or alter predictions

Identify important information

Evaluate comprehension in terms of purposes for reading

relationship to the economy may be covered elsewhere. You begin to formulate questions you would like the class to discuss tomorrow.

Following Reading Behaviors

Finally, following reading, proficient readers continue to confirm or alter their predictions. They work to assimilate or accommodate their background knowledge with the text. Based on their purposes for reading, they identify important information and evaluate their comprehension (Jones et al., 1987), determining whether or not they have met their purposes. If they have not met their purposes, they may decide to consult alternative sources.

Even though the information from the news item was not in the chapter, you decide to share it with the class, connecting it to one of the attempts to decrease the dropout rate. You skim back over the chapter's headings, thinking about the main points in each section. If you cannot remember them, you reread. You continue to refine questions and ideas you would like to share with the class tomorrow.

PRACTICE ACTIVITY 5.3

To make the activities of a proficient reader more understandable, contrast the scenarios presented on page 150 with the following. Consider how these two readers are proficient and identify the strategies they use.

Richard and Lori

Richard and Lori are members of another group in Paulo and Kim's class. Before beginning reading, they think about what they already know about the Anastasi culture, from a movie and from another chapter the class has read. They list the problem, then generate a set of questions they believe will aid them in their task. They then think about what they need to know to respond to the question. Looking over the reading material, they see a chart on the elevation of the region, as well as a map of water sources. Using these, they jot down several features they think they may learn about. Using a heading, they predict that the text will include a weather description. As they read about the Anastasi and the climate and topography of southwestern Colorado, they encounter several concepts they determine are important but are not well understood due to their limited prior knowledge. To better understand these concepts, they consult an encyclopedia. With a better understanding of these concepts and other information acquired from their reading, they modify their original list of questions, then begin to examine additional sources of information.

ACTIVITIES TO PROMOTE INDEPENDENT READING

Learning about strategies that promote independent learning should occur in the context of actual reading of context area texts. The goal of instruction is for the students to be able to select useful strategies, adapt them to the particular texts they read (Pressley, Johnson, Symons, McGoldrick, & Kurita, 1989), and evaluate their success in doing so. They must learn to employ strategies by actually using them with their subject matter texts, first with the help of the teacher, later independently. By doing this, students see how strategies help them understand that particular content (Peters, 1990). Instruction for proficient reading can be framed by the following guidelines:

1. Focus on strategies that are truly helpful for meeting the goals of real tasks in content area learning.
2. Help students learn the strategies while they are also learning the content so they will understand the value of the strategies.
3. Incorporate discussion and sharing of strategies into instruction.

The teaching process to help students develop the ability to use strategies for independent reading follows.

Selecting Strategies to Teach

There are many strategies used by proficient readers. The type of strategy used for a given text depends on the purpose for reading, the characteristics of the reader, and the characteristics of the text. Some texts lend themselves to certain strategies. For example, the strategies used in reading a newspaper editorial differ from those used in reading a novel. The task of reading to study for a test differs from that of reading to get an idea for a term paper, so do the strategies used for completing these tasks. If a text has a clear structure, such as a fairy tale, strategies involving predictions based on text structure can be used. Yet if the text is disorganized and without clear structure, this strategy would not be as helpful.

Students with little background knowledge about particular subject matter will use different approaches to understanding the text than will those who have the ability to connect information in the text to information previously learned. Strategy use is also a matter of personal preference; students should be encouraged to use strategies that work for them.

Palincsar (1986) presents three useful guidelines to follow in selecting strategies to teach. The first guideline is ease of instruction. If teaching a strategy is too complicated, students will not be able to attend to the content they are using the strategy with and thus will not see its value. The second guideline is flexibility of the strategy. Strategies that can be used across a wide variety of reading situations should be taught. The third guideline is use of the strategy for comprehension monitoring, or helping students determine whether or not they are understanding and learning.

By considering the general guidelines and the particular students, the particular text, and the purpose for reading it, strategies for instruction can be identified. Sharing reasons with the students for selecting particular strategies can serve as a model for them in choosing those they will use in their independent reading and studying.

PRACTICE ACTIVITY 5.4

As an example of the personal use of strategies, identify strategies you use when reading to prepare for a report. Do you outline the material, put it on index cards, use color coding? In a small group, share your strategies. It is likely that you and your peers have developed systems that are useful yet quite different.

Teaching for Independent Strategy Use

Instruction for proficient independent reading can be seen as fitting the model of gradual release of responsibility (Pearson & Gallagher, 1983). In this model, the teacher's role can be seen along a continuum of directiveness. When students are first learning strategies, the teacher provides *direct, explicit instruction*. As the students begin to use the strategies on their own to guide their reading, the teacher provides *supportive instruction*, giving them the help they need to use the strategies while reading particular texts. Through this process, the students move toward independent use of the strategies to direct their reading.

Following is a closer examination of direct, explicit instruction and supportive instruction of comprehension activities.

Explicit Instruction.   The teacher provides explicit information to students about comprehension strategies through explanations and mental modeling. The teacher then talks about and demonstrates the thinking processes that he or she uses while working through a text.

Explanations.   Too often, students' and teachers' understandings of the purpose of lessons do not coincide. Perhaps one of the reasons for this is that the purpose has not been clearly explained to the students (Roehler & Duffy, 1986). Roehler and Duffy (1991) define explanations as explicit statements about what is being learned, why it is being learned, why it can be used, and how to use it. Students need to learn the what, why, when, and how of strategy use (Paris, Lipson, & Wixon, 1983) if the goal is for them to use these strategies on their own to control their reading and learning. Here is an example of an explanation about self-questioning using headings that was given to seventh graders in a science class.

Today we are going to learn about a way to check our understanding of what we are reading [what is being learned]. We will use the headings to form questions before we reach each section and then see if we can answer those questions [when to use it]. As you know, headings often give us clues about what the important information in the sections will be. By turning those headings into questions, we can focus our attention on the important upcoming information. Learning the important information will prepare us for understanding upcoming sections. Answering the questions will help us know whether we are understanding the important information. I have found this quite helpful to me in keeping track of my understanding [why it is being learned]. This is a strategy that can be used in any books or articles that have headings [when it can be used]. To use this strategy, we think about the information that the heading tells us is likely to be in the next section, and use one or two question words to begin questions about this information that we think will be answered from reading the section. When we have read the section, we will try to answer the questions [how to use it].

PRACTICE ACTIVITY 5.5

What kinds of information (what, why, when, how) does the teacher include in this explanation of the use of summarizing? What is missing?

Today we will be learning about summarizing chapters. There are three steps in summarizing that you can follow. First, identify important information. Second, put the information in categories. Third, write two to three sentences for each category.

Compare your answer to that in the answer section at the end of the book.

Students can be invited to expand upon the teacher's explanations. In most cases, they will be at least familiar with the strategies introduced by the teacher. Just as it is important to help students activate their background knowledge about subject matter, it is also important to bring to the forefront what they know about strategic approaches to reading. Not only will this prepare them to learn more about strategies, but it will also prompt them to think about ways in which strategies can and do help them to be more proficient in their reading.

Mental Modeling.   Another means of providing information to students is through mental modeling, or thinking aloud. Mental modeling refers to the teacher explaining what he or she is doing, focusing on the reasoning involved while carrying out the task (Roehler & Duffy, 1991). The teacher thinks aloud about strategies as he or she uses them to understand text, sharing with the students thoughts about selecting, using, and evaluating the strategies. Mental modeling differs from explanation in that it occurs while the teacher is actually using the strategy. Like explanations, mental modeling makes the reasoning involved in strategy use clear. In the following example, the seventh-grade teacher models his reasoning while using text structure to identify important information in a selection on mail fraud.

(*Before reading*): I really hope I learn something from this text, as I saw the tail end of a television show on this subject. The commentator was saying that millions of dollars are lost every year through mail fraud and that there are important steps we can take to prevent this from happening. I would like to know what we can do.

(*After reading the first paragraph*): I now understand more about what mail fraud is and who can be affected by it. It sure is a problem. I am expecting, given the title of this article, *Saving Americans From Falling Victims to Mail Fraud*, that I'm going to learn about some solutions to this problem. I sure hope I do. I know in an article like this, once a problem is stated, a solution is often suggested. I sure hope I'm right about this article. I'm going to read to find solutions and jot them down as I come across them to help me remember how I can prevent fraud.

(*While reading*): Here is something I think is a solution: Call the Better Business Bureau if you don't receive what you ordered within eight weeks. I'll bet the people at the bureau could track down the problem. I wonder if we'll read about their track record.

In the above example, the teacher not only was modeling his thinking about what strategy he would use and why he would use it, he was also modeling his use of background knowledge to make predictions and set a purpose for reading. Mental modeling provides a wonderful opportunity to share the reasoning about strategy use in a natural, realistic context.

PRACTICE ACTIVITY 5.6

Thinking aloud can be quite awkward at first. You are expected to explain processes that are often automatic. A metaphor for this is explaining to a new driver how and why you do what you do when you operate a stick shift. To think aloud, you need to become used to examining your own thinking. A good way to do this is to examine what you are doing to understand text while in the process of reading it. For this activity, read an upcoming section of this chapter. While reading it, tape record or jot down the strategies you find yourself using and what you are thinking while using these strategies. Share the experience of completing this activity in small groups, focusing on the strategies you identified as well as the experience of paying attention to your thinking.

Supportive Instruction.   As students become better able to use reading strategies, instruction becomes less directive and more supportive. This support can take the form of guided questions that help students become more aware of how, why, and when to use strategies. For example, you may ask: "What do you know about section headings and, using that knowledge, what do you think we will learn in this chapter?" You can also provide on-the-spot modeling of the use of a strategy in a particular reading situation, as in the following:

The heading indicated we were going to learn to distinguish between Impressionist and Post-Impressionist paintings. I'm not sure I can do that, though. Sometimes it helps me to stop and review. Let's see: How are the two styles alike and how are they different?

Another way to provide support is by offering feedback on the way understanding is affected by the use of a strategy, as in the following:

> Those questions you asked about drilling for oil make sense in light of what we learned about coal mining in yesterday's chapter. Oftentimes, chapters in books are structured similarly. The kinds of information we get from one chapter may give us clues about the kinds of information we'll get in the next one.

Peer Support. Peers working together in cooperative or collaborative groups can also provide a means of support (Conley, 1990). Students working cooperatively on such tasks as creating graphic organizers, writing questions, constructing summaries, and generally sharing their reactions to texts have the opportunity to discuss, justify, and question their own approaches. It is important for students to "discuss their goals with others, help one another understand the tasks required, and help one another to work hard" (p. 121).

While reading and thinking about applying the particular instructional activities to teach independent proficient reading in the next section, consider ways in which cooperative groups could be used to help move the students toward independent strategic reading. The activities presented next are text structure instruction, summarizing, self-questioning, reciprocal teaching, and content processing guides.

Text Structure Instruction

Recall the discussion of the different types of text structures and their use in designing questions and constructing graphic organizers. Text structures can also be used to help students comprehend, remember, and learn from text (Flood, Lapp, & Farnan, 1986; McGee & Richgels, 1985; Piccolo, 1987). Using the structure of texts, students can predict what they will read and ask questions to organize the information as they read it.

Here are some suggestions, adapted from Piccolo (1987), for encouraging students to use text structure to guide their reading.

1. Write prereading questions that correspond to text structures. Share with the students the ways in which you identified the text structure and used it to develop questions. (Questions based on text structures are given in Figure 5.2.)

2. Model for students how to use headings and subheadings to predict the questions the text will answer or what the content will be. Have them make text structure–based predictions in cooperative groups, then justify these predictions to the class.

3. Instruct students to skim for clue words, or words that signify particular structures (see Figure 5.10). The students can use the signal words and the topic sentence to make predictions about the kinds of information they will learn and to formulate prereading questions. As they read the text, they can jot down the answers to the text structure questions.

Summarizing

Summarizing has been shown to be related to increased comprehension of material, recall of text, vocabulary development, and promotion of critical reading (Hill, 1991; Pearson & Fielding, 1991). It is also an excellent means of keeping track of comprehension during and following reading. Although summarizing is difficult for many students, especially if they are reading poorly structured or complicated texts (Hill, 1991), the benefits make it an important strategy to teach.

Summarizing involves the following rules (Brown & Day, 1983):

1. Delete trivial or unimportant information.
2. Delete redundant information.
3. Categorize information.
4. Identify and use the author's main ideas.
5. Create your own main ideas if they are not stated.

FIGURE 5.10   SIGNAL OR CLUE WORDS THAT CORRESPOND
TO TEXT STRUCTURES

Description

- No specific clue words

Collection

- First, second, third, next, last, finally

Causation

- So, so that, because, as a result of, since, in order to

Problem/Solution

- Problem is, solution, solved by

Comparison/Contrast

- Alike, same as, similar to, resembles, compared to, unlike, different from

---

In teaching summarizing, there is much opportunity for both explicit instruction and mental modeling. There is also ample opportunity to demonstrate to students how writing can enhance reading.

GRASP, or the guided reading and summarizing procedure, is an instructional activity designed to help students learn to write summaries for reports as well as to increase their ability to recall information, self-correct, and organize material. The following is a description of GRASP taken from Hayes (1989):

1. **Getting ready.** Hayes suggests using an article from an encyclopedia to teach summarizing, although any reading material may be used. The teacher tells the students that they are going to learn how to summarize the information, then talks about situations in which this strategy may be valuable. The students are told the procedure for writing a group summary is similar to the procedure they can use on their own.

2. **Reading for information.** The teacher directs the students to read the article and remember all that they can. After reading, the class compiles a list of all information remembered. Next, the students are instructed to reread the material to see if there was any other information that should be on the list and to correct any misinformation.

3. **Organizing remembered information.** At this point, the students and teacher attempt to identify the major topics of the text. The topics are used as categories into which the students and teacher group the recalled information. Following this, they discuss and identify relationships among the categories.

4. **Writing the summary.** The teacher now explains that there are three things to do with the material: (a) put important information in the summary and leave out unnecessary details, (b) combine information if possible, and (c) add information to make the summary coherent. The teacher proceeds to model, turning the first category into a sentence, talking about the selection and combination of information. The students write individual summaries for the next category, as does the teacher. Volunteers read their sentences. The teacher and class discuss the strengths of the volunteers' summaries and compare them to the teacher's summary. The teacher's summary is revised based on the students' alternatives. Hayes suggests that a visible record of the revisions be made by crossing out rather than erasing. This makes the revision process more concrete for the students. The class proceeds through each category in the same fashion until a summary of the entire passage is written. In later lessons, the teacher can focus on revising the summaries even further.

Hayes's procedure focuses on the reasoning involved in summarizing. The teacher's modeling, as well as the group discussion of students' ideas for summaries, can make the thinking processes explicit. Working with a real text, students are exposed to the difficulties involved in summarizing. Figure 5.11 is an example of GRASP.

Summaries can help students study for a test, prepare for a presentation, or, more generally, check their understanding. They should be encouraged to use this strategy informally, jotting an outline of a summary, making an orga-

FIGURE 5.11 **EXAMPLE OF THE GUIDED READING AND SUMMARIZING PROCEDURE (GRASP)**

Trade association is a nonprofit organization that represents a group of business firms. Businesses join their associations voluntarily and manage them cooperatively. The companies work together to accomplish goals that no single firm could reach by itself.

A trade association may have only a few members, as in the ironmaking and steelmaking industry. Or it may have thousands of members, as in an association of retail grocers. The size of the trade association's membership has little to do with the effectiveness of the organization. It is more important that the association include most of the companies in the industry. About 3,600 trade associations operate on the national level in the United States.

Trade association activities include promoting business for the industry, encouraging ethical practices in the industry, cooperating with other organizations, and holding conventions. Such associations also work to obtain good relations with the government, the industry's employees, and the general public.

Trade associations sponsor much of the industrial research work in the United States. This research helps improve the quality of goods and services sold by individual firms. Setting industry standardization is another important trade association activity. By obtaining agreements among firms, the trade association sets standards of size and quality for articles and services.

A trade association acts as a source of information about its industry. It may issue bulletins on business trends and provide statistical information. Some publish magazines that are distributed to the public. Trade associations date back to the guilds formed in Europe during the Middle Ages.

From *The World Book Encyclopedia.* ©1993 World Book, Inc. Reprinted by permission of the publisher.

Details Remembered From the Encyclopedia Article

Students' First Recollections	Additions/Corrections
few or many members	information source
do research	*sponsor* research
3,600 trade unions	work for good relations
have conventions	promote business
encourage ethics	cooperative management
voluntary	represents group of firms
nonprofit	
publish magazines	*some* publish magazines
important to have most companies set standards	

FIGURE 5.11 **CONTINUED**

Organization of Remembered Details

Categories	Grouped Information
Description	represents a group of firms
	nonprofit
	cooperative management
	3,600 trade associations
Membership	few or many members
	important to have most of the companies
	voluntary
Activities	have conventions
	some publish magazines
	information source about industry
	work for good relations with government, employees, and public
	sponsor research
Helpfulness to us	encourage ethics
	set standards

Development of the Completed Summary

The First Group of Details Converted to Prose

Trade associations are ~nonprofit~ organizations ~of groups of~ ~whose members are~ business firms, ~which are cooperatively managed.~

The Second Group of Details Converted to Prose

~The organizations are voluntary, but~ It is important to have most companies in the industry ~belong.~ ~in the association and this can be few or many.~

The Completed Summary, as Revised

Trade associations are ~nonprofit~ organizations ~of group of~ ~whose members are~ business firms, ~which are cooperatively managed,~ ~The organizations are voluntary, but~ It is important to have most companies in the industry ~belong.~ ~in the association and this can be few or many.~ ~Trade associations~ ~They~ serve as ~an~ information source~s~ about the industry ~ies~ and ~they~ promote business, sponsor research, and work for good relations. They ~are helpful to consumers by~ promot~ing~ ~e~ ethics and ~set~ ~setting~ standards of size and quality.

nizer that represents categories and details, or identifying the main categories of information. It is an excellent strategy to work on in small groups; the questions raised as the group composes a summary will force the students to verbalize how they are organizing the material they are reading, an important precursor of their doing this on their own.

Self-Questioning

When self-questioning, students ask themselves questions about the text rather than answering questions asked by the teacher. Students' questions can guide their reading of upcoming sections as well as check on their understanding of what they have already read. Questioning gives them purposes for reading. Many instructional studies (e.g., Andre & Anderson, 1978–1979; Davey & McBride, 1986; Singer & Donlan, 1982) have found increased reading performance after instruction in self-questioning.

Like summarizing, question asking is difficult for many students. For much of their school lives, they have become accustomed to answering rather than asking questions. Students are not likely to become proficient at this if only told to practice (Davey & McBride, 1986). Rather, they need to be taught how to ask questions to guide and check their reading. There are a variety of ways to teach students to ask themselves questions as they read. However self-questioning is taught, it is important to focus on why and how questions are used (Wong, 1985), to model the reasoning involved in question generation, and to provide sufficient opportunities for the students to practice asking questions (Balajthy, 1984). Following are several procedures for helping students develop question asking.

Reciprocal Questioning.   The reciprocal questioning, or ReQuest, procedure (Manzo, 1969) was designed to help students set purposes for reading through questioning but could be extended to help them self-check their understanding throughout the reading process. Manzo and Manzo (1990) describe the steps in this procedure.

Step 1:
   The teacher tells the students that they will be learning to set purposes for reading.

Step 2:
   The teacher and students look over the text and read the title and first sentence. The students ask the teacher questions about the first sentence, which the teacher answers. The students are told to ask questions that a teacher might ask.

Step 3:
   The teacher now asks the students questions that focus their attention on the purpose of the selection or key ideas. If the students cannot answer the teacher's questions, they are asked to explain why.

Step 4:

Students and the teacher continue to ask each other questions about each sentence. The teacher begins to model questions that require integration of material across sentences. The process should continue until the students comprehend the first paragraph and have set a purpose for reading the rest of the selection. After reading the selection, the students discuss whether they set a good purpose, then proceed to answer their purpose question.

To make the procedure more understandable, here is an example of a seventh grade interdisciplinary lesson focusing on the formation of hurricanes and the social and economic effects of their destruction.

Step 1: Defining the Purpose for ReQuest

Teacher: As we begin our study of hurricanes—how they are formed, their destructive power, and their effect on people—we will be learning how to set a purpose for reading.

Step 2: Student Questioning

Teacher: Read the title of the selection and the first sentence. When you have finished, create questions that you think a teacher would ask.

A hurricane begins with waves that may form a tropical depression with winds up to 31 miles per hour; it may turn into a tropical storm with winds up to 74 miles per hour, and ultimately may develop into a hurricane with winds over 74 miles per hour.

Student A: In what direction do the waves move from the center of the hurricane?
Student B: Why do these storms produce such strong winds?
Student C: Do all hurricanes start out as tropical depressions or tropical storms?

Step 3: Teacher-Generated Purpose-Setting Questions

Teacher: What are some of the central ideas of this selection?
Student A: It's about hurricanes.
Student B: The selection describes how hurricanes are formed.
Student C: I think that the selection will eventually talk about the movement and destruction of hurricanes.
Teacher: Which has more destructive force—a tropical depression or a tropical storm?
Student A: It must be the tropical storm because the winds are greater.
Student B: I'm not certain either one can really destroy very much.
Student C: I don't know the answer. The sentence doesn't really talk about destruction.
Teacher: It might be useful to focus on the force of winds for a moment to determine how powerful they must be to be destructive. As we recall,

last summer we had a powerful thunderstorm with winds of 50 miles per hour. Remember how many trees went down? How many of you were without power for several days due to power lines that fell down in that storm?

Step 4: Integration of Material Across Sentences

Teacher: Read the following sentences.

Hurricanes move westward along the equator until they fully develop. They then turn northward and pick up speed until they reach temperate latitudes, where they turn east and lose their strength over cool waters.

Teacher: Now, consider this sentence and the first sentence we read. Remember that we learned that hurricanes are formed from the buildup of waves. As the hurricane is building, in what direction are the waves moving?

Student A: In the direction of the hurricane.

Student B: They are moving toward the west because the hurricane moves toward the west, and waves cause the hurricanes.

Reciprocal questioning can also be used when selections of the text are particularly difficult. The students and teacher can question each other about their understanding of what they have read. It is important for the teacher to model questions that require students to focus not only on details but on main ideas and connections among ideas.

Interactive Questioning Activity. The interactive questioning activity (Winn, Ryder, & Netzo, 1993) helps students focus on main points while reading a text with many details. The procedure involves the following strategic routine.

1. Read a segment of the text and write down the information learned. This can be presented to the students as similar to taking notes.

2. Categorize the information and explain why you grouped the information as you did. This can be done in small peer groups, sharing categories generated for the same text.

3. For each category, develop a question that the information can answer. The students can be guided to develop questions that involve putting the information together and making inferences from it. They can be particularly encouraged to use questions beginning with *why* and *how*.

This procedure is similar to Hayes's (1989) summarization instruction discussed in the preceding section; in both, the students begin with details and then organize these into categories, or main ideas. Also in both, the students are encouraged to share their thinking about how the information is organized.

It is important to note that students do not benefit equally from self-questioning instruction. Although this finding has been questioned (Davey &

McBride, 1986), several studies (Andre & Anderson, 1978–1979; Wong & Jones, 1982) have shown that lower achieving or learning disabled students benefited more from instruction in self-questioning than did higher achieving students. Most likely the more proficient learners are already using this strategy; perhaps they could serve as peer tutors and guides for others in the class as this strategy is being presented.

Students can be helped to be more strategic in answering as well as asking questions through learning procedures such as how to determine Question/ Answer Relationships, as described in the next section.

Question/Answer Relationships.   Learning about question/answer relationships, or QARs (Raphael, 1982, 1984, 1986), helps students become aware of and use appropriate sources of information for answering questions. They learn that questions are answered by using

- information that students can find stated directly in the text in one place—these questions are answered by reproducing the stated information.
- information that students can find stated directly in the text but in several places—these questions are answered by combining the information.
- information that is implied in the text—these questions are answered by integrating text information with background knowledge.
- information that is not stated in the text—these questions can be answered by using background knowledge alone.

The first two sources of information are text-based (Anthony & Raphael, 1989), meaning the answers to the questions can be found in the text itself. *Right there* questions have answers that are stated within one sentence of the text. *Think and search* questions can be answered by combining information that is in different places in the text. The next two categories are knowledge-based; students have to use their background knowledge, either together with or supplementary to the text. *Author and you* questions require students to use their background knowledge to make inferences about material in the text. *On my own* questions are related to the topic but can be answered using background knowledge only. Figure 5.12 has examples of the different QARs.

PRACTICE ACTIVITY 5.7

Read the following paragraph and identify the QARs as *right there, think and search, author and you,* and *on my own.* Compare your answers to those in the answers section.

Timing is of the utmost importance when using contingent reward in puppy training. Obviously, your puppy isn't going to know what you mean by the different commands when you first begin to train him, and the only way he'll learn that he's doing the right thing is if he receives a reward the moment he does it. An example is using contingent reward to teach the Sit. If you have a very antsy puppy who much prefers bounding and absolutely hates sitting, you may have to begin by rewarding a bending of the hind legs. If you were to wait until the puppy sits all the way down with his bottom on the floor, you would never get the job done. After a few rewards for partial sitting, the puppy will suddenly sit all the way—at which time you'll not only reward him but tell him how marvelous he is.

From C. Rutherford and D. H. Neil, *How to Raise a Puppy You Can Live With.* Loveland, CO: Alpine Publications, 1981, p. 99.

1. How will a puppy know he is doing something correctly?
2. How long is it likely to take an antsy puppy to learn to sit?
3. What might you give a puppy when he sits on command?
4. Why is it necessary for puppies to learn to sit?

FIGURE 5.12   QAR QUESTIONING STRATEGY

Sleep is the natural periodic suspension of consciousness during which the powers of the body are restored. Most people sleep about 7 or 8 hours a night, but some require only a few hours, while others require 9 or 10. If a person is deprived of sleep, rather profound changes occur. If the individual goes 4 or 5 days without sleep, he may have difficulty concentrating, seeing, or hearing. Some people will hallucinate, or quickly confuse their thoughts with the events around them. It is not uncommon for those who have gone without sleep for 4 or 5 days to become very suspicious of everyone around them. They may believe that others are plotting their death or are attempting to take advantage of them in some way. Scientists believe that sleep is essential for the brain to restore energy and maintain its level of reasoning and psychological adjustment.

Right There

• How many hours do most people sleep each night?

Think and Search

• What happens to an individual's perception of reality after being deprived of sleep for several days?

Author and You

• Why would it be a bad idea to stay up all night to study for a test being given late the next day?

On My Own

• If you take a nap during the day, can you think better after the nap?

Raphael's (1982; Anthony & Raphael, 1989) procedures for teaching students to identify and use QARs include the following.

1. Teacher gives clear descriptions of the different sources of information that can be used in answering questions, as well as examples of each QAR.
2. Teacher demonstrates asking questions, answering them, identifying the category of QAR in which each question belongs, and telling why the questions and answers are in particular categories of QAR.
3. Teacher presents the question, answer, and QAR, and students tell why each question fits into its QAR category.
4. Students identify QARs and answer questions given them by the teacher.
5. Students and teacher discuss when and why QARs are helpful.

Research with students in fourth through eighth grades (Raphael, 1984) has indicated that students who use QARs become more aware of sources of information and produce better answers to questions. Younger students seem to need more instruction on QARs (1 week, with 6 to 8 weeks of practice), while older ones require as little as 10 minutes of instruction.

The instructional activities discussed so far—use of text structure, summarization, and self-questioning—have focused on single strategies. In reality, however, proficient readers coordinate the use of multiple strategies to guide their reading, depending on the purpose of reading the text, and what they know about themselves as learners. It may be constructive to teach one strategy at a time, especially if instruction includes a heavy focus on when and why to use the strategy and if the strategy is a particularly difficult one to learn. However, discussion should include the use of the particular strategy within the context of the use of other strategies.

Multiple-Strategy Approaches

There are also instructional approaches that are based on multiple strategies. One of these is reciprocal teaching (Brown & Palincsar, 1985, 1989; Palincsar, 1986; Palincsar & Brown, 1984). While reading about this approach, think about the way it leads students to be strategic in their reading and how this can enhance their learning. Also think about the explicit and supportive activities of the teacher as the students gradually assume control of using strategies to comprehend the text.

Reciprocal Teaching. Students and teachers participating in reciprocal teaching discuss the text as they are reading it. Their discussions are framed by the use of four strategies: summarizing, self-questioning, clarifying, and predicting. When instruction is first begun, the teacher and class talk about the purposes of reading. Then the teacher instructs the students on the strategies, explaining and modeling their uses. At this time, the teacher provides information about the strategies' role in helping students understand and learn from text. Following the introduction (typically one day per strategy), the group begins to read the text, stopping at designated points to discuss it. The teacher and students take turns serving as the discussion leader; the leader's job is to use the four strategies to discuss the section of the text just read. He or she summarizes the text, asks questions to check understanding of it, asks for clarifications about difficult vocabulary or concepts, and makes predictions about what will be learned next (if what has been previously read leads to a prediction). The teacher's role, when he or she is not the discussion leader, is to provide support—modeling, making suggestions, clarifying questions, and giving feedback. The form of the support varies according to the students' success in using the strategies to discuss the particular text. At times, especially when the students are beginning to learn reciprocal teaching, the teacher may have to provide a high degree of support, perhaps giving a starter word for a question, or thinking aloud about what he or she would include in a summary. At other times, little support may be needed. Gradually, the students become better able to lead discussions through the use of the strategies with very little help from the teacher.

All of the students are encouraged to join in the discussion when it is not their turn to be leader, adding to the summaries, responding to the questions asked, asking for clarifications about points in the text they are unsure of, and making their own predictions. Throughout the discussion, the teacher actively monitors the students' understanding of the content as well as their ability to monitor their own comprehension. There are many opportunities to help the students become more strategic as they work to comprehend the text.

Following is a transcript of a reciprocal teaching lesson on volcanoes. Notice how independent these seventh-grade students are in carrying on the discussion without teacher direction.

> Below the crust is a large layer called the mantle. It is a much heavier layer. The part of the mantle just below the crust is a strange place. Pressure there is very great and the temperatures are very high.

Doug: This told about the second layer of the earth, the one that is under the first one . . .

Sara: The one under the crust.

Doug: Yeah, the crust. It told about what it is like, like how heavy it is and what the temperature is. My prediction is that they will tell us about the next layer because this picture shows another one, and I'll bet it will be cooler because dirt gets colder when you dig.

Chris: That doesn't make sense to me because, because as it's been goin' down, it's been gettin' hotter.

Steph: And heavier too.

Chris: Pretty soon, we'll get to the gooey stuff and it's real hot.

Sam: That's the lava.

Teacher: Well, let's read on and see who's right in their predictions. What will the next layer be like? Who will be the next teacher?

Reprinted with permission of Annemarie Sullivan Palincsar.

A modification of reciprocal teaching (Brown & Palincsar, 1989; Palincsar & Brown, 1986) can also be used in content classes. The students are shown the headings of sections of the text to be read and instructed to write two statements that tell what they think they will learn in that particular section. Then the students and teacher discuss and compare their predictions. After reading a section in the text, the students each write two questions and a summary as well as make notes of anything that needed to be clarified. These questions, summaries, and clarifications can then be discussed by the group.

Reciprocal teaching has been studied extensively with students in elementary and middle school (Brown & Palincsar, 1989; Palincsar, 1986; Palincsar & Brown, 1984, 1986, 1989); students have shown gains in using the strategies as well as in responding to comprehension questions. Note that, in this procedure, the focus of the discussion is on understanding the text, not on mastering strategies. Again, note the use of multiple strategies, simulating what proficient readers do.

Content-Processing Guides.   An important component of proficient reading is evaluating strategy effectiveness; this in turn can lead to selection of effective strategies. The personal aspect of strategy use means that what works for one student in helping him or her understand and learn from a particular text may not be as effective for another. Students can benefit from participating in discussions in which they reflect on the use of particular strategies. Peters's (1990) instruction with content-processing guides provides such an opportunity.

Content-processing guides are teacher-designed study materials that are used during and after reading. The guides model strategies of, or ways of reasoning about, particular subject matter. An example of a content-processing guide demonstrating problem and solution reasoning is presented in Figure 5.13. Notice how the guide focuses on understanding both the subject matter content and the reasoning involved in problem solution.

Peters suggests three activities to follow reading. The purpose of the first is to synthesize important ideas in the text. His example is one in which students analyze two illustrations in the text, determining whether they support what has been read. The purpose of the second activity is to reflect on the usefulness of the reasoning strategy as presented in the study guide. The students discuss why the guide was helpful and suggest ways in which it might be altered to be more so, focusing on the strategy the guide demonstrated. In our example, the students could focus on the effect the guide had on their linking the characteristics of running shoes with the characteristics of the problem of running injuries. They could also talk about the ways of rearranging the guide so they could see the relationships more clearly. In the third activity, the students consider a new chapter or article in the same content area. They identify goals for reading that text, important information that meets their goals, and then compare the organization of the new chapter to ones they have read with guides. Following this, the students decide which strategies to use to read the new material.

By participating in the above activities, the students are led to consider strategies and evaluate their utility for meeting specific goals, as well as to de-

---

FIGURE 5.13   CONTENT-PROCESSING GUIDE
THE EFFECT OF RUNNING SHOES ON INJURIES

Directions: *As you read the article "Running Shoes: Their Relationship to Running Injuries" by S. D. Cook, M. R. Brinker, and M. Poche, complete the information below.*

Causes of Running Injuries

    a. Training errors
    b. _____
    c. Hazards of the road (dogs, cars, potholes, etc.)

Precautions for Running Injuries

Based on the causes above, list things that runners should be aware of in order to prevent injuries. You may want to talk with someone who does a lot of running.

_____

_____

_____

_____

_____

The Role of the Running Shoe in Reducing Injuries

    a. Absorbs shock
    b. Provides control
    c. _____
    d. _____

Things to Look for in Assessing the Condition of Running Shoes

    a. Wear on the sole
        Remedy for this problem: _____
    b. Ability of the shoe to _____
        Remedy for this problem: _____

Source: Based on S. D. Cook, M. R. Brinker, and M. Poche (1990). "Running shoes: Their relationship to running injuries." *Sports Medicine, 10*(1), 1–8.

velop modifications of the strategies. These activities foster students' control of strategy use and ability to use strategies in a way that is personally beneficial.

A System for Studying

Many of the strategies covered earlier in this chapter help readers comprehend text independent of the teacher's assistance. Self-questioning, graphic organizers, summarization, and the use of text structure are also useful and effective strategies to facilitate studying. Each of these activities can be used by students to improve their understanding as they read, review classroom notes, or gather information in preparation for writing activities. This section reviews a comprehensive system for studying.

Proficient readers engage in a number of behaviors as they study. Decisions must be made as to where information can be located, which information is important, and how to organize and make some sort of record of that information so that it may be retrieved and communicated at a later date (Anderson & Armbruster, 1984). While study strategies have been shown to be effective (Alvermann & Moore, 1991; Anderson & Armbruster, 1984; Nist, Simpson, & Hogrebe, 1985), it is evident that most teachers do not teach these strategies (Alvermann & Moore, 1991; Durkin, 1978–1979) and that students who could benefit from them the most (those having difficulty comprehending text) generally do not use them (Simpson, 1983).

As with other types of instruction that focus on the acquisition of strategies, students will be more likely to acquire study strategies when the teacher explains their use, models the process of applying strategies to subject matter material, then eventually assumes a supportive role as students use the strategies in the context of a group process or independent reading.

SQ3R.   SQ3R (Robinson, 1961) is a systematic study strategy that involves prereading, reading, and postreading activities. It consists of the following steps.

> *Step 1:*
> *Survey.* The student examines text headings and titles to acquire a gist of the concepts presented in the reading selection.

> *Step 2:*
> *Question.* The student attends to the headings or titles located during Step 1, then generates a question from each.

> *Step 3:*
> *Read.* The student reads the text with the goal of answering the questions generated in Step 2.

> *Step 4:*
> *Recite.* The student evaluates responses to the questions, then makes notes on important information or concepts that were learned.

> *Step 5:*
> *Review.* The student covers up the notes and reading material and attempts to summarize the important information or concepts learned.

While SQ3R has been in use for over a half century, relatively little is known about the effectiveness of this study system. In a review of six studies that examined the effectiveness of SQ3R with adolescents and adults, Adams, Carnine, and Gersten (1982) report mixed results. Because this is a time-consuming and rather complex study system, it has been suggested that its effectiveness may depend upon extensive training, especially for students who lack effective study strategies (West, Farmer, & Wolff, 1991). This training should consist of (1) modeling the strategy, (2) providing structured guidance with the strategy, and (3) engaging students in cooperative efforts to refine the application of the strategy.

Modeling the Strategy.   The teacher models the steps of SQ3R with a short text passage. This process begins with the teacher defining the purpose of SQ3R, how it will benefit students' ability to learn from text, and finally presenting the students with a handout that lists the various steps of the strategy. Modeling begins as the teacher draws students' attention to each heading or title, then thinks aloud to the students about how the headings are used to anticipate the content of the selection. Thus, if the first heading reads "How the Media Affect the Presidential Campaign," the teacher may want to draw on background knowledge to predict that this section may contain information about how the candidates use the media to their advantage, how the media use controversial issues in the campaign to market the sale of their own products (advertising time or viewer ratings). When a text lacks headings, a heading can be constructed by reading the first sentence of each paragraph and then, on the basis of this information, generating a heading that would seem to define the content of the paragraph or group of paragraphs. The teacher then thinks aloud to the class about how this heading was used to formulate a question, and the question is placed on an overhead or chalkboard. The section of text immediately following the heading is then read aloud to the class; the teacher again thinks aloud about how the question is answered, and the response is noted on the transparency or chalkboard. This question-read-review process is repeated for several headings. Finally, the teacher presents the responses to the various questions on a transparency or chalkboard and demonstrates to students how this information can be summarized; again, the teacher thinks aloud about the process of reviewing information acquired from the selection.

Guidance With the Strategy.   The students are now reading to learn the SQ3R strategy through a step-by-step process directed by the teacher. This should be viewed as a cooperative effort—teacher and students share equally in their effort to learn the strategy. The process begins with the students first reviewing the steps of SQ3R, then examining the heading of the first section of text. Again, in the absence of headings, students may read the first sentence of each paragraph, then generate headings based on the content of the sentence. Having acknowledged the heading, the teacher elicits questions from the students, which are noted on a transparency or chalkboard. It is important to ask students to explain the process they followed in generating their question, paying particular attention to the cues they drew from the headings. It is likely that this step will result in the identification of a wide variety of questions addressing both factual-level information and higher level thinking. It is also important to clarify to students that these questions reflect their personal goals for reading, that SQ3R is a personal study strategy, and that a range of questions is therefore anticipated. With the questions displayed to the students, the teacher can then ask them to select a question, then read to answer that question. Once students have answered the question, they describe what they have learned as the teacher notes this information on the chalkboard or transparency. Once all questions have been answered and the students' responses are displayed, the teacher directs a discussion by asking students to think aloud about the process they used to review and summarize. Finally, the teacher reviews the steps of SQ3R, asks students to comment on its effectiveness, and summarizes the insights gathered from class discussion. These insights may be recorded on a bulletin board, in students' learning journals, or in a handout to be distributed to the students.

Cooperative Efforts.   The final step in training students how to use SQ3R involves their application of the strategy in cooperative groups. The goal here is to promote discussion among students on the process of applying SQ3R to the subject matter content, then reflect upon and describe that process to the class. For each group, the teacher designates an individual to record the group's questions and responses, an individual to direct the group through the steps of the SQ3R, and an individual to summarize the group's insights and evaluation of the strategy. Students are provided a two- to three-page reading selection, then directed to adhere to the following guidelines.

1. The group leader assumes the responsibility of guiding the group through the various steps of the SQ3R.
2. All group members are encouraged to generate questions.
3. As questions are answered, group members should describe the process used to answer questions. The recorder should note these comments.
4. Once all questions have been answered, the reading material should be removed and the group should summarize what they have learned.
5. The group should discuss their views of the effectiveness of SQ3R. These comments should be noted by the recorder so they may be presented to the entire class.

Use of cooperative groups can be an effective means to begin the process of allowing students to apply the SQ3R strategy as they engage in independent studying. By sharing their views on the usefulness of the strategy, students should become more aware of their own thinking as they apply this strategy and should gain additional insights by listening to the comments of their peers.

As noted earlier, SQ3R is a comprehensive strategy. At first, students may find this approach to be tedious or distracting. It may be helpful, therefore, to begin teaching the strategy with short selections or limiting its application to the first few pages of a reading assignment. Over time, as students receive more extended instruction in its use, they should gain a better appreciation of its effectiveness as they listen to the comments of their peers and have the opportunity to evaluate the effectiveness of this strategy in improving their comprehension.

Commentary: Multiple Strategy Approaches.   The research (see review by Pearson & Fielding, 1991) clearly points to the importance of teaching students about strategies they can use to guide their comprehension and studying of text. In this section selected approaches for teaching strategies and strategic approaches to learning within the context of subject matter instruction have been presented. These are starting points for creating an atmosphere in your classroom in which both the subject matter content and process are intertwined, and are discussed and reflected upon. By sharing their approaches to reading tasks, students can become more aware of what they are doing to understand texts and the effects of the strategies, or processes, they use on meeting their purposes. In addition, they can try new approaches based on what their peers have found to be effective.

It is important not to present strategies as ends in themselves. Mastering summarizing is not the point; understanding and learning from the text to meet reading purposes is the goal. Interestingly, it has been reported that, over time, the dialogues in reciprocal teaching focus less explicitly on the use of the strategies and more on content. This indicates that the use of the strategies has become internalized to the point that the students can benefit from their use but need to pay little attention to them. It is also important to consider findings like those in the self-questioning literature (Wong, 1985) indicating that lower achieving students profited more from instruction. Perhaps higher achieving students have developed strategic approaches to reading that are sufficient. Although they can benefit from explaining these to their peers and sharing in dialogues in which they reflect on strategy effectiveness, strategy instruction should not be overemphasized with them. The linking of subject matter content and process instruction, supported in this chapter as a necessary and ideal way to learn to be proficient readers, can serve to avoid an overemphasis on process.

Instruction that links content and process involves multiple considerations and needs to be carefully planned. In the following section, the major considerations that need to be taken into account in planning for subject matter comprehension instruction in today's classrooms are presented.

PLANNING COMPREHENSION ACTIVITIES

Planning for comprehension activities is an extension of planning done for prereading instruction. As discussed in Chapter Four, prereading planning involves considering the nature of the subject matter, the students' prior knowledge, the learning objectives, and the available time and resources. There are additional considerations in planning instruction to facilitate comprehension during reading, considerations that stem from the above. The major planning considerations are shown in Figure 5.14.

FIGURE 5.14   PLANNING CONSIDERATIONS FOR COMPREHENSION ACTIVITIES

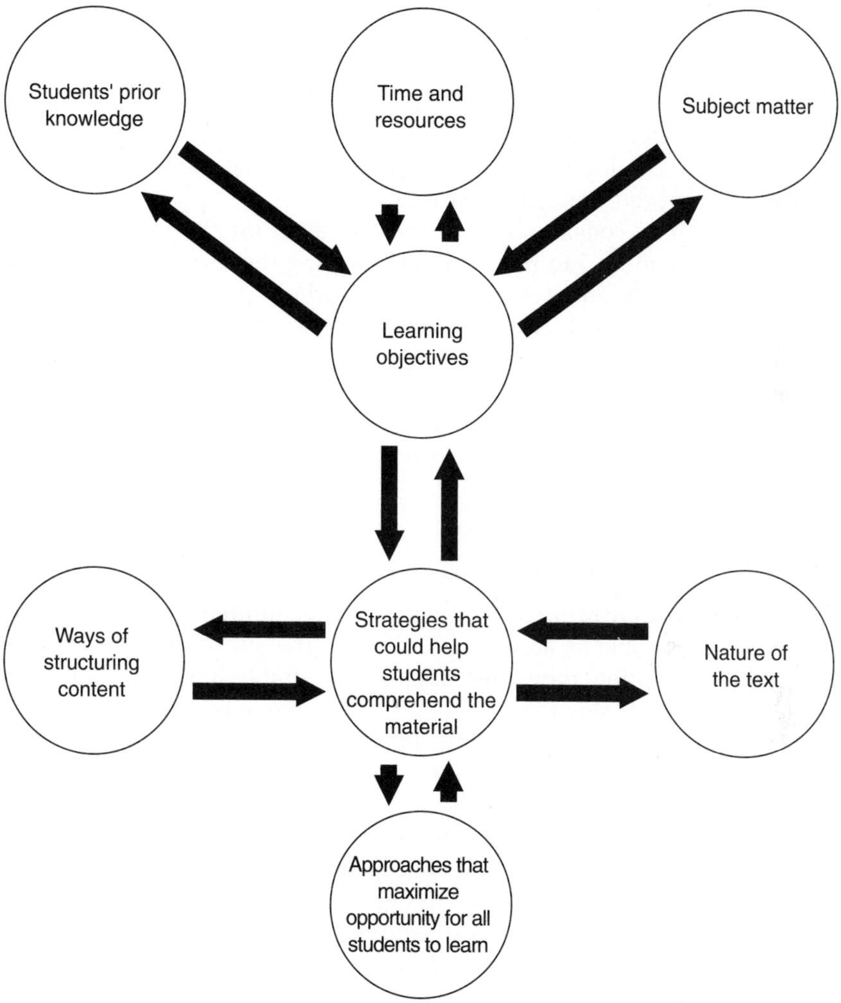

Structuring Learning, Selecting Strategies, and Types of Instruction

One additional consideration is whether you will need to help students structure and organize the information in the text. This decision is made by thinking about your learning objectives as well as the nature of the text and the characteristics of your students. Is the information in the text presented in such a way that the students can organize the information on their own and apply the material to meet the objectives? If not, it becomes necessary to develop a way to help students see the relationships in the text. The next decision is how best to do this. Approaches presented in this chapter were recitation, discussions, and study guides.

Another planning consideration is identifying the strategies that will help the students understand and learn particular reading material and how best to teach or highlight these strategies. The planning decisions here focus on the range of strategies that may be helpful in meeting the learning objectives, the proficiency with which students use these strategies, and the ways in which content and process could be linked in instruction. Once the strategies are identified, decisions revolve around how best to teach them so that the students will develop proficiency in using them and view them as a means to increase comprehension and learning.

The third consideration is the structure for the teaching activity that is most likely to lead to the students' meeting the learning objectives. Decisions must be made about whether to use whole group instruction, cooperative groups, or independent assignments. These decisions are made interactively with all the others involved in planning, in the context of the purpose for reading and the learning objective.

A final planning consideration is the ways in which you can meet the needs of students who have reading difficulties. This consideration is the subject of the next section.

Students With Special Needs

Students with reading difficulties may have limited background knowledge or may have problems accessing and using the knowledge they have (Swanson, 1989). In addition, they often have been found to have less strategic awareness and control of their reading than do students who are not experiencing difficulties (August, Flavell, & Clift, 1984; Baker & Brown, 1984; Garner, 1987). Students with learning disabilities have been viewed as individuals who do not possess certain strategies, who do not select ones appropriate for given tasks, and/or who do not monitor their reading (Swanson, 1989). Another characteristic is the students' poor self-concepts about their reading ability (Butkowsky & Willows, 1980; Johnston & Winograd, 1985). Poor self-concept may appear to be low motivation, disinterest, or disruption. Although difficulties calling up and using relevant background knowledge, problems using strategies to control reading, and poor self-concept do not cause all reading problems, these characteristics are often implicated in reading difficulties.

Many of the instructional activities suggested in this chapter and the previous one are appropriate and helpful for all students, including those with special needs, as they directly address the characteristics noted above. Instructional activities focused on building and accessing background knowledge as well as using strategies to guide reading are particularly helpful. The students with learning difficulties may need the instructional activities to be more explicit, as well as more sustained, but they are not the only ones who can profit from them. Recently, a special education team teacher, whose students with learning disabilities were included in general education classes throughout the day, talked about how she uses study guides: She prepares them for the students with learning disabilities but shares them with any other student who asks for them (and she does get requests).

It is important that students be exposed to rich subject matter content. There has been much attention in the literature about students with reading problems and their lack of exposure to instruction focused on developing the behaviors and attitudes associated with proficient reading, as well as their lack of opportunities to engage in sustained reading (Allington & McGill-Franzen, 1989; Stanovich, 1986). Over the years, instruction for students with reading difficulties has emphasized isolated skills practice; without experience with "real" reading and writing, students miss the chance not only to develop fluency that can come with practice, but to develop rich background knowledge that will facilitate comprehension.

One way to provide opportunities for students with reading difficulties to read subject matter content is to make available alternative material about the topics being studied. The school or community librarian can be very helpful in suggesting and locating sources. Utilizing cooperative learning assignments is another approach to providing exposure to subject matter content; proficient readers can be assigned roles involving explaining the material from the more difficult texts. Other students can profit from the explanations and share what they have learned from alternative sources.

If students with reading difficulties are working with a resource teacher, it is very important to coordinate this instruction with that of the general education classroom. It is critical that subject matter teachers and resource teachers keep close contact and explore ways in which they can coordinate their instruction and guide students in being aware of and benefiting from the connections.

In summary, the following considerations should be addressed when planning for instruction.

1. The subject matter
2. The students' background knowledge of the concepts and processes to be studied
3. The learning objectives
4. The necessity of helping students structure and organize the information in the text
5. The strategies that could help students comprehend the material
6. The structures (whole group, cooperative groups, independent learning) that will best help students meet the learning objectives
7. The approaches that will maximize the opportunity for all students to comprehend the subject matter

These considerations are interactive—they influence each other. Attending to these considerations and their interactions is important in providing a learning environment that enhances students' ability to learn subject matter content and to become independent thinkers capable of constructing knowledge of the world on their own.

PRACTICE ACTIVITY 5.8

To make planning for reading comprehension more concrete, contrast the planning of two seventh-grade math teachers. As you read about them, think about the problems that may arise if all of the planning considerations are not made. Comments are given in the answers section.

Example 1

Ms. Trujillo is planning a lesson in which she wants the students to apply the concept of sets to real-world problems. Examining the text, she finds that the concept of sets is poorly presented, with the examples far removed from the students' prior knowledge; there is also difficult vocabulary. Because the text does not clearly present the defined concepts, Ms. Trujillo obtains two supplemental readings on several levels, provides the students a set of study questions for these readings, and plans for a discussion of the questions once the students have the opportunity to read and respond to the questions independently. After discussion, Ms. Trujillo plans a cooperative learning activity that engages students in the use of material in the text to interpret and solve real-world problems. Following this activity, she plans to have the students share their approaches to these problems with the class. She plans the compositions of her groups carefully, ensuring that the students with reading difficulties are placed with more proficient readers and assigned roles in the groups that will capitalize on their strengths.

Example 2

Ms. Andres is also teaching a lesson on applying the concept of sets to real-world problems. She examines the objectives listed in the teacher's guide and the questions provided for the students at the end of the chapter. Although these questions do not address the concept of sets, she constructs two questions requiring students to apply sets to the everyday world of microbiologists. She provides students an example of sets, instructs them to read the text describing sets, then asks students to individually complete the two questions she has constructed.

CONCLUDING REMARKS

This chapter has presented instructional activities that can be used to help students comprehend and learn from subject matter reading materials. Instructional activities were presented in two categories: activities that focus on structuring and organizing the subject matter content and activities that focus on the process of reading.

Throughout the chapter, the interconnectedness of subject matter content and process was emphasized. In summarizing this chapter, there are three points that we believe are critical to comprehension and learning in subject matter areas.

The first point is the importance of engaging students in higher order thinking about the material they are reading. Comprehension is much more than memorizing facts; it involves students' reasoning about the text as they look for relationships and integrate the material with their background knowledge.

Second is the importance of instruction that aims at making students capable of independent control of their reading. Although subject matter texts are not necessarily written to be read without teacher guidance, students are often asked to read and study them on their own and, in addition, to pursue other reading materials in subject matter areas. To foster the development of independence, it is important that instruction seeks to help students take responsibility for monitoring and regulating their own comprehension.

The final point concerns the importance of creating an atmosphere in the classroom that allows for genuine curiosity and excitement about the information the students are reading and about how they are processing and reasoning about this information. In this kind of atmosphere, students are supported and made to feel secure about freely sharing their interpretations and emotional reactions to the material, as well as their struggles as they work to construct meaning from text.

Reflections

Now that you have learned about ways to facilitate student comprehension of subject matter text, complete the following as a review of the various concepts and activities addressed throughout this chapter.

1. Obtain a copy of a textbook or supplementary instructional material in your subject matter area that contains questions. Examine at least 10 to 15 of these questions and label them according to one of the question strategies presented in this chapter.
2. Select a textbook, article, or other type of printed information for a 30 to 50-minute lesson you might teach in your classroom. Generate questions that are sequenced to present the various question types defined in one of the strategies in this chapter.
3. Select a reading selection from 3 to 10 pages in length that you might teach in your classroom. Examine this selection to identify your lesson objectives. Based on these objectives, construct a three-level study guide, or a study guide in the form of a graphic organizer.
4. Obtain three types of text material used in your subject matter classroom (textbooks, articles, supplementary curricular materials). Examine each of these sources carefully to determine the various types of text structure (description, causation, collection, problem/solution, comparison/contrast). Summarize how frequently these structures are found and the distribution of the various types.
5. Working with a group of your colleagues or by yourself, practice the SQ3R strategy as you engage in reading a subject matter selection. Note

the strengths and limitations of this strategy and discuss your views with your colleagues or an individual familiar with this strategy.

6. Visit a subject matter classroom to observe and monitor questioning during discussion. As you observe classroom questioning, record the number of questions presented, the types of question, and the use of pivotal and emerging questions. Following your observation, write a critique of the questioning activity you observed to include suggestions to modify the lesson.

7. Select a short text selection from a subject matter lesson. Construct a lesson using the GRASP summarization activity to present to your colleagues. Following the presentation of this lesson, solicit your colleagues' comments on the lesson.

REFERENCES

Adams, A., Carnine, D., & Gersten, R. (1982). Instructional strategies for studying content area texts in the intermediate grades. *Reading Research Quarterly, 18,* 27–55.

Allington, R. L., & McGill-Franzen, A. (1989). School response to reading failure: Instruction for Chapter 1 and special education students in grades two, four, and eight. *Elementary School Journal, 89,* 529–242.

Alvermann, D. E., Dillon, D. R., & O'Brien, D. G. (1987). *Using discussion to promote reading comprehension.* Newark, DE: International Reading Association.

Alvermann, D. E., Dillon, D. R., O'Brien, D. G., & Smith, L. C. (1985). The role of the textbook in discussion. *Journal of Reading, 29,* 50–57.

Alvermann, D. E., & Moore, D. W. (1991). Secondary school reading. In R. Barr, M. L. Kamil, P. Mosenthal, & P. D. Pearson (Eds.), *Handbook of reading research* (Vol. 2). New York: Longman.

Anderson, T. H., & Armbruster, B. B. (1984). Studying. In P. D. Pearson, R. Barr, M. Kamil, & P. Mosenthal (Eds.), *Handbook of reading research.* New York: Longman.

Andre, M., & Anderson, T. (1978–1979). The development and evaluation of a self-questioning study technique. *Reading Research Quarterly, 14,* 605–622.

Andre, T. (1987). Questions and learning from reading. *Questioning Exchange, 1,* 47–86.

Anthony, H. M., & Raphael, T. E. (1989). Using questioning strategies to promote students' active comprehension of content area material. In D. Lapp, J. Flood, & N. Farnan (Eds.), *Content area reading and learning.* Englewood Cliffs, NJ: Prentice Hall.

August, D. L., Flavell, J. H., & Clift, R. (1984). Comparison of comprehension monitoring of skilled and less skilled readers. *Reading Research Quarterly, 20,* 93–115.

Baker, L., & Brown, A. L. (1984). Metacognitive skills and reading. In P. D. Pearson (Ed.), *Handbook of reading research.* New York: Longman.

Balajthy, E. (1984). Using student-constructed questions to encourage active reading. *Journal of Reading, 27,* 408–411.

Bellon, J. J., Bellon, E. C., & Blank, M. A. (1992). *Teaching from a research knowledge base: A development and renewal process.* New York: Merrill/Macmillan.

Bloome, D. (1987). Reading as a social process in an eighth-grade classroom. In D. Bloome (Ed.), *Literacy and schooling.* Norwood, NJ: Ablex.

Brown, A. L., & Day, J. D. (1983). Macrorules for summarizing texts: The development of expertise. *Journal of Verbal Learning and Verbal Behavior, 22*(1), 1–14.

Brown, A. L., & Palincsar, A. S. (1985). *Reciprocal teaching of comprehension: A natural history of a program for enhancing learning* (Tech. Rep.

No. 334). Champaign-Urbana: University of Illinois, Center for the Study of Reading.

Brown, A. L., & Palincsar, A. S. (1989). Guided cooperative learning and individual knowledge acquisition. In L. Resnick (Ed.), *Essays in honor of Robert Glaser*. Hillsdale, NJ: Erlbaum.

Butkowsky, I. S., & Willows, D. M. (1980). Cognitive-motivational characteristics of children varying in reading ability: Evidence of learned helplessness in poor readers. *Journal of Educational Psychology, 72*, 408–422.

Conley, M. W. (1990). Instructional planning and teaching in reading and writing. In G. G. Duffy (Ed.), *Reading in the middle school* (2nd ed.). Newark, DE: International Reading Association.

Costa, A. L. (1991). Teacher behaviors that enable student thinking. In A. L. Costa (Ed.), *Developing minds: A resource book for teaching thinking*. Alexandria, VA: Association for Supervision and Curriculum Development.

Davey, B. (1986). Using textbook activity guides to help students learn from textbooks. *Journal of Reading, 29*, 489–494.

Davey, B., & McBride, S. (1986). Effects of question-generation on reading comprehension. *Journal of Educational Psychology, 78*, 256–262.

Dillon, J. T. (1988). *Questioning and teaching: A manual of practice*. New York: Teachers College Press.

Durkin, D. (1978–1979). What classroom observations reveal about reading comprehension instruction. *Reading Research Quarterly, 14*, 481–533.

Flood, J., Lapp, D., & Farnan, N. (1986). A reading-writing procedure that teaches expository paragraph structure. *The Reading Teacher, 39*, 556–562.

Gage, N. L., & Berliner, D. C. (1984). *Educational psychology* (3rd ed.). Boston: Houghton-Mifflin.

Gall, M. (1970). The use of questions in teaching. *Review of Educational Research, 40*, 707–721.

Garner, R. (1987). *Metacognition and reading comprehension*. Norwood, NJ: Ablex.

Good, T. L., & Brophy, J. E. (1987). *Looking in classrooms* (4th ed.). New York: Harper & Row.

Grossier, P. (1964). *How to use the fine art of questioning*. Englewood Cliffs, NJ: Prentice-Hall.

Hamaker, C. (1986). The effects of adjunct questions on prose learning. *Review of Educational Research, 56*, 212–242.

Hayes, D. A. (1989). Helping students GRASP the knack of writing summaries. *Journal of Reading, 32*, 96–101.

Herber, H. L. (1978). *Teaching reading in content areas* (2nd ed.). Englewood Cliffs, NJ: Prentice-Hall.

Hill, M. (1991). Writing summaries promotes thinking and learning across the curriculum—but why are they so difficult to write? *Journal of Reading, 34*, 536–539.

Johnston, P. H., & Winograd, P. N. (1985). Passive failure in reading. *Journal of Reading Behavior, 17*, 279–301.

Jones, B. F., Palincsar, A. S., Ogle, D. S., & Carr, E. G. (1987). *Strategic teaching and learning: Cognitive instruction in the content areas*. Alexandria, VA: Association for Supervision and Curriculum Development.

Manzo, A. V. (1969). The ReQuest procedure. *Journal of Reading, 13*, 123–126.

Manzo, A., & Manzo, B. (1990). *Content area reading: A heuristic approach*. New York: Merrill/Macmillan.

McGee, L. M., & Richgels, D. J. (1985). Teaching expository text structure to elementary students. *The Reading Teacher, 38*, 739–748.

Nist, S. L., Simpson, M. L., & Hogrebe, M. C. (1985). The relationship between the use of study strategies and test performance. *Journal of Reading Behavior, 17*, 15–28.

Ornstein, A. C. (1988). Questioning: The essence of good teaching: Part 2. *NAASP Bulletin, 72*, 72–80.

Palincsar, A. S. (1986). Metacognitive strategy instruction. *Exceptional Children, 53*, 118–124.

Palincsar, A. S., & Brown, A. L. (1984). Reciprocal teaching of comprehension-fostering and comprehension-monitoring activities. *Cognition and Instruction, 1*, 117–175.

_____. (1986). Interactive teaching to promote independent learning from text. *The Reading Teacher, 39*, 771–777.

_____. (1989). Instruction for self-regulated reading. In L. B. Resnick & L. E. Klopfer

(Eds.), *Toward the thinking curriculum: Current cognitive research*. Alexandria, VA: Association for Supervision and Curriculum Development.

Paris, S., Lipson, M. Y., & Wixon, K. K. (1983). Becoming a strategic reader. *Contemporary Educational Psychology, 8*, 293–316.

Pearson, P. D., & Fielding, L. (1991). Comprehension instruction. In R. Barr, M. L. Kamil, P. Mosenthal, & P. D. Pearson (Eds.), *Handbook of reading research: Vol. 2*. New York: Longman.

Pearson, P. D., & Gallagher, M. (1983). Instruction of reading comprehension. *Contemporary Educational Psychology, 8*, 317–344.

Peters, C. W. (1990). Content knowledge in reading: Creating a new framework. In G. G. Duffy (Ed.), *Reading in the middle school* (2nd ed.). Newark, DE: International Reading Association.

Piccolo, J. A. (1987). Expository text structure: Teaching and learning strategies. *The Reading Teacher, 40*, 838–847.

Pressley, M., Johnson, C. J., Symons, S., McGoldrick, J. A., & Kurita, J. A. (1989). Strategies that improve children's memory and comprehension of text. *Elementary School Journal, 90*, 3–32.

Pressley, M., Snyder, B., & Carigula-Bull, T. (1987). How can good strategy use be taught to children: Evaluation of six alternative approaches. In S. Cormier & J. Hagman (Eds.), *Transfer of learning: Contemporary research and applications*. Orlando, FL: Academic Press.

Raphael, T. E. (1982). Question answering strategies for children. *Reading Teacher, 36*, 186–190.

———. (1984). Teaching learners about sources of information for answering comprehension questions. *Journal of Reading, 27*, 303–311.

———. (1986). Teaching question answer relationships, revisited. *Reading Teacher, 39*, 516–522.

Raphael, T. E., Kirschner, B. W., & Englert, C. S. (1986). *The impact of text structure and social context on students' reading comprehension and writing products* (Research Series No. 161). East Lansing: Michigan State University, Institute for Research on Teaching.

Richgels, D. J., McGee, L. M., & Slaton, E. A. (1989). Teaching expository text structure in reading and writing. In K. D. Muth (Ed.), *Children's comprehension of text*. Newark, DE: International Reading Association.

Robinson, F. (1961). *Effective study*. New York: Harper & Row.

Roehler, L. R., & Duffy, G. G. (1986). Studying qualitative dimensions of instructional effectiveness. In J. V. Hoffman (Ed.), *Effective teaching of reading*. Newark, DE: International Reading Association.

———. (1991). Teachers' instructional actions. In R. Barr, M. L. Kamil, P. Mosenthal, & P. D. Pearson (Eds.), *Handbook of reading research: Vol. 2*. New York: Longman.

Rowe, M. B. (1986). Wait time: Slowing down may be a way of speeding up! *Journal of Teacher Education, 37*(1), 43–50.

Simpson, M. L. (1983). Recent research on independent learning strategies: Implications for developmental education (ERIC Document Reproduction Service No. ED 247 528).

Singer, H. S., & Donlan, D. (1982). Active comprehension: Problem-solving schema with question generation for comprehension of complex short stories. *Reading Research Quarterly, 18*, 166–185.

Smith, K., & Feathers, K. M. (1983). The role of reading in content classrooms: Assumptions vs. reality. *Journal of Reading, 27*, 262–267.

Stanovich, K. E. (1986). Matthew effects in reading: Some consequences of individual differences in the acquisition of reading. *Reading Research Quarterly, 21*, 360–407.

Swanson, H. L. (1989). Strategy instruction: Overview of principles and procedures for effective use. *Learning Disability Quarterly, 12*, 3–14.

West, C. K., Farmer, J. A., & Wolff, P. M. (1991). *Instructional design: Implications from cognitive science*. Englewood Cliffs, NJ: Prentice Hall.

Wilen, W. W. (1986). *Questioning skills, for teachers* (2nd ed.). Washington, DC: National Education Association.

Wiley, K. B. (1977). *The status of precollege science, mathematics, and social science educa-*

tional practices in U.S. schools: An overview and summary of three studies. Washington, DC: U.S. Government Printing Office.

Winn, J. A., Ryder, R. J., & Netzo, B. (1993, February). *Using a biography to teach strategic reading.* Paper presented at the annual meeting of the Learning Disabilities Association, San Francisco, CA.

Wong, B. Y. (1985). Self-questioning instructional research: A review. *Review of Educational Research, 55,* 227–268.

Wong, B. Y., & Jones, W. (1982). Increasing metacomprehension in learning-disabled and normally achieving students through self-questioning training. *Learning Disability Quarterly, 5,* 228–240.

Wood, K. D. (1987). Helping readers comprehend their textbook. *Middle School Journal, 18*(2), 20–21.

———. (1988). Guiding students through informational text. *The Reading Teacher, 41,* 912–920.

Wood, K. D., Lapp, D., & Flood, J. (1992). *Guiding readers through text: A review of study guides.* Newark, DE: International Reading Association.

· ·

CHAPTER SIX

Critical Thinking

CHAPTER OVERVIEW

In this chapter we examine ways to teach students strategies they can use to improve their critical thinking. The first section, "Characteristics of Critical Thinking," discusses some of the important elements in higher level cognition, then gives a working definition of critical thinking. The next section, "Guidelines for Teaching Critical Thinking," focuses on the importance of solving practical problems in the context of the subject matter curriculum. The section "An Instructional Framework for Critical Thinking" offers a comprehensive approach to implementing and facilitating critical thinking strategies. The last section, "Strategies for Teaching Critical Thinking," presents four processes to teach students how to engage in critical thinking in the subject matter classroom.

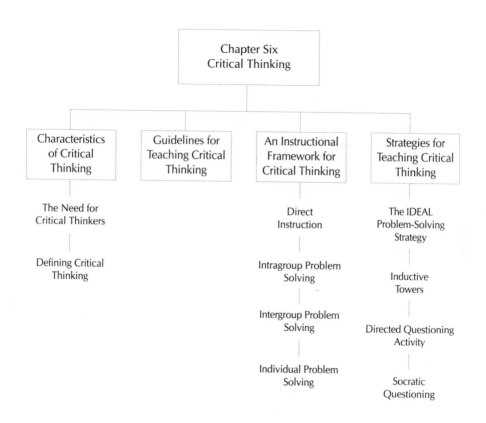

CHARACTERISTICS OF CRITICAL THINKING

This chapter should be viewed as an extension of the comprehension strategies in Chapter Five, in that both chapters focus on improving students' ability to comprehend. Here, however, we restrict our discussion to higher level literacy tasks, such as Costa's higher level questions and the QARs (see Chapter Five), in which students must use their background knowledge in concert with or supplemental to text information.

This section presents the characteristics of critical thinking, a model to describe the critical thinking process, and a definition of that process.

The Need for Critical Thinkers

In recent years there has been increasing recognition that critical thinking should be a fundamental outcome of K through 12 schooling. Citing the need for workers and citizens who can generate solutions to problems and tasks encountered in the workplace and life in the modern world, political, business, and educational leaders have joined forces in efforts to improve the "thinking curriculum." These calls come at a time when we acknowledge the disparity between societal expectations and students' performance. As findings of a recent study by the National Assessment of Educational Progress (Mullis, Owen, & Phillips, 1990) conclude,

> The NAEP results indicate a remarkable consistency across subject areas—students are learning facts and skills, but few show the capacity for complex reasoning and problem solving. Recent assessments indicate that performance is improving, which is laudable, but overall achievement levels remain similar to those posted two decades ago. (p. 33)

In part, students' performance on higher level thinking tasks may be a result of the absence of an agreed upon instructional approach to teaching skills as well as our inability to reach consensus on a common definition of critical thinking. Critical thinking instruction falls into one of three approaches. The first, *isolated skills*, focuses on the instruction of what are believed to be the skills of critical thinking. These skills are generally taught in isolation with the assumption that they will transfer to subject matter curricula. The second, the *infusion approach*, advances the instruction of critical thinking skills within the regular curriculum (Ennis, 1989; Perkins & Salomon, 1989), concentrating both on strategies and the content. The third, the *immersion approach*, focuses on ideas and concepts rather than the process of critical thinking (Prawat, 1991). Inherent in these three approaches are rather different assumptions about the cognitive processes of thinking critically. At one extreme, critical thinking is seen as directed by a set of skills removed from content, while at the other, it is seen as directed by the generation of ideas and concepts richly embedded in content-specific materials. It is not surprising, therefore, to find significant variation in definitions of critical thinking. For some, it is thinking that is reasonable and focused on what an individual should believe or do (Ennis, 1987). For others, it is a step-by-step process that involves (1) identifying a problem, (2) generating a hypothesis, (3) gathering evidence, (4) testing the hypothesis, and (5) drawing conclusions (Haggard, 1988). And for still others, it is the product of an element of intelligence that comprises the mental processes, strategies, and representations that people use to solve problems, learn novel concepts, or make decisions (Sternberg, 1986).

Although there is lack of agreement on the definition of critical thinking or how it should be taught, two general conclusions about the nature of thinking critically can be drawn. First, critical thinking is much more than the ability to recall details and facts at the concrete, surface level of meaning. It involves formal logical procedures, problem solving, and accessing of one's cognitive and metacognitive processes. Second, responses or solutions to critical thinking tasks depend on an individual's knowledge of concepts and ideas in a given subject matter domain. Solutions to these problems, therefore, will vary according to the concepts and ideas that are presented in the student's response.

Defining Critical Thinking

In shaping a definition of critical thinking for this text, consideration is given to three characteristics that could be likened to a "cognitive engine" that propels the critical thinking process. These three elements, shown in Figure 6.1, include (1) the ability of the learner to draw on background knowledge, (2) the ability of the learner to obtain or derive meaning from diverse sources of information, and (3) the ability of the learner to recognize or generate objectives that direct attention and regulate thinking. These elements are used interactively,

FIGURE 6.1   CRITICAL THINKING ELEMENTS

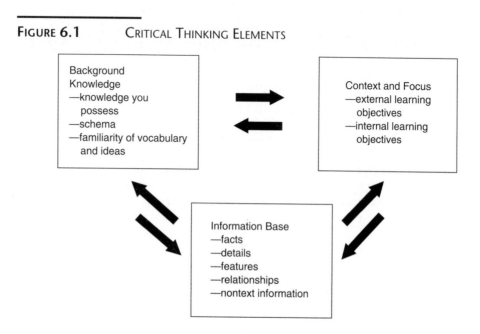

with constant adjustments being made to reach a solution to the problem. Possessing background knowledge for a critical thinking task, for example, a student could define additional information that could contribute to that knowledge and dictate where that information may be found. Yet the student may never engage in critical thinking due to an inability to recognize or generate a critical thinking task. All three elements must be present to generate appropriate solutions to problems. Consider the interactive nature of these elements in the following paragraph.

> For many years, American farmers had relied on chemicals to fertilize the soil, eradicate weeds, and eliminate insects. Yet, as these products became more expensive and as greater amounts of soil were lost to overproduction, farmers began to explore alternatives to chemicals. Ironically, many of the solutions have not been drawn from recent scientific advances but from traditions that have their historical roots thousands of years in the past. Central American Indians, for example, have interplanted corn, beans, and squash to enrich the soil with nitrogen and to reduce erosion and weeds. Other farmers use vacuums attached to tractors to suck up insects, or produce and release insects such as ladybugs that devour aphids and other troublesome insects. And by planting crops in rows that are raised one foot, insects and weeds are reduced, and yields increase as the plants obtain more direct sunlight. Surprisingly, these efforts toward "sustainable" farming appear to increase yields, while simultaneously reducing costs.

This is not a particularly difficult paragraph. Background knowledge derived from planting a garden combined with information about farming most of us have acquired over the years allow a literal understanding of this paragraph. Yet, unless a purpose for reading this paragraph was generated, it is not likely that you engaged in critical thinking. Now, reread the paragraph to determine how the economic costs of sustainable farming differ from those of traditional farming. Make certain you answer this question before you continue reading.

Rereading the paragraph to determine the costs of sustainable farming provided a new focus. Rather than reading for details or to obtain a gist of the selection, reading was purposeful—there was a specific objective in mind. The information base (the paragraph above) provided little insight into the costs of new farming methods. Lacking other text sources, an answer to the question may have been constructed from background knowledge (e.g., estimating the cost of new equipment to vacuum insects or to harvest multiple crops). Ultimately, the lack of additional sources of information and rather limited background knowledge on this method of farming may have minimized the likelihood of processing this question in a manner characteristic of critical thinking.

No doubt, it is now evident that critical thinking involves much more than a set of skills that can be applied to any problem. For the learner, it involves recognizing what he or she knows and what needs to be known to solve a problem, clearly defining the problem or objectives that lead to the solution of the problem, and seeking out information from various sources. With these elements of critical thinking in mind, here is the definition of critical thinking used throughout this chapter.

> Critical thinking is the active use of formal logical procedures involving cognitive and metacognitive processes to understand the world beyond its literal meaning.

This is a rather broad definition. Note that it embodies problem solving—an element of cognition in which the learner has a goal in mind, and a set of mental operations or steps required to reach that goal (van Dijk & Kintsch, 1983). And it involves creative thinking—the ability to form new combinations of ideas to fulfill a need (Halpern, 1984). The definition emphasizes the learner's ability to engage actively in and monitor thinking strategies. Less emphasis is placed on labeling the outcomes of a critical thinking task in favor of defining ways to teach students how they can successfully engage in higher level cognitive tasks. In summary, the definition of critical thinking offered here focuses on the active use of cognitive strategies that extend beyond the reproduction, retrieval, or recognition of literal or factual-level information. Activating these strategies depends on the learner's ability to define a problem, to draw on existing knowledge, to seek additional information, and to develop a logical and reasonable response.

This section has presented the characteristics of critical thinking, a definition of critical thinking, and examples of critical thinking questions. In closing, it is important to emphasize that critical thinking requires background knowledge, the ability to draw on or recognize information presented or obtained from various sources, and the ability to define an objective or goal that directs and regulates the critical thinking process. As such, critical thinking is intentional learning. Students who are proficient at higher level thinking know what they want to learn and know how to redirect their thinking when their goals are not immediately realized. Students who have difficulty with higher level thinking lack many of these same characteristics. Yet, with the teacher's assistance, all students can succeed with critical thinking tasks.

PRACTICE ACTIVITY 6.1

Read the paragraph, then answer the two critical thinking questions that follow. Answers can be found in the answers section at the end of the book.

Acid rain occurs when rainfall reacts with a variety of gases in the atmosphere. Some of these gases or particles are naturally occurring. Forest fires, lightning, and the decomposition of organic matter are all sources of acid-producing substances. As factories, homes, vehicles, and other sources add chemicals to the air by burning fossil fuels, levels of acid rain rise. Acid rain often falls in areas far away from the source of pollutants. Generally, factors that influence where acid rain will fall include temperature, wind direction and speed, humidity, and intensity of sunlight.

1. Would acid rain continue to occur if we no longer burned oil, coal, natural gas, or gasoline?
2. Why are the effects of acid rain in the United States much more visible in the eastern part of the country than in the west?

GUIDELINES FOR TEACHING CRITICAL THINKING

This section presents some guidelines for the instruction of critical thinking in the subject matter classroom. It begins by noting that most students, despite their ability, can succeed in critical thinking tasks. In the past, only the more academically talented students were taught critical thinking. Today, with the ever-increasing need for workers who possess higher level thinking skills, all students must receive critical thinking instruction. As Resnick (1987) has noted, this change in emphasis presents a challenge.

> Although it is not new to include thinking, problem solving, and reasoning in *someone's* school curriculum, it is new to include it in *everyone's* curriculum. It is new to take seriously the aspiration of making thinking and problem solving a regular part of a school program for all of the population, even minorities, even non-English speakers, even the poor. It is a new challenge to develop educational programs that assume that all individuals, not just an elite, can become competent thinkers. (p. 7)

Teaching critical thinking is not easy. It will require you to fill in gaps in students' background knowledge, present reasonable and effective strategies, and sequence instruction over a period of time so that students eventually will be able to engage in critical thinking independent of your assistance. Clearly, critical thinking instruction is not limited to reading. Critical thinking tasks frequently occur during class discussions, recitations, demonstrations, class projects, physical activities, and activities involving the arts. For example, Practice Activity 6.2 poses a question involving the ability to examine and apply visual information to mathematical concepts. The answer appears in the answers section at the end of the book.

PRACTICE ACTIVITY 6.2

Presume that you own a dairy farm and that you are initiating efforts to reduce shipping and packaging costs. You decide to begin reducing costs associated with the half-pint size containers of milk you sell. Presume that the following two containers are made of the same material and that they both contain the same amount of milk. If each of these two types of containers is packed in a 2 ft by 3 ft by 1 ft shipping box, which of the two containers would provide the largest savings in shipping and packaging costs?

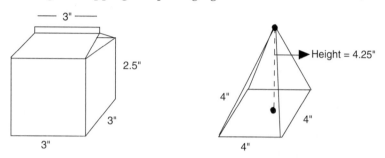

A response to the question in Practice Activity 6.2 requires knowledge of how to compute volumes and areas of a surface and the ability to visualize the arrangement of objects in a specified area (the inside of the container). It also requires prior knowledge (the fact that the top of a half-pint milk container is an empty space). The question is typical of the everyday critical thinking problems that require the application of mathematics.

While it would seem reasonable for students to engage in critical thinking tasks on a regular basis, examinations of classroom practice indicate that students rarely have the opportunity to engage in higher level thinking. It is apparent that the vast majority of questions presented by the teacher require verbatim responses (Alvermann & Hayes, 1989; Armbruster et al., 1991; Wiley, 1977). A similar emphasis on memorization of factual information has been observed in those questions presented in textbooks (Smith & Feathers, 1983). Even when students are presented with higher level questions, their responses are often muted by a reluctance to engage in tasks they perceive as having a high level of failure and ambiguity (Doyle, 1984), seemingly unable to recognize any immediate payoff (Perkins & Simmons, 1988). Realistically, teaching critical thinking will require careful planning and persistence. The following guidelines will be useful in efforts to engage students in critical thinking and to increase the likelihood that students will succeed with higher level thinking.

1. **Critical thinking strategies should be taught in conjunction with subject matter content.** The transfer of critical thinking skills to everyday problem solving rarely occurs unless students are shown when and why specific critical thinking strategies are useful (Brown, Campione, & Day, 1981). The question of whether students can learn critical thinking strategies apart from the content of a specific area of study has generated considerable debate. Resnick (1987), for example, argues that if students lack subject matter knowledge, teaching general critical thinking strategies will be impossible. Critical thinking is not likely to be based on an abstract set of rules that can be applied in any situation. Rather, it is purposeful thinking about information that is familiar (McPeck, 1981). Smith (1990) suggests that critical thinking does not require a set of

learned skills, but knowledge of what one thinks about. An expert in a field of study is likely to be highly successful at critical thinking tasks related to that field. Unfortunately, mastering concepts and skills in a profession does not ensure transfer or understanding its real-world applications (Bransford, Sherwood, Rieser, & Vye, 1986). And mastering a large set of factual information is not likely to generate critical thinking by itself. This problem was addressed many years ago by Whitehead (1929), who noted the dangers of inert knowledge—knowledge used only in a very limited situation or context. Whitehead's concern that educational programs in the early part of this century produced knowledge that remained inert is a condition that still exists today. Much of school learning involves the memorization of unrelated pieces of information rather than the application of that information to real-life problems. It is common, for example, in studying world geography for students to learn the crops, industries, climate, and government of a particular country, but not engage in activities to apply that information to construct new knowledge. It would be unlikely, therefore, for students to engage in problems requiring an understanding of how political, economic, and geographical factors influence a nation's production of durable goods (e.g., how can Japanese companies manufacture so many automobiles when the country doesn't have the natural resources required to produce the basic components of a car?). The challenge to the subject matter teacher is planning an instructional lesson that addresses both the acquisition of information and the application of critical thinking strategies. Meeting this challenge will require the application of the appropriate strategies, and initially it will require some additional planning and preparation.

2. **Critical thinking instruction should present students with real-life problems.** Presentation of instructional activities that reflect real-life problems can increase the likelihood that students will transfer critical thinking strategies to problems encountered outside the classroom and that they will develop methods for identifying and solving these types of problems (Sternberg, 1988). As you plan critical thinking activities, you should consider the following characteristics of real-life problems, adapted from those identified by Sternberg (1985).

- In the real world, it is often hard to recognize that a problem exists.
- In everyday problem solving, it is often harder to figure out just what the problem is than to figure out how to solve it.
- Everyday problems don't always have all the information we need to solve them.
- In everyday problem solving, it is not usually clear just what information will be needed to solve a given problem. Sometimes it is difficult to know where we can find information that helps us solve the problem.
- A solution may work for only that particular problem and circumstance.
- Everyday problems generally have no one right solution.
- The solutions of everyday problems depend on information you know and strategies you use to solve the problem.

- Solutions to important everyday problems have consequences that matter.
- Everyday problem solving often occurs in groups.
- Everyday problems can be complicated, messy, and stubbornly persistent.

Knowledge of these characteristics can increase awareness of everyday problems. Providing each student a copy of the above characteristics and displaying them prominently in the classroom will help maintain an awareness of problem-solving tasks. Students will acquire a better understanding of these characteristics when you discuss each characteristic, explain its importance in solving problems, and provide numerous examples of how the characteristics apply to everyday problems. Finally, you should encourage students to generate examples of everyday problems they encounter, identify the characteristics that apply to those problems, then discuss the importance of developing strategies to solve them.

Engaging students in activities that draw their attention to Sternberg's guidelines enhances both their awareness of the cognitive elements involved in solving problems and the nature of the problems themselves. These characteristics are useful in assessing the incidence of problem-solving activities in individual classrooms. They also can be used to assess questions and activities presented in textbooks or supplementary instructional materials. If you determine that activities fail to exemplify the characteristics of everyday problems, you should develop critical thinking exercises to replace those appearing in existing materials.

3. **Critical thinking instruction may be novel.** Critical thinking instruction is likely to be different from the sorts of activities typically used in most classrooms or those recalled from your own schooling. It is more than asking questions that require students to "think critically." It is an approach to presenting and modeling a strategy, to allowing students guided practice with the strategy, and finally to leading students to the point at which they can apply the strategy independently.

Critical thinking strategies often feature (a) cooperative learning, (b) the use of multiple sources of information, (c) a willingness to allow for a wide range of student responses, and (d) an emphasis on allowing students to become aware of their own cognition. While this may appear to be an excessively complicated effort, it is a natural part of many teachers' day-to-day instruction. On the other hand, if a teacher is accustomed to relying on a single text, regularly having students engage in individual seatwork activities and stressing the memorization of details, then critical thinking instruction will require a concerted effort.

How is critical thinking instruction different from the more traditional forms of instruction? Figure 6.2 compares two techniques for teaching critical thinking in mathematics. The first example follows a very traditional approach, wherein the teacher provides a lecture or discussion of a topic, then directs students to work independently on a series of problems. The second example exemplifies the four aspects of critical thinking instruction. Each involves the presentation of the concept that *distance traveled* equals *rate* multiplied by *time traveled* ($D = RT$).

FIGURE 6.2   COMPARISON OF TRADITIONAL AND CRITICAL
                    THINKING INSTRUCTION

Traditional Instruction

Step 1:
   Teacher introduces the formula *distance* = rate × time ($D = RT$) by first discussing the meaning of each component of the formula, then providing students examples of calculating the formula.

Step 2:
   Students receive the following three problems to complete independently.

   a. If John travels to Lake Elmo in 2½ hours and covers 102 miles in that time, what is his average rate of speed?
   b. United Airlines flight 601 travels 1,200 miles at a speed of 425 miles per hour. How long did the flight last?
   c. Jose's car has enough gas to go 50 more miles. If he has been traveling for 4 hours at an average speed of 52 miles per hour and needs to travel a total distance of 490 miles, will he have enough gas to complete his trip?

Critical Thinking Instruction

Step 1:
   Teacher provides students with the following critical thinking question: You and a friend have decided to drive your automobile from your home in Kansas City to Denver, a distance of 400 miles. Consider that you and your friend will switch from driver to passenger every 2 hours. Unless you learn otherwise, presume that the entire distance will be driven on interstate highways where the posted speed limit is 65 miles per hour. You are driving an auto that gets about 23 miles per gallon. You will leave at 7:00 A.M. Carefully consider the stops you will need to make to eat breakfast, lunch, and perhaps dinner, as well as the time needed to procure gasoline. Also consider construction projects along the way that may delay your travel or cause you to detour from your route. Given all these conditions, what time (to the minute) do you estimate you will arrive in Denver?

Step 2:
   Students are now assigned to cooperative learning groups. They are told that each group will be given a specific task and that they will need to report back to the class on the information they obtained. Students will be directed to solve the entire problem once they have received information from each of the cooperative groups. Hopefully, several groups will respond to each question. Here are the questions for each group.

   a. Determine exactly the time needed to eat breakfast and lunch. In answering this question, you will need to determine the type of place you will be eating (fast food, sit-down restaurant, etc.). You must be able to substantiate your response.

b. Examine the route from Kansas City to Denver. Telephone the Colorado and Kansas tourist departments (they have toll-free lines) to determine if there are any construction projects or detours on the interstate system that will slow your journey. If so, determine the amount of time you will be delayed. Be precise in your calculations.

c. Assuming that your car's gas tank will hold 10.5 gallons of fuel, determine how many fuel stops you will need to make between Kansas City and Denver and the precise amount of time needed for each stop.

d. Your task is to inform the class that your auto will suffer some sort of mechanical problem that will delay your journey for 2 hours. Be prepared to define to the class the type of mechanical problem that would require a 2-hour repair. You may want to consult a book on automobile repair or discuss this problem with an automotive mechanic. Also, you are to inform the class that while repairing your car, the mechanic broke the speedometer cable, which cannot be replaced. You no longer will be able to determine how fast you are going using the speedometer. There are signs on the interstate that will help you determine how fast you are going if you use your watch. How can you monitor your speed?

Step 3:

Each group is then directed to report the information to the entire class. This information is noted by the teacher on the board or an overhead projector. Once all information has been presented, each group is instructed to solve the problem and be prepared to provide a rationale for their response.

Step 4:

Teacher introduces students to the formula *distance = rate × time* (*D = RT*) by first discussing each component of the formula, then providing several examples of calculating the formula. Students should receive a handout containing the formula and examples of its application. Students should have the opportunity to reexamine the problem and their solutions, then modify the solutions based on the teacher's presentation.

Step 5:

Each group presents their response and rationale for solving the problem. Following the group's presentation, the teacher leads a discussion to describe the students' process in solving the problem. The teacher attempts to summarize the process by defining the steps students followed and where applicable, generalizing these steps to other problem-solving situations.

Figure 6.2 demonstrates the application of cooperative learning, the selection of information obtained from various sources, the attention to students' awareness of their own cognition, and the acceptance of a range of plausible responses. Although the problem could be solved by students individually, consider the consequences of that approach. Students would be limited to their own resourcefulness, they would not share ideas with peers who may represent various cultural and intellectual backgrounds, and their opportunity to gain insight into the metacognitive strategies of their peers would be limited. Similarly, the problem could be simplified to reduce the amount and number of sources of information required to reach a solution and to limit the range of plausible responses. However, this would result in a problem unlike those encountered in everyday problem-solving tasks, thus reducing the likelihood that students would transfer problem-solving strategies beyond the context of the problem. And it could reduce the likelihood that students would generate answers based on creative approaches to solving the problem.

This section has presented some suggestions for the instruction of critical thinking in the subject matter classroom. By now, it should be evident that critical thinking instruction is a process to construct knowledge within an area or domain of study. It should not be viewed as a set of skills or strategies to be taught in isolation, but a component of the day-to-day instruction in the subject matter classroom. These assumptions make it clear that critical thinking instruction will require an instructional framework different from what we typically encounter in a classroom setting. The next section presents such a framework to serve as the basis for the presentation of strategies presented later in this chapter.

PRACTICE ACTIVITY 6.3

Here is a problem identified by a seventh-grade student. Take a moment to determine which of the 10 characteristics of everyday problems cited in this section are evident in this problem. The answer can be found in the answers section at the end of the book.

> You have been saving your money for some time to buy a compact stereo system. You are trying to determine if you want to purchase the various components of a system or a system sold only as an integrated unit. The component system sounds much better and has all the features you want but costs about $180 more than the integrated unit. You have exactly enough money for the integrated unit. Right now you own a portable cassette player with a good set of headphones. You have two criteria: You want a system now and you want a great sounding system. What will you do?

AN INSTRUCTIONAL FRAMEWORK FOR CRITICAL THINKING

This section presents a model for critical thinking instruction. Recognize that this is an instructional framework, not an instructional strategy. The purpose here is to present a systematic procedure for teaching critical thinking once a strategy to address particular subject matter objectives has been selected. This framework, based on one proposed by Sternberg and Davidson (1984), consists of four steps. They begin with the teacher presenting a thinking skill to the students and conclude with students engaging in independent problem solving. The four steps are (1) direct instruction, (2) intragroup problem solving, (3) intergroup problem solving, and (4) individual problem solving. The following provides a description of these steps, including a comprehensive example of the process of direct instruction.

Direct Instruction

Direct instruction involves communicating a skill to students. It comprises the following steps:

1. Present and discuss real-world examples.
2. Analyze process of solving examples.
3. Label and define the process.
4. Converge and discriminate from other processes.
5. Analyze more practical examples in process terms.
6. Generate group examples.

Practical, Real-World Examples: Presentation and Discussion. To begin, present students with several everyday problems that require the application of a certain critical thinking skill or strategy. These problems should be relevant and interesting and should require the students' active participation. It should be emphasized that you must focus on the process of the critical thinking strategy as well as the content needed to complete the task.

Group Analysis of Mental Processes Used in Solution of Examples. Once students apply a critical thinking strategy to an everyday problem, you can engage them in a discussion describing the thinking strategies they applied to the problem. By examining their own thought processes, students are more likely to attend actively to the task at hand and to acquire the given strategy. The benefits of group processing become increasingly evident over time. If students are not accustomed to analyzing their own thinking processes, they will require adequate time to develop group dynamics and a dialogue that describes their thought processes.

Labeling and Definition of Process. Next, label and define how the strategy presented is similar to or different from previously learned strategies. This process promotes the use of a common language to describe critical thinking. Having these commonly shared terms assists students in communicating their thought processes to one another and in reaching their own internal conceptualizations.

Convergence With and Discrimination From Other Processes. Now show students how the new process is similar to or different from those learned previously. This step, notes Sternberg and Davidson (1984), is necessary for aiding students in their development of integrated cognitive structures.

More Practical Examples, Analyzed in Process Terms. Here you present practical and relevant problems. This step stresses students' ability to solve problems while simultaneously describing the process of solving the problems. Encourage students to make use of a newly acquired strategy or process or those learned previously. This allows students to compare strategies, noting similarities and differences, then to integrate common elements of those strategies.

Group-Generated Examples.   This is an important element of direct instruction. Stress the importance of constructing problems that require use of the selected critical thinking strategy. This encourages students to consider the application of a selected strategy to various types of problems that are relevant to them.

The steps involved in direct instruction are rather comprehensive. Before proceeding to the next step in the Sternberg-Davidson model, here is an example of a lesson containing direct instruction. This example comes from a high school social studies unit in which students are learning about advertising. The example deals with the techniques of advertising products displayed on grocery store or discount department store shelves. As the example is examined, assume the role of a student and respond to the questions or directions provided. Information presented by the teacher is in italics. Directions for you are in boldface.

Direct Instruction

For the past several days we have been learning about advertising. We have examined several types of advertising, and the purpose of advertising products, and we have examined various advertising media. Today, we will learn techniques for advertising products displayed in stores. Here is a practical problem that I would like you to solve: Let's say you have developed a new soft drink called Limeola Leap. How can you display this product to ensure maximum sales?

In solving this problem, use the strategy we have been examining over the past several weeks. Here are the steps to that strategy.

1. *List everything you know that may be helpful in answering the question.*
2. *Given what you know, what information in the problem do you need to learn more about? Once you have identified these factors, read or talk with me or someone outside class to get the needed information. You may actually want to go through the steps of trying to solve the problem to get a better idea of the things you may need to learn before you can successfully do so.*
3. *Examine what you know and what you have learned from Step 2. Then decide what information is not important and discard it. Using the information that remains, attempt to formulate an answer or several answers to the problem.*

Use this strategy now to formulate an answer to the problem.

Group Analysis of Mental Processes Used in Solution of Examples

Take a few moments to think about how you answered this question. Think about the steps you used to obtain an answer. For now, don't think about the question it-

self, but the steps you used to answer the question. Here are some things to think about.

1. *How did listing what you know about the question help you in your answer?*
2. *With this problem you were asked to determine additional information you needed in order to solve it. Why might this by a useful procedure in solving problems? What might you do differently next time when trying to think about additional information you may need in solving a problem?*
3. *In the final step of this problem you were asked to determine what information was not necessary or useful in answering the question. Think about other problems or questions you have encountered recently. Is this a useful step in solving different types of problems?*

Think about the process needed to obtain an answer to the critical thinking question. Answer the questions to define that process.

Labeling and Definition of Process

The critical thinking strategy we have used here requires you to determine what you know about the problem, what elements you define from the problem itself, and what additional information you may need to solve the problem. Sometimes you may find it useful to repeat the three steps in this process.

Convergence With and Discrimination for Other Processes

Last week we learned a critical thinking strategy designed to help us examine a problem, then decided if each piece of information in the problem was relevant or irrelevant to the problem's solution. Think about the strategy we have learned today. How is this strategy similar to last week's strategy? How is it different? Let's note those differences on the overhead. Note these similarities and differences in your critical thinking strategy journals.

More Practical Examples

Here are three more critical thinking problems. Look at each of these problems to decide if the strategy we learned today would help you solve these problems. You need not solve the problems.

1. *You are touring an art museum. You are asked to decide which medium (oils, watercolors, etc.) allows the richest expression of depth of vision.*
2. *Consider world events over the past 50 years. Has the development of the atomic bomb been a deterrent to military hostilities between countries?*
3. *Why do writers of fiction often address social issues of their times? In answering this question, consider economic, social, or political motives of the author.*

Examine each of the preceding three problems to consider if the strategy presented above would be effective in solving them.

Group-Generated Examples

Create three critical thinking problems that could be answered using the strategy we have discussed today.

Several elements of direct instruction in this critical thinking model are noteworthy. First, students attend to both the content of the problem and the process for solving the problem. The teacher's role is dedicated to constructing critical thinking problems, modeling the strategy, then providing students ample opportunity to learn the selected strategy. Second, this approach is highly flexible. At any point in the process, the teacher can provide additional assistance or clarification. Because the emphasis here is on the problem-solving process and students' needs, the teacher is not restricted by critical thinking tasks presented in a text or workbook. The types of critical thinking problems presented to students should reflect their level of background knowledge, their motivation to learn, and their ability to work cooperatively.

Intragroup Problem Solving

Following direct instruction, students are given a series of rather complex problem-solving tasks. The intent here is to allow students to activate and apply selected strategies within their group. The teacher should emphasize the importance of applying a selected strategy; students' success with the task is secondary. It may be useful at this step to have students monitor their own process of problem solving and to share that process with their peers.

Intergroup Problem Solving

According to Sternberg and Davidson (1984), shared discussions of the mental processes for problem solving allow groups to better monitor and evaluate success of those skills. By analyzing the problem-solving process of their peers, students learn how to monitor critical thinking skills. Monitoring and evaluating are not always natural outcomes of intergroup problem solving. Therefore, consider having each group maintain a log containing summaries of their observations of the problem-solving process. Periodically, these group summaries can be shared and discussed with the entire class.

Individual Problem Solving

The final step in the Sternberg-Davidson model involves individual problem solving. Following intergroup and intragroup problem solving, students should have internalized the critical thinking strategy and the processes for monitoring and evaluating their ability to apply the strategy. Individual problem-solving activities allow the student to engage in self-monitoring of the critical thinking strategy and to seek assistance for problems they encounter.

Commentary: Sternberg-Davidson Model. This instructional framework offers a practical approach to aiding students' critical thinking. The application of direct instruction, inter- and intragroup problem solving, group discussion of students' metacognition, and the individual's use of the strategy to solve practical problems make this a comprehensive approach to teaching critical thinking strategies. Students are likely to respond positively to the diverse activities and share their experiences as they engage in relevant problems. This model contains many of the problem-solving steps students follow in their everyday lives. For that reason, it will be more effective when used in conjunction with content that is both practical and relevant.

Because this is a comprehensive approach to teaching critical thinking, it may seem too time-consuming. Note that the various steps of this framework can be phased in over an extended period. For example, you may devote 30 minutes each week over a period of 4 or 5 weeks to direct instruction. Then, over the next 3 to 4 weeks, you can direct 30 minutes each week to intragroup problem solving. Similarly, intergroup and individual problem solving can be presented for a specified amount of time each week over an extended period. This approach will help you manage the amount of time needed to prepare for this instructional framework, while at the same time ensuring that critical thinking is addressed throughout the curriculum.

STRATEGIES FOR TEACHING CRITICAL THINKING

We turn now to the presentation of four critical thinking strategies. These strategies are flexible—they will apply to a variety of problem-solving tasks in a variety of subject matter areas. The first strategy presented here, IDEAL, is designed to encourage students to learn to solve problems on their own. The second strategy, inductive towers, is a form of cooperative critical thinking used to promote students' ability to form concepts and engage in higher level thinking through a process of inquiry. The third strategy, the directed questioning activity, provides a sequential approach to teaching students a process for generating and answering higher level questions. And the fourth strategy, Socratic questioning, is a method of discussion to promote students' ability to examine their own thinking and evaluate the thinking of their peers.

The IDEAL Problem-Solving Strategy

The IDEAL problem-solving strategy was developed by Bransford and Stein (1984). IDEAL stands for the process of (1) *identifying* the problem, (2) *defining* the problem, (3) *exploring* strategies to solve the problem, (4) *acting* on ideas to solve the problem, and (5) *looking* for the effects of one's thought processes. Here is a description of this five-stage process.

Identifying the Problem. The first step in the IDEAL model is being aware that a problem exists. For the student lacking background information or problem-solving strategies, recognizing the existence of a problem may be a difficult task. Accordingly, you may find it necessary to draw attention to problem identification strategies by encouraging students to discuss aloud the processes they use when identifying a problem. If students hesitate in their response, be prepared to give them a description of this process.

Defining the Problem.   The second step of the IDEAL model involves a precise definition of the problem. Here, the learner must go beyond the recognition that a problem exists; the problem itself must be defined. Consider the following scenario. One day while writing this text, one of the authors decided a bike ride would offer a brief reprieve. Once on his bike, he noticed that he seemed to be exerting an unusually high level of energy. Uncertain if the problem was the bike or himself, he pulled alongside a rider of similar weight and asked that they coast in tandem down a lengthy hill. Within a few minutes, the second rider shot ahead of him. Pulling off the road, the author picked up his bike and spun the wheels, only to discover that the brake pads were rubbing against the rim of the wheel. In this case, the problem was recognized (excessive effort bicycling) and defined (the problem was a mechanical problem with the bike).

Defining problems requires the activation of background knowledge, relating that information to the perceived problem, then isolating those factors that identify the problem.

Exploring Strategies.   The third step of the IDEAL model is to explore the various approaches to solving a problem. Here the student must draw on acquired problem-solving strategies to determine if they are appropriate for the problem at hand. At times, the student may find it necessary to adapt or modify a strategy to meet the requirements of a particular problem. Some students find it difficult to solve problems either because they do not possess the appropriate strategies or because they do not know when to activate and apply an acquired strategy. In their effort to define approaches to solving problems, Bransford and Stein (1984) note that experienced problem solvers adhere to a conscious and systematic approach that includes the following steps:

1. Break down a complex problem into its various parts.
2. Work a problem backward.
3. Rework the problem to solve a simpler, more specific situation.

While these appear to be steps most of us follow in problem solving, they may not always lead to a solution to the problem. For example, these steps are of little use if we do not understand the information necessary to solve the problem. Furthermore, these steps may not be strategies to direct thinking, but artifacts of the thinking process. Recognizing these limitations, Bransford and Stein recommend that problem-solving activities be preceded by the instruction of subject matter concepts required to solve the problem. In a science class, for example, presentation of the concepts of refraction, reflection, and absorption would aid students in solving a problem requiring them to determine how a thermos keeps liquids hot, or how windows might be constructed to provide better insulation for buildings. Conceptualizing and solving problems in all subject matter areas require knowledge of a multitude of concepts. Drawing students' attention to these concepts is an important element in teaching problem solving. Eventually, however, students will need to draw on or locate concepts relevant to the problem at hand on their own. To accomplish this goal, consider the following steps once a problem has been defined:

1. Discuss with students concepts they believe will assist in solving the problem. Have students explain to the class why they selected these concepts.
2. Ask students to identify procedures for locating concepts that may assist in solving the problem. Emphasize to students that identifying the concepts that apply to a problem is an important step in solving it.
3. Model to the students the steps you follow in trying to identify concepts that would aid in the solution of a problem.

Acting on Ideas and Looking at the Effects.   The final two steps of the IDEAL model involve acting on identified problem-solving strategies or solutions and looking carefully at the effects of these strategies. Because these two steps are so closely related, they are combined in the discussion that follows.

Students should realize that generating alternate solutions can actually make problem solving more efficient. Many students, who may fail to act-then-evaluate each step in the problem, either generate an incorrect response or fail to recognize the existence of an error. Without alternatives, they may give up on the task altogether.

Although Bransford and Stein (1984) do not specify how to teach students the final two steps in the IDEAL strategy, you may find the following suggestions useful.

1. Provide students with a handout listing the steps to solving a problem. Direct students, now assigned to cooperative learning groups, to engage in the first step, then reflect upon and evaluate its effectiveness. Once each group has written an evaluation, share and discuss these evaluations and acknowledge any alternate strategies they may have identified. Where applicable, ask students to describe how they derived an alternative strategy.
2. Present a problem to students, then identify the number of steps involved in obtaining an answer. For each step, ask each group to generate a process for solving that component of the problem. These processes can then be shared and discussed with the entire class. During this discussion encourage each group to describe both the process and their rationale for applying a particular strategy.
3. Work backwards through the problem-solving process. Provide students with the problem and the answer to the problem. Then ask students to determine the various steps they would follow to construct an answer.

Commentary: IDEAL Strategy. This strategy presents some general steps to aid students in their understanding of the process of problem solving. It has two notable strengths. First, it is a practical approach for increasing students' metacognitive awareness of the problem-solving process. Each of the five steps of the IDEAL strategy encourages students to think about and define the cognitive processes involved in problem solving. Clearly, this model will encourage students to think about thinking. Second, the IDEAL strategy offers a practical place for the teacher to begin the process of integrating critical thinking within the subject matter classroom. The steps of this strategy can be adapted to almost any subject matter area with minimal preparation. While this strategy increases awareness of the problem-solving process, many students will experience difficulty transferring it to independent reading. Note that this strategy does not monitor each step of the problem-solving process. As a result, students may not know when they make an error and therefore will be unable to activate some sort of fix-up strategy when they fail to solve the problem. Use of this model, therefore, may need to be limited to instances where problem-solving is addressed as a whole-class or cooperative-group activity.

PRACTICE ACTIVITY 6.4

Note the importance of the act and look components of the IDEAL model in the following problem presented by Bransford and Stein (1984). Read the problem, complete the first step of your solution, then refer to the paragraph below for further directions.

> There are 12 cannonballs. All look alike, but one is the "oddball." The oddball is either heavier or lighter than the other balls. You are provided a balance scale that can hold as many cannonballs as you would like on each side of the scale. The problem is, in four weighings (four uses of the scale), find the oddball. (p. 21)

For most people, the first step in solving this problem is to place six cannonballs on each side of the scale. However, this procedure does not lead to a correct response to the problem. Because the oddball can be either heavier or lighter than the other cannonballs, grouping the cannonballs does not advance the problem-solving process. Only by acting on a solution, then looking at the outcome of an initial attempt in the problem-solving process, does it become evident that an alternative solution is necessary. Compare your solution to ours in the answers section.

Inductive Towers

Critical thinking often requires readers to recognize or form conceptual relationships. Inductive towers are graphic representations of the thinking process involved in forming concepts and themes (Clarke, Raths, & Gilbert, 1989). An

FIGURE 6.3   EXAMPLE OF INDUCTIVE TOWER ON ISSUES FACING PUBLIC EDUCATION

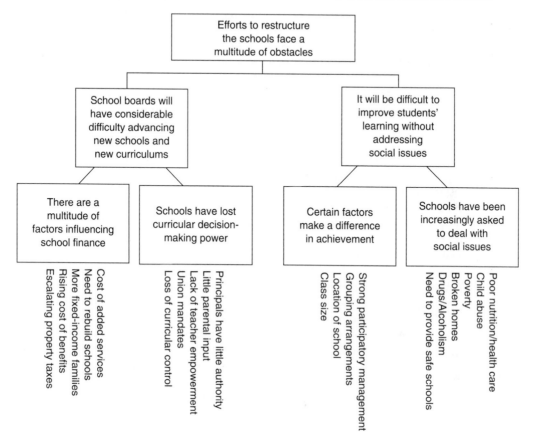

example of an inductive tower is shown in Figure 6.3. Note that this graphic device is a representation of information that begins with the identification of facts and eventually concludes with the construction of a high-level generalization or statement. The steps for constructing a tower, adapted from Clarke and colleagues, follow.

1. Search and retrieve from the information base (from observation, interview, print materials, visual or other media) literal information that appears to be meaningful facts.
2. Link two or more facts that have implied, or logical, relationships to construct a new inferred statement that expresses that relationship.
3. Link two or more of these inferred statements to create a generalization, principle, theory, or rule.
4. Link generalizations, principles, theories, or rules to a new statement that defines a cause/effect relationship, a position of value, or a statement of prediction.

Beginning the Process of Teaching Towers.   Using inductive towers requires students to bring forth information they know or can locate, probe for logical relationships between this information, then generate and define generalizations. Before students construct inductive towers on their own, model the construction of the tower, paying particular attention to linking information through inferences and describing the process of forming generalizations. Limiting the number of facts to four or five should allow students to realize the deductive process of the tower's organization. Once they understand the purpose and construction of the tower, students can begin the process of constructing their own.

Search and Retrieve.   To begin, consider placing students in cooperative learning groups. Working together, students will more readily generate the factual information, and they are more likely to discuss the process of linking that information to construct inferences and generalizations. First, define the problem. Next, ask students to gather facts, statements, quotes, or other surface-level information about a variety of print and nonprint sources. A number of instructional options can be drawn on at this point. One is to ask each group to locate and extract information from numerous sources they are able to locate. Another is to provide each group with a list of a few information sources, with no two groups sharing the same source. Yet another is to direct each individual within a group to certain sources. Once obtained, the information is then brought back to the members of the cooperative group. No matter which option is selected, students should be encouraged to seek information from several sources. Most real-life critical thinking tasks require us to sift through numerous print and nonprint materials. Requiring students to retrieve information from multiple sources not only provides a realistic learning task but makes the students active learners.

Linking Facts.   Now that students have located and defined a body of information, they can begin to construct conceptual linkages. Students begin this process by listing the factual information they have acquired. Consider providing large sheets of paper (butcher paper is excellent) so they will not be hampered by space limitations. Students should contribute information they have located from various sources as well as information that is part of their background knowledge. Once this information is identified, students begin to examine that data to identify or construct logical relationships. For example, consider the following data on the American family between 1960 and 1988:(1) Suicides for teenagers tripled from 3.6 to 11.3 per 1,000, (2) births to unwed mothers rose from 5% to 26% of all births, and (3) the number of children in one-parent families rose from 5.5% to 14.2%. A number of conceptual links can be constructed from this information. Family cohesion has changed markedly; children are more at risk; children today will bring different sorts of problems to school than did children in the past.

Interpreting data and constructing conceptual links require inferential thinking, which may be difficult for some students. If students need assistance in drawing these linkages, the following steps will be useful in creating an awareness of strategies to infer conceptual relationships.

1. **Identify facts or information.** What facts or information seem to be important? Consider how the information is used, where it is used, and who uses it. Discard data or information that is irrelevant or seemingly unrelated.
2. **Look for common qualities.** Based on the preceding step, try to isolate at least two facts or pieces of information that have common attributes or characteristics. Where possible, you as the teacher should draw on your prior knowledge to add information. Attempt to construct a label or heading that describes the relationship between the pieces of information.
3. **Draw conclusions about the labels or headings.** Identify relationships that exist between the labels you have constructed. Try to reach a conclusion about these relationships. Where possible, relate acquired knowledge to the information presented in the lesson.

An example of the application of these steps is shown in Figure 6.4.

Link Inferred Statements to Construct Generalizations.   This step involves linking inferred statements to construct generalizations. Referring to the example on a bird's flight, the following four inferred statements could be constructed:

1. The skeletal system of a bird is lightweight and strong.
2. The respiratory system of a bird allows a constant source of air to enter its body.

FIGURE 6.4   INTERPRETING AND CONSTRUCTING CONCEPTUAL LINKS

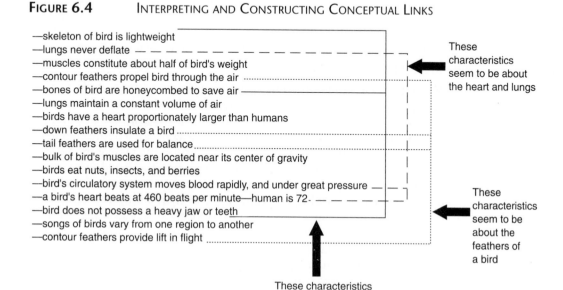

—skeleton of bird is lightweight
—lungs never deflate
—muscles constitute about half of bird's weight
—contour feathers propel bird through the air
—bones of bird are honeycombed to save air
—lungs maintain a constant volume of air
—birds have a heart proportionately larger than humans
—down feathers insulate a bird
—tail feathers are used for balance
—bulk of bird's muscles are located near its center of gravity
—birds eat nuts, insects, and berries
—bird's circulatory system moves blood rapidly, and under great pressure
—a bird's heart beats at 460 beats per minute—human is 72.
—bird does not possess a heavy jaw or teeth
—songs of birds vary from one region to another
—contour feathers provide lift in flight

These characteristics seem to be about the heart and lungs

These characteristics seem to be about the feathers of a bird

These characteristics seem to be about the skeletal system

3. The bird's high metabolic rate is maintained by an efficient circulatory system.
4. Feathers have specialized flight functions.

Understanding common elements in these statements can help in forming generalizations. Note, for example, that Statements 1 and 4 describe characteristics of the bird's physiology that allow it to move through the air, while Statements 2 and 3 describe how the bird produces the energy needed to propel itself during flight. During this step of inferring generalizations, encourage students to vocalize their thoughts. Be prepared to accommodate discussions that allow for risk taking, creativity, and dissension. As noted earlier in this chapter, problem solving can be messy. Answers may not come forth without a great deal of effort, and even when answers are generated, students may not feel comfortable with their response. Recognize in advance that active learning may require group learning processes that promote an open exchange of ideas.

Link Generalizations to Create Themes.   The final step in constructing an inductive tower is defining a theme from the generalizations reached in the preceding step. This theme may be considered to be the central or culminating idea presented in the tower. Once identified, this theme should be logically linked to the subordinate information previously identified in the tower. For example, from the information presented on how a bird flies, one may generate a main theme or culminating idea that a bird's physiology is highly specialized to ensure the survival of the given species.

An inductive tower can provide the framework for promoting students' critical thinking skills in a social context. As students discuss and negotiate the products of each step in constructing the tower, they gain a better metacognitive awareness of the critical thinking process. Sometimes, however, students may experience some difficulty in arriving at an answer. Here are some of the common problems identified by Clarke, et al. (1989).

1. **Mixing facts and abstractions.** As students begin to generate facts, they may present information more appropriately labeled as opinion, conjecture, or generalization. One remedy is to have students cite a source for each of the listed facts. Another is to provide a checklist of the characteristics of facts, then assign a member of the group the task of monitoring to include creating panels of students to review the listed facts, or requesting parents or other teachers to conduct this review.
2. **Omitting or overlooking relevant facts.** In their haste or due to their lack of knowledge, students may fail to locate or identify a variety of sources for obtaining information. One solution to this problem is intergroup discussion. Once a group has identified sources of information, a member of each group consults with another group to discuss and share sources. Students also could be provided direct instruction on the use of library references and online computer databases and document retrieval systems.

3. **Leapfrogging logical steps.** Some groups may leap prematurely to conclusions or link information to infer relationships prior to thoroughly examining the retrieved data. Again, panels of students can examine the constructed tower to critique the groups' interpretations. Students could construct a "justification report" in which they identify a single inferred generalization, then provide a written justification as to why that fact may be linked to the generalization.

4. **Powermongering and acquiescence.** Expect inequalities in the performance of individuals within a group. The range of these inequalities can be reduced by creating groups that are heterogeneous, composed of no more than four to six students, and requiring students to monitor their group's performance (see suggestions for cooperative group evaluations in Chapter Eight).

Commentary: Inductive Towers.   This is an excellent strategy for constructing higher level thinking within a social context. Many students will find the cooperative effort involved in the construction and manipulation of information presented in graphic form an enlightening and enjoyable activity. At the same time, group discussion will increase awareness of the processes involved in critical thinking. Entertaining different points of view, reconciling different approaches to logical constructs or arguments, and reaching a consensus in the context of group learning can get students to think aloud about the process of constructing meaning. As students listen to others and articulate their own thoughts to the members of the group, their attention is focused on their ability to describe their own cognitive strategies. The use of information presented in graphic form provides students with a visual representation of the logical relationships between information that can lead to higher level concepts and themes. An added benefit to constructing inductive towers is that students learn to think from diverse sets of information that they themselves gather. Students should readily engage in a level of inquiry that allows them to locate and then discuss information in an active manner. As active learners responsible for directing their own thinking, students gain a sense of ownership in learning, and they begin to acquire strategies for becoming independent learners.

While inductive towers will stimulate active learning, the tasks presented to students should be reasonable. Information sources should be readily available, and students should have some prior knowledge of the content they are asked to address. Presentation of tasks that are well beyond students' collective level of ability will certainly lead to frustration and a loss of confidence in the ability to succeed with higher level thinking.

Directed Questioning Activity

Students of all abilities can learn to monitor their own comprehension by being shown a process that can improve their understanding and by being encouraged to verbalize this process (Paris, Cross, & Lipson, 1984). Moreover, students can learn higher level thinking strategies when they are taught how to monitor the amount of text information and background information to generate an answer (Raphael & Wonnacott, 1985). The directed questioning activity (DQA; Ryder, 1991) is an instructional process designed to increase students' self-regulation of critical thinking through active involvement requiring the integration of prior knowledge and text information. The DQA is a form of scaffolded instruction—instruction that leads students from a point at which they are dependent on the teacher's guidance to a point at which they function independently. At the beginning of this activity, the teacher constructs questions that will lead students toward higher level thinking. Over time, the teacher's role shifts from generating questioning to coaching students in their efforts to generate and respond to critical thinking questions.

The DQA consists of two instructional components: text-explicit and text-implicit instruction. Text-explicit instruction, conducted prior to reading, builds students' background knowledge and establishes a purpose for critical thinking. Text-implicit instruction occurs during reading to focus students' attention on essential concepts and to provide direct instruction in the process of responding to critical thinking questions. A description of these two components follows.

Text-Explicit Instruction.   This component of the DQA contains activities that build background knowledge and clarify objectives. These activities are limited to a portion of the reading assignment. Preparation for text-explicit instruction involves three steps. First, determine what you want students to learn. Clearly, some of your objectives will require critical thinking. These objectives may be those you construct or those you select from a curriculum or teachers' guide. Second, group content into teachable chunks. The purpose here is to regulate the amount of information students read, to provide a purpose for reading that chunk, and to monitor students' understanding and discuss their interpretation of information contained in the chunk of text read. Third, construct a concept map, frame, or other form of graphic organizer that presents information contained in each chunk of the reading. A detailed discussion of the construction and use of these forms of graphic organizers is presented in Chapter Four. Figure 6.5 gives the overall objectives, the chunked objectives, and the accompanying graphic organizer for a lesson dealing with the Chernobyl disaster.

Text-Implicit Instruction.   In this stage of the DQA you would direct questions to students either prior to or immediately after reading a chunk of text. Questions presented to students prior to reading have been shown to promote active involvement with text and increase comprehension, particularly for those readers who normally do not monitor their understanding as they read (Anderson & Biddle, 1975; Graves & Clark, 1981). Reading with a question in mind also tends to draw the readers' attention to your instructional objectives and promotes the categorization and evaluation of text information (Levin & Pressley, 1981). Students can gain insight into thinking when provided questions that guide their comprehension by making them aware of what they

FIGURE 6.5   GRAPHIC ORGANIZER OF CHERNOBYL DISASTER

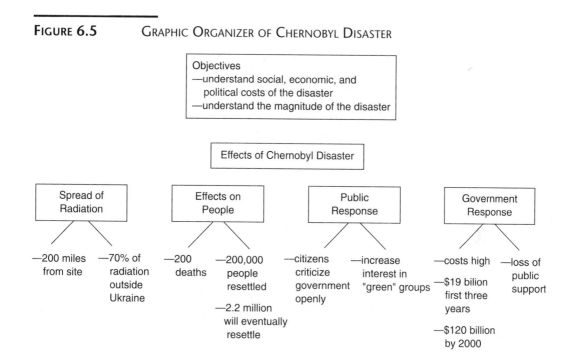

know and what they do not know (Roehler & Duffy, 1984). In general, students read a chapter or section of text, then answer questions included in the text or provided by the teacher. These questions require readers to identify details or construct responses by linking a number of concepts presented in the reading. If readers do not understand a concept presented in the text, or if that concept is not actively recognized during the reading, linking concepts to form generalizations, inferences, conclusions, or hypotheses will be difficult.

The DQA limits the amount of text information students attend to at a given time. Students read a small portion of the reading rather than an entire chapter or section of a text. Questions are presented prior to and during a reading rather than at its conclusion.

Prequestions.   Prequestions are those presented to students immediately before they read. One or two of these questions is usually adequate for each portion of a reading. Additional questions may be distracting. Once students have answered prequestions, have the class discuss them prior to presenting an additional set of questions. In responding to a prequestion, students attend to a small portion of a selection. This may be a paragraph or several pages, depending on the density of concepts in the reading, the students' familiarity with these concepts, and the difficulty of the prequestion itself.

Adjunct Questions.   Adjunct questions are presented to students immediately after an assigned portion of a selection has been read. These are reflective questions; they require the reader to look back and think about an objective different from that presented in prequestions. Often this objective is to respond to a higher level or critical thinking question. Adjunct questions are also cuing questions. The reader is redirected to important concepts or information, and often requested to create some sort of conceptual link.

Both prequestions and adjunct questions are more effective in enhancing comprehension than the traditional questions presented at the conclusion of a reading (Anderson & Biddle, 1975). The conditions for their use are dictated by certain characteristics of the text and the student. Prequestions can be presented when (1) the reading has numerous new or difficult concepts, (2) the reading is poorly written, or (3) specific text information is required in constructing a response to a critical thinking question. Adjunct questions can be presented when (1) concepts are not particularly difficult for the students or (2) it is desirable for students to reflect upon the reading with the purpose of linking information to respond to a critical thinking question. Critical thinking can be facilitated by presenting a series of prequestions that isolate important text information, then presenting an adjunct critical thinking question requiring the application of information acquired from the prequestions. Consider the following example demonstrating the use of prequestions and adjunct questions on the Chernobyl lesson (see Figure 6.5).

Objective: On the basis of the structured overview and information addressed in the prequestions, students will determine the long-term social and economic consequences of the Chernobyl disaster on the former Soviet republics.

Prequestion: How many people will eventually need to be resettled as a result of the disaster?

In 1986 one of the three nuclear reactors in Chernobyl, a city located in the republic of the Ukraine in the Commonwealth of Independent States, overheated and exploded. Results of the disaster had widespread effects on the people, the land, and the economy of the CIS. Recent maps displaying the fallout remaining from the disaster indicate pockets of severe radiation more than 200 miles from the original 19-mile evacuation zone. It is now known that 70% of the fallout actually occurred in the republic of Byelorussia, which borders the Ukraine. In response to this information, the government now plans to permanently resettle 200,000 people over the next several years—effectively doubling the number originally evacuated from the immediate area around Chernobyl. Government officials in Byelorussia now estimate that 2.2 million people will eventually need to be resettled.

Prequestions: How much money will the cleanup of the disaster cost? How many people may eventually die from this disaster?

The economic costs of the Chernobyl disaster will be enormous: more than 600 people have participated in the cleanup, which as of 1991 cost $19 billion. The total cost by the year 2000 is estimated at $120 billion. The cost in human lives thus far has been estimated to be 200. American doctors estimate the eventual toll to be somewhere between 50,000 and 250,000 lives. The public response to the government's handling of the Chernobyl disaster has been widespread. Grassroots movements have been influential in forcing local officials to take nuclear regulation into their own hands, and thousands of protesters have marched throughout the Ukraine and Byelorussia. In response to the public outrage, Russian president Boris Yeltsin signed a decree in 1990 prohibiting the construction of nuclear power plants.

Adjunct Question: Using information that you learned in answering the preceding question, what are the long-term effects of the Chernobyl disaster on the economy and the welfare of the people in the CIS?

This example demonstrates some of the advantages and disadvantages of prequestions. One advantage is their ability to establish a purpose for reading, thus limiting the amount of text information students must learn. This is an important characteristic with text that contains many concepts, or text that is poorly organized. Once a prequestion has been examined, students are likely to ignore extraneous information but attend selectively to concepts addressed in the question. Prequestions also have the advantage of demonstrating to students the importance of self-regulation. Unfortunately, many students read without knowing what information in the text is important (Dole, Duffy, Roehler, & Pearson, 1991). Prequestions can assist readers in setting goals and generating questions that direct attention and regulate thinking. One drawback to the use of these questions, however, is that by restricting students' attention to specific information, other information may not be attended to.

Adjunct questions such as the one presented in the Chernobyl selection engage readers in the critical thinking process. An adjunct question directs students to reread the selection, to restructure the information acquired in the prequestions, then link that information to derive a response reflecting a higher level of thinking. This process of redirecting readers to higher level thinking by applying information from prequestions is referred to here as staging. Answering a staged adjunct question requires inductive reasoning. Readers apply concepts and information acquired from the prequestions and prior knowledge to answer the adjunct question.

In introducing students to the process of responding to staged adjunct questions, these guidelines should be followed:

1. Model the process of answering a staged adjunct question using content familiar to students. Describing strategies to use in responding to the critical thinking question will enhance students' metacognitive awareness of how information obtained from prequestions can be linked to allow for higher level thinking. Continue modeling this strategy over a period of time.
2. Coach students in responding to staged adjunct questions. Present and respond to prequestions with the entire class. Work cooperatively with students in formulating an answer to a staged adjunct question. Encourage students to describe how they use strategies when responding to these sorts of questions.

Moving Toward Independent Critical Thinking.   Up to this point, the DQA is largely directed by you as the teacher. Ultimately, the goal is to have students answer critical thinking questions independently. It is unlikely that the continued presentation of questions alone will aid students in their response to critical thinking required during independent reading. With your guidance, students can create and apply graphic organizers and generate questions to direct critical thinking. This process occurs through scaffolding (Wood, Bruner, & Ross, 1976), a process in which teacher assistance is reduced gradually, eventually leading to the students' independent application of the strategy. Scaffolding the DQA begins with teacher modeling and concludes with student collaborative modeling. Here are some suggestions for beginning the process of teacher modeling.

Structured Overviews

1. Give students an oral summary of a portion of a reading assignment. As the summary is being presented, display terms and concepts on the chalkboard or overhead. Describe the process for organizing this information in the form of a graphic organizer, then create the organizer. Once the graphic organizer displays the key concepts contained in the summary, describe to students the process of drawing on prior knowledge, then add that information to the organizer.
2. Have students skim a portion of a reading to identify key concepts and vocabulary. List these terms on the overhead or chalkboard. Next, describe the process of constructing the superordinate categories from these terms, then direct students to describe the process of generating subordinate categories.

Prequestions

1. Referring to the graphic organizer, model the process of generating questions that require information beyond that provided in the organizer. These sorts of questions generally will require elaboration or the definitions of causal or temporal relationships.
2. Skim the first several sentences in each paragraph from a brief selection. Describe the process of using this information to generate predictions of the passage's content and questions to clarify content or answer the predictions generated from skimming the passage. Explain to students the importance of self-generated questions in regulating comprehension.
3. Modify Step 2 by engaging in question generation as a group process. Encourage students to generate questions from the group's skimming of the passage. Then read to respond to the student-generated prequestions.

Staged Critical Thinking Question

1. Summarize information obtained from the prequestions. Make a list depicting the concepts the questions address. Demonstrate to students how your conclusions can be drawn from conceptual relationships in

this information. Model critical thinking questions by asking and thinking aloud, "What isn't directly stated in that reading that I would like to know?" Emphasize that answers may not be found in the text. Discuss the importance of seeking information from additional sources to respond to these critical thinking questions.

Once you have modeled these steps with your students, the students repeat the process in cooperative groups. Students now coach one another in the construction of graphic organizers, prequestions, and staged critical thinking questions. This step requires you to monitor the groups' progress carefully and provide additional modeling when groups require assistance.

Commentary: DQA. The DQA is an efficient and practical approach to teaching critical thinking strategies in content areas. Like the IDEAL and inductive towers strategies, the DQA involves elements of cooperative learning and group problem solving. The strategy also includes steps to acquaint students with the structure of text, the importance of relating background knowledge to text content, the importance of monitoring the process of higher level thinking, and the process of linking text information and background knowledge to generate inferences. A distinctive element of this form of critical thinking instruction is the chunking of text information. By focusing on smaller portions of a text, students can concentrate on the process of responding to a higher level question and not be distracted by the demands of the information in the text. This process is a form of regulated inductive thinking: Concepts needed for critical thinking are defined through questions, then students are asked to apply that information in answering a higher level question. At first, this process is teacher-directed. Gradually, however, more responsibility is placed on the student to self-direct the process of generating these types of questions.

Initially, elements of this approach, such as preparing graphic organizers and staging questions, may require considerable preparation time. However, with time and continued practice these instructional devices can be generated spontaneously.

Socratic Questioning

Socratic questioning (Paul, 1991) is a strategy to promote critical thinking through classroom discussion. According to Paul, this form of questioning helps students evaluate their own thinking, allows students to compare their own thinking to that of their peers, and promotes consideration of multiple ideas and the interrelationships between those ideas. In this form of discussion, you can promote critical thinking by presenting questions in the following four directions, as identified by Paul.

Their Origin.   Help students focus on the source of information used in the response to a question by asking, "Where did you come up with information that helped you answer this question?" "Can you describe what you were thinking when you originally made this conclusion or learned this information?" "Do you remember if this is something you learned by yourself?" "Is this something you learned in school, from a friend, or from another source of information such as a book or videotape?"

Their Support.   Help students focus on supporting facts by asking, "How do you substantiate this response; do you have proof?" "Where could you locate evidence to support your response?" "Do you think your response is based on fact, or is your response your personal belief?" "Is your response one that would be accepted by a good number of your peers?" "Would someone who is an expert in the area of the question provide a response similar to yours?"

Their Conflicts With Other Thoughts.   Help students anticipate other responses by asking, "What are some counterarguments that people might present to your response?" "Why would some people have a different point of view than that evident in your response?" "Under what conditions would you consider changing your response to this question?" "What additional information would you need to modify your response?" "How would you counter an opposing response?"

Their Implications and Consequences.   Help students consider the implications of their answer by asking, "What are the consequences of this response?" "Is there any evidence for your response in the real world?" "What additional events or information would be necessary for your response to actually be put into effect?"

An example of questions reflecting these four directions is shown in Figure 6.6.

The procedures for planning and administering a Socratic discussion adapted from Paul (1991), are as follows.

Step 1:

Define the underlying concepts and information. First, consider the concepts, information, values, and interrelationships between these elements that underlie the questions presented to the students. You should attempt to predict the sort of insights or values that may be presented by the students. Attention to the underlying concepts and information will enhance opportunities during the discussion to assist students in seeing the relationships among their own thinking, the views of others, and the information obtained from various print and nonprint sources.

Step 2:

Generate a few kernel questions for each of the four question directions. Constructing a few kernel questions for each of the four question directions will increase the likelihood that discussion will proceed smoothly, that questions will cover the various directions represented in the Socratic

FIGURE 6.6   AN EXAMPLE OF SOCRATIC QUESTIONING

CONFLICTING VIEWS

How does this student's thinking conflict with other points of view?

What would you say to someone who said that people basically *want* to accomplish things and learn about things, that people *need* to work and keep busy and feel that they contribute? Could there be other reasons why people seem lazy, like maybe people are afraid of messing up, and that's why they don't go out there and do stuff? Your history book is full of people who did things, worked hard, fought, and so on—how do you explain that?

ORIGIN OR SOURCE

How did the student come to form this point of view?

What makes you say that? Have you always thought that? If not, what made you change your mind? Why did that change your mind?

A STUDENT'S MAIN POINT

For example, "Most people are lazy."

IMPLICATIONS AND CONSEQUENCES

Where does this student's point take us, what follows from it?

If that's true, then should we let people be lazy? If not, how can we get people to do things? What makes some people different, not lazy? If most people are lazy because X (student's reason), then most people must be X—is that true?

SUPPORT, REASONS, EVIDENCE, AND ASSUMPTIONS

Can the student support his or her view with reasons or evidence?

Why do you think so? Are there certain kinds or groups of people that *aren't* lazy? Why are most people lazy? How do you know? How could we find out if that might be so? Do people choose to be lazy, or decide that it doesn't matter if they are lazy, or are they just that way naturally? Do you think most people think of themselves as lazy? Why?

Source: Paul, R. W. (1992). "Critical Thinking: What Every Person Needs to Survive in a Rapidly Changing World." Published by Foundation for Critical Thinking, CA. Second edition (p. 366).

questioning technique, and that structure and organization will be applied to the questioning format. These kernel sentences may be presented to students in advance to allow them ample opportunity to fully consider their response. In addition, a handout displaying these questions can serve as a listening guide for students—as questions are discussed, students note various responses presented by their peers.

Step 3:

Facilitate interdimensional thinking. Questioning proceeds in a manner that allows students to move back and forth between their own ideas and those of their peers, between their own ideas and those expressed in print and nonprint sources, and between various perspectives advanced by you, other students, or an external source. You should attempt to draw attention to various points of view, note, where possible, consistencies and inconsistencies in the responses provided by students, and bring closure to students' points of view.

Step 4:

   Draw on cooperative learning and attend to multicultural variation. Questioning can be enhanced by having students respond to questions in cooperative learning groups. According to Paul (1991), Socratic questioning in cooperative groups promotes students' ability to probe each other's ideas for their support and implication and helps develop a sensitivity to what students are assuming. Note that cooperative grouping also provides an opportunity to draw on an array of cultural or social perspectives present in the classroom. As discussion proceeds through the four directions of questions, you should attempt to draw attention to these perspectives, provide students with positive feedback for voicing them, and encourage all students to seek an understanding and appreciation of different cultural and social points of view.

Here is an example of Socratic questioning conducted with a group of high school students engaged in an interdisciplinary unit dealing with death and aging.

Teacher: Over the past week we have been reading several short stories dealing with aging and death. We have also examined from a scientific perspective some of the physiological and psychological changes that occur during the aging process. Today I would like to begin a discussion on death and the aging process. I would like to start with this question: Do the elderly have the right to die on their own terms?

Carlos: In my family we have been taught that this is not a decision that is made by the individual. Rather, I believe that one must follow one's own religious beliefs.

Tom: I think that there comes a point in time when if there is no chance of recovery, then an individual has the right to determine the process by which he terminates his life. After all, it is the individual who is terminally ill that undergoes the suffering. And if the outcome is clear, then why shouldn't the individual be able to determine the process that leads to a predetermined outcome?

Teacher: (seeking support for the response) Tom, what evidence do you have to suggest the individual has the right to make this decision?

Tom: Individuals have the right to create a living will that directs doctors and nurses to follow certain courses of action in terms of the medical care they receive if they are terminally ill.

Jane: That's right. I had an aunt who had a terminal case of stomach cancer. She was very old and was very sick. She had signed a living will that directed the doctors to stop chemotherapy. Once they stopped treatment with the drugs, she was able to return to her home for her few remaining days of life. If she didn't have the living will, the doctors may have continued treating her, knowing that the cancer could not be cured.

Teacher: (seeking implications and consequences) What are some of the consequences of an individual determining the extent of medical care as expressed in a living will?

Maria: Our grandparents live with us in our home. My sisters and brothers have been taught that we should do everything we can to respect and care for them. If they made a decision to terminate their own life, I think my parents would have the moral obligation to intervene ... to do everything they could to maintain life. After all, if people are very ill, they really are not in a position to make rational decisions.

Pete: But there are also financial decisions. If someone is terminally ill, and if the family must help pay the medical expenses, it may be devastating financially to the parents' children. That happened to my parents when my grandfather had to have chemotherapy. He didn't have insurance and my parents were forced to pay the bills. It really put a lot of pressure on my parents.

Teacher: (seeking to identify conflicts and other thoughts) Well, what are some of the opposing points or views or conflicts we have identified?

Jenny: Well, it seems as though there are legal issues ... who has the responsibility to make decisions ... do the doctors maintain treatment in fear of a malpractice suit? And there are financial issues—will continued treatment place a financial stress on the family members? But I think there are also emotional considerations here. What about the dignity of the individuals who are terminally ill? Don't they have the right to make these decisions? After all, you make the decision whether to smoke ... which could cause cancer ... or whether to wear a seatbelt ... facing great bodily harm in an accident. And think of all the people who know they are ill but never see the doctor. What about elderly citizens who know they have cancer but don't seek treatment. They have made a decision. It seems to me that the issue here is one of commitment; once you commit to medical treatment, then you might be bound to continue that treatment.

Commentary: Socratic Questioning.   Socratic questioning is a strategy to promote critical thinking through classroom discussion. The presentation of the four directions of questioning in a discussion format should serve to advance students' metacognitive awareness of processes involved in responding to higher level questions. Moreover, the teacher's direction of students to the relationships between responses to the four directions of questioning should further their ability to conduct similar strategies independent of instruction. Clearly, this is a strategy that promotes active learning—rather than relying on information in a textbook, the teacher draws on students' knowledge, directing them to reflect on the process they and others followed to generate responses. Students are thus encouraged to consider and judge their own views and the information provided by their peers.

To ensure the success of this strategy, it is important to provide students with the necessary activities prior to and during reading so that they will learn the basic information and concepts necessary to engage in Socratic questioning. While this strategy can stimulate a great deal of discussion, the teacher-to-student questioning may limit the involvement of the entire class. Therefore, consideration must be given to posing questions to cooperative learning groups, allowing the group to reach a consensus on the response to the question, then engaging in a whole-group discussion of the question. This procedure will involve a greater number of students and is more likely to allow students the opportunity to share their views with their peers.

CONCLUDING REMARKS

In this chapter we have presented the characteristics of critical thinking, a definition of critical thinking, an instructional framework for the presentation of critical thinking strategies, and four critical thinking strategies. In summarizing the chapter, we will make four points we believe are essential to promoting higher level thinking in subject matter classrooms.

First, we believe that critical thinking should involve the teacher as a facilitator to promote (1) active learning involving a great deal of teacher talk and modeling and (2) cooperative learning whereby students talk a great deal to one another while the teacher monitors and assists in their collective efforts. Requesting students to complete questions or activities independently without first observing a teacher model and applying and refining that strategy seems to ignore the dynamic process of engaging in higher level cognitive tasks.

Second, as we contemplate subject matter instruction, we picture teachers who themselves practice critical thinking, who see the value of teaching their content by engaging students in practical and challenging problem-solving tasks, and who recognize the importance of educating all students to be more than consumers of surface-level information. This requires conscious and consistent integration of critical thinking strategies within day-to-day instruction. It also requires the perception that teaching should enhance the learner's ability to make sense of the world and to acquire knowledge that can be applied to self-directed learning.

Third, the strategies in this chapter should provide students with a more thorough understanding of the subject matter content. For example, problem-solving activities that require students to form ideas and experiment and observe the application of these ideas will likely increase an understanding of factual information as well as more general concepts or themes.

Finally, like everyday problems themselves, teaching students to solve problems or engage in other forms of critical thinking is sometimes messy—answers may not come readily, students may be hard pressed to formulate any sort of acceptable answer, and the independent application of strategies may be agonizingly slow to develop. These sorts of results can be rather disquieting and the risks may appear too great. At this point, resorting to traditional activities may appear to be an attractive way to restore order and to obtain outcomes that are more "measurable." We would encourage all teachers to be persistent in their efforts, to continue to stress the importance of critical thinking strategies to their students, and to share their efforts with individuals outside the classroom. Ideally, teaching critical thinking will require the cooperation of students, fellow teachers, administrators, and parents. All personnel should recognize the importance and goals of this form of instruction and the process required to develop students' lifelong ability to engage in higher level thinking.

REFLECTIONS

Now that you have become more fully acquainted with critical thinking instruction in the subject matter classroom, complete the following questions as a review of the various topics addressed throughout this chapter.

1. Prepare a critical thinking activity that could be used in your subject matter area. In constructing this activity, consider how you may (a) draw on students' background knowledge, (b) make use of multiple sources of information, and (c) engage students in cooperative learning as they participate in the critical thinking activity.

2. Examine each of the following problems, then determine which of them would display characteristics of real-life problems. You may want to refer to the characteristics of real-life problems presented on pages 216–217.

   a. In an English class the teacher is about to deal with a novel that has an overriding theme addressing people's inhumanity toward one another. To prepare for the novel, students are directed to identify four historical events during the past 100 years that depicted people's inhumanity. At least two of these events must have occurred outside the United States. Students are asked to read at least three different sources for each event, then to compare and contrast the causes and outcomes of each event and to draw generalities across these events.

   b. In a math class the teacher wants students to understand how the calculation of areas of various surfaces can be used in real life. Students are provided tape measures, then asked to calculate the surface area inside the classroom.

   c. In a science class students have been learning about the problems associated with the disposal of low-level radiation from nuclear power plants. As a culminating activity, the teacher invites a group of individuals to serve as a consulting panel to the students. This panel consists of a scientist from the regional power company, an environmental activist, a scientist with the state environmental agency, and an oncologist specializing in cancers caused by radiation. Students are told that they must determine how to dispose of approximately 120,000 pounds of nuclear waste over the next ten years in a manner that is cost-effective and that considers the public's health.

3. Construct an inductive tower by identifying information regarding the effect of television on students' acquisition of knowledge that would be useful in their schooling. You may also want to identify impediments to this learning (what students like to watch, their reason for watching, etc.).

4. Use the IDEAL model to solve the following: Jan, who lives in Minnesota, has stored her car on her brother's farm during the winter because she is afraid of the damage to the body that may occur from salt on the roadways. The car is placed in an old barn which protects it from the weather. She covers the car with a tarp, removes the battery, places a fuel stabilizer in the gas tank, and departs, waiting for spring. When she returns in the spring, she replaces the battery, fills the gas tank with high octane fuel, and cleans the car inside and out. On her way home there is a terrible shudder as she drives down the highway. The shudder becomes worse as she accelerates. What is the problem? How was it caused? What can she do now?

References

Alvermann, D. E., & Hayes, D. A. (1989). Classroom discussion of content area reading assignments: An intervention study. *Reading Research Quarterly, 24,* 305–335.

Anderson, R. C., & Biddle, W. B. (1975). On asking people what they are reading. In G. H. Bower (Ed.), *The psychology of learning and motivation.* New York: Academic Press.

Armbruster, B. B., Anderson, T. H., Armstrong, J. O., Wise, M. A., Janisch, C., & Meyer, L. A. (1991). Reading and questioning in content area lessons. *Journal of Reading Behavior, 23,* 35–59.

Bransford, J., Sherwood, R., Rieser, J., & Vye, N. (1986). Teaching thinking and problem solving: Research foundations. *American Psychologist, 41,* 1078–1089.

Bransford, J. D., & Stein, B. S. (1984). *The ideal problem solver: A guide for improving thinking, learning, and creativity.* New York: Freeman.

Brown, A. L., Campione, J. C., & Day, J. (1981). Learning to learn: On training students to learn from texts. *Educational Research, 10,* 14–21.

Clarke, J. H., Raths, J., & Gilbert, G. L. (1989). Inductive towers: Letting students see how they think. *Journal of Reading, 33,* 86–95.

Dole, J. A., Duffy, G. G., Roehler, L. R., & Pearson, P. D. (1991). Moving from the old to the new: Research on reading comprehension instruction. *Review of Educational Research, 61,* 239–264.

Doyle, W. (1984). Academic tasks in classrooms. *Curriculum Inquiry, 14,* 129–149.

Ennis, R. H. (1987). A taxonomy of critical thinking dispositions and abilities. In J. Baron & R. Sternberg (Eds.), *Teaching thinking skills: Theory and practice.* New York: Freeman.

_____. (1989). Critical thinking and subject specificity: Clarification and needed research. *Educational Researcher, 18,* 4–10.

Graves, M. F., & Clark, D. L. (1981). Effects of adjunct questions on high school low achievers. *Reading Improvement, 18,* 8–13.

Haggard, M. R. (1988). Developing critical thinking with the directed reading activity. *The Reading Teacher, 41,* 526–533.

Halpern, D. F. (1984). *Thought and knowledge: An introduction to critical thinking.* Hillsdale, NJ: Erlbaum.

Levin, J. R., & Pressley, M. (1981). Improving children's prose comprehension: Selected strategies that seem to succeed. In C. M. Santa & B. L. Hayes (Eds.), *Children's prose comprehension: Research and Practice.* Newark, DE: International Reading Association.

McPeck, J. E. (1981). *Critical thinking and education.* New York: St. Martin's.

Mullis, I. V. S., Owen, E. H., & Phillips, G. W. (1990). *America's challenge: Accelerating academic achievement, a summary of findings from 20 years of NAEP.* Princeton, NJ: Educational Testing Service.

Paris, S. G., Cross, D. R., & Lipson, M. Y. (1984). Informed strategies for learning: A program to improve children's awareness and comprehension. *Journal of Educational Psychology, 76,* 1239–1252.

Paul, R. W. (1991). Dialogical and dialectical thinking. In A. L. Costa (Ed.), *Developing minds: A resource book for teaching thinking.* Alexandria, VA: Association for Supervision and Curriculum Development.

Perkins, D. N., & Salomon, G. (1989). Are cognitive skills context-bound? *Educational Researcher, 18,* 16–25.

Perkins, D., & Simmons, R. (1988). Patterns of misunderstanding: An integrative model of science, math, and programming. *Review of Educational Research, 58,* 303–326.

Prawat, R. S. (1991). The value of ideas: The immersion approach to the development of thinking. *Educational Researcher, 20,* 3–10.

Raphael, T. E., & Wonnacott, C. A. (1985). Heightening fourth-grade students sensitivity to sources of information for answering comprehension questions. *Reading Research Journal, 20,* 282–296.

Resnick, L. B. (1987). *Education and learning to think.* Washington, DC: National Academy Press.

Roehler, L. R., & Duffy, G. G. (1984). Direct explanation of comprehension processes. In G. Duffy, L. Roehler, & J. Mason (Eds.), *Comprehension instruction.* White Plains, NY: Longman.

Ryder, R. J. (1991). The directed questioning activity for subject matter text. *Journal of Reading, 34,* 606–612.

Smith, F. (1990). *To think.* New York: Teachers College Press.

Smith, F. R., & Feathers, K. M. (1983). The role of reading in content classrooms: Assumptions vs. reality. *Journal of Reading, 27,* 262–267.

Sternberg, R. J. (1985). Teaching critical thinking: Part 1. Are we making critical mistakes? *Phi Delta Kappan, 67,* 195–198.

———. (1986). *Critical thinking: Its nature, measurement, and improvement.* Paper presented at National Institute of Education, Washington, DC.

———. (1988). When teaching thinking does not work, what goes wrong? *Harvard Educational Review, 89,* 555–579.

Sternberg, R. J., & Davidson, J. E. (1984). The role of insight in intellectual giftedness. *Gifted Child Quarterly, 28,* 58–64.

van Dijk, T. A., & Kintsch, W. (1983). *Strategies of discourse comprehension.* Hillsdale, NJ: Erlbaum.

Whitehead, A. N. (1929). *The aims of education.* New York: Macmillan.

Wiley, K. B. (1977). *The status of pre-college science, mathematics, and social science educational practices in U.S. schools: An overview and summary of three studies.* Washington, DC: U.S. Government Printing Office.

Wood, D. J., Bruner, J. S., & Ross, G. (1976). The role of tutoring in problem solving. *Journal of Child Psychology and Psychiatry, 17,* 89–100.

············

Writing

CHAPTER OVERVIEW

In this chapter we deal with ways in which writing can enhance students' reading and learning in subject matter classes. We begin by discussing the importance of writing. Next, we consider some of the current knowledge about writing—students' writing skills, the sorts of writing done in schools, and the components of the writing process. In the section "Effective Writing Instruction" we discuss the importance of motivating and providing a positive classroom atmosphere, present some general guidelines for writing in subject matter areas, and consider the use of computers in writing. We next describe six types of writing that students can profitably employ in content classes. These are answering questions, taking notes, summarizing, writing to encourage critical thinking, expressive writing, and extended and formal writing. In the last section of the chapter, we take up the matter of responding to students' writing, stressing approaches that minimize the time teachers need to spend at this task, and the matter of assessing students' writing.

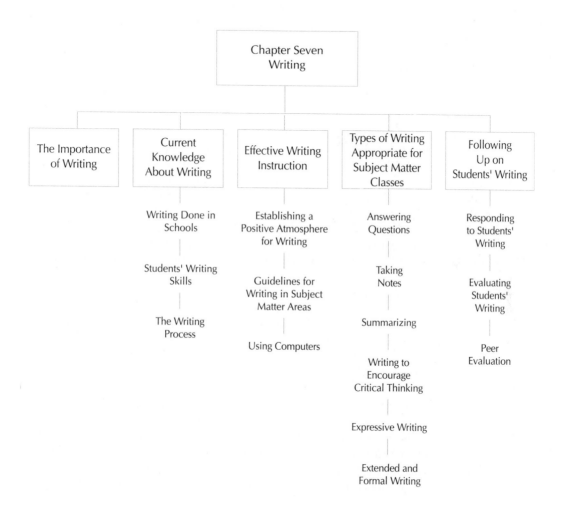

Chapter Seven
Writing

The Importance of Writing

Current Knowledge About Writing

Writing Done in Schools

Students' Writing Skills

The Writing Process

Effective Writing Instruction

Establishing a Positive Atmosphere for Writing

Guidelines for Writing in Subject Matter Areas

Using Computers

Types of Writing Appropriate for Subject Matter Classes

Answering Questions

Taking Notes

Summarizing

Writing to Encourage Critical Thinking

Expressive Writing

Extended and Formal Writing

Following Up on Students' Writing

Responding to Students' Writing

Evaluating Students' Writing

Peer Evaluation

THE IMPORTANCE OF WRITING

Over the past 10 to 15 years, educators have learned a good deal about the relationships among reading, writing, speaking, and listening; furthermore, the importance of recognizing and building on the interrelationships among the language arts has become an increasingly frequent and significant theme. However, today's scholars are certainly not the first to recognize the importance of these connections. It was nearly 300 years ago when Francis Bacon coined his now famous aphorism: "Reading maketh a full man, conference a ready man, and writing an exact man." Current scholars would hardly agree with Bacon's observation.

Current scholars would also agree with the view of writing expressed by William Zinsser (1988), the widely published Yale University writing teacher, novelist, essayist, and editor. "Writing," says Zinsser, "is not just a special language that belongs to English teachers and few other sensitive souls who have a 'gift for words.' Writing is the logical arrangement of thought. Anyone who thinks clearly should be able to write clearly, about any subject at all" (p. 11). Moreover, Zinsser explains, writing, thinking, and learning are very closely related. By writing, students often find out what they know about a topic or what they want to say about it. And by teaching writing across the curriculum—by engaging students in writing in social studies, art, music, science, mathematics, and other subjects—teachers can do much more than encourage students who are afraid of writing to write; teachers can encourage students who are afraid of learning to learn.

Writing also serves students in other ways. As Bacon's statement suggests, it can help students be precise about what they know and what they do not know. Additionally, as Vacca and Linek (1992) point out, writing gives students an opportunity to interact with the material they are learning, to become personally involved with a text, and to use their background knowledge and experiences to make sense of the ideas and information they encounter in classes. All subject matter areas offer students such opportunities. In mathematics, for example, students might write about a real-life situation in which they could use trigonometry to determine a distance they need to know. In physical education, students might write about some specific rule changes that they believe would improve high school basketball. Or in French class, American students might write to French students, perhaps describing some of the slang used by American teenagers and asking about the use of slang by French teens.

Moreover, writing is not something that is useful just in school. Writing is useful throughout life. Not everyone, of course, writes a lot; but most people write something each day. Teachers write lesson plans, memos to principals or department chairs, letters to parents, reports of various sorts, and essays about teaching and learning. Those in business and industry write memos, reports, documentation for goods or services, descriptions of upcoming events, and newsletters. Those in politics and various other public positions write reports, position papers, news releases, and speeches. And almost everyone will have occasion to write for personal reasons—notes to family members, letters to friends, directions for doing something or getting someplace, and the like.

Thus, writing serves multiple functions: Not only does it help students learn about what they know and what they do not know and help them to get involved in their work and their studies, but it also enables them and the adults they become to communicate with friends, colleagues, business associates, and constituencies. In the remainder of this chapter, we first consider how much students write, how well they write, and the writing process. Next, we discuss the importance of establishing an atmosphere that encourages writing, present some guidelines for writing in content areas, and consider some of the most powerful uses of computers for writing. After that, we discuss the various types of writing teachers might use in subject matter classes. Finally, we consider some matters involved in responding to and evaluating students' writing.

CURRENT KNOWLEDGE ABOUT WRITING

The topic of students' writing proficiency has received a good deal of national attention. Recent surveys of the sorts of writing done in school, national assessments of students' writing skills, and research and theorizing about the writing process have provided a great deal of useful information on the topic. Each of these matters is considered below.

Writing Done in Schools

Current orientations to teaching writing generally endorse process approaches, approaches which focus on specific components of writing—topic selection, prewriting, drafting, revising, and editing. Such approaches underscore the importance of students engaging in these various practices and suggest that less attention should be given to the finished written products of writing. However, as first indicated in Applebee's (1981) national survey of writing in secondary schools and as verified in subsequent reports, such as that of Graves and Piché (1989), discussion of process approaches and the recent interest in writing appear to have had limited influence on actual classroom practices.

In few classrooms do students engage in prewriting activities, generate their own topics, and share their writing with peers. The suggestions teachers give students for editing and revising their writing continue to emphasize mechanical correctness more than matters of content and style. And extended writing—writing of paragraph length or longer—is a very infrequent activity. Secondary school students, for example, spend only about 3% of their school time writing paragraphs and longer pieces, and even in English classes less than 10% of class time is devoted to extended writing. In fact, only about a third of the teachers in Applebee's survey reported ever asking students to write at length.

Corroborating these figures, something over 30% of the 17-year-olds and 40% of the 13-year-olds in Applebee's survey reported receiving no writing instruction at all. Even when students are required to write at length, they are provided with a very limited number of tasks, usually producing informational writing. Although there are some differences in emphasis across grades and subjects, writing in all subjects is predominantly expository, typically done in response to material previously presented, and written for the purpose of demonstrating knowledge about topics that have been dealt with in class. Clearly, students need to do more writing, and they need to engage in more kinds of writing.

Students' Writing Skills

Since students do relatively little writing, it is not surprising that many of them do not write well. Results of National Assessment of Educational Progress (NAEP) periodic reviews of students' writing have been summed up in this way: "On average, American students do not write well, and their writing performance has not improved in recent years" (U.S. Department of Education, 1991, p. 68). A few figures and one example from a recent NAEP report suggest the depth of the problem. Only 27% of 12th graders were able to write an effective persuasive letter to their senator arguing for or against cutting funds for the space program, only 35% could successfully write an analytic essay examining their favorite story, and only 56% could successfully write an imaginative ghost story (Mullis, Owen, & Phillips, 1990).

The following response is typical of the weak responses many students wrote for the persuasive task.

Dear Senator:
I don't think there should be cuts in the funding but I do think the problems we have here should be taken care of first. Then you should work on the space program.

The lack of thinking skills evidenced in such writing—the student's illogical position that the present funding in the space program should be maintained and spent elsewhere—and the student's inability to support a position simply do not demonstrate the sort of thinking and writing skills that Americans will need in the 21st century. Since writing achievement and critical thinking must be products of schooling, these distressing levels of performance underscore the need for significant steps to improve students' writing.

PRACTICE ACTIVITY 7.1

Pause at this point and answer two series of questions—in writing. First, consider the information presented in the chapter and answer these questions: How much writing do students typically do? What sorts of writing do students typically do? How well do students write? Next, consider your experiences as a student in the intermediate and secondary grades and answer these questions: How much writing did you do in school? What sorts of writing did you do in school? How well did your experiences in school prepare you for the writing you do now?

The Writing Process

Until recently, teaching writing often consisted primarily of teaching grammar, and learning to write was largely defined as gaining control over linguistic conventions, many of which were mechanical. The concern was almost exclusively with the finished product, and instruction was largely divorced from considerations about the context of the writing, the writer's purpose, or the audience to whom the writing was addressed. A good deal of recent thinking about writing represents a very different view, and much of this thinking has contributed to a major shift in teachers' understanding of the writing process and the objectives of writing instruction. This view has led to wide acceptance of cognitive process models of writing, the realization that writing is a social process, and concern with what the writer can learn about a particular subject from writing about it. The view has also led to the realization that a writer can learn much about himself or herself during the writing process. Each of these matters is considered next.

Writing as a Cognitive Process. Cognitive process models of writing deal with the thought processes that writers engage in as they write. Flower and Hayes (1981) developed the most influential of these models; Figure 7.1 shows some of its components. As can be seen, the model includes the mental operations of *planning, drafting,* and *reviewing,* as well as several subprocesses. As indicated by the arrows, the model is recursive; that is, the various subprocesses

---

FIGURE 7.1   SOME COMPONENTS OF THE WRITING PROCESS

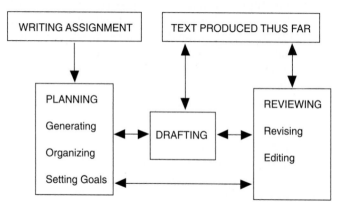

occur and reoccur in a variety of orders. A writer may begin with planning, translate some of his or her thoughts into a preliminary draft, pause to do some additional planning and drafting, and pause again, perhaps this time to set some different goals. Alternatively, the writer may begin drafting immediately without planning, finish a draft and review it, and only in the process of reviewing the draft really begin to think about setting goals. These, of course, are only two of the possible paths a writer may take with a particular piece of writing. Thus, the model emphasizes that writing is a complex, multifaceted process, something quite different from the step-by-step, mechanical, and formulaic process suggested in many traditional textbooks.

Not surprisingly, there are major differences between the writing processes of mature writers and novices. Skilled writers are knowledgeable about a variety of discourse types, purposes of writing, and audiences for writing; and they make conscious use of this knowledge as they write. They do a lot of deliberate planning and goal setting. Many school-age writers, on the other hand, lack such knowledge and do little conscious planning and goal setting. They tend to employ a greatly simplified version of the planning component of the process and often begin writing without much thought, simply treating a writing assignment as a request to tell everything they know about the topic without giving much attention to the purpose of their writing or its audience, or to how they might accomplish their purpose. Attention to writing as a cognitive process has shifted the concern of writing teachers from addressing mechanics and correcting surface features of writing to providing instruction that deliberately engages students in the various subprocesses that mature writers employ.

PRACTICE ACTIVITY 7.2

1. Assume that you are going to be taking an essay test that will include a question on the cognitive process model of writing. Look back through this section of the chapter and take the sorts of notes that would help you prepare for such a question.
2. One important tenet of the process model of writing is that there is no single writing process but a variety of processes that writers use at different times and for different purposes. Outline some of the processes that you go through when doing different sorts of writing, then write a comment on the extent to which your writing process differs from one situation to another.

Writing as a Social Process.   In addition to the concern with writing as a cognitive process, there has been an increased interest in writing as a social process. This view of writing as a social process focuses on the role of the context in which writing takes place and the audience for whom it is written in shaping both the requirements of writing and the composing strategies students use.

As noted earlier, the most frequent purpose of writing in school is for students to tell teachers what they know about topics they have read about or have been taught. This is certainly one legitimate purpose, but it is important to understand that mature writing skills develop best when students' writing engages them in genuine problem-solving activities centering on topics and issues in which they have some real sense of ownership. Students are best aided in becoming competent writers when they produce material that has real communicative purposes and that requires them to plan and make choices as they shape their writing so that it is appropriate for their purposes, their readers, and the social circumstances in which it will be read.

Such a view emphasizes the fact that writing is an appropriate and useful activity in all content areas, not just in English classes. All teachers need to tap students' own interests and ask them to write for various purposes, for a variety of audiences, from different perspectives, and about diverse topics.

Writing to Learn and Feel.   A third concern is that students need to realize that not all writing is directed to some outside person. One very important audience is the individual writer, and frequently the writing one does for himself or herself does not result in a polished product. Students can write to find out what they know about a topic. Students can also write to engage with a topic—to gain some feeling for, appreciation of, and interest in the topic. Both are very legitimate uses of school writing.

This latter type has been called *expressive writing* (Britton, Burgess, Martin, McLeod, & Rosen, 1975), and it has been contrasted with the more typical type of school writing, which has been called *transactional writing*. Transactional writing is the objective, informational writing that people use in transacting business with each other. Virtually all the writing typically done in the subject matter classroom is transactional, and most of this writing is relatively formal. Expressive writing, on the other hand, is closely tied to talk. It employs the everyday language often used to discuss thoughts, feelings, and opinions with friends or family. In school, students can use expressive writing to consider what they are learning and to make some sort of commitment to it. They can use their background knowledge, their experiences, and their personal feelings to deal with the ideas they are exploring. Through expressive writing, students can try to understand these ideas better, assess for themselves how well they understand them, and generate some sort of personal involvement with them. At least some of the writing students do in school—and quite possibly a good deal of it—should be expressive.

PRACTICE ACTIVITY 7.3

These last two sections have been short ones, but in fact they can be made even briefer. Try writing a summary of the two sections. As much as possible, do this in your own words because that will help you better understand and remember the ideas.

EFFECTIVE WRITING INSTRUCTION

Here we consider three facets of effective writing instruction: establishing a positive classroom atmosphere, following guidelines appropriate for content area writing, and using computers for what they do best.

Establishing a Positive Atmosphere for Writing

Because writing is hard work and because many students do not write well, it becomes doubly important for teachers to motivate students to write and to create a classroom atmosphere in which they feel free to write. There are a number of things you can do to contribute to such an atmosphere. They are not hard and they will not take long to point out, but they are vitally important.

The starting point in establishing a positive atmosphere for writing is to have students do a substantial amount of writing in which they do not attempt to produce a polished product to be handed in, judged, and graded. This means giving students opportunities to write to discover what they already know about a topic, to jot down notes as they read, or to write to engage themselves with the topic.

A closely related approach is to allow students to submit only a selected portion of the writing they produce for your comments. This gives students some sense of power, and it gives them valuable practice in evaluating their writing. After all, they will want to hand in their best work.

Also, before students hand in papers for your comments, and perhaps a grade, the papers should usually have gone through several rounds of peer review. As is the case with selecting which work to hand in, peer review offers valuable practice in evaluating writing. It also gives students practice in listening to each other closely and communicating with each other precisely.

Finally, when you do get papers, use a coaching tone rather than a judgmental one in your response. This will go a long way toward convincing students that writing is a risk they can afford to take.

PRACTICE ACTIVITY 7.4

Consider to what extent the classroom atmosphere and practices just described are similar to those you encountered in school. Then, briefly contrast how you would feel about writing if you were in a class where an atmosphere like this prevailed with one in which the teacher's attitude toward your writing was almost always judgmental and critical.

Guidelines for Writing in Subject Matter Areas

The following guidelines include suggestions that both we and others (Tchudi & Huerta, 1983; Vacca & Linek, 1992) have found useful in dealing with writing in subject matter areas. They are consistent with a number of points that have already been made about writing and constitute a review and extension of many of those points.

1. Keep the content of students' writing—what they are saying—as the central focus. Treat the form of their writing—how they say it—after dealing with the content.
2. Design writing activities to help students structure and synthesize their knowledge. Also, provide opportunities for students to write in order to record and recall ideas from their reading.
3. Give students varied audiences to write for. Their audiences should include themselves, their classmates, other students in your school and perhaps other schools, the community outside school, and yourself. Be doubly sure that you are not the only audience for their writing.
4. Create writing activities that give students opportunities to play the roles of learners and researchers.
5. When students are doing formal writing assignments, provide them with the time to engage in the full writing process. That is, give them adequate prewriting time so that they can formulate and organize their thoughts, give them sufficient writing time to get their thoughts down on paper, and assist them and let their peers assist them in honing and revising their work. Avoid situations in which students do not get much assistance and feedback until they hand in their writing for a grade.
6. Make peer response a frequent activity. Students need a lot of feedback on their writing—much more than you can give them—and peers are an extremely valuable resource. Remember, though, that students need assistance in responding to writing. Providing them with guidelines, giving mini-training sessions, and discussing the sorts of responses that are most likely to be helpful to others will prove useful.
7. Differentiate between revising and editing, and make revising your students' first concern. Revising consists of modifying a piece of writing to make it clearer, more powerful, more gripping, more interesting, and the like. Editing consists of making sure that such matters as spelling, punctuation, and usage are correct. It is probably best to save editing for after revision, because otherwise editing may replace revision. Also, much of the writing students do in content classes does not need editing because the writer will be its only audience.
8. Whenever possible, publish, display, or otherwise publicly acknowledge students' formal writing. Students will be a lot more interested in polishing and honing their formal writing if it is likely to be circulated among others.

PRACTICE ACTIVITY 7.5

Select one of the guidelines for writing in the subject matter classroom and list the advantages and disadvantages of the idea. Consider both the advantages and disadvantages you have listed, then state your position on the matter succinctly in a paragraph or so.

Using Computers

Over the past decade, computers and computer applications have proliferated in schools. Catalogs and brochures now list thousands of different programs targeted for students at all grade levels and in all subject matter areas. However, for fostering students' writing skills in subject matter classes and for making subject matter writing as feasible and productive as possible, a very small number of computer applications are far and away superior.

The best of these applications, by a huge margin, is word processing. Word processors make the planning, generating, drafting, revising, and editing so necessary to learning to write effectively and to producing accomplished pieces of writing feasible and acceptable to students. Everyone seems to have their favorite word processors. *Microsoft Word* from Microsoft is probably the most popular package for Macintoshes; for IBM and compatible computers, *WordPerfect*. Undoubtedly, some word processors are superior to others, and money spent on good programs and relatively powerful computers is likely to be well spent. However, any program and any computer represent immeasurable advantages over writing by hand or typing. Thus, the first step in using computers effectively is finding out what equipment and programs are available in your school and arranging for students to spend significant amounts of time with them.

The next step is to become thoroughly familiar with the program and then instruct your students in using it. Many students will already be adept at word processing, but others will not; without specific instruction, many students will not get the maximum benefits that word processing can give them. It does not matter whether you provide the instruction or have a teacher particularly skilled in word processing do it; but in either case, instruction should proceed from basic functions, such as keying in text and saving and retrieving files, to more advanced functions, such as replacing words and larger units of text, to still more advanced functions, such as indexing, outlining, and adding headers and footers.

Students will certainly profit if they learn to use the spell check and thesaurus features that are included in many programs. Many students who would almost never consider employing a dictionary or thesaurus will readily run their writing through spell checkers or use an electronic thesaurus to search for more colorful and appropriate words.

Another extremely motivating feature of many of the more powerful word processors is the desktop publishing capability. Using a word processing program's resources for different fonts, type sizes, and styles, such as bold or shadowed print, makes it possible for students to produce work they can be truly proud of. Using other features, such as printing multiple columns, printing horizontally rather than vertically on a page, and importing graphics, offers students additional opportunities to produce creative and compelling final versions of their writing. The opportunity to produce professional-looking material will often provide students with the motivation to do the sort of drafting and revising that mature writers do.

In addition to word processors, three other software applications seem particularly useful to developing writers. One of these is an electronic dictionary, something like the *American Heritage Electronic Dictionary* from Houghton Mifflin or *Definition Plus* from the Word Science Corporation. Like an electronic thesaurus, an electronic dictionary puts the information students need where they can and will use it. Another type of software that can be helpful for developing writers is a grammar and style checker. Prentice Hall's *RightWriter* and *Sensible Grammar* from Sensible Software are two such programs. These utilities are quite sophisticated and check such diverse matters as grammar, usage, punctuation, spacing, level of formality, sentence diversity, and readability. A third type of useful software is a drawing program. *SuperPaint* from Silicon Beach Software and *Aldus Freehand* from the Aldus Corporation are among the better known ones. Programs such as these that enable students to create graphics make it possible for them to summarize and synthesize information and to present it as an attractive and informative part of their writing.

TYPES OF WRITING APPROPRIATE FOR SUBJECT MATTER CLASSES

As you have probably noticed, up to this point in the chapter you have been asked to do quite a bit of writing. In fact, you have been asked to engage in five of the six sorts of writing that are particularly useful in content classes. Here we discuss these six types—answering questions, taking notes, summarizing, writing to encourage critical thinking, expressive writing, and extended and formal writing. The first three of these are fairly common activities in subject matter courses, while the last three are less often used. Although not all of them need to be part of every subject matter course, you should consider the potential of each and choose several to include in your repertoire.

Answering Questions

Answering questions is an extremely frequent activity that students undertake in conjunction with reading. As long as the questions are not objective ones, such as true-false or multiple-choice items, they require at least some writing. Writing out answers generally will be more beneficial to students than simply selecting from among choices because writing forces students to really grapple with the meaning of the answers they are constructing. Thus, writing out answers to questions is a valid and useful activity. Attention to several matters can make questions more effective learning tools.

The most basic guideline is to pose questions that lead students to the most important information in a text. In discussing questions on narrative material, Beck and McKeown (1981) refer to a story map. Specifically, a story map is a set of questions that, when answered, will provide the essential information of a story. Beck and McKeown also suggest that questions be asked in the order in which they are addressed in the story so that, in answering them, students build a model of the story in their minds. This makes good sense. Moreover, the same basic guideline holds for expository material: Questions should lead students to the most important content of the selection, and the order should follow that in which the information occurs in the text. Generally, sets of questions that get at the essence of a story include the three types presented in Chapter Five—*gathering and recalling information, making sense of gathered information*, and *applying and evaluating actions in novel situations.*

A second guideline is to sometimes have students write out answers in complete sentences in relatively polished prose, and at other times to have them simply jot down phrases capturing the gist of answers. Writing out answers fully gives students practice in composing and often prompts them to more fully consider and formulate their responses, quite possibly producing fuller learning. Jotting down brief responses, on the other hand, gives students an opportunity to appreciate the value of such informal writing and allows them to answer more questions in less time.

A third guideline is to allow opportunities for cooperative learning. In particular, the jigsaw approach (Aronson, Blaney, Stephan, Sikes, & Snapp, 1978), which is described in more detail in Chapter Eight, can be very useful. In this approach, a class of 30 is divided into five groups of six students. The groups are given material that has been broken into six subsections, each of which is assigned to one student in each group. Thus, for example, in a lesson on chemical elements, one student in each group might write down the characteristics of one element, another in each group the characteristics of a second element, another the characteristics of a third, and so on. After studying and writing about his or her section individually, the member of each group who has written about a particular element gets together with the members from other teams who have written about the same element. Then, the five students in each of these "expert" groups discuss their element and compose a description of it. Next, the experts return to their own groups, share their descriptions of each of the elements, and write out the final description of the elements for their group's response.

PRACTICE ACTIVITY 7.6

Refer back to the section "Guidelines for Writing in Subject Matter Areas" and note which of the eight guidelines given there are being followed in the jigsaw example just described.

Taking Notes

Note taking is another writing activity that students engage in frequently, although for the most part not as frequently as they might. Students need to learn to use this important study strategy if they are to become proficient at understanding and remembering what they read. As Devine (1987) has pointed out, "Observations of many teachers and students through the years indicate that passive listening or reading leads to minimal learning" (p. 2). Learning new information, whether it is from an oral presentation or a text, requires the student to do something more than simply listen or read. Notes are certainly one aid to learning. In the remainder of this section, we discuss taking notes from lectures and taking notes while reading. First, however, we consider what is probably the most important aspect of assisting students in becoming able note takers—convincing them that the time and energy involved in note taking are well spent. It is certainly the case that many students are not highly skilled note takers; however, it is even more the case that many simply do not choose to take notes. Unless students can be convinced that taking notes is worth their time and effort, showing them how to do it is of little use.

Three steps are useful in motivating students to take notes. First, let them in on the secret. Explain to them that when learning new information from either a lecture or a reading selection, some form of actively manipulating the material—doing something with it other than simply listening or simply reading—is absolutely essential. Tell them that learning does not just happen; learners need to actively engage with the material they are dealing with if they are to learn much.

Second, explain why note taking works, why it helps them learn and remember information. For example, give these reasons: Taking notes forces them to pay attention to the lecture or text and to avoid daydreaming, and attending to something is certainly a necessary step in learning. Taking notes also forces them to put information in their own words, and putting information in their own words makes them rather than the lecturer or the text the owner of the information. Finally, notes are an abbreviated permanent record of the lecture or text, something they can study and review when they need to.

A third step in motivating students is to involve them in demonstrations of the effect of taking notes versus not taking notes. That is, give them brief lectures or selections from which they take notes, then give them other brief lectures or selections from which they do not take notes. Two or three classes later, allow them time to review their notes—which, of course, cover only some of the lectures or texts they have dealt with—then quiz them on all of the material. After they have completed the quiz, have them compare their performance on material for which they took notes with that on material for which they did not. Their performance should be hugely superior on the material on which they took notes. You should point this out, celebrate it, and encourage them to make note taking a frequent activity.

Once students understand the value of notes, help them become skilled note takers. One sequence for doing so is to first instruct them in using one specific procedure for taking notes from lectures and another specific procedure for taking notes during reading, then give them opportunities to practice with the procedures. Once students have learned and practiced the procedures, invite them to modify them according to their own learning styles and the demands of a particular lecture or reading situation.

The best known and most widely recommended note-taking procedure is the Cornell format (Pauk, 1989). The particular version of the Cornell format described here is based on the suggestions of Olson (1989). Here are guidelines for implementing it, phrased as they would be for students.

1. Using 8½-by-11-inch lined paper, draw a vertical line about 3 inches from the left margin.
2. The wider section of the paper is for your notes, the narrower section for questions you write about the notes. Writing questions that are answered in your notes and then attempting to answer the questions without looking at the notes is an excellent way to study.
3. You don't need to use a regular outline format, but you should indent details under main points.
4. You don't need to write in complete sentences; phrases are fine.
5. You can't possibly write down every word I say; instead, listen for main ideas and important details.
6. Listen for verbal cues, such as "The definition is . . . " or "The three major causes were. . . ."
7. Once you have completed the notes in the right-hand column, write the questions that are answered in your notes in the left-hand column. Do this as soon as possible after taking the notes. Most forgetting takes place very soon after you hear a lecture.
8. When studying your notes, cover up the left-hand column and practice answering the questions. It's a good idea to answer them out loud; it's even better to answer them out loud to a partner.

Present these ideas to students on an overhead or the board, discussing them one by one and taking any questions students have. During this discussion, include a reminder of the importance of active processing, telling students that using the Cornell format gives them the opportunity to write down the notes during a lecture, think up questions on the notes and jot them down, then ask and recite the answers to the questions. Stress the value of doing the reviewing with a partner, and suggest that students form cooperative groups for reviewing their notes. In such groups, one student could ask the questions, another could answer them, and a third could keep a written record of the review, particularly noting any questions that caused problems.

Following this initial presentation, construct a sample Cornell format outline for a particular lecture (such as that shown in Figure 7.2), actually writing in the main points and some of the important details as an aid to students the first time they use the format. Give the lecture, having students complete the Cornell format outline as they listen. Next, have students write their marginal questions, then get together with partners and review their questions. Finally, have a class debriefing session in which you discuss stu-

FIGURE 7.2   EXAMPLE OF CORNELL NOTE-TAKING SYSTEM

	Shock
What is shock?	*Definition:* a temporary depression of vital life processes
What causes shock?	*When it happens:* (1) severe injuries because of blood loss; blood pressure drops; (2) when body is stunned and loses control of circulatory system
How can I tell if someone is in shock?	*Symptoms:* cold and clammy skin; fast, weak pulse, then increase in rate; falling blood pressure; paleness; dizziness; dilated pupils
Is shock life-threatening?	*Severity:* can be serious threat to life; longer condition worsens—greater the threat to life
What do I do if someone goes into shock?	*Treatment:* lie victim down; elevate legs; keep warm with blanket; take pulse every 5 min.; comfort victim

dents' questions and comments about using the system and try to solve any problems that arise.

The next step in the Cornell format will depend on how well students performed. If they did well, you can have them work without the support of a partially completed outline. If they struggled, however, again construct some of the outline yourself to serve as a scaffold for their note taking. Also, hold debriefings after each attempt to be sure they are on track and to provide help and encouragement as needed. In general, instruction should follow the gradual release of responsibility model (Pearson & Gallagher, 1983) presented in Chapter Five. As you may recall, using that strategy you first demonstrate how to do a task, then gradually give students the responsibility of doing more and more of the task on their own, until eventually they are doing it independently.

Taking notes from reading selections is different from taking notes from lectures. The former is somewhat easier because students are not under pressure to keep up with the speaker and can go back and reread if necessary. As was the case with assisting students in learning to take notes from lectures, teach a specific procedure, give students a number of opportunities to practice it, then let students modify it if they find that they need to. Our recommendations here draw on the Cornell format (Pauk, 1989) and the suggestions of Olson (1989). Additionally, recent texts by the National Education Association (Rafoth & DeFabo, 1990) and the Association for Supervision and Curriculum Development (Gall, Gall, Jacobsen, & Bullock, 1990) have provided helpful suggestions. Once again, the guidelines are phrased as they would be for students.

1. As in the approach for taking notes for lectures, use 8½-by-11-inch lined paper and draw a vertical line about 3 inches from the left margin. Use the wider section for your notes and the narrower section for questions.

2. Read each section of a chapter through before you begin taking notes; there is no other way of knowing what will be important to remember.
3. As with lecture notes, you should probably indent details under main points.
4. Whether you write in phrases or complete sentences is up to you. Choose the form that best suits you and the material you are reading.
5. Whichever form you use, jot down notes in your own words. This is vital because writing things in your own words forces you to think about them.
6. Write questions as soon as possible after taking the notes; study by covering up the notes and attempting to answer the questions without looking at them; answer the questions out loud and with a partner, if possible.

As with lecture notes, present these ideas on an overhead or the board, discuss them and take questions, then remind students of the importance of active processing and the value of doing the reviewing with a partner or in a cooperative group. Again, use the gradual release of responsibility model in teaching the technique.

Summarizing

Summarizing is not a common content area writing activity. This is unfortunate, because it should be a very frequent activity when reading. Summarizing is an extremely valuable study strategy because, even more than note taking, it forces active processing. Summarizing requires a student to understand a text, identify the most important information, and put that information into his or her own words.

One approach to teaching summarizing was presented in Chapter Five; a second approach is described here. Summarizing can be taught much like note taking. Begin by motivating students, in this case urging them to use written summaries as part of their studying and learning. First, tell them that summarizing is an important skill. Next, explain why it is an important skill: It is important because it forces them to pick out significant information and recast it in their own words, and this means that the information is more likely to be understood and remembered. Finally, give them demonstrations of what they remember when they do summarize as well as what they remember when they simply read; that is, have them summarize some texts, simply read others, take some sort of quiz on the texts they did and did not summarize, then compare their results.

After these motivational activities, move to specific instruction in summarizing. Brown and Day (1983) have developed and tested some practical rules for summarizing. In fact, summarizing is one of the best understood and most effective learning strategies (Pressley, Johnson, Symons, McGoldrick, & Kurita, 1989). Here are the rules for summarizing.

1. Read the whole selection before you attempt to summarize it. Then, summarize first smaller and then larger units.
2. Summarize paragraphs by following these rules:

- Delete unimportant and redundant information.
- Use categories and terms that are more general. For example, if the author mentions *perch, trout,* and *salmon,* you might write down *fish.*
- Identify a topic sentence for the paragraph.
3. Summarize complete passages by first summarizing the individual paragraphs. Then, construct an overall summary of the complete passage.

As in dealing with note taking, present these ideas on an overhead or the board, discuss them and take questions, then remind students of the value of active processing. It is also useful to remind students that if they summarize an author's ideas for a paper or a speech, they need to be sure to give the author credit for his or her ideas. Instruction here should again follow the gradual release of responsibility model. Finally, tell students that, as with other techniques they are likely to use, they get out of summarizing what they put into it. That is, hard work and effort pay off. This message is likely to be most effective with students if you are candid and admit that hard work and time are costs, and summarizing is a relatively costly procedure. Thus, it is appropriate to suggest that students select writing summaries as a learning activity when the material they are reading is challenging and important and when they want to know it well.

Writing to Encourage Critical Thinking

There are many ways in which students can practice critical thinking. One of the writing activities already discussed, answering questions, gives students an opportunity to both gain knowledge from what they read and manipulate and react to that knowledge in various ways, including thinking critically about what they have learned. However, as explained in Chapter Six, critical thinking is extremely important and something that students can profit from doing more of. Writing offers excellent opportunities for critical thinking, and for this reason we have included this separate section on writing to encourage critical thinking.

As noted in Chapter Six, critical thinking requires students to use cognitive and metacognitive processes to go beyond what is explicitly stated in any single text. Critical thinking requires students to draw on their background knowledge, derive meaning from several different sources of information, and recognize or generate objectives that will direct their thinking and completion of a task. Writing, particularly extended writing, gives students the time and the space to think critically and to record both the process and the results of their thinking.

As Resnick (1987) has pointed out and as we have repeatedly stressed, critical thinking is something that all students need to and can do. All students can think critically if they are given appropriate topics and appropriate assistance in dealing with those topics. Topics, for example, can vary from practical and concrete problems, such as deciding what sorts of plants are likely to grow well on the north side of a house in the Pacific Northwest, to philosophical problems, such as to what extent the public school system ought to teach youngsters to examine the political system in the United States. The resources you give can vary from simply presenting students with the critical thinking task and telling them they can use libraries and any other sources of information they find useful to actually giving them all the materials they will need to complete the task.

In leading students to become critical thinkers, there is a place for both relatively easy and more difficult tasks, as well as for directed and independent learning. Initially, give students topics and the amount of support that they need to succeed, then gradually challenge them by presenting them with more complex tasks and less support; that is, follow the gradual release of responsibility model. In the remainder of this section, we present examples of a simple task with much teacher support and a fairly difficult task that allows for independent learning.

As an example of a simple task, consider directing students in a consumer education class to make a decision about what sort of VCR to buy. The writing task is for students to document the process they went through in making the decision, to state the decision, and to explain why they made that decision. As resources, give students a profile showing the income and expenditures of the family they are to represent, a half dozen or so ads for VCRs, and an issue of *Consumer Reports* that evaluates VCRs. Then ask them, individually or in groups, to analyze the situation and come up with a report in which they (1) define the problem, (2) describe the resources they have used to make their decision, (3) describe the process they used to reach their decision, and (4) state their decision. Also, as a further exercise in critical thinking, ask them to discuss how principled or arbitrary their decision was.

Of course, this task could be made more challenging and require more critical thinking if you provided students with fewer resources. For example, it would become a great deal more challenging if you simply presented students with the problem of choosing a VCR and asked them both to determine what information they needed to make a reasonable decision and to find that information themselves.

As a more difficult task, consider some particularly talented senior high students in a social policy class that is dealing with the issue of public health care. The particular matter to be considered in this critical thinking and writing activity is the advisability of mandatory large-scale testing for various communicable diseases. The issue has come up in some of the class readings and has elicited a good deal of debate among the students, but this debate has produced a lot of heat without a great deal of light. In introducing the activity, you note this and tell them you think the issue is one worth their time and effort. You can also provide them with a single resource, a chapter on risk benefit analysis from Eugene Robin's (1984) *Matters of Life and Death: Risks and Benefits of Medical Care.* The chapter presents a fascinating scenario of the risks and benefits of large-scale diagnosis.

Next, tell students that they can work alone or in groups, but that beyond that they are on their own for a while. For this activity, they will need to start from the beginning and identify the specific problem they want to address. Then, they will need to engage in at least some of the following steps and prepare a report in which they record some of these steps. The steps include (1) defining the problem, (2) explaining how they decided what resources they would need to solve it, (3) describing the resources they used to make their decision, (4) describing the process they used to reach the decision, (5) stating the decision, (6) justifying it, and (7) assessing how certain they are of their decision. As suggested in the previous exercise, you can provide additional experience with critical thinking by asking them to discuss how principled or arbitrary their decision was. The decision as to just which of these steps to record in their reports is one the students will need to make as part of the critical thinking process in which they are engaging.

It is important to recognize that these two assignments represent a great range of difficulty and that the latter would challenge many students. It may be too difficult for some, and you may need to provide more resources. At the same time, the problem is representative of the large, complex, and unbounded decisions that life presents; learning to deal with such problems is the essence of critical thinking.

PRACTICE ACTIVITY 7.7

Brainstorm a list of half a dozen topics in your subject matter that invite critical thinking. Include both easier topics and more challenging ones, but definitely choose topics that require the complex sorts of thinking illustrated in the VCR and testing for communicable disease examples just given. If possible, ask a colleague to join you in this activity.

Expressive Writing

As noted earlier, although there is not very much writing done in subject matter classes, most writing that is done is addressed to the teacher and is transactional, meant to convey information. Students need more opportunities for expressive writing, writing that gives them opportunities to articulate their thoughts, feelings, and opinions about the topics they are studying.

Sometimes the expressive writing students produce will be directed to you as their teacher, to other students in the class, or to some wider audience beyond the classroom. Often, however, students will write for themselves, and their efforts will not be passed on to others. Partly for this reason and partly because students need the opportunity to make these personal responses without having to give a lot of thought to such matters as mechanics and usage, expressive writing should be informal, not subject to rules, nor to criticism and revision. This makes your task in promoting and fostering expressive writing an easy one; there is not a lot of teaching or correcting that needs to be done here.

However, your task is also likely to be a challenging one just because students are unlikely to have done very much expressive writing in the past, particularly in content classes.

Students' lack of experience means that several practices will be useful when you introduce expressive writing in your classes. First, explain to students what expressive writing is and why you are having them do it. This type of writing gives them the opportunity to voice their personal feelings about topics that come up in their readings and in class; doing so will help students become more involved with the topics and better understand them.

Second, model expressive writing, then share both the composing process and what is written with students. For example, after reading a chapter about the Great Depression, you might write something like this: "I've read about the Great Depression before, and every time I read about it and see the pictures of the men and women doing nothing, just looking tired and without hope, I wonder how they survived. I also wonder how I would survive in their situation." Although this writing is neither profound nor vivid, it is an honest personal response to the topic, and that is what students should communicate in their expressive writing.

Third, let students know that they are being asked to present their own feelings and responses, that recording them as they occur is okay, and that, unless you suggest otherwise, they do not need to share what they have written with anyone. Because writing for themselves is a new experience for many students, this may need to be repeated several times. You need to demonstrate your sincerity by giving students time for expressive writing and by letting them keep such writing to themselves.

One sort of expressive writing that has been widely discussed and advocated is journal writing (Anson & Beach, 1994; Atwell, 1987). As described by Fulwiler (1982), journal writing occupies a place midway between diaries and class notebooks. The subject of a diary is simply the writer, while the subject of a class notebook is the course content. A journal, on the other hand, deals with the relationship between the student and the course content. In the sort of journal writing considered here, students—and, in some cases, teachers—record relatively informal comments responding to class topics. Every class offers students numerous opportunities for journal responses to important topics. Students in geometry classes, for example, might speculate about practical uses of the formulas they are learning. Students in music classes might write about the awe certain composers or certain music inspires in them. And students in computer classes might consider parallels between the incredibly rapid growth of the computer industry and the growth that has occurred in other industries during this century.

Three matters are particularly worth consideration when designing journal activities. One is whether anyone other than the writer should read them. Opinions differ here, but if students spend fairly substantial amounts of time on journals, then you should read at least some of the entries. Of course, it may be necessary to sometimes guarantee students that certain journal entries will remain private.

Another matter is who should read them. You and other students are both viable audiences. At some points you probably will want to read students' journals, but students should sometimes be allowed to read each others' entries.

The third matter is choosing between individual and dialogue journals. Individual journals are simply journals kept by individual students. Dialogue journals, on the other hand, are extended conversations in which pairs of students respond at length to each others' entries. In such journals, students deal with both the course topic they are reading about and their partners' responses to the course topic. For example, two students reading the same novel might discuss the theme of the book and at the same time each other's interpretation of that theme.

As already noted, the sort of expressive writing done in content classes does not require much instruction. However, once the notion of expressive writing has been introduced, it may be necessary to point out opportunities for it. Here are just a handful of topics students might want to write about:

- The geological age of the earth, which one recent estimate put at 3.8 billion years
- Abstract art, photography as art, or the right to freedom of expression
- Jazz, rap, or any other style of music
- The assassination of John Kennedy, Robert Kennedy, Malcolm X, or Martin Luther King, Jr.
- The impact of Darwin's theories
- Raising the speed limit to 65 mph on some interstates
- Experiencing a tornado, hurricane, or other major storm
- The impact of genetic engineering
- Cars, toasters, or other products designed to become obsolete

PRACTICE ACTIVITY 7.8

The above list of topics for expressive writing is a short one. It is also one that is not specifically tailored to your content area or students. Before you go on to the next section, jot down half a dozen or so topics in your content area that are likely candidates for students' expressive writing. Then, write a sentence or two of your own for each of these topics.

Extended and Formal Writing

Although most of you reading this book are subject matter teachers rather than writing teachers and will therefore be using writing primarily as a vehicle to further students' success with your subject rather than as an end in itself, there are still occasions when you want students to engage in extended and relatively formal writing. Two approaches to writing—approaches consistent with the cognitive process model discussed earlier—are particularly worth considering. These are the process approach and the environmental approach, which are discussed next.

The Process Approach.   The process approach was briefly discussed in the section on the cognitive process models of writing. This approach (see, e.g.,

Graves, 1983) is currently the most widely discussed and advocated method of teaching writing. The approach draws its name from its emphasis on the process of writing, on the activities that a writer pursues as he or she plans a writing task, drafts the writing, then reviews, revises, and edits it. The approach stresses that students need time and a good deal of freedom to engage appropriately in these tasks.

In using the process approach, students often engage in a series of activities:

1. Freewriting or prewriting—brainstorming that allows them to choose and explore a topic of interest, then search for what they want to say about it.
2. Initial drafting, the emphasis here being on the content rather than the form of expression (there may be several drafts or parts of drafts done along with some peer discussion).
3. Sharing writing with classmates and getting some response from peers.
4. Rewriting the first draft as something closer to a final product (in many cases, students then meet individually with the teacher to review the writing).
5. Completing a final draft.
6. Sharing completed writing with other students in the class or with an outside audience.

Often in classrooms in which the process approach is used, students do not hand in all their final drafts but pick some of their best work to be read and evaluated by the teacher. As noted before, this is an excellent practice, since it gives students a sense of control, provides them with an opportunity to evaluate their own writing, and leaves the teacher with fewer papers to read. Finally, whenever possible, students in process writing classrooms should write for audiences other than the teacher.

In employing the process approach, a music teacher, for example, might ask students to describe a particular style of music and a selection exemplifying that type, then explain why they liked it. Initially, students might meet in small groups to share their initial thoughts about styles of music. Then, they might prewrite—quickly jotting down a number of types of music and their reactions to them. Next, they might select one type of music and write rough drafts. They could then share these drafts with their peers, getting feedback and revising as needed. In their second drafts, they would probably pay more attention to form, producing writing that was more like a final product. After completing these drafts, they might again share their writing with others, probably looking for comments on form and mechanics as well as further comments on content. Next would come the third, possibly final, drafts. As a concluding activity, each student might read his or her paper and play a tape of the musical selection used as an example. After this, students might hand in their papers for the teacher's response, or they might not. The major purposes of the assignment—thinking about types of music, engaging with the topic, planning and drafting a piece, revising and editing it, and sharing their writing with an audience—have already been accomplished.

Of course, this is a rather lengthy assignment and not something most subject matter teachers would engage in frequently. Note, however, that it is not necessary to present a full-blown assignment such as this to take advantage of the insights provided by the process approach. Any of the individual activities students did while completing this assignment could be of value by themselves. That is, discussion, writing about something interesting, prewriting, drafting, peer reviewing, revising, editing, and sharing finished products with an audience are all activities that could be engaged in independently in subject matter classes.

PRACTICE ACTIVITY 7.9

Consider some extended writing that you might employ in your content area using the process approach. First, decide on some topics. Next, decide on how long you might devote to the writing. After that, determine an audience for the writing. Then list the prewriting, writing, revising, editing, and sharing activities that students would do. Finally, decide on what sort of culminating activity you could provide.

The Environmental Approach.   The other writing approach that has received a good deal of attention has been termed the environmental approach. The name was chosen to reflect the fact that in using the approach, the teacher carefully structures the writing environment—the materials that students work with and the activities they engage in—in order to help students reach specific objectives. This approach, while not as widely used or advocated as the process approach, has a good deal of support from research (Hillocks, 1986). Although the environmental approach shares a number of features with the process approach, it also differs from the process approach in a number of ways. Compared to the process approach, the environmental approach is more structured, and both the activities students engage in and the outcomes of those activities are more deliberately planned. Teachers using the environmental approach have clear and specific objectives, they deliberately select materials and problems that will engage students in specific writing processes, and they employ such activities as small group problem-centered discussions that are conducive to high levels of engagement and peer interaction.

A typical environmental writing experience might begin with a brief lecture on a topic. Very soon, however, you would involve students in concrete materials and experiences that let them work with the ideas presented in the lecture. Most of the time should be devoted to allowing students to manipulate ideas rather than to your presenting them. The following example is based on one Hillocks (1986) provides. As described here, it might be used in a junior high art class.

The goals for this assignment are for students to recognize and appreciate the myriad of details in a still-life display and for them to appreciate the task of communicating to a particular audience and being precise and detailed in their writing. As a prompt, bring to class a slide showing 30 or so seashells arranged on a table. Then explain to students that they are to write a composition in which they describe one of the shells in sufficient detail that another student can identify it. At this point, you may briefly point out one or two distinguishing features students will need to take into account, but introductory comments should be brief. Next, have students get into small groups and brainstorm about the set of features they need to consider to accomplish their task. After this, they should separate and write their drafts. Next, probably in small groups, have them try out their compositions, seeing if their peers can indeed pick out the shell they are describing. They can then revise as necessary. As a concluding activity, they can present their identifications and let the class identify the selected shells. Finally, they should discuss the intricate details of still-life displays and just what was and was not needed to accomplish the identification task, then attempt to arrive at some generalizations for related writing tasks in which things need to be identified.

As with the process approach, content teachers need not use all of the environmental approach in any single writing activity. One particularly useful insight of the environmental approach is that students often need some starting point, some relatively concrete prompt or stimulus that serves as a basis for their writing and gives them materials to manipulate and transform. Thus, for example, a geography teacher might bring in maps of three or four cities and the area surrounding them and ask students to brainstorm, then draft lists of locational advantages that the cities have in common. Somewhat similarly, a science teacher might present three or four demonstrations of the effect of friction on bodies of different shapes, then ask pairs of students to draft their speculations about the forces operating in the demonstrations.

PRACTICE ACTIVITY 7.10

Since you have just read about the environmental approach, this is a good time to design an environmental writing assignment in your content area. Doing so requires a fair amount of work, so you might want to work on this with a partner or even get together in a small group and let different members of the group handle different parts of the assignment. As you are doing the assignment, keep notes. Then, write up a final description so that you will have the assignment ready to use when you need it.

FOLLOWING UP ON STUDENTS' WRITING

Once students have produced some writing, you will probably be faced with a stack of papers that cry out for attention. We discuss here a number of matters to consider in responding to students' work and several approaches to evaluating writing.

Responding to Students' Writing

At the beginning of the chapter, we noted that during the past 10 to 15 years scholars have been reassessing the conception of writing and approaches to teaching it. During this same period, a number of writing teachers began to consider response to student writing. It appears that one of the reasons students do not write well and one of the reasons teachers do not assign a lot of writing can be found in the ways teachers typically have responded to students' writing. Briefly, in the past teachers have almost always responded with criticism, nearly filling papers with red marks and such angry shorthand as *awk* (awkward) and *frag* (sentence fragment). Most of that criticism has been of mechanical features—grammar, punctuation, spelling, and the like—with very little attention given to content. Often, students have received papers without a single positive comment. Furthermore, almost the only ones to respond to students' papers has been teachers.

Today, those who deal with students' writing have adopted a very different approach. Based on a variety of considerations of appropriate modes of response (see, e.g., Anson, 1989), a very telling article on the importance of praising students' writing by Daiker (1989), and the experiences we have had as instructors for projects in which college students respond to high school students' writing via telecommunications (Graves & Duin, 1992; Ryder, 1991), we offer the following guidelines for response. Following these guidelines not only makes good sense as a method of improving students' writing, but it also makes for a lot less work for you; this, of course, increases the feasibility of having students write in your classes.

Much of what students write does not require a formal response. A great deal of the writing students do is done to learn the material, to find out what they already know about it, or to engage with it. Moreover, even when students write formal papers, it is not necessary for you to respond to everything they write. Many teachers have found that letting students select what they think is their best work from a set of three or four papers and submit only that one for formal response works well. There are fewer papers to grade and more time available for each paper. Students get better feedback on their writing, they get an opportunity to evaluate their own writing and decide which paper they want to hand in for a grade, and they are put in a much less taxing situation than when everything they write must be graded.

You need not be the only respondent to students' writing; instead, you should allow students to respond frequently to each others' writing. Since there will probably be about 30 students and just one teacher in most classes, students can respond to each others' writing in much more detail than the teacher can. Also, the process of responding to each others' writing offers some valuable lessons. Finding out what sorts of response other students want on their writing and what sorts of response students give to each others' writing will teach students a great deal about writing.

Whether it is students responding to each other or your responding to students, a central concern in any response should be to give students positive feedback. As noted above, in the past, the vast majority of teachers' responses to students has been criticism. In fact, Daiker (1989) reports that in most studies of how teachers respond to students' writing the ratio of criticism to praise is about 9 to 1, and in one study 15 of 25 teachers responding to a student essay found nothing to compliment. This simply is not the way to get students to do their best. Students need compliments on their writing. In fact, both you and peer respondents should try to provide at least one compliment for each critical comment made. Moreover, it is important to be specific and to include praise throughout, not simply at the beginning or end of comments.

In addition to being specific with praise, it is important to include both explicit comments and examples and general comments and prompts in responses. In some cases, students need to be shown just what to do; they may even need to be given models, a sentence or two showing how you or a peer reviewer might make a point. In other cases, they just need to be pointed in a direction and should be given the freedom to find their own solutions to the challenges writing presents.

It is usually a good idea to limit the number of comments on students' papers, and to limit the length and complexity of them. No matter how many comments you make, students will respond to only a limited number of them. Making more comments than students will respond to is a waste of time, and it does not help students. Selecting a few really important matters to comment on saves time, focuses students' attention, and does not present them with a paper discouragingly filled with suggestions for revision. This same suggestion applies to peer reviewers.

Finally, the most effective tone to adopt in responding to students' work is very often that of a coach, a co-worker, or even a cheerleader. Think of a coach talking to a young man or woman during a time-out. The individual is playing fairly well, almost as well as he or she can, but might be able to do a little better with some encouragement. This is a position students often find themselves in when writing. It is up to you to provide that encouragement and offer a few hints.

Evaluating Students' Writing

Writing assessment in subject matter classes should provide information on students' ability to reason and assign relevance to the content of their reading. This is not to negate the importance of mechanical elements, but attention to mechanics should come after students have had ample opportunities to construct and revise the content of their writing.

Writing assessment in subject matter classrooms presents several challenges. First, you must determine the method of assessment that will be used. Writing assessment traditionally has been directed at elements of mechanics, grammar, style, and the quality or sophistication of the content. Assessment of all of these factors can be unwieldy and is often not necessary in subject matter classes. Writing should be viewed as a tool for the communication of knowledge that is constructed by the learner, a process that is parallel to the construction of meaning from reading (Tierney & Pearson, 1983). Assessment approaches consistent with these tenets need to be used.

A second challenge in evaluating students' writing is the time it requires. If, for example, you have five classes of 30 students and 10 minutes is required to read and comment on a paper, you would be faced with 25 hours of grading. Dedicating this amount of time to writing assessment is simply unrealistic. Thus, you need to evaluate writing with techniques that offer students meaningful feedback, but require a minimum of time. Holistic methods of evaluating students' writing meet these requirements.

Holistic evaluation examines students' writing as a whole rather than as isolated elements. It can be done quickly, is based on impressions of the written piece, and does not require marking corrections or making suggestions for revision. The value of holistic scoring lies in its ability to present a sense of what is essential in a written piece (Cooper, 1977).

Three types of holistic writing assessment—general impression marking, dichotomous scales, and analytic scales—are described here. Each is useful in subject matter classrooms and requires a minimal amount of preparation and practice. They address different elements of writing and yield different degrees of precision. When used appropriately, these holistic assessments can provide meaningful feedback that will improve the quality of students' writing and their understanding of the content studied. Additionally, holistic assessment techniques can be used by students for evaluating each others' writing.

General Impression Marking. General impression marking is a relatively easy form of assessment. It requires no analysis of specific mechanical, grammatical, or stylistic features of the writing. Instead, it considers the number and depth of appropriate concepts in students' writing. Scoring is done using a numerical scale, typically ranging from 1 to 8 or from 1 to 10. Shown here are the criteria that could be used for evaluating a U.S. history assignment on the First Amendment.

	Low							High
Knowledge of the First Amendment	1	2	3	4	5	6	7	8
Ability to relate historical events to the First Amendment	1	2	3	4	5	6	7	8
Ability to relate other constitutional rights to the First Amendment	1	2	3	4	5	6	7	8

When returned to students, such a rating sheet can direct them to specific conceptual elements of the writing that are strong as well as those that require further work. Students can then seek additional information, clarify previously acquired information, or restructure information that may have been misunderstood.

PRACTICE ACTIVITY 7.11

Shown here is a portion of an eighth grader's essay on the agriculture of the Midwest. Take a few moments to read this sample and mark the scoring scale below. Our scoring is shown in the answers section at the end of the book.

The farmers in the Midwest grow most of the corn and wheat produced in the U.S. Increasingly over the past several decades, soybeans have also become an important crop. These crops grow well in this part of the country because the summers are hot and humid. Other parts of the country grow wheat and corn but the temperature in those areas is not as warm as the Midwest. The stability of the small family farm has been threatened during the 1980s as worldwide demand for corn and wheat decline. The lack of demand was also accompanied by many years of high production. As a result, prices of these crops declined significantly. Individual farmers were also hurt because they borrowed a lot of money from banks so they could buy more land. This added land produced crops that brought little profit and farmers were unable to make their payments. As a result, many of them lost their farms.

	Low						High	
Knowledge of primary crops grown in the Midwest	1	2	3	4	5	6	7	8
Ability to recognize climatic and soil conditions for crop production in the U.S.	1	2	3	4	5	6	7	8
Ability to define conditions contributing to the decline of family farms	1	2	3	4	5	6	7	8

Dichotomous Scales.   A dichotomous scale is a set of descriptors to which the evaluator responds with a simple yes or no. This scale does not quantify elements of the writing but indicates only whether an element is present. Although the dichotomous scale provides a rather general assessment, it does direct students to specific aspects of their writing that are strong and specific aspects that need revision.

One advantage of the dichotomous scale is its flexibility. For example, on one writing assignment you may limit assessment to stylistic elements, whereas on another you may focus on content. Selective use of the scale will reduce the amount of time spent on evaluating a writing assignment and allow students to focus on and improve specific elements of their writing. The dichotomous scale is also useful as part of the process approach to writing. Applied to students' first drafts, the scale first directs them to areas in need of revision. Applied to students' second drafts, the scale can draw attention to improvements as well as identifying elements that still need revision.

Figure 7.3 is a dichotomous scale that examines cognitive, organizational, and mechanical elements of students' writing.

FIGURE 7.3   DICHOTOMOUS SCALE

	Yes	No
Cognitive Elements		
Information is valid.	___	___
Ideas are contemporary and display insight and intuition.	___	___
Ideas are well integrated.	___	___
Writer notes similarities and differences between ideas and information.	___	___
Information and ideas are clearly presented.	___	___
Information is drawn from reliable sources.	___	___
Writing displays logic and coherence.	___	___
Organizational Elements		
Overall themes or hypotheses are clearly stated.	___	___
Themes are elaborated throughout the writing.	___	___
Paragraphs have controlling ideas.	___	___
Paragraphs have supporting details.	___	___
Logical transitions are provided.	___	___
Summaries are provided.	___	___
Mechanical Elements		
Punctuation is generally correct.	___	___
Subjects and verbs agree in number.	___	___
Pronouns agree with antecedents.	___	___
Pronoun referents are clear.	___	___
Unclear modifiers are avoided.	___	___

Analytic Scales.   Like a dichotomous scale, an analytic scale deals with specific aspects of students' writing. For example, an analytic scale might deal with content, organization, and mechanics. However, unlike a dichotomous scale, an analytic scale does not simply indicate whether or not a particular feature is present. Instead, an analytic scale includes descriptions of several levels of performance in each of the areas considered, and the evaluator rates students' performance in each area by comparing their performance to the descriptions given. Thus, students are ranked from high to low on each of the aspects considered. Figure 7.4 is a modified version of an analytic scale origi-

FIGURE 7.4 ANALYTIC SCALE

Content

Low		Middle		High
2	4	6	8	10

High: The writer has given some thought to the topic and writes what he or she really thinks. The writer discusses each main point long enough to show clearly what he or she means. The writer supports each main point with arguments, examples, or details; the writer gives the reader some reason for believing it. Points are clearly related to the topic and to the main idea or impression the writer is trying to convey.

Middle: The writer gives the impression that he or she does not really believe what is written. The writer does not fully understand the topic and tries to guess what might be appropriate for the essay, then writes what he or she thinks will get by. The writer does not explain points very clearly or make them come alive to the reader. The writer writes what he or she thinks will sound good, not what he or she believes or knows.

Low: It is hard to tell what points the writer is trying to make or if he or she is trying to make any particular point. The writer is only trying to get something down on paper. He or she does not explain points, only asserts them and then goes on to something else, or repeats them in slightly different words. The writer is not concerned with supportable information.

Organization and Structure

Low		Middle		High
2	4	6	8	10

High: The writer has developed an introduction that clearly defines the topic and the point the writer is making about the topic. The writer has also developed a conclusion that restates the topic and brings closure to the paper. The writer orders ideas in clearly formed paragraphs. The paper flows smoothly through the use of transitions.

Middle: The writer has developed an introduction that either defines the topic or the point the writer is making about the topic, but not both. The conclusion is not differentiated from the body of the text, but there is closure. Paragraph structure does not show good reasoning. Too many things may be included in one paragraph. Some paragraph breaks seem to be arbitrary. Transitions are used sparingly. There is some choppiness from idea to idea.

Low: The writer has used no introduction or conclusion. If the writer has made an attempt at an introduction or a conclusion, it is a haphazard try, not necessarily containing a thesis or topic. There is little or no regard for paragraph structure. The paper has choppy organization due to a lack of transitions.

Style and Voice

Low		Middle		High
2	4	6	8	10

High: The writer establishes a clear, consistent voice and point of view. The writer seems to have a firm grasp of his or her audience. The writer uses a style that is interesting, holds the reader's attention, and motivates him or her to continue to read.

FIGURE 7.4   CONTINUED

Style and Voice (continued)

Middle: The writer's voice is difficult to identify or may be inconsistent or confusing. The writer lacks awareness of audience. The style seems simple and not very interesting.

Low: The writer shows no recognizable voice in the piece. The style seems flat and lifeless and shows no concern for audience. The paper fails to hold the reader's attention.

Sentence Clarity

Low		Middle		High
2	4	6	8	10

High: The writer shows confident control of sentence structure. There are no run-on sentences or inappropriate sentence fragments. The paper reads smoothly from sentence to sentence. Sentences are varied in length and structure.

Middle: The writer shows some control of sentence structure and there are almost no run-on sentences or sentence fragments. The writer only occasionally writes a sentence that is awkward or puzzling.

Low: The writer has many problems with sentence structure. There are several run-on sentences and sentence fragments. Sentences are short and simple in structure, somewhat repetitious in their patterns or simply rambling.

Word Choice

Low		Middle		High
2	4	6	8	10

High: The writer's words are employed in a unique and interesting way. Most vocabulary is appropriate to support style, clarity, and usage.

Middle: The writer uses common words in a standard way. The paper may have some trite, overworked expressions. The writer, on the other hand, may work so hard at being different, that he or she uses words in ways that do not sound natural. Some of the vocabulary might be inappropriate to support style, clarity, and usage.

Low: The writer's word choice is limited and inappropriate for the paper. Sometimes words are used incorrectly or the wrong word is used.

Mechanics and Usage

Low		Middle		High
2	4	6	8	10

High: The writer consistently uses appropriate punctuation, capitalization, spelling, and usage (no more than two errors in mechanics and usage per page).

Middle: The writer uses proper punctuation, capitalization, spelling, and usage most of the time (no more than five errors in mechanics and usage per page).

Low: The writing contains many errors in punctuation, capitalization, spelling, and usage (more than five errors in mechanics and usage per page).

nally developed by Diederich (1974). It can be used with transactional writing students might do in almost any content area. If you wanted to focus on only some aspects of students' writing, then you would use only selected parts of the scale. (As described here, the scale is most appropriate for senior high students, but modifications could make it appropriate for younger students also.)

When an analytic scale is used, students should be given the scale and told the various criteria that are going to be considered in evaluating their writing. Once they are familiar with the criteria, students can gain excellent feedback from the scale, and can use this information to examine their writing and make revisions. At the same time, no markings, corrections, or extensive comments are required. Of course, this scale will not draw attention to specific words, sentences, or paragraphs; and some students will need assistance with these parts of their writing. These students are likely to benefit from a sort of peer editing and assessment described at the end of this section of the chapter.

PRACTICE ACTIVITY 7.12

Here are two writing samples addressing the impact of global warming. Examine each sample carefully, then complete the analytic scale that follows for each essay. Our responses are given in the answers section at the end of the book.

Sample 1

The earth's atmosphere is getting hotter. Because we burn a lot of gasoline and other fuel the air is warmed up. The heat goes up in the air. If the air keeps getting hotter the ice caps will melt and it will flood. If it floods then we will have no place to live or grow food to eat. Animals will die because they will get hot and the trees will die. Most animals don't know how to keep cool when they get hot. We need to make it cooler for them to live. I keep cool in summer by going to the pool, but animals can't. We need to plant more trees.

Sample 2

Global warming is caused by gases that are released into the atmosphere. When gases like carbon dioxide are released, they trap heat in the atmosphere just as heat is trapped inside a greenhouse. These same gases also reduce the amount of ozone in the atmosphere. This ozone protects the inhabitants of the earth from dangerous ultraviolet light rays that can be dangerous to humans and animals. Reduction of global warming can be accomplished by significant reductions in the burning of fossil fuels that emit large amounts of carbon dioxide, through reforestation of the planet, and through the careful control of chemicals such as CFCs that can deplete the ozone layer.

	Low		Middle		High
General Merit					
Content	1	2	3	4	5
Organization	1	2	3	4	5
Clarity	1	2	3	4	5
Word choice	1	2	3	4	5
Mechanics					
Grammar and usage	1	2	3	4	5
Punctuation	1	2	3	4	5
Spelling	1	2	3	4	5

Peer Evaluation

As noted earlier, the responsibility for evaluating writing can often be shifted from the teacher to students. Like the cooperative learning experiences described in Chapter Eight, peer assessment allows students to learn from each other. Peer evaluation can also reduce the time you devote to grading, thus making it feasible for students to write more frequently. Students may pay more attention to what their peers tell them than what you suggest. Finally, peer evaluation provides a social context that makes the evaluation more meaningful to students.

Typically, peer review is conducted by small groups of students who examine the content, organization, style, and mechanics of a written piece. Through the use of questions or a checklist provided by the teacher, the groups make suggestions for revisions and rank final drafts. Note that peer review gives students an excellent context in which to improve their critical thinking and organizational skills and increase their appreciation of writing (Nystrand, 1986).

To begin peer evaluation, walk students through a writing assessment. First, select an analytic, dichotomous, or general observation scale. Then, present the rationale for the assessment scale and a brief description of its use. Next, model use of the scale with a writing sample. As the scale is being marked, it is important to provide a thorough rationale to students so they understand the evaluation criteria being applied. Equally important, students need an opportunity to discuss the elements being evaluated.

In addition to using these scales or as an alternative to using them, Beaven (1977) has described procedures that will promote small-group dialogue and begin to direct students' attention to important elements of writing.

1. Identify the best section of the composition and describe what makes it effective.
2. Identify a sentence, a group of sentences, or a paragraph that needs revision and revise it as a group, writing the final version on the back of the paper.
3. Identify one or two things the writer can do to improve his or her next piece of writing. Write these goals at the top of the first page.

Following these guidelines will acquaint students with elements of writing to attend to as they conduct holistic assessments. Following them also initiates a process by which students can better understand the components of good writing. Finally, following them will ensure that students get some positive feedback from each other. Listed here are some other suggestions for assisting students in becoming effective peer evaluators.

1. Certain individuals within a group may "specialize" in particular elements of writing. Such a division of labor may speed up the evaluation process, provide more reliable feedback, and increase the likelihood that students will enhance their knowledge of the elements evaluated.

2. Students may sometimes wish to use colored markers to highlight particularly well written sentences or paragraphs. Highlighting should be limited to the identification of the strengths of the written piece.

3. Attempt to set time limits for an evaluation and enforce these limits so that students stay on track.

4. Hold the group accountable for completing their evaluation. Have groups make oral presentations or provide written summaries of their findings to share with the class.

5. Initially set length limits on writing assignments to increase the likelihood that students will complete their evaluations.

6. Maintain portfolios of students' written work. These records contain samples of the students' writing collected throughout the year and the holistic evaluations applied to the writing.

7. Periodically direct all groups to conduct a holistic evaluation of the same writing sample to build consensus in scoring.

One excellent way to use peer evaluation is to use it along with teacher sampling of students' writing. Each time students use peer evaluation, you may evaluate one or two papers, then compare that evaluation to those the peer groups have done. Over time such sampling will provide a good sense of students' writing ability, their ability to communicate the content of the subject matter through writing, and their evaluation skills.

CONCLUDING REMARKS

We began this chapter by noting the importance of writing, then discussed how much writing secondary students do and how well they write. The central theme is that writing is important not just in English classes or special writing classes, but in all classes. It is also important to realize that most students do not write very often nor very well and that changing this situation is an important goal for all teachers.

The next section considered current conceptions of writing as a complex psychological process, a social process, and a means for students to converse with themselves. Each of these ideas—the view of the writing process as a recursive set of planning, drafting, and revising episodes; the view that one learns to write well by trying to communicate real messages to real audiences; and the view that the writer is sometimes the primary and sole audience for his or her writing—should influence the way content teachers work with writing in their classrooms.

Another section dealt with the vital importance of providing students with a positive classroom atmosphere, some of the most effective uses of computers in writing, and some general guidelines for content area writing. These included focusing on content, designing activities that require structuring and synthesizing, including varied audiences, letting students write as learners and researchers, providing adequate time for writing, using peer feedback, differentiating between revising and editing, and publishing students' writing.

The longest section of the chapter described six sorts of writing that are appropriate in content classes: answering questions, taking notes, summarizing, writing to encourage critical thinking, expressive writing, and formal writing. Consider all of them as you plan your classes and use those that seem to fit best with your students.

The final section offered guidelines for responding to students' writing and some evaluation methods. Following these guidelines will create an atmosphere in which students are willing to face the challenges of writing and work to improve their writing and their understanding of the content you teach. Using the evaluation methods will result in evaluation that is fair, practical, and sensitive to what is important in students' writing. Moreover, using these methods will enable you to spend less time on evaluation and therefore make it easier to assign more writing activities.

REFLECTIONS

Now that you have considered students' writing and ways that writing can be used as an aid to reading and learning, complete the following activities in order to review and strengthen what you have learned in the chapter.

1. Summarize the information about how much students write and what sort of writing they do. Then, consider the subject matter you teach and compose statements describing how much writing and what sorts of writing students should be doing in your subject area.

2. Generate a list of 20 or so topics typically dealt with in your subject area. Select six that you think would be good topics for expressive writing and create writing prompts for each of them.

3. One of the central points made about effective writing instruction is that students need the experience of writing for various audiences. Describe some of the audiences that students might write to when dealing with

topics in your subject area. In some cases, it may be useful to have students assume a persona, for example, a particular historical figure, and write to an audience that figure might address.

4. Select a short section from a text in your subject area and write a set of questions that tap students' understanding of the most important content in the section. Go through your list and see if they include questions that require students to gather and recall information, make sense of gathered information, and apply and evaluate actions in novel situations. If any of these types are missing, see if you can add some questions representing them. However, do not add questions unless they deal with important matters.

5. Review the description of the Cornell format for taking notes from lectures and the procedures for teaching the system. Choose some lecture topics from your subject area that could be used in instructing students to use the Cornell system, and sketch out a plan and a time line for teaching it.

6. The chapter repeatedly stressed the importance of giving students positive responses to their writing. Select several of your students' papers or obtain some papers from students about the grade level you plan to teach and generate a list of positive comments for each paper.

7. Different methods of evaluating students' papers have both advantages and disadvantages. Select two of the three types of methods described—general impression marking, dichotomous scale, and analytic scale—and describe the advantages and disadvantages of each. Indicate which of them you are likely to use in your classes.

REFERENCES

Anson, C. M. (Ed.). (1989). *Writing and response: Theory, practice, and research.* Urbana, IL: National Council of Teachers of English.

Anson, C. M., & Beach, R. W. (1994). *At the center: Using journals in the classroom.* Norwood, NJ: Christopher-Gordon.

Applebee, A. N. (1981). *Writing in the secondary school: English and the content areas.* Urbana, IL: National Council of Teachers of English.

Aronson, E., Blaney, N., Stephan, C., Sikes, J., & Snapp, M. (1978). *The jigsaw classroom.* Newbury Park, CA: Sage.

Atwell, N. (1987). *In the middle: Writing, reading and learning with adolescents.* Portsmouth, NH: Boynton/Cook.

Beaven, M. H. (1977). Individualized goal setting, self-evaluation, and peer evaluation. In C. R. Cooper & L. O'Dell (Eds.), *Evaluating writing.* Urbana, IL: National Council of Teachers of English.

Beck, I. L., & McKeown, M. G. (1981). Developing questions that promote comprehension: The story map. *Language Arts, 58,* 913–918.

Britton, J. N., Burgess, T., Martin, N., McLeod, A., & Rosen, H. (1975). *The development of writing abilities.* New York: Macmillan.

Brown, A. H., & Day, J. D. (1983). Macrorules for summarizing text: The development of expertise. *Journal of Verbal Learning and Verbal Behavior, 22,* 1–14.

Cooper, C. (1977). Holistic evaluation of writing. In C. R. Cooper & L. O'Dell (Eds.), *Evaluating writing.* Urbana, IL: National Council of Teachers of English.

Daiker, D. A. (1989). Learning to praise. In C. M. Anson (Ed.), *Writing and response: The-*

ory, practice, and research. Urbana, IL: National Council of Teachers of English.

Devine, T. H. (1987). *Teaching study skills* (2nd ed.). Boston: Allyn & Bacon.

Diederich, P. B. (1974). *Measuring growth in English*. Urbana, IL: National Council of Teachers of English.

Flower, L. S., & Hayes, J. R. (1981). A cognitive process model of writing. *College Composition and Communication, 35*, 365–387.

Fulwiler, T. (1982). The personal connection: Journal writing across the curriculum. In T. Fulwiler & A. Young (Eds.), *Language connections: Writing and reading across the curriculum*. Urbana, IL: National Council of Teachers of English.

Gall, M. D., Gall, J. R., Jacobsen, D. R., & Bullock, T. L. (1990). *Tools for learning: A guide for teaching study skills*. Alexandria, VA: Association for Supervision and Curriculum Development.

Graves, D. H. (1983). *Writing: Teachers and children at work*. Portsmouth, NH: Heinemann.

Graves, M. F., & Duin, A. H. (1992). *Tutoring via telecommunications*. Minneapolis: University of Minnesota, Center for the Interdisciplinary Study of Writing.

Graves, M. F., & Piché, G. L. (1989). Knowledge about reading and writing. In M. C. Reynolds (Ed.), *Knowledge bases for the beginning teacher*. Oxford, England: Pergamon.

Hillocks, G., Jr. (1986). *Research on written composition: New directions for teaching*. Urbana, IL: ERIC Clearinghouse on Reading and Communication Skills.

Mullis, I. V. S., Owen, E. H., & Phillips, G. W. (1990). *Accelerating academic achievement: A summary of findings of 20 years of NAEP*. Princeton, NJ: National Assessment of Educational Progress, Educational Testing Service.

Nystrand, M. (1986). *The structure of written communication: Studies in reciprocity between writers and readers*. Orlando, FL: Academic Press.

Olson, P. S. (1989). *Study skills across the curriculum*. Brunsville, MN: Reading Consulting.

Pauk, W. (1989). *How to study in college* (4th ed.). Boston: Houghton Mifflin.

Pearson, P. D., & Gallagher, M. (1983). The instruction of reading comprehension. *Contemporary Educational Psychology, 8*, 317–344.

Pressley, M., Johnson, C. J., Symons, S., McGoldrick, J. A., & Kurita, J. (1989). Strategies that improve children's memory and comprehension of text. *The Elementary School Journal, 90*, 3–32.

Rafoth, M. A., & DeFabo, L. (1990). *Study skills*. Washington, DC: National Education Association.

Resnick, L. (1987). *Education and learning to think*. Washington, DC: National Academy Press.

Robin, E. (1984). *Matters of life and death: Risks and benefits of medical care*. Stanford, CA: Stanford University Press.

Ryder, R. J. (1991, June). *Application of analytical writing strategies to computer-based tutorial writing instruction*. Paper presented at the meeting of the National Educational Computer Conference, Phoenix, AZ.

Tchudi, S. N., & Huerta, M. C. (1983). *Teaching writing in content areas: Middle school/junior high*. Washington, DC: National Education Association.

Tierney, R. J., & Pearson, P. D. (1983). Toward a composing model of reading. *Language Arts, 60*, 568–580.

U.S. Department of Education. (1991). *Youth indicators 1991: Trends in the well-being of American youth*. Washington, DC: Author.

Vacca, R. T., & Linek, W. M. (1992). Writing to learn. In J. W. Irwin & M. A. Doyle (Eds.), *Reading/writing connections: Learning from research*. Newark, DE: International Reading Association.

Zinsser, W. (1988). *Writing to learn*. New York: Harper & Row.

Cooperative Learning

CHAPTER OVERVIEW

In this chapter we examine cooperative learning and suggest ways to incorporate it in subject area reading activities. We begin with a brief definition of cooperative learning, contrasting it to both competitive and independent learning. Next, we examine cooperative learning in more detail, highlighting five necessary components of effective cooperative learning situations. Following this, we build a case for using cooperative learning. The case comes from both theoretical considerations and research findings, and it is a very strong one. Next, we describe five different types of cooperative learning, different ways of putting students together and arranging activities to promote successful learning. In the section that follows this, we present ways to teach students to work cooperatively. This section contains principles for teaching procedural skills, a list of cooperative skills that students need to learn, guidelines for establishing cooperative groups, and specific methods of teaching cooperative skills. Then, in the longest section of the chapter, we give specific examples of cooperative tasks that are appropriate in subject matter classes. Finally, we describe three procedures for assessing cooperative learning.

Chapter Eight
Cooperative Learning

What is Cooperative Learning?

Positive Interdependence

Face-to-face Promotive Interaction

Individual Accountability

Interpersonal and Small-Group Skills

Group Processing

The Case for Cooperative Learning

Theoretical Support

Support from Reasearch

Types of Cooperative Learning

Formal Cooperative Groups

Student Teams Achievement Divisions

Jigsaw

Base Groups and Informal Cooperative Groups

Teaching Students to Work Cooperatively

Teaching Procedural Skills

Cooperative Skills to Be Taught

Establishing Cooperative Groups

Teaching Cooperative Groups

Cooperative Activities for Subject Matter Classes

Cooperative Poetry: "I, Too"

The Vocabulary of Glacier Park

The Life and Works of Beethoven

The Scientific Method

Choosing and Financing an Automobile

A Flyer on the Yearbook

Assessing Cooperative Learning

Simple Checklist

In-depth Assessment

Student Assessment

In describing cooperative learning, Johnson, Johnson, and Holubec (1990) compare it to two other sorts of learning that are often used in classrooms—competitive and independent learning. They explain that teachers can structure lessons for students in three ways. Students can "engage in a win-lose struggle to see who is best." They can "work independently at their own goals at their own pace and in their own space to achieve a present criterion of excellence." Or, they "can work collaboratively in small groups, ensuring that all members master the assigned material" (p. 1).

Morton (1988) describes the same contrast using sports metaphors. One option is for students, "like Rocky Balboa in the ring," to compete to see who is best. Another option is for students to work independently, "like long-distance runners." Finally, students can work interdependently and collaboratively in small groups, assisting each other in mastering the assigned material—"like mountain climbers attempting to scale a curricular mountain, they succeed or fail together" (p. 35).

Many classrooms employ all three approaches, often intermixing them. Including a combination of these and other approaches in providing subject matter instruction is definitely appropriate. However, cooperative learning merits special attention because it is a very powerful approach that deserves to be used more frequently than it often is. In this chapter, we describe cooperative learning in detail and explain how to include cooperative learning activities as one important part of subject matter instruction.

WHAT IS COOPERATIVE LEARNING?

Cooperative learning is easy to define. Johnson and colleagues (1990) define it as "the instructional use of small groups so that students work together to maximize their own and each other's learning" (p. 4). Slavin (1987) notes that the term refers to "instructional methods in which students of all performance levels work together toward a group goal" (p. 8).

However, although these definitions are clear and concise, by no means do they fully explain cooperative learning. Not every small group is a cooperative group. Even more to the point, not every small group is an *effective* cooperative group. Johnson et al. (1990) list five necessary components of effective cooperative learning situations—positive interdependence, face-to-face promotive interaction, individual accountability, interpersonal and small group skills, and group processing. Each of these is discussed below.

Positive Interdependence

Positive interdependence refers to a situation in which each member of a group is dependent on each other member for his or her success. As one example of positive interdependence in the world of sports, Johnson et al. (1990)

give the example of a quarterback and a receiver: It takes the best efforts of both players to complete a pass; neither can do it alone.

In positively interdependent groups, each student has two responsibilities: He or she must learn the assigned material or procedure and must ensure that every other student in the group also learns it. Moreover, the student must be aware of this positive interdependence and consciously coordinate his or her efforts with those of others in the group.

Face-to-Face Promotive Interaction

Face-to-face promotive interaction consists of direct interchanges in which students promote each other's successful completion of cooperative tasks. For example, in a group cooperatively writing an essay on wetlands preservation, one student might say to another, "That's a great introduction that will really wake up people to our cause. Now we need some sort of transition to our first example of what we can do to preserve wetlands." It is vital to have such direct interactions because the interpersonal and verbal interchange that occurs in them is the driving force that prompts students to assist, support, encourage, praise, and challenge each other on their way to achieving the assigned goals of the group.

Individual Accountability

Those unfamiliar with cooperative learning may believe that it is based on a naivete that assumes that all students in a group will naturally contribute their parts and work toward common goals. This is not always the case. In effective cooperative learning groups, each individual is evaluated, and the results of his or her evaluation are given back to the individual and to the other members of the group. This is done for two primary purposes. First, if group members are to help each other, they must know who needs help and what they need help on. Second, each individual needs to understand that cooperative learning groups are not opportunities for a "free lunch"; that is, students need to know that each person is held responsible for his or her learning and for his or her contribution to others' learning. Students who do not participate fully are not given credit for contributing.

Interpersonal and Small-Group Skills

Having or gaining appropriate interpersonal and small-group skills is a prerequisite for effective participation in cooperative learning groups. Simply putting students together and telling them to cooperate is not likely to accomplish much; in fact, simply putting students together and telling them to cooperate is likely to have a negative outcome and thus spell the death of efforts at cooperative learning. Among the skills students need in order to work successfully in small groups are getting to know and trust each other, communicating accurately, accepting and supporting each other, and resolving conflicts constructively.

Group Processing

As used here, group processing refers to the members of cooperative groups discussing how they functioned as a group—how effective they were in achieving their goals and in working together to do so. In group processing, students reflect on their working session and consider things they did that worked, things they did that did not work, and things they can do to improve their group's efforts in the future. This sort of group processing should be a frequent part of cooperative learning.

Figure 8.1, which Johnson et al. (1990) use to clarify the differences between cooperative and traditional learning groups, summarizes this section of the chapter and highlights some additional characteristics of cooperative learning.

FIGURE 8.1   DIFFERENCES BETWEEN COOPERATIVE AND TRADITIONAL LEARNING GROUPS

Cooperative Groups	Traditional Groups
Positive interdependence	No interdependence
Individual accountability	No individual accountability
Heterogeneous membership	Homogeneous membership
Shared leadership	One appointed leader
Responsible for each other	Responsible only for self
Task and maintenance emphasized	Only task emphasized
Social skills directly taught	Social skills assumed and ignored
Teacher observes and intervenes	Teacher ignores group
Group processing occurs	No group processing

PRACTICE ACTIVITY 8.1

1. **Positive Interdependence.**   Try to fix the concept of positive interdependence in your mind by coming up with an example of your own. An exam-

ple we developed is given in the answers section at the end of the book. To better understand cooperative learning, do as many of these exercises as possible in groups. As you proceed through the chapter and learn more about what makes an effective cooperative group, try to make yours a model group. Also, as emphasized in Chapter Seven, whenever possible write down your responses to better remember the material.

2. Promotive Interaction.   The example of face-to-face promotive interaction given here is verbal. Extend the concept by developing an example of face-to-face promotive interaction that is nonverbal. Our example is in the answers section. Again, make this a group activity if possible.

3. Individual Accountability.   Individual accountability is not something unique to cooperative learning situations. To what extent are students held individually accountable in typical classrooms? How is this usually done? Our response is in the answers section.

4. Interpersonal Skills.   One of many arguments supporting cooperative learning is that people need to use the same sort of interpersonal and small-group skills practiced in cooperative learning in the world outside school. Do you find this to be true? Name half a dozen jobs in which interpersonal skills are crucial to success. Our response is in the answers section.

5. Group Processing.   Pause for a moment here and jot down a note or discuss with your classmates how often groups in which you have participated have processed their group work. Our response and some brief thoughts on the matter are included in the answers section.

The Case for Cooperative Learning

A very strong case for using cooperative learning can be made by considering several theories and the results of a huge body of research. Here, each of these is briefly considered.

Theoretical Support

According to Vygotsky (1978), a major part of children's learning occurs within what he calls the zone of proximal development, which he defines as "the distance between the actual developmental level as determined by independent problem solving and the level of potential development as determined through problem solving under adult guidance or in collaboration with more capable peers" (p. 86). Students who are more capable in a particular area can improve the learning of those less capable. One assumption motivating cooperative learning is that the members of a group differ in their skills and knowledge, with some members having advanced skills and knowledge in one area and others in another. What happens in a group, then, is that a student's zone of proximal development is extended by the others in a group, and he or she is led to accomplish tasks he or she could not accomplish without the aid of others in the group.

Further theoretical support for cooperative learning comes from the construct of metacognition. As defined by Flavel (1976), "metacognition refers to one's knowledge concerning one's own cognitive processes and products or anything related to them" (p. 232). Accomplished learners have metacognitive knowledge about themselves, the learning tasks they face, and the strategies they can employ in completing these tasks. The discussing, questioning, summarizing, and puzzling over problems that are parts of cooperative learning put students in the position of repeatedly having to be metacognitive. And being metacognitive—being actively aware of what one does and does not understand about a learning task and being able to use some sort of fix-up strategies when learning breaks down—are absolutely crucial for students to become effective learners.

Additional theoretical support for cooperative learning can be found by considering how cooperative work affects cognition. Listed here are three of the cognitive effects Johnson and Johnson (1991a) discuss. First, students in cooperative groups recognize that they will have to summarize what they have learned, explain it, and teach others in their group. Second, being in a cooperative group means that students will frequently need to ask questions of others, rephrase the responses others give, and elaborate on what they know. Third, the fact that there are several students in a group and that groups are generally heterogeneous means that students who do not know something can turn to others for assistance. Moreover, students can assist each other in a number of ways. Different students know different facts; different students offer different perspectives on the same facts; and different students have different strategies that they can use and can assist each other in using. Thus, cooperative groups offer students a myriad of opportunities to engage in the sorts of problem solving they will need to use in the world outside school.

Support From Research

Over the past several decades, the value of various sorts of learning by teaching—participating in cooperative learning and in various other sorts of tutoring—has become increasingly clear (Bargh & Schul, 1980). Not surprisingly, studies of tutoring demonstrate that both the students tutored and those who serve as tutors gain a better understanding of the subject matter covered and more positive attitudes toward the subject matter itself (Cohen, Kulik, & Kulik, 1982). As one group of educators (McKeachie, Pintrich, Lin, Smith, & Sharma, 1986) put it, "students teaching other students" is one of the most powerful methods of instruction available. "There is," McKeachie and his colleagues continue, "a wealth of evidence that students teaching other students is extremely effective over a wide range of content, goals, students, and personalities" (p. 63).

Much of that evidence comes from research on cooperative learning. In fact, according to Johnson and Johnson (1989), cooperative learning is one of the most thoroughly researched areas of instruction, with over 600 studies having been conducted in the past 90 years. Slavin (1987) echoes these sentiments, noting that cooperative learning approaches are "among the most extensively evaluated alternatives to traditional instruction in use in schools today" (p. 18).

In the majority of these studies, cooperative methods are compared to more traditional ones, the majority of which would be classified as competitive and a lesser number as individualized. The evidence from these studies is extremely compelling. In one comparison, Slavin (1987) found that 57% of the studies favored cooperative learning, 41% found no differences, and a single study favored the group that did not engage in cooperative learning. In another comparison, this one including only studies in which the cooperative learning groups were working to achieve some goal and the success of the group depended on the individual learning of each group member, Slavin found that 83% of the studies favored cooperative learning.

Of particular note is that the advantages of cooperative learning occurred in a variety of domains. Students in cooperative groups showed superior performance in academic achievement, displayed more self-esteem, accommodated better to mainstreamed students, showed more positive attitudes toward school, and generally displayed better overall psychological health. In addition, students in cooperative groups displayed better interpersonal relationships; these improved interpersonal relationships held regardless of differences in ability, sex, ethnicity, or social class. Johnson and Johnson (1989) provide a detailed review of this literature.

Certain sorts of cooperative learning offer some particular advantages for teaching critical thinking. As tasks become more conceptual in nature, as increasing amounts of problem solving are required, as more creative answers are needed, as long-term retention is required, and as higher level thinking and critical reasoning are increasingly demanded, the superiority of cooperative learning over competitive and individualized learning becomes even greater (Johnson & Johnson, 1991a).

Given the theory and research supporting cooperative learning, it is important to include at least some cooperative learning experiences in subject matter classrooms.

PRACTICE ACTIVITY 8.2

List three theoretical arguments supporting cooperative learning. Then, list several areas in which students in cooperative groups have outperformed those not in cooperative groups. Our response is given in the answers section.

TYPES OF COOPERATIVE LEARNING

With the large number of investigations that have been done on cooperative learning and the many teachers interested in the approach, it should come as no surprise that there are many types of cooperative learning groups. Here, we describe five types of groups, at least some of which have a place in your classroom.

Formal Cooperative Groups

Formal cooperative learning groups are the basic type used in Johnson and Johnson's approach. These are heterogeneous groups of three or four students, who typically differ in ability, ethnicity, social class, and gender. Such groups incorporate the five defining characteristics of cooperative learning—positive interdependence, face-to-face promotive interaction, individual accountability, the use of interpersonal and small group skills, and group processing—and generally last for several class sessions. Appropriate tasks for formal groups include problem solving and decision making, reviewing homework, solving specifically assigned problems, performing and writing up lab experiments, studying for exams, writing and editing, and making class presentations. They are particularly effective in promoting problem solving, creativity, and critical thinking.

Student Teams-Achievement Divisions

Student teams-achievement divisions (STAD) is the most frequently used of Slavin's approaches. STAD is a stylized approach in which groups of four students, differing in ability, ethnicity, social class, and gender, work together. STAD groups work as follows:

1. The teacher initially presents the lesson.
2. Students work together to ensure that each individual in the group masters the material. For example, group members encourage each other, compare answers, work out discrepancies, suggest approaches to solving problems encountered, and quiz each other.
3. After preparing as a group, students are quizzed individually and receive points based on the extent to which each exceeds his or her previous performance.
4. Individual points are then totaled for a team score, and students are rewarded for both their individual and team scores.

The whole process generally takes three to five class periods. STAD has been used in a variety of subject areas, including English, social studies, and mathematics. According to Slavin, the procedure is best suited to learning well-defined objectives with single correct answers. Thus, it is particularly well suited for mathematical computations, first language mechanics and vocabulary, second language vocabulary, geography and map skills, and science concepts. It is important to recognize that formal cooperative groups and STAD serve two different functions, the former being more appropriate for higher level tasks, the latter for more basic tasks.

Jigsaw

Jigsaw was originally developed by Aronson and his colleagues (Aronson, Blaney, Stephan, Sikes, & Snapp, 1978). Like STAD, it is a stylized approach, yet it is quite different. In the jigsaw approach, a class of 30 would be divided into five heterogeneous groups of six students each to work on material that the teacher has broken into subsections. Here are the major steps of the approach.

1. Each student in a group learns one part of the material being studied. For example, in studying a particular state, one student in each group might investigate major cities, another the state's agriculture, another its industries, and so on.

2. After studying his or her section individually, the member of each group who has studied a particular subpart of the topic gets together with the members from other teams who have studied the same subpart.

3. The students in each of these "expert" groups discuss their subtopic, refining their knowledge about it.

4. The experts return to their own groups and teach their classmates about their sections. Because classmates afford the only opportunity for students to learn about sections other than their own, students are necessarily interested in and motivated to attend to each others' presentations.

5. Students take individual exams on all of the material, both the material they taught and what they learned from others.

Jigsaw, of course, must be used in a situation in which a subject can be broken into subparts for students to teach. With that single exception, the procedure is widely applicable.

Base Groups and Informal Cooperative Groups

Base groups and informal cooperative groups are special function groups recommended by Johnson and Johnson. Base groups are heterogeneous, long-term groups of four or so students who are likely to remain together for a semester or a year. The primary purposes of such groups are to provide support, encouragement, help in completing particular assignments, and general assistance for members of the group. Typically, base groups meet weekly at the beginning of the class session and go through several routines. These are likely to include checking how each group member is keeping up with the demands of the class and is feeling about the course, reviewing the reading assignments for the past week, planning study topics and a study schedule for the upcoming week, reviewing for upcoming quizzes, and bringing any group members absent the previous week up to date on the class. According to Johnson et al. (1990), using base groups helps to "improve attendance, personalize the course, improve the quality of the learning experience, enhance overall achievement and mastery, and ensure that higher-level reasoning and critical thinking take place within the course" (p. 15).

Informal cooperative groups (Johnson, Johnson, & Smith, 1990) are pairs of students who work together for a single class session to better learn from a lecture, which, for example, might be given as an introduction to an upcoming reading selection. The general plan is for the teacher to build a lecture around a set of focusing questions and several brief lecture segments. The approach gives students an opportunity to prepare for the lecture, actively consider the content of the lecture as it is progressing, and formulate some sort of closure. Here are the steps for using informal cooperative groups.

1. Prepare half a dozen or so guiding questions. Give these questions to the pairs before the lecture, then allow students about 5 minutes to discuss what they know about the topic, thereby creating a sort of advance organizer for the lecture.

2. Deliver the first segment of the lecture, taking no more than 10 to 15 minutes. Have the pairs construct 2- to 3-minute, "turn-to-your partner" discussions on the lecture, perhaps answering a guiding question covered in the segment.

3. Deliver the other parts of the lecture, again limiting each segment to 10 to 15 minutes and again having the student pairs conduct brief discussions on each segment.

4. Give the pairs a concluding discussion task of perhaps 5 to 6 minutes that allows them to summarize the lecture and identify the essential learnings it conveyed.

While using informal cooperative groups will shorten the lecture time available, this loss of time will be more than made up by students' increased involvement and interest in the class. Indeed, using such groups forces students to prepare for the lecture, to attend to it because they will need to discuss it, to review it several times as they discuss it with their partner, and to review and synthesize it a final time immediately after its completion. Moreover, the procedure is extremely easy to implement, fosters active learning, and is widely applicable.

PRACTICE ACTIVITY 8.3

This section of the chapter described five types of cooperative groups. Name and very briefly describe each of these. If you are presently teaching, take one of your class lists and divide the class into groups for any of the cooperative methods except informal cooperative groups. Then, jot down the general guidelines you followed in choosing students for the groups. We cannot, of course, show you how to group your students. However, we have given guidelines we follow in creating groups in the answers section.

TEACHING STUDENTS TO WORK COOPERATIVELY

Regardless of which type of cooperative learning you plan to use in your classroom, one thing remains constant: Students need to be taught how to engage effectively in cooperative learning. Here, we present guidelines for teaching procedural skills, list the cooperative skills to be taught, provide guidelines for establishing cooperative groups, and make specific recommendations for teaching cooperative learning skills. Following these guidelines will enable you to introduce and use cooperative learning while maintaining a smoothly running classroom. The section draws heavily on the work of Johnson et al. (1990).

Teaching Procedural Skills

To begin, recognize that the task of learning cooperative skills is a procedural rather than declarative one; that is, students need to learn how to actually do something, not merely learn about something. Procedural tasks are typically more difficult to learn and more time consuming than declarative learning tasks, and learning to engage in cooperative learning is no exception. This means, first of all, that both you and the students need to spend time and energy preparing for cooperative learning. It also means that your time and energy will be best spent if you follow some well-established techniques for teaching procedural skills. The following four steps have proven useful.

1. Explicitly teach the skill. If, for example, the skill is expressing support and acceptance for others' ideas, students need to know just how to do this. One way of expressing support is to do it verbally, saying something such as "Nice idea. I really think that will work." Another is nonverbally, perhaps with eye contact, a pleasant look, or a nod.

2. Direct students to engage in the skill; have them get in groups that have assigned tasks to accomplish and overtly try to show support for each others' ideas.

3. Give students feedback on their successes and failures so that they know when they are and are not engaging in supportive behavior. Initially, you as the teacher will need to give this feedback; later, students will become increasingly able to give feedback to each other.

4. Since students need to be able to use the procedures without conscious attention, allow them to practice frequently. You will need to continue to give feedback during these periods of practice and consolidation.

PRACTICE ACTIVITY 8.4

Because this section contains quite a few new ideas, it is worth reviewing. At this point, explain the difference between declarative knowledge and procedural skills. Then, list the four general guidelines for teaching procedural skills. Our response is in the answers section.

Cooperative Skills to Be Taught

Johnson et al.'s (1990) list of procedural skills to be taught includes forming, functioning, and formulating skills. The authors note that, as a prerequisite to engaging in these skills, you and your students need to have forged a cooperative context in which positive interdependence exists and is encouraged by all. This section deals first with fostering positive interdependence and then with forming, functioning, and formulating skills.

Fostering Positive Interdependence.   Positive interdependence exists when students fully understand that they cannot succeed unless others also succeed and that, similarly, others cannot succeed unless they do. Johnson et al. (1990) capture both the cognitive and affective aspects of the concept in their frequently repeated phrases "We sink or swim together" and "None of us is as smart as all of us" (p. 81). Positive interdependence is fostered by first explaining the concept to students, then structuring your class in such a way that positive interdependence is repeatedly demonstrated to students. That is, students need to understand the concept *and* they need to see it demonstrated repeatedly in the classroom.

There are several types of positive interdependence that you can employ. Goal interdependence exists when each member of the group recognizes that he or she can achieve his or her goals for the lesson only if all others in the group also achieve their goals. It is the primary sort of interdependence needed and should be an attribute of all cooperative lessons. Methods of creating goal interdependence include explaining that each student must attain a prescribed mastery level before anyone in the group will be given credit for completing the assignment and before anyone can proceed to another assignment.

Reward interdependence is created when students receive a reward only if all members of the group reach some criterion of performance. For example, you might give bonus points to each member of a group if all answer at least 9 out of 10 items correctly on a weekly quiz.

Resource interdependence exists when each member of the group has only one part of the information or other resources necessary to complete the task. The jigsaw approach described in the previous section is an example of resource interdependence.

Role interdependence involves giving each student a particular specialty within the group. Roles often used in cooperative groups include those of reader, writer or recorder, checker, and prober. The reader, of course, reads the material aloud, the recorder takes notes, the checker examines the notes to make certain that the record is correct and nothing is omitted, and the prober prods his or her fellow students to go beyond their initial formulations.

As you work to establish a cooperative context in which positive interdependence is recognized by all, you can simultaneously teach forming, functioning, and formulating skills.

Forming Skills.   Forming skills are beginning skills that are prerequisite to effective group functioning. They include (1) moving into cooperative groups without bothering others in the room, (2) staying with the group, (3) talking quietly, and (4) encouraging everyone to participate in the group's activities.

Functioning Skills.   Functioning skills are those that students use as they participate in group work. They include (1) giving directions, (2) expressing support and acceptance of others' ideas, (3) asking for help or clarification when needed, (4) offering to explain or clarify a matter when another student needs assistance, (5) paraphrasing others' responses, (6) energizing the group if it begins to bog down, and (7) describing one's feelings, particularly when there is a problem that needs to be solved.

Formulating Skills.   Formulating skills are needed to perform the various roles of group members. These roles include those of (1) the summarizer, who summarizes the groups' learning—typically from memory; (2) the corrector, who checks the correctness and completeness of the summary; (3) the elaboration seeker, who elicits further information and explanation from group members; (4) the memory helper, who prompts group members to use memory aids to remember the material they are learning; and (5) the checker, who demands that group members make explicit the implicit reasoning behind their thinking.

PRACTICE ACTIVITY 8.5

Form a group that includes a summarizer, a checker, and an elaboration seeker. Then define forming, functioning, and formulating skills; give a specific example of each. After each member of the group has performed his or her role, compare your examples to those we give at the end of the book.

Establishing Cooperative Groups

As you prepare to use cooperative groups in your classroom, several very practical questions undoubtedly come to mind. Among them might be how large groups ought to be, which students ought to be grouped together, and what characterizes good learning objectives. Each of these topics is considered here.

Deciding on Group Size. One of the first questions that come to mind in setting up groups is how large to make them. There is no single answer to this question for two reasons. First, as indicated in the section of the chapter on types of cooperative groups, there are several different kinds of groups and not all of these are the same size. Informal cooperative groups, for example, are pairs of students; base groups are likely to be composed of five or six students. Second, the optimal size of groups varies with the specific task to be completed, your experience and expertise with group work, and your students' experience and expertise.

Although there are no absolute guidelines regarding group size, there are several general ones.

1. With the exception of a few special purpose groups, such as informal cooperative groups, groups seldom have fewer than three students.

2. Six students is often considered about the largest group size one would typically work with. Having more than six students in a group often becomes unwieldy.

3. Start out using small groups, then gradually move to larger groups as you and your students gain experience. This probably means starting with groups of three. Moreover, there is no hurry in moving to larger sizes.

4. Give careful consideration to the task the groups are going to complete. How many subtasks are there? Is there enough work for four or five students? Is there too much work for three or four students? Do students need to meet outside class? Will having larger groups make it difficult for students to find meeting times?

Recognizing that most groups contain between three and six students, that smaller groups are easier to handle when you are just beginning cooperative work, and that the specific task of the groups needs to be considered will usually provide you with the information you need to make effective decisions on group size.

Assigning Students to Groups.   Other questions to consider when establishing cooperative groups concern which students should comprise groups and who should decide which students to include in particular groups. There are several factors that should be considered in answering these.

The first thing to recognize is that one major purpose of using cooperative groups is to assist students in meeting, understanding, working with, and having empathy for the diverse people and cultures that make up our society. In any society, it is crucial that people learn to work with each other. However, in our multicultural society, just learning to work with others is not enough. Students need to learn to work with, understand, appreciate, and respect others who may be quite different from them in a variety of ways. Thus, one recommendation for grouping students for cooperative work is to deliberately group together students representing diverse cultures, races, ages, genders, abilities, interests, and levels of motivation.

Are there any limits to the amount of heterogeneity you should seek for groups? Of course there are! The groups have to function, and the individual students in the groups have to feel comfortable and believe that the group can function and that they can contribute to its success. This means paying particular attention to which combinations of students will work well together as you first begin group work. As you and your students become more accomplished with group work, you can move toward more heterogeneous groups.

Closely related to the matter of what sorts of students make up groups is that of how groups are assigned. For the most part, since you know what sort of mix you want in groups, you should assign them. Occasionally, you might use random assignment, which generally will result in heterogeneous groups. Sometimes, you will want to let students choose their own groups, although this will often result in fairly homogeneous groups and in groups that may have a larger social than work agenda.

Also related to the matter of assigning groups is that of how long to keep groups together. Both common sense and compromise are required in making decisions here. On the one hand, groups should stay together and work together long enough to learn to function well together. On the other hand, ideally, over the course of a semester or year, each student should have the opportunity to work with and get to know every other student in the class. Obviously, achieving both goals will require compromises.

To summarize, groups should be heterogeneous (but not so heterogeneous that they do not function well), you generally should be the one to assign students, and groups should stay together long enough that they become effective but not so long that students get to work with only a few of their classmates.

Specifying Learning Objectives.   Specifying learning objectives is always important, but with cooperative group work, specifying objectives becomes doubly important. Since students are working in various groups and you are not directly supervising them as you might be with whole-class instruction, students need to have a very clear idea of what they are trying to accomplish. Moreover, since mutual interdependence and individual accountability are central to cooperative learning, every student needs to understand clearly both what he or she is expected to accomplish and what his or her group is expected to accomplish.

Good objectives for cooperative learning groups have several definable characteristics. Learning objectives should be precise, concise, limited in number, and multidimensional. In addition, most assignments ought to allow students to set and pursue some objectives of their own. Keep in mind that cooperative learning groups have two sorts of objectives—academic and group-processing. Most considerations here are relevant to both sorts of objectives, but at the end of the section are a few comments specifically dealing with group-processing objectives.

Precise objectives are those that students can clearly understand and recognize as being met or not met. For example, in teaching vocabulary, simply telling students to learn five words is not very precise. To be more precise, you could tell them to learn the two most common meanings of each of the five words and be able to produce a sentence employing each meaning. Concise objectives are those that are deliberately stated in relatively few words. This does not mean that they should be too brief, but it does mean that you should check your initial phrasing of objectives to see if there is a briefer and perhaps clearer way to state them. First attempts to phrase objectives are often rather wordy and sometimes fail to fully capture the intended meaning.

The advice to limit the number of objectives means just that. A long list of objectives is often inappropriate. How many is enough? That varies with the situation, particularly with the length of the assignment: Usually a 2-week assignment would have more objectives than a 2-day task. However, having two to four objectives is often appropriate.

Multidimensional objectives tap various levels on a continuum leading from immediate and specific objectives to more distant and general ones. For example, you would certainly have some specific objectives when dealing with a history chapter on the Great Depression. You would want students to know who Franklin Delano Roosevelt was, and you would want them to know some of the major features of the New Deal. Moving toward somewhat broader objectives, you might want students to be able to draw some comparisons between conditions in the United States at the beginning of the depression and conditions just before the 1990 recession. Another objective for your study of the Great Depression—one much further along the continuum—would be for students to appreciate the hardships that their grandparents and others who lived through the depression experienced and perhaps speculate about how today's Americans would react to such hardships. Finally, you might suggest some optional objectives. Students interested in art might choose to investigate what sort of paintings were produced during the 1930s; those interested in athletics might try to find out what sort of attention sports received during this difficult time; others interested in movies might research the contents and themes of films of the period.

With respect to group-processing objectives, special attention should be given to choosing those that will best contribute to students' success in their group work. Johnson et al. (1990) give the following set of seven group-processing objectives. These should be introduced to students one at a time. Explain and model the strategy, then give students ample opportunity to practice it and get some feedback before moving on to another one.

1. Having each member explain how to get the answer.
2. Asking each member to relate what is being learned to previous learnings.
3. Checking to make sure everyone in the group understands the material and agrees with the answers.
4. Encouraging everyone to participate.
5. Listening accurately to what other group members are saying.
6. Not changing your mind unless you are logically persuaded.
7. Criticizing ideas, not people. (p. 54)

PRACTICE ACTIVITY 8.6

This is a good point to do some work with learning objectives. Form a small group with others in your subject area. Together, identify a short segment of text in your subject, something students might deal with in two or three days, and list three academic objectives you might have them work toward. Make one of them specific and immediate, another somewhat more distant, and the third more distant and general. Perhaps one or two members of the group could work on each of these and then share. Finally, list two group-processing objectives you might have for this assignment.

Teaching Cooperative Groups

As noted earlier, teaching cooperative skills is a procedural teaching task rather than a declarative one, and consequently it is demanding and will take time. Including cooperative learning in your repertoire of instructional approaches may be particularly challenging because doing so means handing over classroom control and responsibility for learning to students. The challenge, however, is well worth the effort because engaging in cooperative learning can result in students learning more, in their developing better attitudes toward learning, and in their becoming better prepared to deal with today's increasingly interdependent world. Moreover, although teaching cooperative skills takes considerable time and energy, it is a task that every teacher can complete successfully. It is simply something that needs to be done carefully and thoroughly. Johnson et al. (1990) offer the following step-by-step guidelines for successfully teaching students to work cooperatively.

1. Show students the need for cooperative learning.   Create a bulletin board featuring cooperative learning. Tell students that cooperation is an important skill to learn. Discuss the fact that much of their adult life will be spent working with others. Cite research showing the effectiveness of cooperative learning. Tell students that no one of them is as smart as all of them. Then validate what you say. Show that you think cooperative learning skills are important by giving credit for students working cooperatively as well as for the learning that the cooperative groups produce.

2. Make certain that students really understand each skill you are teaching.   If you are teaching students to encourage each other in their groups, give them some specific examples of encouraging language—"That's right." "I think you really have something there." "Exactly!" "All right!" Model the behavior for them. Get in a group that is working on a task and demonstrate encouragement—verbally, through eye contact, nodding assent, or even rapping on the desk to show approval. Then let students model the behavior, possibly through role playing—"Assume that Jake here has just come up with a solution to a problem your group has been working on for 20 minutes without success. What do you say to him, Tim? How can you show your appreciation?"

3. Have students repeatedly practice the skill.   Remember, the goal here is automatic performance of the skill, doing it without having to think about it. The literature on fostering automatic behavior is clear and straightforward (LaBerge & Samuels, 1974). Behavior becomes automatic when it is practiced repeatedly in nontaxing situations. Having thoroughly explained a skill, modeled it, and had students role play its use, tell them you are going to be looking for the skill as they work in their groups. Or tell them that you want each member of the group to practice that particular skill during the day's group work—"Today, in your groups, I want each of you to give verbal encouragement to other members of your group at least twice. I'm going to assign a recorder to each group to keep track of each instance of verbal encouragement and then report back to you on what he or she found when you process your group work at the end of the hour."

4. Ensure that students process their group work and attend to their use of the various skills as part of this processing.   In the above example, the teacher ensured group processing of the skill being stressed by specifically telling students to use a certain skill, then assigning a student to record the use of the skill and report to the group on it. This sort of teacher-directed processing of skills should be a frequent feature of group work when you are initially helping students to work cooperatively. Moreover, even after students have developed cooperative skills, you will still need to highlight certain ones and tell them to focus on these skills as they process their work as a group. Ultimately, however, the goal is for the group to routinely process their work and pay attention to their group skills without your having to remind them. Tell them this, then check from time to time to be sure they are using these skills.

5. Make certain that students continue to practice their skills.   Group work can be demanding and may not seem rewarding. Students need to be told that group work, like anything else, does not always succeed. And they need to be given the time, practice, and encouragement to repeatedly practice their cooperative skills and to learn that cooperative learning very frequently does produce large learning dividends.

Once students are actively and successfully working in groups, there is still important work to be done. Groups need to be monitored, and when something goes awry or groups simply become stalled, you will need to intervene to get things back on track.

Eventually, students need to monitor their own groups, but when you begin group work, you will probably need to assume the bulk of the responsibility for monitoring them. Regardless of whether it is you or your students doing the monitoring, there are certain things to look for, certain questions to ask. Here is a beginning set of questions. As you become increasingly familiar with cooperative learning, you will undoubtedly add some questions of your own.

- Are students physically in their groups?
- Are students courteously attending to each other?
- Are they talking quietly and otherwise behaving so that they are not bothering other groups?
- Do any students seem to be left out and ignored by their groupmates?
- Do students appear to understand the task?
- Are they making progress? Are parts of the assigned work completed or at least visibly in progress?

If students are just learning to work cooperatively and your answer to any of these questions is no, then your intervention is definitely called for. Later, as students become more experienced with group work, you may want to let groups struggle a bit so that they learn to solve their own problems. Later still, when students are doing the monitoring, they should be the ones to intervene to get groups on track.

When you do intervene to facilitate students' success, two strategies are particularly useful. First, explain what you perceive to be the problem and how it can be corrected, being as direct and explicit as possible. Second, whenever the behaviors you are attempting to elicit are likely to be difficult, model them. Thus, for example, if you notice that in debating an issue students tend to criticize each other, sit in on the group for a time and make it a point to respond to issues rather than people. Then, after you have modeled several instances of responding to issues and after some students in the group have given responses that are directed to issues rather than people, stop and discuss what you have been attempting to do and why it is important to criticize issues rather than individuals.

PRACTICE ACTIVITY 8.7

As a way of reviewing this section of the chapter, list the five steps for teaching cooperative skills. Once you have the five steps clearly in mind, discuss the answer to the following question with your classmates: To what extent are these same guidelines applicable in areas other than cooperative learning? As you will see if you check our response in the answers section, we have some definite thoughts on the matter.

COOPERATIVE ACTIVITIES FOR SUBJECT MATTER CLASSES

In this section, we present specific examples of cooperative learning activities for subject matter classes. The activities are selected to represent a range of cooperative learning opportunities and therefore vary in a number of ways. They exemplify four sorts of cooperative learning—formal cooperative learning groups, informal cooperative learning groups, student teams-achievement divisions, and jigsaw. Some of them are targeted for middle school or junior high students, others for senior high students. They are directed toward various content areas, including English, geography, music, social studies, science, consumer math, and journalism. Finally, some of them were constructed specifically for this book, while others were constructed by teachers who have worked with David and Roger Johnson, two University of Minnesota professors who are among the foremost authorities on cooperative learning. The teachers' activities differ from those constructed for the book in two ways: First, they are more detailed and include specifics on such matters as ensuring positive interdependence, teacher monitoring of groups, and group processing. Second, they exemplify formal cooperative learning groups rather than all types of cooperative groups.

Although each of these activities deals with a specific topic that would be taken up in specific classes, each also serves as an example of an activity that could be modified for your classroom. As you study them, consider how they could be modified to be appropriate in your subject area.

Cooperative Poetry: "I, Too"

This activity, a formal cooperative learning group lesson, was created by Edythe Johnson Holubec (1987), an English teacher in Taylor, Texas. Note that suggested teacher dialogue is set in quotation marks.

Subject Area: English

Grade Level: Junior and senior high

Lesson Summary: Students read a poem and answer questions about it.

Instructional Objectives: Students gain practice in reading and understanding poetry, in sharing their interpretations of a poem, and in listening to and considering other interpretations and other points of view.

Materials:

Item	Number Needed
Copy of Langston Hughes's "I, Too" (with discussion questions and agreement form)	One per student
Observation sheet	One per group

Time Required: One class period

Decisions

Group Size: Four (five if an observer is used)

Assignment to Groups: Teacher assigned, with a high-, two medium-, and a low-achieving student in each group. Also, each group should contain males and females and a mix of racial and cultural backgrounds.

Roles: **Encourager**: Watches to make certain all group members are contributing and invites silent members in by asking them for their opinions or help.
Reader: Reads the poems to the group. Also serves as the *Praiser*, who praises good ideas or helpful suggestions of group members.
Recorder: Records the group's answers and summarizes each until the group is satisfied with it.
Checker: Checks to make certain group members can explain each answer and the group's rationale for it.

From *Structuring Cooperative Learning: The 1987 Lesson-Plan Handbook* by D. W. Johnson, R. T. Johnson, and Edythe Johnson Holubec. Edina, MN: Interaction Book Company, 1987.

I, Too

by Langston Hughes

I, too, sing America.

I am the darker brother.
They send me to eat in the kitchen
When company comes,
But I laugh,
And eat well,
And grow strong.

Tomorrow,
I'll be at the table
When company comes.
Nobody'll dare
Say to me,
"Eat in the kitchen,"
Then.

Besides,
They'll see how beautiful I am
And be ashamed—

I, too, am America.

1. What are the emotions expressed by the poem?

2. What do you think/feel about what the poem says?

3. What are the three key words in the poem? (Be able to defend your choice.)

4. What is the poem saying?

To group members: When you sign your name for the answers to these questions, it means that you have participated in the assignment and understand the questions and the answers. You also must agree with the answers and be able to explain them.

Observer: (Optional) Does not take part in the discussion of the poem but observes the group's interactions, records the behaviors on the observations sheet, and reports to the group during the processing time.

The Lesson

Instructional Task

"Your task will be to read a poem and answer the questions. I want you to come up with three possible answers for each question, then circle your favorite."

Positive Interdependence

"I want one set of answers from the group that you all agree upon."

Individual Accountability

"I will ask each of you sometime during the class period to give me the rationale for your group's answers."

Criteria for Success

"Your group will start with a grade of 100 on this assignment. I will pick someone at random to explain one of your group's answers to me. If he or she can do that, you will keep your score. If not, you will lose 10 points. I will check at least three of you on at least three of the questions."

Expected Behaviors

"I want to see each of you contributing and helping your group, listening to your group members with care, and pushing the group to look for all the possibilities before deciding on an answer. Also, your group will get a set of role cards. Pass them out randomly, read your role, and make certain you know how to do it before the Reader starts reading the poem. The Observer will report on how well he or she saw you performing your roles during the processing time." (If necessary, go over the roles to make certain the students understand them.)

Monitoring and Processing

Monitoring

Circulate among and listen to the groups. Check to make certain the groups are doing the task right (coming up with at least three possible answers, then agreeing on their favorite) and that group members are performing their roles.

Intervening

Feel free to interrupt while the groups are working. Push groups to explore interesting answers and elaborate on superficial ones. Praise examples of good

	Group Members			
OBSERVATION SHEET				
Contributes ideas				
Encourages others				
Praises good ideas				
Summarizes				
Pushes deeper				
Other helpful behaviors noticed:				

group skills. If you see an interaction problem, encourage the group to stop and solve it before continuing.

Closing

After the groups have finished answering the questions, have a class discussion over the answers. Pick group members at random to explain answers, keeping track of contributors and groups and grading groups accordingly. List the groups' answers on the board, then see if the class can decide on answers all members agree on.

Processing

After the class discussion, have the groups get back together to process. Have the observer report on what he or she saw and show each group their marks on the observation sheet. Then have the groups write down their answers to the following questions:

1. What behaviors did we do well?
2. What behaviors do we need to improve upon?
3. How well did we perform our roles?
4. What would help us perform our roles better?

If there is time, have the groups share some of their answers with the whole class.

The Vocabulary of Glacier Park

In Chapter Three we described a number of approaches to vocabulary instruction. One of those was the concept/relationship procedure. Here, the approach is used with the student teams-achievement divisions version of cooperative learning to help students learn vocabulary from the selection they are studying. The group considered is a middle school or junior high U.S. geography class, which, although not formally tracked, includes a number of students for whom reading is often a challenge. The text for this unit, *Glacier* (Root, 1988), is a very short book on Glacier National Park specifically designed for middle school and junior high students who experience some difficulties with reading. It contains only about 8,000 words and could be read in less than 1 hour by students reading at about 150 words per minute and less than 90 minutes by students reading at about 100 words per minute. A class might spend a 5-day week working with the text and related activities. Here, only the vocabulary aspect of the lesson is considered. The context/relationship procedure itself is described first, then how it can be used with STAD.

The concept/relationship procedure is a fairly substantial approach for teaching new words that do not present difficult conceptual challenges. It is frequently appropriate for teaching a set of 10 or so words from a chapter-length text students are studying, which is what *Glacier* is. The heart of the procedure is a brief paragraph that uses the word to be taught three of four times. The paragraph is followed by a multiple-choice item that checks students' understanding of the word. A sample paragraph and multiple-choice item for the word *glacier* and the steps for presenting it are shown here.

Glacier

A *glacier* is a huge mass of ice and snow that builds up gradually in extremely cold weather. At one time, *glaciers* covered much of what is now the U.S. Although they move slowly, *glaciers* actually do move, and when they move they carve up the land that they pass over. The rugged peaks and valleys of Glacier National Park were formed millions of years ago by *glaciers*.

Glaciers are:

_____ a. types of rugged mountain peaks.

_____ b. huge masses of ice and snow.

_____ c. violent winds that blow from north to south.

In presenting the context/relationship procedure, the following steps are used:

1. Explain the purpose of the procedure—to learn words important to understanding the upcoming selection.
2. Pronounce the word to be taught.
3. Read the paragraph in which the word appears.
4. Read the possible definitions, and ask students to choose the best one.

5. Pause to give students time to check a definition, give them the correct answer, then answer any questions they have.
6. Read the word and its definition a final time.

For this selection on Glacier National Park, preteach these eight terms before students read the selection: *avalanche, chinook, continental divide, crevasse, glacier, hibernate, moraine,* and *tundra.* This should take about 10 minutes.

Following this initial presentation, tell students that they will be working in STAD groups, and explain the STAD procedure. The task for each group is to ensure that all members have mastered these words. Students will be quizzed individually at the end of the week, and points will be awarded based on the extent to which they meet or exceed their average score on previous vocabulary quizzes. Also, the total points they receive will be based on the points they receive individually *and* the average points received by other students in their group. Thus, to do well, each student must do well individually, and he or she must do everything possible to see that other students in his or her group do well. It is vital that students understand this fully.

Next, assign students to heterogeneous groups of four. For this first group session, have students match vocabulary words and their definitions. The session ends when all members of the group can successfully match all eight terms and their definitions.

Later in the week, hold a second group session. This time students should first ensure that all in their group can still match words and definitions—something they can probably do with little additional work. Then, students should ensure that all members of their group can write out appropriate definitions for the terms. This production task is more difficult than the recognition task of matching, but actually producing definitions will serve to better fix the definitions in students' memory.

At the end of the week, give students a vocabulary quiz made up of the multiple-choice items constructed for the initial instruction. Calculate points and award them as soon as possible.

The Life and Works of Beethoven

This activity, a formal cooperative learning group lesson, was created by Larry Stone (1987), a teacher at Tisbury School in Vineyard Haven, Massachusetts.

Subject Area:	Music
Grade Level:	Junior high
Lesson Summary:	Students receive clues about the life of Beethoven, which, if shared with their group, will help them answer questions about Beethoven.

From *Structuring Cooperative Learning: The 1987 Lesson-Plan Handbook* by D. W. Johnson, R. T. Johnson, and E. J. Holubec. Edina, MN: Interaction Book Company, 1987.

Instructional Objectives:	Students will learn specific facts about the life and works of Beethoven. They will also gain practice in using logic and in sequencing.	

Materials:

Item	Number Needed
Beethoven's life worksheet	One per student
Beethoven's life answer key	One for teacher
Clue cards containing relevant and irrelevant facts about Beethoven	One set per group
Student checklist	One per student

Time Required:	One class period or less

Decisions

Group Size:	Four
Assignment to Groups:	Teacher assigned, based on the teacher's prior knowledge of the students' varying levels. Make each group as heterogeneous as possible.
Roles:	None

The Lesson

Instructional Task

Using the clue cards, students will read about the life and works of Beethoven. The set of clues will be dealt out by one member of each group until all the clues are distributed. No member may look at any clues other than his or her own. By asking each other questions about the clues, the students are to answer the six questions concerning Beethoven's life. Each student is to write the answers on his or her own worksheet. When every member of the group is satisfied that their answers are correct, they should sign their names to all of their group's answer sheets.

Positive Interdependence

Each student receives only part of the information needed to complete the assignment. Everyone in the group must agree on the answers before the group is finished, and all group members will receive the same grade, based on their answers.

Individual Accountability

Everyone will write the answers on their own paper and must signify that they agree with their group's answers by signing each of the group's answer sheets.

CLUE CARDS

Beethoven did not visit the United States or Italy.	Beethoven was born in 1770.	Beethoven visited M. Pfeiffer's hometown and saw the Tower of London.
One of Beethoven's teachers was very interested in church music.	His father was one of seven children, two of whom were Johanne and Wolfgang.	Beethoven was born in a European country.
Mr. Zimmerman was not one of Beethoven's teachers.	Van der Eder was a very rich patron of church music.	Germany, Italy, and Austria are all in Europe.
The town of Wahring is about 20 miles west of Berlin, Germany.	Mozart, a great composer, lived in Germany.	London is in England, where Queen Elizabeth reigns.
Beethoven is buried in a German town west of Berlin.	Beethoven wrote fewer than 15 symphonies.	Beethoven visited one of the three European countries listed on one clue card.
It is fair to say that Beethoven did not visit the country he was born in.	Beethoven wrote more than seven symphonies.	One of Beethoven's teachers was from England.
One of Beethoven's teachers was from Austria.	M. Pfeiffer and F. Zimmerman were both from Austria.	The United States.
Wolfgang's brother helped Beethoven study the violin.	Beethoven was 57 years old when he died.	Beethoven was not born in Italy or Austria.
Johanne never met Beethoven.	Carl Olsen was born in France.	To get the number of symphonies he wrote, add the number 7 to the least number of symphonies that Beethoven might have written according to the clues.
The city of Berlin is 150 miles from the western border of Germany.	Beethoven wrote more than two symphonies.	
	Beethoven visited Carl Olsen's home country.	

Criteria for Success

There are a total of 10 answers. Any group that correctly answers all questions or misses only one will be given an A, two wrong answers a B, three wrong answers a C, and four incorrect answers a D. More than four wrong answers will receive a failing grade.

Expected Behaviors

Tell the students that each group member is to be allowed to have his or her say about the questions and each group is to help members understand the material covered in the lesson.

Monitoring and Processing

Monitoring

Walk around and observe the cooperation of the members of each group. Take notes on how the students are working to use while processing their work as a group.

Intervening

Intervene only if the procedure is not being followed.

BEETHOVEN'S LIFE WORKSHEET

1. In what country was Beethoven born? _____
2. How many symphonies did he write? _____
3. In what year did he die? _____
4. What are the names of three of Beethoven's teachers? _____
   _____ _____
5. Name three countries that Beethoven visited during his lifetime.
   _____ _____ _____
6. In what town was Beethoven buried? _____

BEETHOVEN'S LIFE ANSWER KEY

1. In what country was Beethoven born?	Germany
2. How many symphonies did he write?	Nine
3. In what year did he die?	1827
4. What are the names of three of Beethoven's teachers?	His father, M. Pfeiffer, van de Eder
5. Name three countries that Beethoven visited during his lifetime.	England, France, Austria
6. In what town was Beethoven buried?	Wahring

STUDENT CHECKLIST

Place a check beside each sentence you feel you fulfilled.

_____ 1. I followed the directions given by the teacher.

_____ 2. I shared the contents of my clues with the other group members.

_____ 3. I helped other members in my group to understand and answer the questions.

_____ 4. I received help from other members of my group when I needed it.

_____ 5. I asked other members of my group about their clues.

_____ 6. I felt that the task was finished or accomplished satisfactorily.

_____ 7. I felt that everyone in my group helped solve the answers to the questions.

Processing

Review the behaviors observed during the lesson. Use anecdotal notes to describe behaviors you saw that helped the groups work together effectively. To ensure that groups do not become competitive, during this feedback use the phrase *I saw a group (do)* . . . or *One group member (did)*. . . . Direct each student to complete the checklist individually and sign the paper. Then ask each student to name a social skill that he or she performed effectively that day. Ask the group to name a social skill that they performed effectively during the activity.

PRACTICE ACTIVITY 8.8

This lesson (The Life and Works of Beethoven) can be readily adapted for other content areas. Pick an important, memorable, and perhaps colorful historical figure from your content area, develop half a dozen or so questions on him or her, then make up sets of clues for two of the questions. Once you have done this, share your two questions and clues with a colleague, and see how he or she does in using the clues to answer the questions.

The Scientific Method

This activity, an informal cooperative group lesson intended for a senior high science class, would be used near the beginning of the course in preparation for reading a selection on the scientific method.

The first step is to plan the lecture, focusing on half a dozen or so questions students will be asked to deal with. Here are some questions.

1. About when did the scientific method originate? Who is generally credited with originating it?
2. What sorts of approaches preceded the use of the scientific method?
3. What is the scientific method? Define *theories, hypotheses, data, observations, experiments,* and *scientific laws,* and note how each is a part of the scientific method.
4. Who uses the scientific method today? How widespread is its use? What are some opposing methods of inquiry?

This lesson can be given in a single period, with a little class time allowed on the following day for students to prepare for and take a short quiz. During the full period, allow students about 5 minutes for a focused discussion before the lecture, divide the lecture into two segments of about 5 minutes each, give students 2 to 3 minutes for turn-to-your partner sessions following each of the two lecture segments, then give them about 15 minutes for a classification task following the lecture. On the following day, give students about 5 minutes to prepare for the quiz and 5 minutes to take it.

Once the lecture is planned and the questions set, it is time to establish groups. Simply having each student pair up with a partner in an adjoining desk is fine for this sort of work. After students have partners, tell them that the scientific method and related concepts are central to the course and that they will have a quiz on this material the following day. Note also that each student will take the quiz individually but will receive a grade based on the average score obtained by both students in the group. Give students the focusing questions, probably on an overhead, and tell them that they have 5 minutes to write out the answers to as many of the questions as they can. Also, tell them that if they have any ideas at all about the answers, they should write them down. (Note that the scientific method is an appropriate topic for this sort of prelecture brainstorming because senior high students will have been exposed to the scientific method in the past and will know something about it. There are a number of other science topics about which students are apt to know very little and which do not lend themselves well to brainstorming.)

Once the 5 minutes is up, tell students that the first segment of the lecture will provide answers to the first two questions and that they will want to check their answers against those given in the lecture. Then give the first segment of the lecture. At the end of the lecture, tell students that each group will have 2 to 3 minutes to write one final answer to each of the first two questions. When this time is up, randomly call on one group to read their answer to one of the questions and another group to read their answer to the other question.

Next, tell students that this second segment of the lecture will provide answers to the third and fourth questions and that they should again check their answers against information given in the lecture. Give the second segment of the lecture and have each group write out a single answer to each of the two questions. Again, after students have had time to write out their answers, randomly call on one group to read their answer to one of the questions and another group to read their answer to the other.

As the last prompt for the day, give the groups four situations, then ask them to classify each situation as a theory, a law, an experiment, or an observation. Tell students that each group can pick only one classification for each situation and that they should be prepared to give their reasons for each classification as well as the classification itself.

Here are the situations, adapted from Wilbraham, Staley, Simpson, and Matta (1987).

1. The ashes of a campfire weigh less than the wood that was burned. Therefore, it appears that mass is destroyed (lost) when wood is burned.
2. A body at rest tends to remain at rest.
3. Using a portable burner, you find that it takes 10 minutes for a pint of water to boil in the lab at school, which is located close to sea level. However, when you use the same burner to heat water at your cabin in the mountains, you find that it takes 12 minutes to boil.
4. All matter is composed of atoms. Atoms, in turn, are composed of protons, electrons, and neutrons.

Classifying these is not an easy task, and groups will need a good 10 minutes to agree on the classifications and jot down their reasoning. Once they have finished this task, randomly call on groups for their answers and their reasoning, and provide enough feedback so that you are convinced that students understand the concepts and are free of misconceptions.

Toward the end of the period, give the reading assignment on the scientific method as homework—pages 3 through 5 of Wilbraham et al. (1987)—noting that the assignment is brief and essentially reviews the material dealt with during the period. Remind students that there will be a quiz the next day and that they will take the quiz individually but receive a grade based on the average score of their group.

At the beginning of the next class period, allow the groups about 5 minutes to review the material, then give the quiz.

Choosing and Financing an Automobile and Computing Transportation Costs

This activity, a formal cooperative group lesson, was created by Lucille Groulx (1987), a teacher at Loy Norrix High School in Kalamazoo, Michigan.

Subject Area:	Consumer Math
Grade Level:	Secondary

From *Structuring Cooperative Learning: The 1987 Lesson-Plan Handbook* by D. W. Johnson, R. T. Johnson, and E. J. Holubec. Edina, MN: Interaction Book Company, 1987.

Lesson Summary:	Using information sheets about the costs of buying and running an automobile, students must agree on the most economical car to buy for a family of four and must work math problems based on their decision.
Instructional Objectives:	Students will gain practice in decision making and mathematical computation, and will build their awareness of automobile fuel conservation.

Materials:

Item	Number Needed
Situation and Decisions Worksheet	One per group
Transportation Fact Sheets 1 and 2	One per student
Average Driving Statistics	One per student
Math Problems Worksheet	One per student
Observations Sheet	One per group

Time Required:	Three to four class periods

Decisions

Group Size:	Four
Assignment to Groups:	Random, by counting off, or teacher assigned to ensure that heterogeneous racial, sex, and math competency factors exist in each group.
Roles:	**Checker:** Makes sure that everyone has completed his or her share of math problems and that all group members know how to do each of the math problems. **Recorder:** Reads the situation narrative to the group, records the group's decisions on the decision worksheet, and records the group's math computations on one math problems worksheet to be submitted to the teacher. **Questioner:** The only person in the group who is to direct group questions regarding the assignment to the teacher. This person will return to the group and inform members. **Observer:** Records the actions of each group member on the observations sheet; does not participate in the group while observing.

The Lesson

Instructional Task

When the groups are in place, distribute the materials and randomly assign the roles. Explain that each group is to hand in one decisions worksheet, one math problems worksheet, and one observations sheet. Clearly state that all computation work must be shown. Motivate the students to consider fuel and money conservation by offering a prize to the group that succeeds in saving the most money under the budgeted transportation amount.

Positive Interdependence

Explain that you want one paper from the group that all members agree on and on which they can explain the answers. Remind them that everyone is to cooperate in the decisions involving car choice, size, number of cylinders, type of transmission, and length of financing. No one is finished until all members of the group are finished.

Individual Accountability

Make certain that students understand that you expect them to divide the math problems among group members, with each teaching the other group members how to complete the problems.

Criteria for Success

Groups will get 10 points for each math problem and will receive one group grade.

Expected Behaviors

Tell students that you expect them to work together and to help each other understand how to do the math involved.

Monitoring and Processing

Monitoring

While the students are working, move from group to group to observe the degree of cooperation occurring and to assist students in needed math skills. Respond to Questioners from groups and observe how the Questioners share the information upon their return to the groups.

Intervening

Reteach math skills as needed. Also, point out problems in the social skills of the groups and help the groups resolve the problems.

Processing

Each day, have each Observer report to his or her group the interaction patterns observed and have the group decide what they do well and what they need to improve upon.

Closing

Have the group teach the Observer how to complete the math problems. Then score the math worksheets and inform all groups of the grades they received.

SITUATIONS AND DECISIONS WORKSHEET

Situation

A family of four (two parents and two children—ages 8 and 10) need to buy an automobile. They have $10,000 in a savings account from which they can withdraw $\frac{1}{4}$ of the price of an automobile to cover the down payment. They also have a yearly budgeted amount of $7,500, which must cover their transportation costs.

Your goal is to spend less than this budgeted amount ($7,500) for the year on transportation costs. The group that saves the most money to be deposited in the family's savings account will win the prize.

You are to discuss the decisions below that must be made and come to agreements with at least three other people. You are also to work the math problems dealing with transportation costs cooperatively, and share the information with each other. Only one decision paper and one math worksheet is to be turned in for each four people. All four persons are to sign the decision sheet and the math problem worksheet to show that you agree as to the decisions and answers, and that you all understand how to work the problems.

Decisions

Date _____   Group Number _____

1. The automobile of our choice is _____ (make of car).
2. It is a minicompact _____ subcompact _____ compact
   _____ mid-size _____ large/full-size _____ . (Check
   one)   Number of cylinders _____
3. This automobile has an automatic _____ manual _____ transmission. (Check one)
4. The total price of this car is _____ .
5. Its estimated gas mileage for urban (city) driving is _____ . (Deduct 5 miles from the highest estimated mileage.)

Signatures

_____   _____

_____   _____

TRANSPORTATION FACT SHEET 1

Minicompacts

Ford Fiesta	$7,850	Suzuki Swift	$7,600	Subaru Justy	$8,350
Geo Metro	$6,700	Toyota Tercel	$8,500	Hyundai Excel	$7,500

Subcompacts

Toyota Corolla	$13,000	Mercury Topaz	$11,300	Saturn Sedan	$10,400
Pontiac Sunbird	$11,500	Mazda Protege	$11,850	Volkswagen Golf	$12,000

Compacts

Honda Accord	$16,850	Buick Skylark	$14,550	Chevrolet Cavalier	$13,900
Mazda 626	$14,050	Saab 900	$26,500	Chrysler LeBaron	$14,900

Mid-size

Lexus LS400	$42,200	Buick Regal	$17,900	Cadillac Eldorado	$32,450
Mazda 929	$27,800	Ford Taurus	$19,850	Audi 100	$30,700

Full-size

Chrysler Imperial	$28,450	Pontiac Bonneville	$23,600	Ford Crown Victoria	$21,800
Cadillac DeVille	$33,700	Oldsmobile 98	$27,600	Lincoln Town Car	$34,350

TRANSPORTATION FACT SHEET 2

Vehicle Selection: Automobile Mileage Guide

Size			City	Highway	Combined
Minicompact	4	Manual	20–36	31–48	23–40
Minicompact	4	Automatic	23–29	28–38	25–32
Subcompact	4	Manual	17–35	25–46	20–39
Subcompact	4	Automatic	17–30	20–36	18–33
Subcompact	6	Manual	14–20	23–28	17–23
Compact	6	Manual	18–20	25–28	19–23
Subcompact	6	Automatic	14–20	21–27	17–22
Mid-size	6	Manual	16–21	25–33	14–24
Compact	6	Automatic	16–20	21–27	18–23
Compact	8	Manual	15–16	21–25	17–19
Mid-size	6	Automatic	17–19	22–27	19–22
Compact	8	Automatic	10–16	17–22	13–19
Mid-size	8	Manual	15–20	22–29	18–23
Mid-size	8	Automatic	10–19	14–27	11–22
Full	8	Automatic	10–18	15–25	11–21

AVERAGE DRIVING STATISTICS

- The average driver travels 15,000 miles per year.
- The average driver spends $1.20 for a gallon of gas.
- Car insurance costs approximately $1,030 per year.
- There will be five oil changes over the year amounting in cost to $100.

MATH PROBLEMS WORKSHEET

All work must be shown.

1. The down payment for your automobile choice is $\frac{1}{4}$ the total cost of the car. What is this amount? _____

2. The rate of interest on the car loan is 8% on the remaining cost of the car. What will this amount to for a 1-year financing period? _____

3. You are financing the car for 3 years, and so you need to pay off $\frac{1}{3}$ of the remaining cost of the car each year. What will this amount be for a year? _____

4. The average number of miles driven per year is 15,000. What is the average number of miles driven per month? _____

5. Find the cost of fuel for your car choice by month. Use Fact Sheet 2 and deduct 5 miles from the highest estimate when figuring your fuel mileage.

   $$\frac{\rule{3cm}{0.4pt}}{\text{(miles per month)}} \div \frac{\rule{2cm}{0.4pt}}{\text{(mpg)}} \times \frac{\rule{2.5cm}{0.4pt}}{\text{(price of gas)}} = \frac{\rule{3cm}{0.4pt}}{\text{(cost of fuel per month)}}$$

6. What will be the average fuel cost per year for your model? _____

7. How much will car insurance and five oil changes cost you per year? _____

8. What will car insurance and five oil changes cost per month? _____

9. What is the total cost for your model per month? Per year?
   Car payments _____
   Insurance   _____   _____
   Oil changes _____   (Total cost per month)
   Fuel costs   _____   _____
                                    (Total cost per year)

10. Is the year cost more than your budgeted amount for transportation? _____

11. How much money have you saved from your transportation budget amount which can be deposited in your savings account? _____

Group Member Signatures

_____   _____

_____   _____

OBSERVATION SHEET				
	Group Members			
Contributes ideas				
Asks for help				
Gives direction to group's work				
Encourages				
Checks to make sure everyone understands				
Praises				

A Flyer on the Yearbook

This activity, a jigsaw lesson intended for a high school yearbook or journalism class, entails the writing, editing, and production of a 2-page flyer or set of flyers advertising the upcoming yearbook. The activity would occupy about a week's class time, although during some of this time only one group member will be actively working on the project. Thus, other activities need to be available for the other group members.

The first step is to select the groups. For this activity, heterogeneous groups of four would work well, and thus there will probably be six or seven groups in all, each of which will construct a flyer. There are two phases to the activity, and each student in a group has a specific but different role during each phase.

In the first phase, each student writes the initial draft of one section of the flyer. One student writes the introductory section—a general statement about the yearbook and why students should buy it. A second student writes a feature section—a preview of an article that will actually be in the yearbook, perhaps a focus on volleyball, or the prom, or school dress. The author should decide what to preview, and the criteria he or she uses should be that the topic previewed is representative of the articles in the yearbook and that it is likely to be interesting and exciting to a lot of students. A third student in the group writes a second feature section—another preview of an article that will be in the yearbook. This should complement the other feature section, showing another side of the yearbook and perhaps appealing to different students than did the first feature. The fourth student writes the concluding section of the flyer. This should sum up the information that has been covered so far, plug the yearbook again, and tell students exactly how to place their orders.

During the second phase of the activity, students actually construct the flyer. In this phase, three students in the group each use different computer software programs to prepare the text for printing; a fourth student monitors and coordinates the work and has the completed flyers printed.

First, one student enters the drafts of the group members on a word processor, perhaps Microsoft Word by the Microsoft Corporation. This student is also responsible for using the spelling checker that is a part of Word, calculating the length of the completed draft to fit a 2-page flyer format (Word will also do this), and correcting any obvious errors.

Second, another student takes the word-processed draft and runs it through a grammar and style checker, something like Sensible Grammar by Sensible Software. As noted in Chapter Seven, Sensible Grammar checks a myriad of text features. Among other things, it looks for poor phrasing, misused verbs and pronouns, passive voice, repeated words, capitalization errors, punctuation errors, incorrect verb tenses, and faulty spacing. Any of the features can be turned off, and dealing with all of them at once may make the task too complicated; so you may want to have only some of the features turned on for this activity.

Third, another student takes the draft that has now been word-processed, checked for spelling, checked for length, and checked for various aspects of grammar and style, and uses desktop publishing software to produce the actual layout of the flyer. Here, the student might use Pagemaker by the Aldus Corporation, one of the most popular and powerful desktop publishing programs. Like Sensible Grammar, Pagemaker performs a myriad of functions. The student can use it, for example, to create a banner headline, to employ different type styles and sizes for various parts of the flyer, to set the number of columns to be used, even to import graphics and arrange the print so that it wraps around the graphics. Whatever the student chooses, he or she is responsible for the initial layout of the flyer.

Finally, the fourth student, who is the manager, is responsible for keeping a record of how well the group worked together and for leading the discussion when the group processes their work at the conclusion of the activity. The manager's tasks include setting up a schedule for completing each task, sharing and, if necessary, negotiating that schedule with you, getting each group member's output to the member who is handling the next phase of production, calling the group together once the initial layout is completed so that each member of the group can check the draft before it is printed, getting the flyer printed or photocopied, and calling the group members together at the conclusion of the activity to process their work.

Once the groups are selected, explain the procedure and assign group members to specific roles for each phase. This is a fairly complex set of activities, so written instructions would be useful. At this time, you will also need to give students the evaluation criteria. Give a single grade for each completed flyer, and base that grade on the quality of the writing and mechanical correctness of each of the four sections of the flyer, the audience appeal of each of the four sections, and the layout of the flyer as a whole.

You also have a decision to make here—whether to print and distribute the flyers of all the groups or to have a contest to see which flyer is printed and distributed. In either case, you need only one flyer for each student in school, so the total number of flyers printed would be the same. The question is whether or not you want to introduce some competition into the activity. As Aronson et al. (1978) point out, a little competition can sometimes be useful to build cohesion within groups. However, as they also point out, a little competition can go a long way when your ultimate goal is to teach cooperation, and you would not want to create competitive situations very often.

Once you have made a decision on this—you could make this decision on your own or share the decision making with students—the next step is to set a due date for the completed flyers. At this time, you should also schedule a total class metting to share, discuss, and perhaps vote on the flyers. This meeting will give you an opportunity to have the class as a whole process the groups' work.

The concluding steps are to hold the final meeting, grade the flyers and return them to students with plenty of feedback, and distribute the flyers to all students in the school.

PRACTICE ACTIVITY 8.9

At the beginning of this section, we asked you to think about how each of the cooperative lessons described could be modified to make it appropriate for your subject area. At this point, we have a more demanding assignment. Identify one of the four types of cooperative learning described here—formal cooperative groups, student teams-achievement divisions, jigsaw, or informal cooperative groups—and make up a cooperative lesson of your own, one appropriate for a class you have now or the sort of class you are likely to have in the future. You can complete this assignment at any of three successively more challenging levels. The first option is to simply write down a 1- or 2-paragraph description of the activity. The second option is to create a detailed description of the activity, similar to those given here. The third, and in many ways best, option is to actually create the activity and use it in a class. Each successive option demands more time and effort from you, and each will prepare you more fully to use cooperative groups. Whichever option you choose, if at all possible do complete this activity in a cooperative group.

ASSESSING COOPERATIVE LEARNING

In this section we describe three successively more sophisticated procedures for assessing cooperative learning. Both teachers and students can profit from such assessments. Teachers can use the results to adjust the composition or structure of groups, provide students with additional assistance in specific cooperative procedures, or assist individual students who may have difficulty functioning within a group. Students can use the results to become more familiar with cooperative learning, acquire a better understanding of the strengths and weaknesses of their group's performance, and learn to assist other students in understanding their contributions to the group's learning.

An excellent form of assessment to begin with is a simple observations sheet, such as Figure 8.2, suggested by Johnson and Johnson (1991b).

FIGURE 8.2   SIMPLE CHECKLIST OF OBSERVED COOPERATIVE BEHAVIORS

	Yes	No
1. Do students understand the task?	_____	_____
2. Have students accepted the positive interdependence and individual accountability?	_____	_____
3. Are students working toward appropriate criteria?	_____	_____
4. Are students demonstrating the specified behaviors?	_____	_____

This checklist is particularly useful for teachers who are just becoming acquainted with cooperative learning in their classroom. It will provide a reasonable indication of how well students exhibit the desired behaviors and demonstrate the importance of deliberate and systematic monitoring of students' behaviors during cooperative learning.

Once you are thoroughly familiar with this checklist, a more elaborate assessment of students' participation can be conducted. Figure 8.3 assesses participation patterns noted by Johnson and Johnson (1991b) and patterns we have found useful.

Monitoring students' cooperative performance at this level provides the degree of insight necessary to fine-tune a group's efforts and offer feedback to individual students. In addition, comparing students' cooperative learning behaviors at the beginning of the school year with those toward the end provides a valuable indication of the changes of behavior over an extended period of time.

Assessment of this sort, of course, will require considerable time. Therefore, the form given in Figure 8.3 should be used with one group at a time. As you become more familiar with cooperative learning in your classroom, you

FIGURE 8.3   IN-DEPTH COOPERATIVE LEARNING ASSESSMENT

	Not Observed	Exemplary	Successful	Needs Improvement

Contributing Ideas

Group members provide opportunity for all members to contribute their information to the group.   _____   _____   _____   _____

Group members share equally in providing ideas and information to the group.   _____   _____   _____   _____

The group displays behaviors that encourage the contribution of ideas from group members.   _____   _____   _____   _____

Asking Questions

Group members ask questions of one another.   _____   _____   _____   _____

Group members ask questions that reflect a range of thinking abilities.   _____   _____   _____   _____

Group members ask questions that prompt other members to elaborate or justify the responses.   _____   _____   _____   _____

Expressing Feelings Toward One's Own Performance

Members are given the opportunity to evaluate their own performance in the group.   _____   _____   _____   _____

Members are able to communicate to the group their evaluation of their own performance.   _____   _____   _____   _____

Group members share their successes and frustrations.   _____   _____   _____   _____

Group members honestly share their evaluations of their personal performance.   _____   _____   _____   _____

Encouraging All Members to Participate

Group members are supportive of each others' active participation in the group's efforts.   _____   _____   _____   _____

FIGURE 8.3   CONTINUED

	Not Observed	Exemplary	Successful	Needs Improvement
Group members appear willing to engage in discussion.	——	——	——	——
Group members provide verbal and nonverbal cues to support members' participation.	——	——	——	——

Seeking External Assistance

	Not Observed	Exemplary	Successful	Needs Improvement
Group members obtain information or assistance from teacher when necessary.	——	——	——	——
Group members seek assistance from other groups when necessary.	——	——	——	——
Group members obtain sources of information other than those provided in class.	——	——	——	——

Promoting Group Members' Involvement

	Not Observed	Exemplary	Successful	Needs Improvement
Members actively listen to each others' questions and comments.	——	——	——	——
Members provide encouragement to others in the group.	——	——	——	——
The group acknowledges and provides positive feedback at the conclusion of an activity or at the end of a learning session.	——	——	——	——
Group members are supportive and accepting of one another as individuals.	——	——	——	——
Group members respect each other.	——	——	——	——
Group members exhibit behavior indicating mutual trust.	——	——	——	——

Guiding the Group's Effort

	Not Observed	Exemplary	Successful	Needs Improvement
Group members remain on task.	——	——	——	——
Group members adhere to their assigned tasks.	——	——	——	——
Collective efforts are taken to ensure successful completion of tasks.	——	——	——	——

FIGURE 8.3   CONTINUED

	Not Observed	Exemplary	Successful	Needs Improvement

Evaluating Group Performance

The group regularly sets aside time to discuss and evaluate collective performance.   ___   ___   ___   ___

Individuals in the group are regularly provided the opportunity to formally evaluate their performance in the group.   ___   ___   ___   ___

Group members provide closure at the conclusion of the lesson through summarization and review.   ___   ___   ___   ___

may want to simplify the form to make it less time consuming or add to it to investigate behaviors that are of particular importance for a particular group of students.

The last form of cooperative learning assessment we present in this section deals with student self-assessment. Groups must be given opportunities to conduct discussions of their performance. One common error of collaborative learning arrangements is to provide too brief a period of time for students to process and discuss the qualitative aspects of their cooperation. Teachers need to remind students that assessment of their effort is an important part of their task. Emphasizing the importance of assessing their efforts may require that an assessment form be turned in along with the assignment itself. If students see tasks and assessment as a continuous process, they are more likely to hold each other accountable for fulfilling their roles as group members.

The sample form given in Figure 8.4 is intended to serve as a basis for group evaluation at the conclusion of a lesson.

This form may be used for discussion purposes only, or it may be completed and turned in with the group's assignment. When the form is first introduced, it may be useful for you to use it to evaluate the entire class's performance. This approach allows you to discuss the use of the assessment form, to clarify the intent of the questions, and to give students the opportunity to actively share and discuss procedures for examining their performance. As soon as possible, however, students should begin using the form themselves.

In this section we have provided three procedures for teachers and students to use in assessing cooperative learning. Both students and teachers can

---

FIGURE 8.4 STUDENT ASSESSMENT OF COOPERATIVE LEARNING

Directions: *For each of the following questions, circle the number that best describes how you feel. If you feel that your group never does what the question is asking, then circle 1. If you think your group occasionally does what the question is asking, circle 2. If you think your group sometimes does what the question is asking, circle 3. If you think your group usually does what the question is asking, circle 4. And if you think your group always does what the question is asking, circle 5. Finally, if you don't know or can't answer the question, circle 6.*

1. In our group we openly share ideas and information.

1	2	3	4	5	6
Never	Occasionally	Sometimes	Usually	Always	Don't Know

2. In our group we help each other by praising each member's work.

1	2	3	4	5	6
Never	Occasionally	Sometimes	Usually	Always	Don't Know

3. In our group no one person takes charge, we all contribute to the task.

1	2	3	4	5	6
Never	Occasionally	Sometimes	Usually	Always	Don't Know

4. In our group we are honest, but we also support each other.

1	2	3	4	5	6
Never	Occasionally	Sometimes	Usually	Always	Don't Know

5. In our group we can learn more than if we work independently.

1	2	3	4	5	6
Never	Occasionally	Sometimes	Usually	Always	Don't Know

6. In our group we all know what to do when we are given an assignment.

1	2	3	4	5	6
Never	Occasionally	Sometimes	Usually	Always	Don't Know

7. In our group we conclude our work by summarizing what we learned and by evaluating how well we worked together.

1	2	3	4	5	6
Never	Occasionally	Sometimes	Usually	Always	Don't Know

benefit from conducting these types of assessment. Sometimes, a teacher may be misled by concluding that since students "are really busy in their groups," the groups are functioning effectively. Like any new approach, cooperative learning will require the teacher to continually modify, refine, and perhaps reteach the procedures. Thorough monitoring of students as they are engaged in their groups will increase the likelihood that problems can be addressed before they become obstacles and that student successes can be capitalized on to instill greater interest and participation. Similarly, students will gain a more thorough understanding of the roles and responsibilities of group members when they attend directly to what they did that was successful and what they need to work harder on.

CONCLUDING REMARKS

We began this chapter by defining cooperative learning and discussing its most important characteristics. Next, we made a case for cooperative learning, citing both theory and research, then described five different types of cooperative learning. Following this, we discussed procedures for instruction in cooperative skills: First, we presented some general principles for teaching procedural skills; then we gave a list of cooperative learning skills students need; next we discussed some matters to consider when first establishing cooperative groups; finally, we described specific teaching methods. In the longest section of the chapter, we described six examples of cooperative learning lessons. We then presented several methods of assessing cooperative learning.

Two points are worth stressing here. The first is that cooperative learning skills are not easily or quickly taught, nor are they easily or quickly learned. Simply putting students together in groups does not constitute effective cooperative learning. Effective cooperative learning demands that students internalize certain attitudes and employ certain skills, with the prerequisite attitude being students' acceptance of their positive interdependence with other members of their group. Like most worthwhile learning, learning cooperative skills takes substantial amounts of time and energy, on both students' and the teacher's part. If you feel that you want additional information on teaching cooperative learning skills, we can particularly recommend three books that we have found lucid and helpful—Johnson et al.'s (1990) *Circles of Learning: Cooperation in the Classroom,* Aronson et al.'s (1978) *The Jigsaw Classroom,* and Slavin's (1987) *Cooperative Learning: Student Teams.*

The second point is that teaching students to use cooperative skills is well worth this effort. Remember, cooperative learning can produce gains in academic achievement, better acceptance of students of diverse backgrounds and personalities, improved attitudes toward school, more positive self-concepts, and enhanced interpersonal skills. The potential payoff from using cooperative learning in your classroom is distinctly worth the cost.

REFLECTIONS

This section of the chapter gives you the opportunity to reflect on cooperative learning, to consider what sorts of cooperative learning you want to implement in your class, to consider how you will implement cooperative learning, and to think about some topics in your subject matter area that lend themselves particularly well to cooperative learning.

1. As noted early in the chapter, competitive learning is frequently used in classrooms. Think back to your own experiences in high school or experiences you have had in college and identify the class you remember as the most competitive. Explain what made it competitive and assess the contribution that the competitiveness made to your enjoying the class.

2. Again, think back to your experiences in high school or experiences you have had in college, but this time identify a class in which independent learning was emphasized. Then list two or three simple ways in which some of that independent work could have been done cooperatively.

3. Look back at the five necessary components of effective cooperative learning and identify the component you plan to emphasize first when introducing students to cooperative learning. Explain why you would emphasize this component first, then describe how you would begin working with it in a classroom.

4. Consider the five types of cooperative learning described and identify the type you would introduce first to a group of students. Explain why you would introduce this type first. Now consider the five types again and identify the type you are likely to use most often with students. Explain why this is the type you would use most often. Finally, consider the five types once again and list any other types you will probably use at least occasionally.

5. As noted, the task of learning cooperative skills is a procedural one; learning to work cooperatively requires students to learn to do something, not just learn about something. Think about some procedural skill you have learned to do well. Explain how you learned it and consider which of the guidelines for teaching procedural skills you followed in learning it.

6. List half a dozen topics in your subject area that lend themselves to cooperative learning. From this list, select the one that best lends itself to cooperative learning and explain why it is particularly well suited.

7. The chapter described three procedures for assessing cooperative learning. Identify the procedure you are likely to use most frequently and explain why you would tend to use it. Consider whether you are likely to use either of the other procedures and how frequently you might use them.

REFERENCES

Aronson, E., Blaney, N., Stephan, C., Sikes, J., & Snapp, M. (1978). *The jigsaw classroom*. Newbury Park, CA: Sage.

Bargh, J., & Schul, Y. (1980). On the cognitive benefits of teaching. *Journal of Educational Psychology, 72,* 593–604.

Cohen, P. A., Kulik, J. A., & Kulik, C. C. (1982). Educational outcomes of tutoring: A meta-analysis of findings. *American Educational Research Journal, 19,* 237-248.

Flavel, J. H. (1976). Metacognitive aspects of problem solving. In L. B. Resnick (Ed.), *The nature of intelligence.* Hillsdale, NJ: Erlbaum.

Groulx, L. (1987). Choosing and financing an automobile and computing transportation costs. In D. W. Johnson, R. T. Johnson, & E. J. Holubec, *Structuring cooperative learning: Lesson plans for teachers.* Edina, MN: Interaction Book Company.

Holubec, E. J. (1987). Cooperative poetry: "I Too." In D. W. Johnson, R. T. Johnson, & E. J. Holubec, *Structuring cooperative learning: Lesson plans for teachers.* Edina, MN: Interaction Book Company.

Johnson, D. W., & Johnson, R. T. (1989). *Cooperation and competition: Theory and research.* Edina, MN: Interaction Book Company.

———. (1991a). Collaboration and cognition. In A. Costa (Ed.), *Developing minds: A resource book for teaching thinking* (2nd ed.). Alexandria, VA: Association for Supervision and Curriculum Development.

———. (1991b). *Learning together and alone* (3rd ed.). Englewood Cliffs, NJ: Prentice Hall.

Johnson, D. W., Johnson, R. T., & Holubec, E. J. (1987). *Structuring cooperative learning: Lesson plans for teachers.* Edina, MN: Interaction Book Company.

———. (1990). *Circles of learning: Cooperation in the classroom* (3rd ed.). Edina, MN: Interaction Book Company.

Johnson, R. T., Johnson, D. W., & Smith, K. A. (1990). Cooperative learning: An active learning strategy for the college classroom. *Baylor Educator, 15*(2), 11–16.

LaBerge, D., & Samuels, S. J. (1974). Toward a theory of automatic information processing in reading. *Cognitive psychology, 6,* 293–323.

McKeachie, W. J., Pintrich, P., Lin, Y., Smith, D. A., & Sharma, R. (1986). *Teaching and learning in the college classroom.* Ann Arbor, MI: NCRIPTL.

Morton, T. (1988). Fine cloth, cut carefully: Cooperative learning in British Columbia. In J. Golub (Ed.), *Focus on collaborative learning.* Urbana, IL: National Council of Teachers of English.

Root, P. (1988). *Glacier.* Mankato, MN: Crestwood House.

Stone, L. (1987). The life and words of Beethoven. In D. W. Johnson, R. T. Johnson, & E. J. Holubec, *Structuring cooperative learning: Lesson plans for teachers.* Edina, MN: Interaction Book Company.

Slavin, R. E. (1987). *Cooperative learning: Student teams* (2nd ed.). Washington, D.C.: National Education Association.

Vygotsky, L. (1978). *Mind in society: The development of higher psychological processes.* Cambridge, MA: Harvard University Press.

Wilbraham, A. C., Staley, D. D., Simpson, C. J., & Matta, M. S. (1987). *Addison-Wesley chemistry.* Menlo Park, CA: Addison-Wesley.

. . . .

Cultural and Linguistic Diversity

—By Susan M. Watts and Judith L. Peacock

CHAPTER OVERVIEW

This chapter focuses on cultural and linguistic diversity in the classroom. The first section defines cultural diversity and explains why content area teachers need to be concerned with this topic. It also sets forth the goals of multicultural education. The next two sections describe two groups of culturally and linguistically diverse students: students who speak English as a second language and students who speak a nonstandard form of English. One purpose of these sections is to help content area teachers appreciate the linguistic achievements of these students. Another is to suggest ways teachers can help these students be successful learners in the content area classroom. The fourth section presents the idea that the classroom itself is a culture and that students from cultures that differ from the classroom culture may encounter difficulties learning in this environment. The final section describes a multicultural curriculum and examines current textbooks in light of cultural diversity.

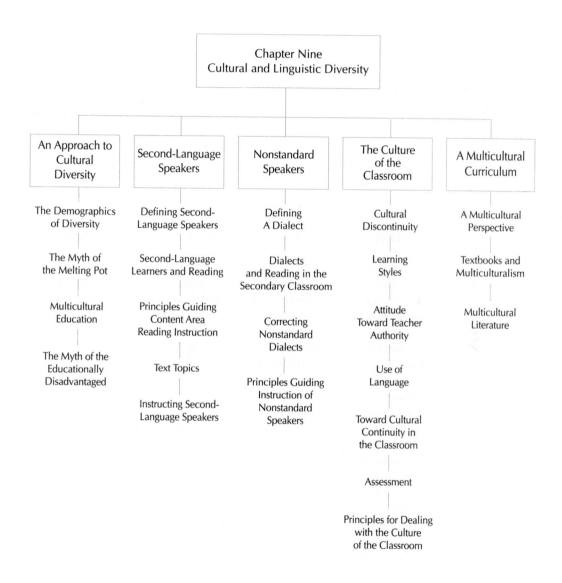

Chapter Nine
Cultural and Linguistic Diversity

An Approach to
Cultural
Diversity

The Demographics
of Diversity

The Myth of
the Melting Pot

Multicultural
Education

The Myth of the
Educationally
Disadvantaged

Second-Language
Speakers

Defining Second-
Language Speakers

Second-Language
Learners and Reading

Principles Guiding
Content Area
Reading Instruction

Text Topics

Instructing Second-
Language Speakers

Nonstandard
Speakers

Defining
A Dialect

Dialects
and Reading in the
Secondary Classroom

Correcting
Nonstandard
Dialects

Principles Guiding
Instruction of
Nonstandard
Speakers

The Culture
of the
Classroom

Cultural
Discontinuity

Learning
Styles

Attitude
Toward Teacher
Authority

Use of
Language

Toward Cultural
Continuity in
the Classroom

Assessment

Principles for Dealing
with the Culture
of the Classroom

A Multicultural
Curriculum

A Multicultural
Perspective

Textbooks and
Multiculturalism

Multicultural
Literature

An Approach to Cultural Diversity

This first section explains the rationale for including a chapter on cultural diversity in a text on reading in subject matter areas and describes the philosophy underlying the teaching suggestions included here. The term *cultural diversity* is used to describe a class in which the teacher and students represent a variety of languages, values, life experiences, and habits. In general, cultural diversity results from variations in racial and ethnic identity or socioeconomic class. The aim here is not to promote one culture over another; nor is cultural diversity viewed as a problem for teachers to overcome. Instead, the culturally diverse classroom provides an opportunity to enhance and enrich the learning of all students.

The Demographics of Diversity

Over the years, the American high school classroom has been a popular setting for TV series. Depending on your age, you may remember "Our Miss Brooks" and "Mr. Peepers" from the 1950s. Then there were "Room 222" and "Welcome Back, Kotter," in the 1960s and 1970s, and in the late 1980s "Head of the Class."

Although situation comedies are not known for their realistic portrayal of everyday life, they do, in this case, reflect a genuine trend in American public education—a trend toward greater ethnic, racial, and socioeconomic heterogeneity in the classroom. Thus, when Miss Brooks taught English in the 1950s, her classes consisted of white, middle-class students, as typified by the irrepressible Walter Denton. Thirty years later, Charlie Moore's history students—Darlene Merriman, Eric Mardian, Jawaharlal Shoudhury, Simone Foster, Maria Borges, and Alan Pinkard (to name a few)—were African-American, Asian-American, European-American, and Hispanic. They were wealthy and working class, preppy and streetwise.

Recent statistics from the U.S. Census Bureau confirm that greater ethnic, racial, and socioeconomic diversity is a fact of life for every part of the country. Focusing on racial data, we find that during the 1980s the nonwhite population grew to 25% of the total population, up from 20% at the beginning of the decade (Lewis, 1991). This was the most rapid increase in the minority population during this century. The largest growth numerically was among the Hispanic population—up 53% to 7.7 million people (Lewis, 1991). In addition to a generally higher birth rate among nonwhite Americans (Banks, 1991), changes in U.S. immigration laws ensure that the diversification of the population will continue—of the 700,000 legal immigrants who enter this country each year, three out of four now come from non-European countries (Lewis, 1991). *One-Third of a Nation*, a report issued by the American Council on Education and the Education Commission of the States (1988), predicts that one in three Americans will be nonwhite by the year 2000.

As suggested by the TV sitcoms, a corresponding demographic shift is occurring in public schools, especially those located in large urban areas. The

Census Bureau projects that 46% of school-age youths will be minority by the turn of the century (Pallas, Natriello, & McDill, 1989). The shift toward classrooms composed of students of heterogeneous racial and cultural backgrounds is noted by Simpson (1992).

In the 1990s, those now called minorities will constitute a majority in U.S. colleges and, after the year 2000, in public schools. Many will need special assistance to succeed in high school and college and will not realize their potential unless educators become more aware of the unique needs of individual students.

Current research suggests that students' native culture affects their learning and their attitudes toward school. At the same time, a multitude of reports and studies suggest that traditional classroom teaching—which is oriented to white, Anglo, middle-class culture—is not meeting the needs of a sizable number of students who belong to a minority racial or ethnic group, live in a poverty household, or have a non–English language background. For instance, results from the National Assessment of Educational Progress (NAEP) show that the reading and writing skills of black and Hispanic children are substantially lower than those for white children at each of grades 3, 7, and 11 (Beaton, 1986; NAEP, 1985). In addition, statistics from the Census Bureau (1991) reveal that black and Hispanic youth are less likely to complete high school than white youth. More and more, educators are realizing that when students' nonmainstream cultural values and experiences conflict with the cultural values and experiences that dominate the American classroom, identification becomes more difficult, resulting in nonparticipation, misbehavior, poor achievement, and high dropout rates (Schlosser, 1992). Interestingly, during the period in which U.S. public school classrooms are growing more racially diverse, teachers have remained overwhelmingly white and female (NEA, 1992).

Growing heterogeneity in American classrooms creates an urgent need to find appropriate ways for educating culturally diverse students and thus presents new challenges to teachers. In a just society, all teachers—including secondary content teachers—have a responsibility to help all students reach their potential and be successful in school and the society at large. Even if you teach in a culturally uniform environment, you need to be concerned with cultural diversity. Your students will most certainly live in a global society, and they will need the skills and knowledge to live harmoniously with various cultural groups.

There is also a practical, less noble, rationale for being concerned with cultural diversity. This reason concerns the economic future of America. By the year 2000, people of color will constitute a disproportionate share of the work force (Banks, 1991). If their current level of educational achievement does not increase, they will not have the knowledge and skills to compete in a primarily service-oriented, global job market. Corporations will export even more jobs to skilled workers overseas, leaving American workers unemployed and powerless and opening the door to economic depression and social unrest.

The Myth of the Melting Pot

The question remains as to how to approach cultural diversity in the classroom. Dealing with cultural diversity is nothing new for American public schools. As a nation of immigrants, the United States through the years has depended on its public schools to educate children from varied backgrounds. What is different, however, is the magnitude of diversity. As already suggested, whereas U.S. Schools once taught children from primarily European backgrounds, they now teach children from Asian, African, Latin American, and Native American backgrounds. (And not just Asian, for example, but Laotian, Cambodian, Vietnamese, Japanese, Korean, and Chinese.) Different, too, is the way in which many schools now view their role in educating students from many cultures.

The view that dominated America from the turn of the century to the 1960s was that of assimilation. This was the idea that America was to be a melting pot, a nation in which all cultural differences would combine to form a new and superior American culture. In actuality, however, the culture of the dominant immigrant group at the time rose to the top of the pot, while the cultures of other groups stuck to the bottom (Banks, 1977). Thus, as agents of assimilation, schools weaned immigrant students, black students, and Native American students away from their own cultures and replaced their cultures with the English language and Anglo customs. Assimilation worked reasonably well for ethnic people who were white—such as Swedes, Poles, and Germans—but not so well for darker-skinned people.

Running counter to the idea of assimilation was that of cultural pluralism. Instead of being a melting pot, America was to be a salad bowl. Just as shredded lettuce, croutons, bacon bits, tomato wedges, and other ingredients retain their identity when tossed together in a salad, so, too, people had the right to retain their cultural identity within the American society. Whereas assimilationists asserted that to be strong America needed a unified culture, cultural pluralists asserted that to be strong America needed cultural democracy, with every ethnic culture contributing to and enriching the total society. Although a few writers and philosophers had espoused cultural pluralism at the beginning of the century, the concept did not take hold in America until the black Civil Rights Movement of the 1960s. Tired of assimilationist promises of blending in, black leaders demanded more control over institutions in their communities and fuller representation of their culture. For schools, this meant more black teachers and administrators and textbooks reflecting black culture. Inspired by the Civil Rights Movement, other nonwhite groups began to make similar demands, and even white ethnic groups began to reclaim cultural pride (Banks, 1977).

Multicultural Education

The concept of cultural pluralism led to the movement known as multicultural education. According to Banks (1977), the overarching goal of multicultural education is to help individuals better understand themselves by looking at their culture and behavior through the perspectives of other cultures. Multicultural education includes studying different ethnic cultures, providing equal educational opportunities, and promoting the concept of ethnic diversity. However, it is not something that can simply be added to the curriculum; instead, it must permeate the curriculum. It is not just for African American students or Native American students—it is for all students. Multicultural education is an attitude, a philosophy, a way of being with others rather than a set of rules or a curriculum. As one teacher put it, "For me, multicultural awareness means to infuse this awareness and knowledge of others, their culture, and history into the instructional content and classroom climate rather than teach it" (Watts, personal communication, June 24, 1992).

In Banks's view the total environment of the ideal school would reflect the ethnic diversity of American society. Thus, the multicultural school would have a racially and ethnically mixed school staff that respects and values ethnic diversity. Teachers and administrators would have positive attitudes toward all youth and high academic expectations for them. The curriculum in the multicultural school would help students view American society and history from a variety of perspectives, not just the perspective of Anglo American historians and writers. Furthermore, not just humanities and history teachers would be concerned with cultural content, but science, music, home economics, physical education, and other teachers as well. Teaching strategies and methods would reflect the notion that students' background and specific language affect the way they learn. The school's testing and counseling program and expectations for student behavior would also reflect ethnic diversity.

To achieve the multicultural school, writes Banks (1977), systemwide reform is needed. Just using multiethnic materials, for example, is not enough. While ascribing to Banks's ideas, this chapter can only address a few of the issues and topics in multicultural education. The following sections address the needs of two groups of culturally and linguistically diverse students in the classroom: students who speak English as a second language and students who speak a nonstandard form of English. In addition, the final section discusses the relationship of multiculturalism to the total curriculum. The hope is that you, as an individual teacher, will do what you can to create a multicultural environment in your classroom.

The Myth of the Educationally Disadvantaged

An important issue needs to be addressed before proceeding with specific teaching suggestions. For a number of years racial minority or ethnic students, students from poverty homes, and students who speak limited English or nonstandard English have been labeled "educationally disadvantaged," "educationally deprived," or "at risk." Many teachers have been trained to believe that these students lack a viable culture, lack language skills and knowledge, and lack parental support for school success (Garcia, 1978). Their generally poor performance on standardized assessments (discussed later in this chapter) seems to affirm academic deficiency. As a result of these deficit views, an entire bureaucracy of compensatory education (Flores, Tefft Cousin, & Diaz, 1991) has evolved in which minority and low-income students are disproportionately separated into remedial and low-track classes to receive instruction in basic skills (Sleeter, 1992).

Recent research suggests that labels such as "educationally disadvantaged" and "at risk" are myths. As noted by Flores et al. (1991), researchers are discovering that so-called disadvantaged children have functional cultures, are proficient users of their native language, and bring a great deal of knowledge into the classroom. Labels such as "educationally disadvantaged" and "at risk" tend to keep schools from being creative in the education of nonmainstream students. The labels may also be used to rationalize failure. If students are labeled "at risk" at the beginning of their school career, then no one is surprised when they later fail. If students *are* at risk, it may be because educators have disadvantaged them. It is, in fact, the educational system that is at risk of failing if it does not keep up with the movement of the nation toward increasing heterogeneity.

PRACTICE ACTIVITY 9.1

Read the following descriptions of adolescents of various racial, ethnic, and socioeconomic backgrounds. As a teacher, rank these adolescents from those you would *most like* to those you would *least like* to have in class (1 = *most like*). If you feel comfortable doing so, discuss your rankings with your classmates. Some comments are given in the answers section at the end of the book.

1. _____ Song Vang came to the United States from Laos when she was a small child. She and her parents live in the local Hmong community. Since her parents have had difficulty learning English and adjusting to American ways, Song must be the family interpreter and decision maker.

2. _____ Laurie Dobson, a white teenager, lives with her mother and brother in a downtown shelter for the homeless. Although their living situation is difficult, Laurie's mother wants her children to get an education. She does the best she can to get Laurie to school every day.

3. _____ José Sierra, his parents, and his brothers and sisters have just moved into the local Hispanic community. His parents were able to find seasonal work in the pea-canning factory. José has attended schools in several states and speaks both Spanish and English fluently.

4. _____ Marissa Sarawak is an exchange student from Malaysia. The daughter of a Kuala Lumpur businessman, Marissa speaks English quite well and is frequently asked to speak to civic and church groups about her native land.

5. _____ Mustafa Hajrulahovic, a Muslim, is a recent refugee from ethnic violence in Eastern Europe. He and his family arrived in this country with only the clothes on their backs. Mustafa speaks no English.

6. _____ T.J. Thomas lives in the black community on the city's north side. His father is an attorney and his mother is a schoolteacher. T.J. enjoys playing hockey and baseball in the city's recreation program.

SECOND-LANGUAGE SPEAKERS

Imagine this scenario. You're a seventh-grade geography teacher. The school counselor has just informed you that beginning Monday you will have three new students in your second-hour class. These students, part of a large family of Vietnamese refugees being sponsored by a local church, speak only limited English. Their ability to read in English consists of recognizing such words as *Coca-Cola* and *Nike*. On hearing this news, you begin to panic. How on earth can you teach geography to these students? After all, you don't speak their language, and you certainly don't have materials they can read. What are you supposed to do? As emphasized in the previous section, such a scenario is becoming more and more common in American public schools. This section attempts to help subject matter teachers understand and deal with the second-language speakers in their classrooms. It defines second-language speakers, discusses the relation of reading to second-language learners, and presents principles guiding instruction for second-language learners. It also considers the relationship between second-language learners and topics described in this text and ends with a set of principles for working with second-language learners.

Defining Second-Language Speakers

Second-language speakers have in common the fact that the first language they learned to speak was not English. Beyond that they are a diverse group. Some are fluent in both English and their native language, while others know little or no English. Some learn to speak English quickly, while others learn more slowly. In a school setting, students may take from 4 to 8 years to become proficient users of English (Allen, 1991). The more similar the first language is to the second, the more readily the person is likely to acquire the second language (Fries, 1945). Thus, students who speak French, Spanish, or Italian generally will have an easier time learning English than students who speak Chinese or Japanese. Like first-language learning, second-language learning is creative and constructive (Allen, 1991). Rather than being passive receptacles of a second language, students are active interactors with that language. They constantly hypothesize about the rules of the language, test their rules, and revise them based on the feedback they receive.

School districts provide varying instructional programs for second-language students. One type of program, which is really no program, is submersion. Students must either "sink or swim" as they are thrown into the regular classroom with no special help. Another type of program is immersion. The language of the classroom is English, but the teacher knows the students' native language. Another type of program is bilingual; in the bilingual classroom, instruction is carried on both in English and in the students' native language. The most common type of program, and the one forming the backdrop of this section, is the English-as-a-second-language (ESL) curriculum, in which the ESL teacher spends time team teaching with the regular classroom teacher to address the needs of students with limited English skills.

Even if second-language learners are receiving excellent instruction from well-qualified ESL teachers, they need the assistance of the regular classroom teacher. For one thing, the goal of ESL programs is to help students master English, not to help them learn math, science, or history. While learning English, students still must advance cognitively. Subject matter teachers possess the knowledge these students need. For another thing, ESL students require much more practice in developing English speaking, reading, and writing skills than the ESL program can provide. Although your goal is not to teach English, integrating the acquisition of English with learning content and establishing a language-rich classroom can do much to facilitate language growth. Finally, isolating students in ESL programs, as with any other kind of tracking, can lead second-language speakers to perceive themselves as poor learners or as failures.

Too often limited English proficiency is equated with limited intelligence. We assume that because people do not speak English fluently they must be less intelligent. In considering the task students face in learning a second language, however, we can gain a new respect for their accomplishment. Already they have developed a vast knowledge of their own language. Not only are they learning the forms and structures of a new language, but they are also learning how to use that language with different persons, in different settings, and for different purposes (Allen, 1991).

Second-Language Learners and Reading

In working with second-language learners, teachers naturally wonder what to do about reading. In relating reading to second-language content area learning, the following discussion uses the framework of reading presented in Chapter One. It also comments on topics presented throughout this text.

A Model of the Reading Process.   You will recall that Chapter One presented a model of the reading process at the secondary level. According to this model, the reading process must consist of three elements in order for readers to construct meaning from printed text: automaticity, metacognition, and schemata. These elements will be discussed here in relation to second-language learners.

Automaticity.   Automaticity refers to the parts of the reading process that the reader performs instantaneously and without conscious attention. It includes processing information at the letter, word, phrase, and sentence levels. Many second-language learners in your classroom will not have accomplished automaticity. They will still be in the beginning stages of reading—decoding the printed symbols, matching sounds to symbols. Interestingly, since decoding strategies are transferable across languages (Burns et al., 1992), second-language learners who already know how to read in their first language may have an easier time learning to read English than beginning readers who are native speakers of English. In other words, once students have learned how to learn, they can transfer those skills to their new language (Cummins, 1979). By the same token, students who are proficient in their first language are likely to become proficient in English as well.

One way to compensate for a lack of automaticity on the part of second-language learners would be to use simplified texts to teach content. Ask your school's ESL teacher, reading teacher, or librarian to help you locate lower level textbooks or trade books on the subject. Other ways would be to record portions of the class textbook or highlight key sentences in the textbook and help students read them. You might also have other students help second-language learners with the text.

Metacognition.   Metacognition, you remember, refers to the reader's awareness of his or her comprehension of a text, as well as the reader's regulation of the processes that lead to comprehension. Second-language learners employ a strategy known as code switching (Garcia & Padilla, 1985). Code switching might be considered a form, albeit more subconscious, of metacognition. During reading, second-language learners will read the text orally or silently in English, but then mentally translate it into their native language for comprehension. Obviously, the implication for instruction is to allow students time for code switching. To respond orally to questions or discussion based on their reading, these students must retranslate the information into English. You should not assume that they do not know the answer or have misunderstood the question if they do not respond immediately. Presuming that the students are proficient in their first language, they may actually be performing at a high level of cognition. As second-language learners advance in their decoding of English, metacognition might become a matter of their recognizing when cultural differences are interfering with comprehension, then asking for help in understanding the text.

Schemata.   Schemata are the "chunks of knowledge" that exist in our head. We activate these schemata to help us make sense of the world. As mentioned repeatedly in this text, students have difficulty comprehending materials based on experiences and concepts outside their background. This is even more true for students coming from nonmainstream cultural backgrounds. Hmong students, for example, come from an agricultural society in which commerce is carried on through bartering. Until they have learned the concept of a monetary system, doing math problems about dollars and cents will be complex and abstract. Quite often the schemata are there, and the teacher must simply help students make the connection to their native culture. One teacher made math problems more meaningful for Haitian students by changing liter containers to calabashes (Richards, 1991). If teachers do not have knowledge about specific cultures, they might ask students themselves to think of similar objects, events, persons, or places in their own culture ("Can you think of anything like this?"). A study by Lipson (1983) underscores the effect of culturally specific prior knowledge on students' reading comprehension. Compared with culturally unfamiliar text, students read culturally familiar text faster, recalled the text better, comprehended it at a higher level, and made fewer distortions in comprehension.

In helping second-language students learn to read, teachers need to create a classroom environment rich in printed material. Flood your classroom with trade books, magazines, newspapers, and brochures and encourage students to become comfortable with them. When possible, use these sources in your teaching. Although reading will be difficult at first, understanding will gradually improve as students become more automatic in their response to text and attain greater understanding of their own metacognition and as they enrich and develop their schemata.

Principles Guiding Content Area Reading Instruction

Also in Chapter One, five principles for content area reading instruction were presented. These principles, along with their application to second-language learners, are reviewed here.

1. **Content area reading instruction is based on the assumption that students acquire meaning through the application of strategies, skills, and prior knowledge to text material.** As noted in Chapter One, this principle includes the idea that content reading "is a functional skill driven by the learner's need to acquire knowledge . . . to the student, content reading is a strategic process to acquire meaning, not a set of skills or exercises taught in isolation of content." Similarly, Krashen (1981) distinguishes between language acquisition (subconsciously acquiring a language in informal settings because there is a need to learn the language) and language learning (consciously learning the rules of a language in a formal setting). The implication is that the former will be more meaningful and useful to students, whereas the latter will allow them chiefly to edit their own language output. Your task as a teacher is to motivate second-language students to learn content—and, in the process, learn the language—by providing them with purposeful tasks. Moll and Diaz (1987) describe how a teacher in San Diego engaged Hispanic students in learning English language skills. Knowing the students were interested in finding out the community's opinion on bilingualism, the instructor had them develop and administer a questionnaire, then write a report on their findings.

2. **The classroom is a dynamic social and intellectual environment where students acquire knowledge.** As stated in Chapter One, "instruction within this environment draws on students' knowledge collectively and individually . . . teachers should acknowledge the cultural and social diversity of the classroom on an ongoing basis." It must be emphasized that the discussion in the present chapter is not an attempt to extinguish students' first language. In

fact, bilingualism should be encouraged, and students' first language and culture should be used as a resource to widen the perspective and enrich the learning of mainstream students as well. For example, in the case of the Vietnamese students introduced earlier, you might have them describe similarities and differences between their native culture and the mainstream culture and teach common Vietnamese words and expressions.

3. **Content area reading instruction allows students to learn from numerous sources of information.**   The lack of automaticity among second-language learners often means that using printed materials—especially the more complex texts of the secondary classroom—is not an option. In these instances, other resources will be needed to teach your subject matter content. Alternative resources might be visual teaching techniques, such as conducting an experiment in science, acting out math problems, or showing films as part of social studies. Hands-on activities, such as having students draw maps or make models, will often need to be used to teach content. Alternative resources might also be people. Ask second-language students who have a better mastery of English to explain assignments to other students, or have students work in cross-language pairs. Another possibility is to invite English-speaking adults from the students' home community to tutor. This would be an excellent way to build support between the school and home.

4. **Content area reading instruction is directed at the learner. According to this principle, learners do not passively absorb knowledge.**   Instead, they actively relate their existing knowledge to incoming information and organize and interpret that information in a manner that allows for construction of meaning. This principle has an important implication for second-language learners. In interpreting a text, they may use perfectly sound reasoning. However, if their background knowledge is different from that of the teacher, they may give an "incorrect" answer. Teachers need to be careful not to reject answers that on the surface seem wrong. They need to find out how students arrived at an answer and focus on their process of thinking. It may be that, by presenting the student with a few probing questions, it will be evident that he or she has arrived at a different, yet legitimate, answer. Here again, second-language learners can be a resource for mainstream students, as they share their unique perspective during group problem solving.

5. **Instructional strategies and activities in the content areas are adaptable to the constraints of the classroom.**   Having second-language learners in the classroom does not necessarily mean more demands on teacher time. In a review of the literature on teaching subject matter to second-language students at the secondary level, Reyes and Molner (1991) describe strategies that have proven successful with this linguistically diverse group. In each case the strategies were effective with mixed groups of language-majority and language-minority students enrolled in regular content area classrooms. This suggests that what benefits linguistically diverse students benefits mainstream students as well—proving the maxim "Good teaching is good teaching is good teach-

ing." Among the successful strategies they cite are Langer's PreReading Plan, or PReP (described in Chapter Four of this text), semantic mapping (similar to the list, group, label strategy also described in Chapter Four), the experience-text relationship method (similar to the directed questioning activity discussed in Chapter Six), and student teams-achievement divisions (STAD) and jigsaw approaches to cooperative learning (both described in Chapter Eight).

Text Topics

The preceding chapters have dealt with a variety of topics. Here are a few comments connecting these topics to second-language learners.

Assessment.   As mentioned in Chapter Two, the use of formalized tests to assess the aptitude and achievement of students with limited English proficiency, students of a minority group, and students of low income has been criticized. More will be said on this aspect of assessment in the section titled "The Culture of the Classroom." For now, a comment on assessing the readability of texts for second-language learners is in order. Some research suggests that for these readers the structure of the text is more important than the length of words and sentences. Rigg (1981), for example, found that Southeast Asian children had no difficulty understanding a story that followed a familiar narrative format but had great difficulty understanding a story that shifted back and forth between narrative and expository text. Thus, analyzing text structure rather than applying readability formulas may be more appropriate when selecting reading materials for ESL students. A discussion of the various types of text structures can be found in Chapter Five.

Cooperative Learning.   Two theories of second-language acquisition are of interest here. Cummins (1980) distinguishes between school language (the language of textbooks and teachers) and social language (the language of hallways and cafeterias). According to Cummins, school language can be difficult for second-language speakers to learn because it tends to be abstract and distant. Social language, on the other hand, is easier to learn because it is rich in context and immediate. Dulay and Burt (1977) note that high-anxiety situations raise a filter between the language input the learner is receiving and the learner's language-processing center, thereby inhibiting language learning. School language is thus likely to create anxiety for the learner, and the teacher must be careful to ensure that accommodations are initiated, where possible.

Both of these theories point to the value of linguistically heterogeneous cooperative learning groups for second-language learners. Not only do these students learn language more quickly in informal peer groups, but they also are relieved of the pressure of having to perform independently. In discussing cooperative learning strategies for second-language speakers, Reyes and Molner (1991) state:

> In an extensive review of the benefits of cooperative learning for language minority students, Kagan (1986) notes that in cooperative classrooms minority students of-

ten make strong gains, are more involved in activities, receive more practice with learning concepts, spend more time on task, and become motivated to learn. Kagan offers several explanations for these findings. First, cooperative learning is more "culturally congruent" with students from Mexican American and Asian backgrounds, for example, because these cultures value cooperation and group interaction. Second, in a cooperative classroom, all students receive equal amounts of teacher attention and have equal opportunities to learn. Finally, peer and group rewards serve as strong motivators. (p. 101)

Vocabulary. Chapter Three identified six word-learning tasks. Two of these—learning new words representing known concepts and learning new words representing new concepts—are particularly important to keep in mind when teaching vocabulary to ESL students. Language expresses the ideas, values, experiences, and environment of a culture. Oftentimes, once a concept is presented, students can identify the word or words in their first language that describe the concept. Other times, this will not be possible because the concepts—and the words—do not exist in the students' native culture. For example, an art instructor might be explaining the terms *azure* and *aquamarine* to a linguistically diverse class. If there are Navajo students in the class, they will have no idea what the teacher is talking about because blue and green are not distinguished in their color spectrum (Brown et al., 1958). By knowing about students' cultures, a teacher can be sensitive to these differences.

Prereading Instruction. A great deal has already been said regarding prereading instruction. One note to add would be the importance of dialogue between you and your second-language learners. A back-and-forth interchange will help you determine differences or gaps in students' prior knowledge and be a means for developing students' understanding of the mainstream culture. This dialogue might occur during a formal instructional strategy, such as KWL, as described in Chapter Four, or it might occur during informal conversations with students before class, in the hallways, or in the school cafeteria. You might want to paraphrase or restate what students say to make sure you are understanding their prior knowledge.

Comprehension Instruction. For many years it has been assumed that students need to master a hierarchy of basic skills before being exposed to more advanced skills in comprehension. Language-minority students, in particular, were thought to need drill in phonics, vocabulary, and word decoding. Oftentimes, these skills were taught as discrete skills with no relation to a meaningful whole. And, oftentimes, students became bored and frustrated with instruction. In recent years, however, cognitive psychology has shown that students with limited English proficiency can benefit from comprehension instruction that develops problem-solving and reasoning abilities. The reciprocal teaching strategy discussed in Chapter Five has been cited as particularly effective (Means & Knapp, 1991).

Chapter Five also describes how to conduct class discussions. The value of discussion for second-language learners—not only for assessing students' understanding of their reading but also for tapping their prior knowledge— should be emphasized. By definition, a discussion encourages multiple points of view, and this fits well with the concept of a multicultural classroom. In a discussion, participants are free to change their points of view, and this too fits well with the concept of multicultural education. In contrast to responding to rapid-fire questions, a class discussion allows ESL students to practice their verbal skills more naturally and easily. Recognize, however, that ESL students may be reluctant to participate in discussions due to ridicule or the fear of failure. Also, some of these students may adhere to cultural values that do not promote discussion or competition between individuals. That being the case, students should engage in small-group discussions or activities that promote cooperative rather than competitive learning.

Critical Thinking.   The concept of instructional scaffolding discussed in Chapter Six is particularly pertinent to ESL students. To accomplish more complex tasks, second-language learners at first will need the assistance of special materials and the assistance of the teacher and other students. One difference between scaffolding for first- and second-language secondary students is that scaffolding for second-language secondary students must be supplied for the decoding process as well as for developing critical thinking strategies. This is done, for example, when teachers read text orally to students, allowing them to practice critical thinking skills before they have fully mastered word decoding.

Writing Instruction.   Studies have shown that second-language learners can begin to write in English long before they become fluent speakers. In fact, writing activities aid the development of oral language (Hudelson, 1984; Rigg, 1981; Urzua, 1987). As in reading, second-language learners often will employ code switching during writing activities. For example, native speakers of Spanish will interject Spanish vocabulary and spellings, especially if they are having difficulty communicating their meaning. As a subject matter teacher, you will want to focus more on the content of second-language learners' writing than on the form. Too much emphasis on mechanics can discourage the writing endeavors of ESL students with fragile English skills. The general impression marking system, which focuses on the content of writing, discussed in Chapter Seven may be particularly useful with ESL students. Look in their writing for indicators of how far along they are in language acquisition rather than for indicators of how far they have yet to go.

Instructing Second-Language Speakers

In summary, the following principles should be useful in guiding instruction of second-language speakers.

1. Integrate the learning of content with the learning of language skills by using such techniques as class discussion.
2. Incorporate a wide variety of materials at a variety of levels of difficulty that help create a language-rich classroom that entices students to read and helps build their knowledge of the mainstream culture.

3. Motivate students to learn content by providing purposeful tasks that are meaningful to the students' daily lives and background experiences.
4. Develop a respect for and knowledge of students' native culture and use it as a learning resource for all students.
5. Establish learning situations, such as linguistically heterogeneous cooperative learning groups, that allow students to practice their new language skills in nonthreatening ways.
6. Engage students in learning tasks that require higher level thinking.
7. Use nonprint resources and human resources to scaffold, or mediate, instruction.

PRACTICE ACTIVITY 9.2

Imagine that you are a science teacher. You have a class of 25 students. Five of these students are Hispanic. They speak English with varying degrees of fluency, and their English reading and writing skills are minimal. Today's lesson is on photosynthesis. Your textbook contains a good description of this process. Using instructional strategies and ideas suggested in the foregoing section, explain how you would teach photosynthesis to your class. Our response is given in the answers section.

NONSTANDARD SPEAKERS

You may have students who regularly speak a dialect of English. It may be black English—"We be working after school, man" or "Don't nobody want no friends like that" or "I got two book." On hearing such speech, the general public may cringe at what it perceives to be poor English and wonder why the schools aren't doing a better job of educating students. This section defines dialect, describes the relation of nonstandard dialect to reading, and discusses the issue of correcting students' nonstandard English. Because of its prevalence in American classrooms, the focus will be on black English. Before proceeding, however, you should note that racial, ethnic, or socioeconomic identity does not necessarily dictate the dialect a person speaks; specifically, not all African-Americans speak, or even know anything about, black English.

Defining a Dialect

A dialect is a variation of a language, sufficiently different from the original to be considered a separate entity, but not different enough to be classified as a separate language (Burns et al., 1992). Differences occur in phonology, intonation, grammar, syntax, and vocabulary. In effect, dialects are the languages of subcultures. They vary by geographical region, socioeconomic class, and age. There may even be many versions of a single dialect. We all speak a dialect of English, and many of us are bidialectal; that is, we speak more than one dialect.

In addition to black English, some of the better known dialects spoken in this country are Appalachian English, Pennsylvania Dutch, and Yiddish.

Dialects are complete and functional language systems. The grammatical rules, or predictable patterns, of black English have been well documented since the 1970s. For example, the verb *be* is used to denote habitual or ongoing action ("We be working after school, man"); multiple negatives are used in one sentence for emphasis ("Don't nobody want no friends like that"); the plural marker *-s* is omitted when there are other words in the sentence that indicate plurality ("I got two book") (Alexander, 1980). In addition, in recent years researchers have called attention to the fact that black English is rich in figurative language. For example, "playing the dozens," a verbal game of one-upmanship by insult especially common among black male adolescents, involves hyperbole and other creative uses of language (Delain, Pearson, & Anderson, 1985):

> *Jesse:* Man, you so ugly that when you walk down the streets the dogs die!
> *Duane:* Well, man, you so ugly that when you walk down the streets blind folks turn their heads!
> *Jesse:* Well, you so ugly that when you were born the doctor slapped your face!
> *Duane:* Well, you so ugly that when you were born the doctor slapped your momma!
> *Jesse:* Well, at least my momma don't look like she snorted a basketball!

A study by Delain and colleagues (1985) suggests that the experience of black youth with figurative language outside school enhances their understanding of figurative language in school texts.

While no dialect is inherently superior for the purposes of communication, one dialect must be chosen as the standard in a region so that every one can understand each other. The dialect chosen is usually the one spoken by the people with political and economic power. Their dialect then becomes the most prestigious. In the United States, the most prestigious dialect is standard English. This is the dialect used in business, in government, in entertainment, and in most public classrooms.

Dialects and Reading in the Secondary Classroom

A main concern here is whether or not speaking black English or another nonstandard dialect affects a student's ability to comprehend oral and written standard English in the classroom. For example, when nonstandard speakers read orally, they may substitute their dialect features for the standard English of the text. Or after reading a portion of standard English text, they may summarize the information or respond to a question in nonstandard dialect. Does this mean they are having trouble reading and comprehending? If so, what should be done to help them?

All speakers have a range of comprehension that extends beyond the limits of their own dialect (Goodman, 1969a). Research has shown that speakers of black English are generally able to comprehend oral and written standard English, even though they may choose not to use it. They have "receptive control"

(Goodman & Buck, 1973). This is a major difference between nonstandard speakers and second-language speakers who are just beginning to learn English. Exposure to television is a major factor in nonstandard speakers' ability to comprehend standard English (Alexander, 1980).

Numerous researchers (Bean, 1978; Goodman, 1968; Rigg, 1975; Sims, 1972) have shown that nonstandard speakers' dialect-involved "errors" do not interfere with comprehension. In fact, there is some evidence that nonstandard speakers are actually performing at a high level of cognition as they translate standard English text into black English (Goodman, 1969b). Ironically, many teachers, especially at the primary level, spend a great deal of time correcting the oral reading pronunciations of children who speak black English and thereby underestimate their potential for comprehension instruction. In some instances, perceived mispronunciations have even been the basis for assigning students to remedial reading classes.

It would seem, then, that at least mechanically students' dialect should not present problems with comprehending oral and written standard English. However, misunderstanding may develop out of differences in background and cultural knowledge. For example, Reynolds, Taylor, Steffenson, Shirey, and Anderson (1982) had a group of white eighth graders and a group of black eighth graders read the same passage. The passage could be interpreted as describing "sounding" (another name for "playing the dozens") or as describing a physical fight. The black students applied their knowledge of sounding to interpret the text, while the white students thought the text was about a fight. In a classroom setting, comprehending this text would present a problem to the black readers if it were about fighting and, conversely, to the white readers it if were actually about sounding.

Correcting Nonstandard Dialects

In the musical *My Fair Lady*, Professor Henry Higgins spends a great deal of time and effort attempting to change the dialect of flower girl Eliza Doolittle. As the story goes, if Professor Higgins can just get Eliza to stop squalling in that infernal cockney and adopt the more "cultured" speech of the British upper class, she will be acceptable in high society. Much the same issue occurs in teaching nonstandard speakers in the American classroom. Should you be a Henry Higgins and attempt to change the dialect of the students in your class?

The answer is yes and no. On the one hand, students should be taught the truth: Their dialect is a valuable, unique, and colorful expression of their culture and should be retained. They should be taught that the way they speak makes them neither bad nor good persons. On the other hand, students should be taught the reality: They need to be able to use standard English to participate fully in many areas of our society. Not teaching standard English conventions and not insisting that students practice them denies students access to what Delpit (1988) calls "the culture of power."

Issues of language diversity and power need to be discussed openly and honestly. All subject matter teachers should be ready to point out how standard English may be appropriate in some situations and dialect in others. They should allow students to use their dialect in reading and speaking in the classroom, but model the standard and encourage them to use it. In addition, social studies and English teachers might use the following activities suggested by Alexander (1980).

Activities for Helping Students Increase Their Awareness of Dialects and Value Their Own Dialect

1. Discuss the major dialect areas in the United States.
2. Read passages in other English dialects to your students to help them appreciate the variability of English and the legitimacy of their own dialect. (Also have students read books that reflect their dialect.)
3. Have students conduct a television survey and note which programs use noticeable dialects.
4. Play recordings of speeches of Dr. Martin Luther King, Jr., who was a bidialectal master. See if students can hear in his speeches the call-response style of the black preacher as well as the standard English dialect style of the statesman.

Activities for Helping Students Become Proficient in Standard English

1. Discuss and role play different situations in which vernacular black English dialect and standard English dialect would be used.
2. Use pattern practice drills to help students develop understanding of both black English dialect and standard English dialect.

    I talked to Mary Ellen every day.
    I been talkin' to Mary Ellen.
    I talked to Mary Ellen a *long* time ago.
    I been done talked to Mary Ellen.

3. Examine your own speech patterns and read to your students regularly.

Black folklore, idioms, proverbs, and other language patterns might be used as the basis for reading and writing activities and for motivating students to learn about other language patterns. In other words, teachers can capitalize on the language resources that students bring to the classroom. For example, have students work in cooperative learning groups to compose rap lyrics, which are no different from a sonnet in terms of having a set structure (Griffin & Cole, 1987).

Principles Guiding Instruction of Nonstandard Speakers

In summary, the following principles should be useful in guiding instruction of nonstandard speakers of English.

1. Develop and transmit respect for your students' dialect as a language system that reflects a culture that is valued.
2. Allow students to use their own dialect in the classroom, but model standard English and encourage students to use it.

3. Teach students about the arbitrariness of the dialect selected as "standard."
4. Show students that you believe they are capable of bidialectism.

PRACTICE ACTIVITY 9.3

Read the following interaction between a teacher and a student. What does it say about the environment that has been established in this classroom?

Scene: Vanessa is looking for something in her desk.
Mr. Ross: What are you doing?
Vanessa: Nuttin'.
Mr. Ross: (laughingly) What!
Vanessa: Oh, nuthin'.
Mr. Ross: What!
Vanessa: Oh, nothing.
Mr. Ross: Now . . .
Vanessa: (interrupting) I know, *nuthin* is nonstandard English, and that's all right when I'm outside playing with my friends. *Nothing* is standard English, and that's what I need to use in the classroom.

Now compare the following interaction to the one above. What is the difference? Why?

Scene: Mr. Ross is conducting a health lesson.
Mr. Ross: How many kinds of bones does your body have?
Theo: They be three bone, man.
Mr. Ross: What are they?
Theo: Long bone, short bone, and flat bone.
Mr. Ross: Have you ever broken a bone?
Theo: I ain't never broken no bone.
Mr. Ross: Well, that's good!

Our comments are given in the answers section.

THE CULTURE OF THE CLASSROOM

The premise of this section is that the classroom itself is a culture (Villegas, 1991). The American classroom is a community composed of a teacher and students with their own language (typically standard English or the teacher's version of standard English), their own values (do your own work, don't copy anyone else's paper), and their own habits (when the bell rings, take your seat and be quiet). Villegas describes the traditional classroom culture more fully as follows:

> The dominant form of interaction is the teacher-directed lesson in which the instructor is in control, determining the topics of discussion, allocating turns at speaking, and deciding what qualifies as a correct response. Verbal participation is re-

quired of students. Implicitly, teaching and learning are equated with talking, and silence is interpreted as the absence of knowledge. Students are questioned in public and bid for the floor by raising their hands. They are expected to wait until the teacher awards the floor to one of them before answering. Speaking in turn is the rule, unless the teacher specifically asks for choral responses. Display questions prevail. Individual competition is preferred to group cooperation. Topics are normally introduced in small and carefully sequenced steps, with the overall picture emerging only at the end of the teaching sequence. (p. 20)

The public school classroom generally reflects the culture of the teacher, the school district, or the dominant cultural group in the community. For most classrooms the culture will be that of white, Anglo, middle-class Americans. There is nothing wrong with this classroom culture. Teacher and students must share some commonalities for the classroom to function, and students who come from this background generally adjust to classroom routines and practices with no problems. Students, however, who come from different cultural backgrounds—with different learning styles and different patterns of communication—may have more difficulty. Unless there is sensitivity and accommodation to their needs, they will not be fully engaged in learning. As a result, they may become disruptive, or fall silent, or even drop out.

Cultural Discontinuity

This section presents examples of learning styles that differ from those of the mainstream culture in the classroom. It should be noted that these are examples of broad groups of students and not necessarily descriptive of every individual in the group.

As a teacher or prospective teacher, it may be difficult to imagine how students would have trouble with traditional ways of learning. Thinking of your own culture shock in going from the high school classroom to the college classroom may help. If you were like most freshmen, you probably had some difficulty adjusting to college classes. Things were quite different from high school. Instead of involving you in question-and-answer dialogue, the professors lectured for an hour. You were expected to take copious notes on which you would later be tested. You had homework in high school, but nothing like the extensive reading lists in college. You were expected to keep up with the reading without anyone checking on your progress. Altogether, the instruction was much more impersonal. If you had a question or problem to discuss with a professor, you had to make an appointment to see him or her during office hours. Unable to adjust to this new classroom culture, many students drop out of college after the first semester.

Learning Styles

As noted by Villegas (1991), learning in the typical American classroom, especially at the secondary level, is teacher directed. The teacher decides on the objectives of instruction, assigns chapters to read, asks students questions on their reading and controls discussion, and tests students' achievement of the objectives. This method of classroom organization may present difficulties to students who come from backgrounds where learning is more self-directed and more peer directed. Philips (1972, 1983), for example, investigated the learning patterns of children from the Warm Springs Indian Reservation in central Oregon. In school these children were extremely quiet, a quality often attributed to shyness or linguistic deficiency. Philips found that at home these children were accustomed to a high degree of self-determination. If they needed assistance in learning a task, they turned to other children or to older siblings. On the few occasions when they did learn from adults, they did so through observation rather than through verbal instruction. On their own initiative, the children then practiced the skill privately and did self-testing. When faced with interacting directly with the teacher at school, the children were at a loss as to what to do and fell into a silent role.

Other researchers have found peer interaction to be similarly important in the learning of various cultural groups. Wong Fillmore (1986) reported that opportunities for Hispanic children to interact with their English-speaking peers were an important factor in helping them acquire speaking and comprehension skills. On the other hand, for Chinese children interactions with the teacher were more helpful. When the teacher's lessons were clear and well organized, the Hispanic children did well, but they became inattentive when the teacher was unclear. The Chinese children, on the other hand, became even more attentive when the teacher was unclear.

Attitude Toward Teacher Authority

Students view the authority of the teacher differently from culture to culture. According to Erickson and Mohatt (1982), Odawa Indian students react more favorably to teachers who avoid exercising direct social control. This reflects the Odawa value that one person should not openly try to control the behavior of another. Thus, rather than ordering students around or waiting for everyone to do the same thing at the same time, teachers were more effective if they gave orders less directly and allowed students to shift from one activity to another gradually. According to Delpit (1988), the opposite is true for black students. They expect teachers to act authoritatively. Teachers who are soft-spoken or chummy appear to be weak and ineffectual and not worthy of respect. Whereas white, middle-class children are taught to obey teachers simply because they are teachers, black children obey because teachers constantly demonstrate the ability to control the class and push students to succeed.

Use of Language

In addition to varying learning styles and attitudes toward teacher authority, the use of language differs from culture to culture, and this may affect communication in the classroom. Heath (1983), for example, investigated the learning difficulties of children from Trackton, an African-American working community in the Appalachias. She found that the linguistic environment of the classroom was quite different from that of the children's homes. One major difference was in the use of questions. In the traditional classroom, teachers ask "display" questions, questions that require students to show off their academic knowledge (e.g., "What color is this crayon?"). Teachers already know the answers to the questions they ask. Trackton parents, however, asked their children more open-ended questions, with answers unknown to the adults (e.g., "What are you going to do with this color?"). Unaccustomed to a test style of questioning, the Trackton children were frustrated by their teachers' questions and did not know how to respond. As a result, they appeared academically incompetent. Differences in the use of questions are particularly significant since so much of instruction in the traditional classroom is carried on through interrogative dialogue.

Another difference Heath noted was in the use of commands. Compared with middle- and upper-class parents, working-class families, both black and white, give more direct commands to their children (e.g., "Put the book on the shelf"). Middle-class teachers tend to give indirect, or veiled, commands (e.g., "Is this where the book belongs?"). Children from the same background as the teacher understand that they are really being told to put the book on the shelf. Accustomed to directives, children like those from Trackton believe the teacher is offering them a real alternative; that is, they can put the book on the shelf or they can put it somewhere else. Misinterpreting the teacher, these children seem to be disobeying when they don't put the book on the shelf.

Au and Mason (1983) provides another example of cultural differences in language use. These researchers examined the difficulties some teachers encountered during reading lessons with Polynesian children in Hawaii. A common speech event in the culture of these children is the "talk story" in which two or more individuals jointly narrate a story. Accustomed to collective turn taking, the children responded poorly when teachers attempted to enforce the one-speaker-at-a-time rule of mainstream classrooms.

Toward Cultural Continuity in the Classroom

Recognizing that learning styles may differ across cultures, we are still faced with the problem of how to bridge the gap between students' native culture and the culture of the classroom. It is not possible to duplicate every student's home background in the classroom. Nor is it possible, or even desirable, to assimilate every student into the mainstream culture—that would contradict this chapter's approach to cultural diversity. Instead, we might follow a "model of mutual accommodation" (Villegas, 1991). According to this model, both teachers and students adapt their actions to the common goal of academic success with cultural respect. Thus, with Heath's help, Trackton teachers adjusted their questioning strategies to correspond to the type of questions Trackton parents asked. These questions drew many more responses from the children. Then, as the children became more engaged in learning, the teachers taught them how to respond to middle-class question-answer routines.

Helping students accommodate their actions to the culture of the classroom means that teachers must make that culture explicit (Delpit, 1988). The classroom culture is understood and taken for granted by students who share the teacher's cultural background. For students outside that background, however, the classroom culture is not fully understood. Just as traveling in a foreign country is much easier if someone tells the traveler appropriate ways of acting, dressing, and speaking, so, too, students find it much easier to adapt to the classroom culture if the teacher fully explains classroom rules and expectations.

Accommodating the classroom to the students' culture, on the other hand, requires that the teacher know something about that culture. There is no one way to teach culturally diverse students—that would contradict the very notion of *cultural diversity*. Teaching must be adapted to local circumstances. Just as traveling in a foreign country is the best way to learn about another culture, so, too, teachers should visit their students' homes, attend events in their students' communities, and talk with parents and community leaders. As part of inservice or preservice training, teachers should experience ethnicity firsthand through field trips to schools in culturally diverse settings and through teacher exchanges.

Assessment

Providing culturally responsive instructional strategies demands providing culturally responsive assessment strategies as well. For a number of years, educators and researchers have acknowledged that standardized, norm-referenced tests are culturally biased (refer to Chapter Two for a discussion of purposes and types of assessment). Culturally biased means the tests reflect, and thus favor, the dominant culture. Again, as with traditional instruction, students from a white, Anglo, middle-class background tend to perform better on these tests than do students from racial and ethnic minority and lower socioeconomic backgrounds. Results of standardized tests have been used to place nonmainstream students in lower track classes, where instruction typically focuses on decontextualized subskills and bypasses higher level cognitive skills.

Norm-referenced tests are culturally biased in several ways. First, culturally diverse students are generally not represented in norming populations. Students' test scores have meaning only if their background is similar to the background of the student population on which the test was normed. Second, test topics and vocabulary tend to be unfamiliar to culturally diverse students (see Dove Counterbalance Intelligence Test in Figure 9.1). Although publishers have attempted to make their tests more objective and authentic, no test can escape being influenced by the values and experiences of its writers and developers. Third, culturally diverse students tend not to be as testwise as mainstream students; that is, they are not as experienced in the characteristics and formats of tests, such as answering multiple-choice questions, nor are they as experienced in the test-taking situation. For example, working within time limits, especially if they must code switch, is difficult and takes more time. These

---

FIGURE 9.1   THE DOVE COUNTERBALANCE INTELLIGENCE TEST

Directions: *If questions such as the following appeared on an intelligence test, what would your IQ be? The Dove Counterbalance Intelligence Test was written as a tongue-in-cheek example of the cultural bias inherent in standardized intelligence tests. Try answering a few items from this test.*

1. Who did "Stagger" Lee kill (in the famous blues legend)? (a) his mother (b) Frankie (c) Johnny (d) his girlfriend (e) Billy
2. Cheap chitlins (not the kind you purchase at the frozen-food counter) will taste rubbery unless they are cooked long enough. How soon can you quit cooking them to eat and enjoy them? (a) 15 minutes (b) 8 hours (c) 24 hours (d) 1 week (on a low heat or flame) (e) 1 hour
3. What is Willie Mae's last name? (a) Schwartz (b) Matauda (c) Gomez (d) Turner (e) O'Flaherty
4. "Money don't get everything it's true _____" (a) but I don't have none and I'm blue (b) but what it don't get I can't use (c) so make with that you've got (d) but I don't know that and neither do you
5. Many people say the "Juneteenth" (June 19) should be made a legal holiday because this was the day _____. (a) the slaves were freed in the U.S. (b) the slaves were freed in Texas (c) the slaves were freed in Jamaica (d) the slaves were freed in California (e) Martin Luther King was born (f) Booker T. Washington died

---

same criticisms can be applied to commercially produced criterion-referenced tests. Even typical end-of-the-unit or end-of-the-chapter teacher-constructed tests are culturally biased.

Because of the bias inherent in formal standardized tests, informal testing that is flexible and ongoing may be more appropriate for culturally diverse students. The primary purpose in assessing these students should be to determine their strengths and weaknesses and then to tailor instruction to meet their needs. The following methods can be used to provide qualitative information about student achievement that can be used to make instructional decisions.

- **Performance-based testing.** Have students demonstrate their knowledge or mastery of a skill. They might conduct a science experiment, solve a math problem, or draw a picture. You might even use drama as a means of assessing students' understanding.
- **Open-ended responses.** Use probing questions rather than multiple-choice questions. Such questions should encourage students to elaborate on a response using their background of experiences. Encourage students to write their responses. Allow students to respond in their first language if you have access to interpretation.
- **Teacher/student interaction.** If culturally appropriate, dialogue with students.
- **Teacher observation.** Simply watching students' reactions to your instruction—a puzzled look, a frown, or a smile—will often tell you whether or not you need to adjust instruction.

- **Portfolios.** Portfolios are collections of students' work over time. They might include essays, reports, daily work, artwork, audiotapes—almost anything that indicates learning. Various stages of a project, such as rough drafts of an essay, should be included, not just final products. Both students and teachers can select items for the portfolio.
- **Anecdotal records.** Briefly record when individual students accomplish a certain skill or show understanding of a certain concept. Anecdotal records focus on what students can do.

Principles for Dealing With the Culture of the Classroom

In summary, the following principles should be useful as a guide in implementing a model of mutual accommodation.

1. Be explicit with students about the culture operating in the classroom. Don't assume that students possess the same cultural framework as you do.
2. Learn about the cultures to which the students belong in order to expand the classroom culture as a whole.
3. Develop a repertoire of teaching styles (direct, indirect, and collaborative) so that you can teach students in culturally appropriate ways. For example, use cooperative learning groups for students who learn better through peer interaction.
4. Ask questions of students and hear their answers. Instead of making assumptions about why students react or behave or answer as they do, ask them, "Why?" or "What makes you say that?"
5. Provide assessment that is situational—informal, flexible, ongoing practices that help you adjust your instruction to students' needs. Establish a risk-free environment so that students feel at ease in trying new skills, asking questions, or expressing their ideas and opinions.
6. Use a variety of assessment strategies so that there are opportunities for students of diverse backgrounds to succeed.

PRACTICE ACTIVITY 9.4

Read the following anecdote adapted from Garcia (1978). Explain what you would have done if you were the teacher. Compare your response to ours in the answers section.

> Mary Walking Tall, a student from the White Pine reservation, returned to her social studies classroom after lunch. She and her best friend, Leslie, were busy talking as they took their seats next to each other. The teacher began to prepare the class for the weekly quiz on current events.
>
> "Okay, class, it's time to get started," he announced. "Take out a piece of paper and number from 1 to 10. I'm only going to read each question once, so listen carefully."

After reading the third question, the teacher noticed that Mary was whispering to Leslie. "No talking during exams, Mary. If you talk to Leslie again, I'll assume you're cheating and throw your paper in the wastebasket."

After reading the fourth question, the teacher saw Mary pass a note to Leslie. "Mary, what's in that note you're passing to Leslie?"

"I'm just giving Leslie the answers to the questions."

"You're what! You're not supposed to cheat."

"I'm not cheating," exclaimed Mary. "Leslie doesn't know the answers, so I'm just helping her out."

"I'll bet you are," said the teacher, grabbing Mary's paper and tossing it in the wastebasket.

A MULTICULTURAL CURRICULUM

Curriculum refers to the topics studied in the classroom and the materials used to present those topics. This last section describes a multicultural curriculum. It also evaluates current textbooks in relation to multiculturalism and discusses the value of the use of multiethnic literature in subject matter classrooms.

A Multicultural Perspective

As mentioned in the first section, multiculturalism should be an integral part of the curriculum and not an additive. According to Banks (1977), multiculturalism is not merely adding ethnic minority heroes, such as Martin Luther King, Jr., or César Chavez, to the curriculum. The "hero" approach does not describe the total experience of the cultural group. Nor is multiculturalism simply studying the customs and behaviors of ethnic groups. Activities such as building tepees and igloos and preparing ethnic foods tend to reinforce stereotypes and convey the idea that ethnic groups are not integral parts of American society. Nor is multiculturalism black studies for African Americans, Native American studies for Native Americans, Puerto Rican studies for Puerto Ricans. This approach only tends to separate groups further.

A multicultural curriculum goes beyond these approaches to examine issues, events, and concepts from the perspective of more than one culture. In 1992 the United States observed the 500th anniversary of the arrival of Christopher Columbus in America. This quincentennial event is a rich example of a multicultural perspective. As might be expected, in many classrooms across the country teachers led their students in honoring Columbus for his achievement in discovering the New World. According to the traditional viewpoint, Columbus was a hero because he opened the way for the settling of the continent. In other classrooms, however, teachers led their students to see another side to this event—from the viewpoint of Native Americans. To the American Indians, Columbus's arrival meant disease, death, and the destruction of their societies. After reading about the quincentennial event in tradebook selections and newspaper and magazine articles, students took the roles of Europeans and American Indians and debated the pros and cons of Columbus's voyages. They assumed the role of sailors in Columbus's crew or natives on shore and wrote stories and diary entries about the landing from their respective points of view. In some classes students even held a mock trial in which Columbus was accused of genocide, and comparisons were made to other historical events in which genocide occurred.

As much as possible, teachers should incorporate a multicultural perspective into reading and writing activities. Social studies teachers will have many opportunities to help students examine historical events from a variety of viewpoints. For example, the colonial period in American history is usually studied from the viewpoint of the English colonists; but American Indians, African Americans, Spaniards, and other groups were living in America at the time, and students should also read to learn about their experiences. In studying feudalism, students might read about the feudal system in Japan as well as in Europe. English teachers can have students read the stories, poems, and plays of various cultural groups. Literature can be used to discover how diverse groups have interpreted such themes as creation and power. Examples of multicultural reading and writing activities for other subject matter areas include the following.

- **Science.** In studying environmental issues, have students research and report on the ecological perspective of Native Americans, who are known for their reverence of natural resources. Have students hypothesize how some current environmental problems would have been addressed differently if Native Americans had the legislative power to affect U.S. laws.
- **Civics.** Have students find out how many people of color serve in the U.S. Congress, their state legislature, and their local government. They might display their findings in a graph. Discuss reasons for underrepresentation of minorities in governmental bodies and the effect the lack of a minority perspective may have on legislation.
- **Health.** Have students find alcohol and tobacco advertisements featuring racial minorities and blue-collar workers. Discuss issues related to targeting products to these groups.
- **Home economics.** Have students research the attitude of various cultures to food and hospitality. They might compile their information in a class chart. Examine the diets of individuals from various cultural groups, then determine the nutritional value of these diets. Examine health risks or incidents of illnesses among various cultural groups and discuss the relationship between nutrition and health factors.

Textbooks and Multiculturalism

Textbooks have a tremendous impact on what is taught in the classroom. In many instances, they serve as the mainstay for the structure and content of a subject matter course. Thus, it is important to examine how well current textbooks support a multicultural perspective.

During the past 20 years—largely as a result of pressure from the Civil Rights Movement (Banks, 1991)—textbook publishers have done a better job of incorporating cultural diversity. More attention is being paid to the achievements of ethnic and racial minority groups, and there is more sensitivity toward stereotyping these groups. Much still needs to be done, however. Textbooks, by and large, are still predominantly Eurocentric or Americentric; that is, they are written from the perspective of the white, Anglo, middle class.

Inaccuracies regarding other cultures are not uncommon; for example, Chinese and Korean cultures are frequently and inaccurately treated as one and the same. Little space is given to describing the impact of historical events on various groups, such as the Civil War on African Americans. Examples presented in textbooks often do not reflect students' experiences—word problems in a math textbook might talk about people traveling around the world in jet planes when problems about taking the subway might be more meaningful or realistic. In many instances, cultural diversity in textbooks is only cosmetic—photos and artwork might show people of color, but the discourse within the text may not address these groups. The checklist in Figure 9.2 is designed to help you evaluate subject matter textbooks for their treatment of cultural diversity.

Because of the limitations of many textbooks currently in use in the subject matter classroom, the following list highlights ways to supplement or correct a text to facilitate the presentation of a multicultural curriculum.

1. Supplement the text with information from other resources such as films, filmstrips, trade books, magazines, and newspapers. Newspapers and magazines are excellent sources of updated information in all content areas.

2. Ask parents, members of the local community, and the students themselves to comment on or add to information presented in the text. Give students an opportunity to bring their community and their culture to the classroom.

3. Reexamine the topic under study by discussing ways it would apply to the local community.

4. Have students use their notebooks as a forum for responding to their reading in a more personal manner. They might draw correlations between the reading and their own lives, state their feelings about the reading, or think about how a historical event affected them or members of their culture.

5. Address stereotyping directly. Make students aware of the subtle stereotypes contained in the text. This will help students examine their own values. The class does not need to come to consensus on a particular value, but students do need to observe the consequences of stereotypical information and how it affects our society.

6. Encourage class discussion of what is read. This allows for multiple perspectives to emerge. Always ask students to think about who wrote the text and what that person's perspective might be. Help them see that they should not blindly accept everything they see in print.

FIGURE 9.2   CHECKLIST FOR EVALUATING TEXTBOOKS FOR USE IN A
                   MULTICULTURAL CLASSROOM

Does the Textbook . . .

	Yes	No
1. Acknowledge and reflect multiple perspectives where appropriate?	____	____
2. Allocate adequate space for discussing the experiences of ethnic and racial groups (e.g., the slave trade or the detainment of Japanese Americans during World War II)?	____	____
3. Include the achievements of ethnic and minority groups?	____	____
4. Portray ethnic and racial groups accurately and avoid stereotyping?	____	____
5. Use examples that reflect the experiences of culturally diverse students?	____	____
6. Contain photos and artwork showing people of color?	____	____
7. Lend itself to accommodating limited-English-proficiency students (e.g., including photo essays, graphs, and other pictorial aids)?	____	____
8. Include other resources for further reading in specific areas?	____	____
9. Have a clear glossary of terms for nonnative speakers?	____	____
10. Make cultural diversity seem interesting and exciting?	____	____

7. Have students read about a specific topic in several sources. You might divide the class into cooperative learning groups and assign a different resource to each group. Then have the groups come together and discuss similarities and differences in the information presented. Students should see how information can vary across sources and how an author's perspective affects the perception of information.

8. As you use a particular textbook, keep track of inaccuracies, omissions, or offensive statements. Note students' reactions to the material and whether they think particular groups have been treated fairly. Comments might be written on index cards and kept in a file box in the school library for other teachers' reference. (Also note positive things about the text.)

The extent to which textbooks should incorporate cultural diversity is a controversial issue. At one extreme is the view that only one culture should be represented. Eurocentrists, for example, argue that since American institutions are based on Western civilization, students should first of all become literate in the history, literature, and music of Europe. This position recalls the assimilationist argument. At the other extreme is the view that all cultures should be represented. Since more than 100 ethnic groups now make up today's America (Hamilton, 1991), incorporating every group would be difficult and could amount to what has been called "ethnic cheerleading" (Tifft, 1990). Instead of these extremes, the standard perhaps should be to select materials that teach students the skills and knowledge they need to live in a multicultural society and that fairly, accurately, and honestly represent a culturally rich society.

Multicultural Literature

Multicultural literature refers to trade books, both fiction and nonfiction, that portray individuals belonging to nonmainstream ethnic, racial, or socioeconomic groups. Having students read about their own culture helps develop positive attitudes and a sense of dignity and self-worth. Reading about cultures other than their own helps students gain understanding and appreciation of diverse groups. English and social studies teachers in particular might use multiethnic literature to build mutual respect and a sense of community in culturally diverse classrooms. In recommending books for independent reading or in selecting books for class discussion, choose books that approach cultural diversity positively and accurately. Burns et al. (1992) suggest the following guidelines for evaluating multiethnic books.

1. Do the illustrations and text depict the character in the story as a distinct individual or as a stereotype of a particular ethnic group?
2. Do the settings always show conditions of poverty?
3. Are dialects used as a natural part of the story, or are they contrived to reinforce a stereotype?
4. Is the minority culture treated respectfully or portrayed as inferior?
5. Are minorities described authentically?
6. Is there diversity among characters within a particular ethnic group?

Figure 9.3 summarizes reasons for using trade books in subject matter classrooms and lists resources for locating appropriate multicultural literature.

PRACTICE ACTIVITY 9.5

Read the following statements from textbooks. Explain why each statement is inappropriate from a multicultural perspective. Our response is given in the answers section.

1. Thomas Walker was the first man to explore the Cumberland Gap.
2. When the Europeans arrived in North America, there were fewer than 500,000 natives.
3. Father Hennepin helped the Indians learn farming skills so that they could support themselves.

FIGURE 9.3   **WHY USE TRADE BOOKS IN CULTURALLY DIVERSE CONTENT AREA CLASSES?**

- Trade books can motivate students to read. Written on a wide variety of topics, trade books can appeal to individual interests. Students can choose books that appeal to them.
- Trade books are available on a variety of reading levels. While limited-English-proficiency students may not be able to read the class textbook, they may be able to read about the subject in a trade book.
- Trade books help develop critical reading skills. Students learn to analyze printed material by comparing information presented in trade books with information presented in their textbooks.
- Trade books can examine topics in more depth. Since textbooks must cover a wide range of topics, only a limited amount of space can be given to each. Students can extend their knowledge of diverse cultural groups by reading trade books.
- Trade books tend to be more up to date. Since trade books are smaller and easier to produce, they can be published more frequently than textbooks. Trade books can respond more quickly to current issues and events.
- Trade books can make concrete what was abstract. Topics discussed in textbooks become more vivid and meaningful when students read biographies and historical fiction. Students can identify more easily with diverse groups by reading novels, stories, and plays with multicultural characters and settings.
- Trade books can present a variety of perspectives. By reading several books dealing with a specific topic, students can discover varying points of view. Textbooks are often single-sided in describing events and issues.
- Trade books can help students see similarities between historical and modern-day events. For example, a history textbook might describe child labor in the early 1990s; a trade book could help students see parallels to migrant labor today.

For help in identifying and using multicultural trade books, consult the following resources:

Harris, Violet J. (Ed.). (1992). *Teaching multicultural literature in grades K–8.* Norwood, MA: Christopher-Gordon Publishers.

Minnesota Humanities Commission. (1991). *Braided Lives: An anthology of multicultural American writing.* St. Paul: Minnesota Council of Teachers of English.

Stenland, Anna Lee. (1979). *Literature by and about the American Indian: An annotated bibliography* (2d ed.). Urbana, IL: National Council of Teachers of English.

Concluding Remarks

As the United States becomes even more culturally and linguistically diverse, teachers increasingly will need to be cognizant of the variety of values, experiences, and learning styles that students bring to the classroom. This chapter has not presented a single formula or recipe for teaching subject matter content to diverse groups. Instead, it has attempted to make you sensitive to the needs and achievements of nonmainstream students so that you can make wise instructional decisions for your situation. The chapter has also encouraged you to establish a multicultural classroom—a classroom that celebrates and values a variety of cultural perspectives and encourages students to share their cultural identity with you and their peers. Teaching in a culturally diverse classroom will require careful preparation—but, then, good teaching has always required this. As we have noted, many of the activities presented throughout this book will enhance a multicultural perspective as you engage students in learning activities in your subject matter classroom. As you integrate these activities in your curriculum, we encourage you to consider their value not only in promoting students' learning but in enhancing appreciation of your students' cultural diversity.

Reflections

1. Research current and projected ethnic, racial, and socioeconomic demographics for your school district. You might illustrate this information with charts and graphs. Is the population of your district becoming more culturally diverse? If so, what is being done to meet the needs of this changing population?
2. Interview an ESL teacher. Discuss materials and methods used to instruct second-language speakers. Ask how subject matter teachers can help ESL students learn content as well as improve their language skills.
3. Find out more about the grammar of a dialect present in your community. Prepare a list of rules implicit in this dialect. Include a list of vocabulary words common in the dialect.
4. Visit a culturally diverse classroom. Observe whether or not the teacher's instructional style and communication patterns differ from those of the traditional classroom. Discuss your findings with your peers.
5. Read about Marva Collins and Jaime Escalante, two teachers famous for their ability to motivate culturally diverse students, or interview teachers or administrators in your community about teachers who are able to motivate culturally diverse students. Write a report describing the characteristics and teaching style of these successful teachers.
6. Research current educational programs or models of instruction that seem to be meeting the needs of culturally diverse students. Share your findings with your peers.

7. Along with two or three of your peers, assume that you are a member of a textbook selection committee for your local school district. Using cooperative learning techniques, evaluate textbooks currently on the market for their treatment of diverse cultures. Contact a local school district to obtain minutes of their textbook committees or the district's criteria for textbook adoption. Examine this information to determine their procedures for dealing with various cultures.

8. Design a multicultural reading or writing activity for your subject matter area. Share this product with your peers.

9. Read one or more fiction books featuring a minority character or culture. Write a description of this character's portrayal in the text.

10. Explore your own cultural perspective on such topics as the organization of the family, interaction between adults and children, the role of women in society, the importance of work, attitude toward material possessions, and attitude toward the environment. Discuss your perspective with your peers.

REFERENCES

Alexander, C. F. (1980). Black English dialect and the classroom teacher. *The Reading Teacher, 33,* 571–577.

Allen, V. G. (1991). Teaching bilingual and ESL children. In J. Flood, J. M. Jensen, D. Lapp, & J. R. Squire (Eds.), *Handbook of research on teaching the English language arts.* New York: Macmillan.

American Council on Education and the Education Commission of the States. (1988). *One-third of a nation: A report of the Commission on Minority Participation in Education and American Life.* Washington, DC: American Council on Education.

Au, K. H., & Mason, J. M. (1983). Cultural congruence in classroom participation structures: Achieving a balance of rights. *Discourse Processes, 6,* 145–167.

Banks, J. A. (1977). *Multiethnic education: Practices and promises.* Bloomington, IN: Phi Delta Kappa Educational Foundation.

———. (1991). Multicultural literacy and curriculum reform. *Educational Horizons, 69,* 135–140.

Bean, T. W. (1978). Decoding strategies of Hawaiian Islands dialect speakers in grades 4, 5, 6. *Reading World, 17,* 295–305.

Beaton, A. E. (1986). *National Assessment of Educational Progress 1983–1984: A technical report.* Princeton, NJ: Educational Testing Service.

Brown, R. W., Copi, I. M., Dulaney, D. E., Frankena, W. K., Henle, P., & Stevenson, C. I. (1958). *Language, thought, and culture.* Ann Arbor: University of Michigan Press.

Burns, P. C., Roe, B. D., & Ross, E. P. (1992). *Teaching reading in today's elementary school.* Boston: Houghton Mifflin.

Cummins, J. (1979). Linguistic interdependence and the educational development of bilingual children. *Review of Educational Research, 49,* 222–251.

———. (1980). The cross-lingual dimensions of language proficiency: Implications for bilingual education and the optimal age issue. *TESOL Quarterly, 14,* 175–187.

Delain, M. T., Pearson, P. D., & Anderson, R. C. (1985). Reading comprehension and creativity in black language use: You stand to gain by playing the sounding game! *American Educational Research Journal, 22,* 155–173.

Delpit, L. D. (1988). The silenced dialogue: Power and pedagogy in educating other people's children. *Harvard Educational Review, 58,* 280–298.

Dulay, H., & Burt, M. (1977). Remarks on creativity in language acquisition. In M. Burt & M. Finocciaro (Eds.), *Viewpoints on English as a second language.* New York: Newbury House.

Erickson, F., & Mohatt, G. (1982). Cultural organization of participation structures in two classrooms of Indian students. In G. B. Spindler (Ed.), *Doing the ethnography of schooling: Educational anthropology in action.* New York: Holt, Rinehart & Winston.

Flores, B., Tefft Cousin, P., & Diaz, E. (1991). Transforming deficit myths about learning, language, and culture. *Language Arts, 68,* 369–379.

Fries, C. C. (1945). *Teaching and learning English.* Ann Arbor: University of Michigan Press.

Garcia, E. E. & Padilla, R. V. (Eds.). (1985). *Advances in bilingual education research.* Tucson: University of Arizona Press.

Garcia, R. L. (1978). *Fostering a pluralistic society through multi-ethnic education.* Bloomington, IN: Phi Delta Kappa Educational Foundation.

Goodman, K. S. (1969a). Dialect barriers to reading comprehension. In J. C. Baratz & R. W. Shuy (Eds.), *Teaching black children to read.* Washington, DC: Center for Applied Linguistics.

———. (1969b). Analysis of oral reading miscues: Applied psycholinguistics. *Reading Research Quarterly, 5,* 9–30.

Goodman, K. S., & Buck, C. (1973). Dialect barriers to reading comprehension revisited. *The Reading Teacher, 27,* 6–12.

Goodman, Y. M. (1968). A psycholinguistic description of observed oral reading phenomena in selected young beginning readers. (Doctoral dissertation, Wayne State University, 1967). *Dissertation Abstracts International, 29,* 60A.

Griffin, P., & Cole, M. (1987). New technologies, basic skills, and the underside of education: What's to be done? In J. A. Langer (Ed.), *Language, literacy, and culture: Issues of society and schooling.* Norwood, NJ: Ablex.

Hamilton, D. (1991, January 31). L.A. district examines new textbooks amid charges that the state-approved series is flawed by cultural biases. *Los Angeles Times,* p. B1.

Heath, S. B. (1983). *Ways with words: Language, life, and work in communities and classrooms.* London: Cambridge.

Hudelson, S. (1984). Kan yu ret an rayt en Ingles: Children become literate in English as a second language. *TESOL Quarterly, 18,* 221–238.

Krashen, S. (1981). *Second language acquisition and second language learning.* Oxford, England: Pergamon.

Lewis, A. C. (1991). Washington news. *Education Digest, 56,* 51–53.

Lipson, M. Y. (1983). The influence of religious affiliation on children's memory for text information. *Reading Research Quarterly, 18,* 448–457.

Means, B., & Knapp, M. S. (1991). Cognitive approaches to teaching advanced skills to educationally disadvantaged students. *Phi Delta Kappan, 73,* 282–289.

Moll, L. C., & Diaz, S. (1987). Changes as the goal of educational research. *Anthropology and Education Quarterly, 18,* 300–311.

National Assessment of Educational Progress. (1985). *The reading report card.* Princeton, NJ: Educational Testing Service.

National Education Association. (1992, July 7). Few men, minorities are public school teachers. *Minneapolis Star Tribune,* p. 7a.

Pallas, A. M., Natriello, G., & McDill, E. L. (1989). The changing nature of the disadvantaged population. *Educational Researcher, 18,* 16–22.

Philips, S. (1972). Participant structures and communicative competence: Warm Springs children in community and classroom. In C. Cazden, V. P. John, & D. Hymes (Eds.), *Functions of language in the classroom.* New York: Teachers College Press.

———. (1983). *The invisible culture: Communication in classroom and community on the Warm Springs Indian Reservation.* New York: Longman.

Reyes, M., & Molner, L. (1991). Instructional strategies for second-language learners in the content areas. *Journal of Reading, 35*, 96–103.

Reynolds, R. E., Taylor, M. A., Steffenson, M. S., Shirey, L. L., & Anderson, R. C. (1982). Cultural schemata and reading comprehension. *Reading Research Quarterly, 17*, 353–366.

Richards, J. J. (1991). Commentary. In B. Means, C. Cheemer, & M. S. Knapp (Eds.), *Teaching advanced skills to at-risk students: Views from theory and practice*. San Francisco: Jossey-Bass.

Rigg, P. S. (1975). A psycholinguistic analysis of the oral reading miscues generated by speakers of a rural black dialect compared to the miscues of speakers of an urban black dialect. (Doctoral dissertation, Wayne State University, 1974). *Dissertation Abstracts International, 35*, 7624A.

———. (1981). Beginning to read in English the LEA way. In C. W. Twyford, W. Diehl, & K. Feathers (Eds.), *Reading English as a second language: Moving from theory*. Bloomington, IN: Indiana University.

Schlosser, L. K. (1992). Teacher distance and student disengagement: School lives on the margin. *Journal of Teacher Education, 43*, 128–140.

Simpson, R. J. (1992, January). Education 2000: A peek into the future. *USA Today Magazine*, pp. 86–88.

Sims, R. (1972). A psycholinguistic description of miscues generated by selected young readers during the oral reading of text material in black dialect and standard English (Doctoral dissertation, Wayne State University, 1972). *Dissertation Abstracts International, 33*, 2089A.

Sleeter, C. E. (1992). Restructuring schools for multicultural education. *Journal of Teacher Education, 43*, 141–148.

Tifft, S. (1990, September 24). Of, by and for—whom? *Time*, p. 95.

Urzua, C. (1987). "You stopped too soon": Second language children composing and revising. *TESOL Quarterly, 21*, 279–304.

U.S. Bureau of the Census. (1991). *Statistical abstract of the United States* (11th ed.). Washington, DC: Author.

Villegas, A. M. (1991). *Culturally responsive pedagogy for the 1990s and beyond*. Princeton, NJ: Educational Testing Service.

Wong Fillmore, L. (1986). Research currents: Equity or excellence. *Language Arts, 63*, 474–481.

Answers to Practice Activities

Chapter One

Practice Activity 1.1

There are a number of instructional techniques and activities to facilitate students learning. Here is a partial list of activities to prepare students for learning, to assist them while they are engaged in the learning task, and to extend students' thinking after the lesson.

Preparing to Learn

- Discuss key vocabulary used in the lesson.
- Present key ideas or concepts to enhance students' background knowledge.
- Establish discussion groups in which students can identify from their prior knowledge information that relates to the lesson; allow students the opportunity to generate a written summary of their ideas.
- Present a film, videotape, or other form of visual display that will acquaint students with concepts contained in the lesson.
- Ask students to respond to a series of statements that address concepts, values, or beliefs contained in the lesson.

As Students Are Learning

- Present students with questions that direct their attention to the lesson content.
- Direct students to work in cooperative groups to examine and respond to questions they may generate as they engage in the lesson.
- Ask students to generate their own questions as they engage in the lesson—these questions can then be examined and discussed by the class as a whole at the completion of the lesson.
- Present students with higher level thinking questions that force them to go beyond the literal information in the lesson.

At the Conclusion of the Lesson

- Have students give written summaries of what they learned.
- Initiate a classroom discussion to clarify lesson objectives and extend understanding.

- Direct students to obtain additional information on the lesson content from sources they believe to be useful—this information can be used to extend understanding through discussions, demonstrations, or writing activities.
- Apply the lesson content to real-world activities or events.

Practice Activity 1.2

Responding to the stated goal, your attention should have been directed to information pertaining to gutters. As you encountered information on downspouts, that information was localized and examined to determine if it aided you in accomplishing your goal. You may also have noted voids in your understanding of metal or wood gutters at the conclusion of the reading. To obtain additional information, it may have been necessary to reread. It is likely that you drew on prior knowledge before, during, and after reading. Prior to reading, you may have attempted to note the durability of metal and wood, particularly if you live in an area of the country that has extremes in weather. During reading, you most likely constructed a better understanding of the durability of metal gutters, and an understanding that wood gutters are more difficult to install and maintain. After reading, you may have realized that metal is most likely stronger, requires less maintenance to maintain its visual appearance, and is less expensive (presuming you have some sense of the cost of clear cedar, cypress, and redwood). You may also have noticed that given a purpose for reading, your attention was focused on goal-directed information. Finally, lacking the figures that are referenced in the reading, you most likely had to fill in that omission with some sort of visual image from prior experience, or you may have reread that section in an attempt to create some sort of visual image.

There is one more mental scheme you may have experienced in the preceding example of metacognition: noncompliance. Gutters, for most of us, are not a particularly stimulating topic. Lacking a commitment to carrying out the goal as described, you may have decided to proceed to the next heading, thinking that the discussion of the example had concluded.

Practice Activity 1.3

This example demonstrates the importance of automaticity in the reading process. By inverting the words, your automatic recognition of words was reduced; as a result, your fluency and comprehension were likely reduced. In fact, you may have sounded somewhat like a remedial reader. You also may have noticed that on the first reading you had little recall other than a few isolated facts; your understanding of the gist of the reading was likely to have been limited. Due to the inverted text, you may have found that certain words were processed at the level of individual letters or letter clusters to construct a pronunciation. Again, when this occurred, your processing of the text was slowed and your comprehension of the sentence fragmented. By the third trial, the context had become more familiar, as had the rather unique "shape" of the words. You most likely doubled your rate from the first trial, and by the conclusion of the third trial you may have constructed a relatively sound understanding of the passage.

CHAPTER TWO

Practice Activity 2.1

Yes; percentile scores are sensitive to the performance of students at a specific grade level.

Yes; in a normal distribution of scores, the average raw score represents the 50th percentile.

No; stanines range from 1 to 9 and represent an unequal number of scores in each stanine.

Yes; if a test has a large standard error of measurement, care should be taken in using these scores for curricular or instructional decisions.

No; a standardized, norm-referenced achievement test is not a good measure of a student's mastery of the various skills or content taught in a subject matter area.

Practice Activity 2.2

Until relatively recent times, displaying one's suntan was not an attribute widely accepted by the population. In fact, for many years having a suntan denoted one as a laborer. Over time, however, a <u>suntan</u> became fashionable as those <u>who</u> could afford to travel <u>could</u> maintain their tan by <u>sunning</u> in distant locations. More <u>re-cently</u>, however, many individuals in <u>the</u> medical community have warned <u>that</u> excessive sun can cause <u>melanoma</u>, premature aging of the <u>skin</u>, and small wartlike growths. <u>An</u> individual's resistance to the <u>amount</u> of sun is determined <u>by</u> the thickness of the <u>skin</u> and the amount of <u>melanin</u>. Individuals who have thicker <u>skin</u> are less likely to <u>burn</u>. The extent of the <u>natural</u> color is determined by <u>melanin</u>, a human skin pigment. <u>The</u> skin pigment is made <u>of</u> skin cells called melanocytes. <u>It</u> is these cells that <u>produce</u> melanin, the pigment that <u>protects</u> the skin from the <u>harmful</u> rays of the sun. <u>Individuals</u> who have large concentrations <u>of</u> melanin are less likely <u>to</u> be affected by the <u>sun's</u> rays. Suntan as well <u>as</u> sunburn is caused by <u>the</u> invisible ultraviolet rays of <u>the</u> sun. These UV rays <u>are</u> the most intense between 10:00 A.M. and 2:00 P.M., at which time the sun's rays are less likely to be deflected by the earth's atmosphere. The effects of the sun are particularly strong the first time one is outdoors after a prolonged period of time indoors, such as the winter months. For those individuals who burn quickly, the first exposure to the sun should be limited to no more than 15 minutes a day. During subsequent exposures, the duration of exposure can be increased by increments of 15 minutes. Protection from the sun's UV rays can be obtained from sunscreens. These products contain chemicals to screen out portions of light in the UV spectrum to prevent the skin from burning.

Practice Activity 2.3

Part 1: Components of a Textbook

1. Page 162
2. No. It only addresses the problems of maintaining the ideal weight.
3. Page 133

Part 2: Reference Skills

1. Encyclopedias
2. Databases that provide references on nutrition
3. Government publications
4. Card catalog or computerized card catalog

Part 3: Vocabulary Knowledge and Strategies

1. **heredity:** b. one's genetic makeup
2. **malfunction:** a. not working correctly
   obesity: b. being overweight
   noncaloric: prefix: non = not   **root:** caloric = having calories
   undernutrition: prefix: under = less than   **root:** nutrition = available vitamins, minerals, fats, proteins
   appetite: a desire for food or drink
   diet: food and drink considered in terms of nutritional qualities

Part 4: Comprehension

1. Fats and protein have the greatest satiety value.
2. Diets that have a balance of carbohydrates, proteins, and fats are the best for most people because they are less likely to become monotonous and because they provide an appropriate level of nutrients for maintaining health and weight.
3. Losing weight involves more than watching what you eat. If your body has a set point, you must lower the set point. This means that you must burn more calories through exercise. Many diets don't work for long periods of time because once individuals have lost weight, they will go back to their normal weight established by the set point.

CHAPTER THREE

Practice Activity 3.1

Words for 8th Graders

fling: a new meaning
rationale number: a new word for a known concept
pneumonia: a word in students' oral vocabularies
finite: a new concept

Words for 11th Graders

fluke: a new word
languish: a new word for a known concept
fugue: a new concept
taxonomy: a new concept

Practice Activity 3.2

Words for Junior High Students

Harmony is likely to be at the acquainted level.
Languid is likely be at the unknown level.
Fast food is almost certainly at the in-depth level.
Triangle is likely to be at the established level.

Words for Senior High Students

Examinations is almost certainly at the in-depth level.
Pi is likely to be at the established level.
Erstwhile is likely be at the unknown level.
Aerobic is likely to be at the acquainted level.

Practice Activity 3.3

_____ sensationalist   a. not favoring a particular side
_____ surreal   b. fantastic and unreal
_____ inflated   c. increased beyond what it should be
_____ neutral   d. poorly organized
                           e. designed to arouse strong reaction

Practice Activity 3.4

1. Semantic Map Activity

Reactions to Fearful Places

terror	cemetery
fainting	forest
screaming	haunted house
shaking	cave
running	dark alley
freezing	deserted island

FEAR

Antonyms	**Synonyms**
certainty	horror
courage	fright
boldness	dread
confidence	alarm
assurance	panic

2. Frayer Model Activity

1. **Define the new concept with its necessary attributes.**   A textbook is a book specifically written to be used for formal instruction in a particular subject.

2. **Distinguish between the new concept and similar but different concepts with which it might be mistaken.**   Nonfiction books that are written for the general public, workbooks and worksheets in which you write responses to various questions and exercises, and instructions that come with products are not considered textbooks.

3. **Give examples of the concept, and explain why they are examples.**   *A Nation Grows* (Scholastic, 1987), *Exploring American History* (Globe, 1986), *Chemistry* (Addison-Wesley, 1987), *World Geography* (Glencoe, 1989), *Keys to Reading and Study Skills* (Holt, Rinehart & Winston, 1985), and *Literature* (McDougal, Littell, & Company, 1984). All of these are texts specifically constructed for use by secondary students in typical high school classes.

4. **Give nonexamples of the concept, and explain why they are nonexamples.**   *Robinson Crusoe* by Daniel Defoe: This is a novel, a fictional work written primarily to entertain the reader. *All the President's Men* by Carl Bernstein and Bob Woodward: This is a nonfiction work designed primarily to inform and written for individuals to read on their own. *New York Times:* This is a newspaper. *Newsweek:* This is a weekly news magazine.

5. **Present students with examples and nonexamples, ask them to identify which are and are not instances of the concept and to state why, then give feedback.**

Washington Post (nonexample)
TV Guide (nonexample)
Adventures in Reading, published by Harcourt Brace Jovanovich (example)
America, America, published by Scott, Foresman (example)

3. Semantic Grid Activity

	Characteristics					
Planet	**Closer to Sun Than Earth**	**Larger Than Earth**	**Has Moon(s)**	**Has Rings**	**Orbits the Sun**	**Inner Planet**
Earth	−	−	+	−	+	+
Jupiter	−	+	+	+	+	−
Mars	−	−	+	−	+	+
Mercury	+	−	−	−	+	+
Neptune	−	+	+	+	+	−
Pluto	−	−	+	−	+	−
Saturn	−	+	+	+	+	−
Uranus	−	+	+	+	+	−
Venus	+	−	+	−	+	+

4. Answers will vary.

5. Available Concept or New Concept?

12th grade   *medium*   sources of information, such as print,
                                                            television, and radio
This almost certainly represents an easily available concept.

7th grade   *review*   a critical report
Here, the difficulty of teaching the new meaning depends on whether you
want students to know that a *review* is a critical report or to be able to write
a critical report. Simply teaching the meaning only requires students to deal
with an easily available concept, while teaching the procedure requires
concept learning.

7th grade   *issue*   children
Here, the concept is readily available.

12th grade   *force*   the capacity to do work or cause change
If you want students to do something other than parrot a definition, concept
teaching is going to be necessary in this case.

9th grade   *scan*   to mark poetic meter
Here again, the difficulty of teaching the new meaning depends on whether
you want students to know what it means to scan a piece of poetry or to
actually be able to do it. Both tasks are difficult, but the latter is even more
difficult. Teaching the meaning may well require students to learn the
concept of meter, which is not an easy one to learn. On the other hand,
teaching the procedure of scanning poetry to determine its meter would be
time-consuming.

Practice Activity 3.5

Answers will vary.

Practice Activity 3.6

Answers will vary.

CHAPTER FOUR

Practice Activity 4.1

Economic Costs	Environmental Costs	Health Costs
Cleanup	Destruction of animals and plants	Polluted water
Polluted water supply		supply
Reduced tourism		

Chapter Five

Practice Activity 5.1

"How can China become more industrialized?" is the pivotal question. Developing mineral resources is one way China can become more industrialized and improve its economy; thus, Question 2 focuses on the learning objective. This question could be asked first. Questions 1 and 3 may need to be asked to support Question 2. They would serve as emerging questions.

Practice Activity 5.2

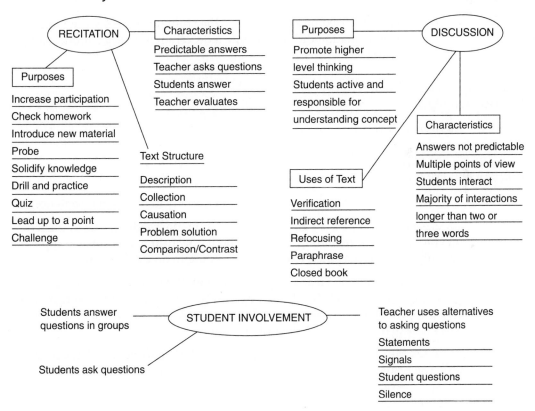

Practice Activity 5.3

Richard and Lori used at least the following strategies to guide their reading:

1. Thinking about what they already know about the topic.
2. Identifying the purpose for reading (listing the problem).

3. Generating questions.
4. Thinking about what they need to know to respond to questions.
5. Predicting from the graphics and headings.
6. Consulting other sources when they realized they were having comprehension problems.
7. Modifying their original questions.

Practice Activity 5.4

Answers will vary.

Practice Activity 5.5

The explanation focused on *what* strategy the students were learning and *how* to use it. The explanation did not include a description of *why* summarizing is helpful and *when* to use it.

Practice Activity 5.6

Answers will vary.

Practice Activity 5.7

1. *Right There.* The answer can be found directly in the second sentence.

2. *Think and Search.* To answer this question, the reader needs to go across several sentences, including the one about rewarding the antsy puppy for bending its hind legs and the one about needing to do this a few times.

3. *Author and You.* To answer this question, the reader needs to use his or her background knowledge as well as information in the text. The text states that puppies should be rewarded. From background knowledge, the reader will know that rewards are generally food treats.

4. *On My Own.* The reasons puppies should learn to sit are not given in the text. The reader must rely totally on his or her background knowledge.

Practice Activity 5.8

While Ms. Andres designed questions that matched her goal of application of the material, she did not focus on the characteristics of the text or of her students that would help or hinder her students. Her instruction does not seem likely to result in the students' successful application of the concept of sets. Ms. Trujillo, on the other hand, carefully considered the text in relation to the learning goal and what she knew about her students; from this, she was able to design instruction that provided the support they needed as well as actively engage them in the reading process as they worked toward successfully meeting the goal. She attended carefully to the needs of students with reading difficulties. Her plan to use alternative sources, study questions, and discussion, as well as her cooperative grouping considerations, provided the means for these students to comprehend and apply the material.

CHAPTER SIX

Practice Activity 6.1

In this example, the first question is relatively easy to answer if you have the requisite background knowledge: Acid rain would fall without pollutants produced from fossil fuels. Lightning and the decomposition of organic matter, for example, contribute to the production of acid rain. According to our definition, answering this question requires critical thinking because the reader must comprehend the definition of fossil fuels, know that burning fossil fuels contribute to acid rain, and understand what sources other than fossil fuels contribute to the production of acid rain. Some of this information must be accessed from prior knowledge, while other information can be obtained from the paragraph. The second question, also requiring critical thinking, is more difficult. The reader must be selective in gathering a greater amount of information from prior knowledge (more industries and homes in the East burn types of fossil fuels that pollute more than natural gas, which is prevalent in the West and South), and must be able to relate that knowledge to information in the reading (factories contributed to the increase in acid rain, the burning of fossil fuels increases acid rain). Note how both questions require much more than the recognition or retrieval of literal information.

Practice Activity 6.2

In this problem the amount of liquid in the two containers is identical. To solve this problem, you need to determine the amount of volume available in each container and the actual volume of the milk. If the container's volume is greater than the milk's, then space is wasted. Note that the top of the milk container (the fold-out spout) is empty space. Another factor in this problem is the packing of the containers. The pyramidlike containers fit neatly together with no wasted space, while the common half-pint containers do not.

Practice Activity 6.3

The following elements of everyday problems were found in the stereo problem.

1. **In everyday problem solving, it is not clear what information will be needed to solve a given problem.** In this case, the seventh grader was

not certain the existing cassette and headphones could be used with the component system. Not recognizing this, the student faced the problem of either buying the affordable system or delaying the purchase.

2. **The solutions to everyday problems depend on the information you know and strategies you use to solve the problem.** Again, the student was not aware of the potential to run the cassette with the integrated system, or could continue to use the headphones rather than purchase speakers.

Practice Activity 6.4

There are several possible solutions to this problem. One involves separating the balls into groups of four. The first two groups are placed on the scale (four balls on each side). If the scale balances, the oddball is not among the eight balls being weighed. If on the first weighing the scale does not balance, remove one group and place another on the scale. If the scale now balances, the oddball is in the group set aside. If the scale still does not balance, the oddball is on the side of the scale where the balls have not been replaced. The group containing the oddball can now be halved, as can the group on the other side (which now serves as the "standard" weight). The balls in the oddball group can now be weighed against the standard, and through a process of elimination the oddball will be identified.

CHAPTER SEVEN

Practice Activities 7.1–7.10

Answers will vary.

Practice Activity 7.11

	Low							High
Knowledge of primary crops grown in the Midwest	1	2	3	4	5	**6**	7	8
Ability to recognize climatic and soil conditions for crop production in the U.S.	1	2	3	**4**	5	6	7	8
Ability to define conditions contributing to the decline of family farms	1	2	3	4	5	6	7	**8**

This is a well-written piece. The section on the decline of the family farm is very complete, and we gave it a high rank of 8. The section on primary crops of the Midwest is also good, but the student says nothing about the relative size of those crops, so we did not rate that as high. The section on climate and soil conditions said nothing on soil, so we ranked it slightly below the midpoint of the scale.

Practice Activity 7.12

Sample 1

	Low		Middle		High
General Merit					
Content	1	**2**	3	4	5
Organization	1	2	**3**	4	5
Clarity	1	2	**3**	4	5
Word Choice	1	2	**3**	4	5
Mechanics					
Grammar and Usage	1	2	3	4	**5**
Punctuation	1	2	3	**4**	5
Spelling	1	2	3	4	**5**

Sample 1 contains a few important concepts, and all of the content is related to the central idea. However, after the first few sentences it trails off in a set of observations that are neither fully explained nor necessarily the most important points to make. We gave it a 2 on content, although we could also have given a 3. It is organized reasonably well, so we gave it a 3 on organization. It is not always clear (e.g., the need for trees isn't explained), so we gave it a 3 on clarity. Finally, word choice is adequate, so we gave it a 3 on word choice. In terms of general merit, our assessment is that it is an average paper. With respect to mechanics, we ranked it higher. We saw no errors in grammar, usage, or spelling, and awarded it a 5 in those categories. Several introductory phrases could usefully be set off with commas and are not, so we gave it a 4 on punctuation.

Sample 2

	Low		Middle		High
General Merit					
Content	1	2	3	4	**5**
Organization	1	2	3	4	**5**
Clarity	1	2	3	**4**	5
Word choice	1	2	3	4	**5**
Mechanics					
Grammar and Usage	1	2	3	4	**5**
Punctuation	1	2	3	4	**5**
Spelling	1	2	3	4	**5**

Sample 2 is considerably stronger than Sample 1. It contains a number of important concepts, the writing is well organized, the paper is clear, and the word choice is appropriate to the general topic. Importantly, the paper shows the student's strong understanding of cause-and-effect relationships and a generally high level of conceptualization. In terms of general merit, we gave it top marks for everything except clarity. With respect to clarity, we thought that some matters (e.g., what gases besides carbon dioxide are harmful, what ozone is, and how ultraviolet rays are dangerous) might be more fully explained. With respect to mechanics, we gave the paper top marks on every count. We found no grammatical, spelling, or punctuation errors. All in all, we found this a very well written short essay.

CHAPTER EIGHT

Practice Activity 8.1

1. **Positive Interdependence.** The two of us writing this book constitute a definite instance of positive interdependence. Neither of us has the expertise to do the book alone, and neither of us had the time to get the book done by the target date. Together, though, we did it, and we both know that we could not have done it alone.

2. **Promotive Interaction.** Face-to-face promotive interaction can be shown by something as simple as a nod of agreement, a smile of encouragement, or an okay signaled by the thumb and forefinger. Simple, quick, and unobtrusive as such responses are, they mean a lot.

3. **Individual Accountability.** In typical classrooms today, students are almost always individually accountable. They are individually accountable for a lot—for getting to class on time, for paying attention during class, for doing their work, and for passing quizzes and exams. The latter, of course, is the most frequent method of requiring individual accountability.

4. **Interpersonal Skills.** There are probably a number of jobs in which small-group skills are not needed, but interpersonal skills are almost always needed. We certainly need them in our work as teachers. Administrators need them, whether they are school officials or business and industry leaders. Barbers and beauticians need them. Salespeople certainly need them. Travel agents need them. And executives of all sorts and at all levels need them. There are not, in fact, many jobs in which interpersonal skills are not needed.

5. **Group Processing.** In our jobs as university teachers, we do a lot of group work. It is not very unusual to have three or four small group meetings a day. And how often do we process our group work? In our collective years as university teachers, neither of us can remember a time when group processing was a part of our group work. On reflection, we think this is a shame. Obviously, without processing our group work, the chances that it will become more effective are much reduced.

Practice Activity 8.2

Theoretical support for cooperative work comes from Vygotsky's (1987) notion of the zone of proximal development, the notion that teaching something is an excellent way to learn it, and the notion of metacognition. Areas in which students working cooperatively have outperformed others include academic achievement, self-esteem, accommodation to others, attitudes toward school, interpersonal relationships, and higher level skills.

Practice Activity 8.3

Formal cooperative learning groups are heterogeneous groups of three or four students who work together on a project over several class sessions. These groups incorporate all five defining characteristics of cooperative learning.

Student Teams–Achievement Divisions are heterogeneous groups of four students who study together, are quizzed individually, and receive individual and group points based on the extent to which they exceed their previous scores.

Jigsaw groups are heterogeneous groups of 6 or so students operating in a class of 30. Each student in a group is given part of an assignment, learns the material in cooperation with the students from the other groups who have been given the same part of the assignment, then teaches that part to his or her group. Finally, students take individual quizzes on the entire assignment.

Base groups are long-term, heterogeneous groups of four or so students who typically remain together for a semester or year and provide support, encouragement, and assistance to each other.

Informal cooperative groups are temporary pairs of students who work together for a single class session to master the material of a lecture.

In assigning students to groups, the principal criterion is that the groups be heterogeneous—made up of students of different genders, social classes, abilities, and races. In addition, students should be able to work together. It would seldom be appropriate to put all students who are inattentive in the same group.

Practice Activity 8.4

Declarative knowledge is knowledge about things, knowing, for example, that the Civil War ended in 1865. Procedural skills are the skills a person needs to actually do something; a skilled welder or the driver of a car displays procedural skills. So, too, do students who can function well in cooperative groups.

The guidelines for teaching a procedural skill are (1) teaching students what the skill is, (2) having them actually engage in the skill, (3) giving them feedback on their performance, and (4) giving them sufficient opportunities to practice.

Practice Activity 8.5

Forming skills are the beginning or prerequisite skills that students need just for groups to function; they include talking quietly. Functioning skills are those that students use as they work in groups; they include paraphrasing others' responses. Formulating skills are the role or functions that group members have in their groups; they include roles such as summarizing the group's learning.

Practice Activity 8.6

Answers will vary.

Practice Activity 8.7

- Show students the need for cooperative skills.
- Make sure that students thoroughly understand each skill.
- Have students practice the skills.
- Make certain that students process their group work.
- Ensure that students continue work on the skills over time.

Our belief is that these guidelines are broadly applicable for teaching in situations in which we as teachers know the answers to the questions we are asking, understand the concepts we are teaching, or know how we want the skill performed. They are less widely applicable when the answers to the questions are unclear, the concepts are fuzzy, or the skill can be performed in a variety of ways.

Practice Activity 8.8

Answers will vary.

Practice Activity 8.9

Answers will vary.

CHAPTER NINE

Practice Activity 9.1

There are no right or wrong answers. The purpose of the exercise is to help you think about your own response to culturally diverse students. If you were able to rank these students, then consider the attitudes, values, and perceptions underlying your decisions. For example, you might feel most uncomfortable having a homeless student in class because of the instability you perceive in this child's life or the difficulty this child might have fitting in with middle-class children. Another teacher might not see having a homeless child in class as a problem.

Practice Activity 9.2

Answers will vary. You might introduce the topic by demonstrating photosynthesis or by asking students to describe their experiences with growing flowers or vegetables. Hispanic students might read about the process in simplified texts. The one who is the most proficient in English could explain the concept to the others. The class could work in linguistically heterogeneous cooperative learning groups to discuss the text and answer questions. They could work in cross-language pairs to draw diagrams of the photosynthesis process.

Practice Activity 9.3

Vignette 1. This is a risk-free environment in which the student feels free to speak in her nonstandard dialect. It's also an environment in which the teacher has been explicit about the difference between standard and nonstandard dialects. The teacher and student have developed a rapport—the student knows the teacher is not making fun of her.

Vignette 2. This interaction takes place within the context of instruction, whereas the preceding interaction takes place spontaneously. In Vignette 2 the teacher is more interested in assessing the student's understanding of content. Asking the student to rephrase his answer in standard English might discourage him—and others—from responding. If the teacher wants students to practice standard English, he should state this at the outset of discussion.

Practice Activity 9.4

The teacher should have considered Mary's cultural background before judging her actions. As a Native American, Mary has probably been taught to share her things and put others ahead of herself. Competition and individual accomplishment are foreign to many native cultures. The teacher might have ignored Mary's whispering and later spoken to her privately about her actions.

Practice Activity 9.5

1. The statement should read that Thomas Walker was the first white man to explore the Cumberland Gap. The likelihood that Native Americans were the first people to walk there should be acknowledged.

2. This statement may suggest that since there were fewer than 500,000 Native Americans it was all right for the Europeans to take over their land.
3. This statement suggests that the Indians had not been able to support themselves before the arrival of Father Hennepin, which, of course, would not be true.

ABOUT THE AUTHORS

Randall Ryder received his Ph.D. from the University of Minnesota in 1978. Prior to this he was a Title I reading teacher in the Poudre R-1 School District in Fort Collins, Colorado. He currently is a Professor in the Department of Curriculum and Instruction at the University of Wisconsin—Milwaukee where he teaches courses in content area reading and secondary developmental reading. His research interests include vocabulary development, staff development, and comprehension instruction. He has worked extensively in professional development schools in the Milwaukee Public School District and is presently a member of a school board in suburban Milwaukee. He has published *High Interest Easy Reading: Book Series and Periodicals for Less Able Readers* for the International Reading Association and has published widely in journals such as the *Journal of Reading, Elementary School Journal, Journal of Educational Research, Journal of Educational Psychology*, and *Reading, Research and Instruction*.

Michael Graves is a Professor in the Department of Curriculum and Instruction at the University of Minnesota, where he chairs the Literacy Education program and teaches courses in content area reading, reading research, and secondary remedial reading. Prior to receiving his Ph.D. from Stanford in 1971, he was a composition instructor at Long Beach State College and a secondary English teacher in the Long Beach and Fountain Valley School Districts in California. His research and development interests include vocabulary development, comprehension development, and effective instruction. He is the former editor of the *Journal of Reading Behavior*, the former associate editor of *Research in the Teaching of English*, and the coauthor of two forthcoming books—*Scaffolding Reading Experiences* and *Essentials of Classroom Teaching: Elementary Reading*. His articles have appeared in such journals as *American Educator, Child Development, Elementary School Journal, English Journal, Journal of Educational Psychology, Journal of Educational Research, Journal of Reading, Reading Research Quarterly*, and *Review of Research in Education*.